Handbook of
Counseling
& Psychotherapy
with Men

Handbook of Counseling & Psychotherapy with Men

MURRAY SCHER

MARK STEVENS

GLENN GOOD

GREGG A. EICHENFIELD

SAGE Publications
International Educational and Professional Publisher
Newbury Park   London   New Delhi

For information address:

 SAGE Publications, Inc.
2455 Teller Road
Newbury Park, California 91320

SAGE Publications Ltd.
6 Bonhill Street
London EC2A 4PU
United Kingdom

SAGE Publications India Pvt. Ltd.
M-32 Market
Greater Kailash I
New Delhi 110 048 India

Printed in the United States of America

Library of Congress Cataloging-in-Publication Data

Handbook of counseling and psychotherapy with men.

Includes bibliographies.
1. Counseling.   2. Psychotherapy.   2. Men—
Counseling of.   I. Scher, Murray.   [DNLM: 1. Counseling.
2. Men.   3. Psychotherapy.   WM 420   H2312]
BF637.C6H313   1987   159é.3   87-16578
ISBN 0-8039-2991-9 (cloth)—ISBN 0-8039-5355-0 (pbk.)

95 96 10 9 8 7 6 5 4 3

Contents

Acknowledgments

Although we are responsible for the conception and final preparation of this book, we are deeply appreciative of everyone who has had a role in its preparation and realization. The list of those who influenced and aided us is very lengthy and stretches back into our formative years, but we will be brief in our acknowledgments. We greatly appreciate the network of men in this country dedicated to a new conception of how men might be. The National Organization for Men Against Sexism is the organized proponent of that view, and it was at its Tenth National Conference on Men and Masculinity in St. Louis in 1985 that this book was conceived. We also very much thank Kathleen Copeland for her pleasant willingness to handle a ridiculous amount of correspondence, thus greatly easing our work.

Individually, we also wish to make some acknowledgments. Murray thanks his wife, Rita, and daughter, Elena, for allowing him to be the man he wants to be and Art Brownell, Harry Canon, Earl Koile, and Bob Murff for teaching him how. Mark thanks The Ohio State University's Counseling and Consultation Services and the University of Southern California's Student Counseling Services for their support. He also acknowledges the men in his life who have been wonderful role models and sources of motivation to stay connected to the men's movement and men's issues—his father, Jerry, Grandpa Max, Uncle Ed, Scott Blish, Ted Weiser, Quinn Crosbie, Glenn Good, Stephen Colladay, Bucky Jackson, and Dick Stranges. Mark also acknowledges the loving support of his wife Jawaii and his three terrific children—Jamie, Jeremy, and Shawn—who have taught him much about masculinity. Glenn acknowledges the significant intellectual and personal contributions provided by his partner, Dr. Laurie Mintz, of the University of Missouri at Columbia. She shared in many aspects of this work and offered her insights, patience, and support generously. He also thanks his parents, Drs. Jeanne and Bob Good, and his friends for their encouragement and assistance along the way. Gregg thanks his mother, Shirley, for her continued support of his academic and professional career. Having raised three boys, she has been an unending source of information and understanding about men. He also thanks his brothers, Harvey and Ira, for helping him to understand the pain, joy, and myriad other emotions that boys, men, and brothers experience. Dorothy Foster, his former boss at the University of Oklahoma, has respected him in his work with and about men; she allowed him to grow, make mistakes, and learn that men and women really can work together effectively.

Finally, we acknowledge our debt to each other. We have trusted, supported, and encouraged one another thus learning and stretching ourselves, and, in doing so, discovered that men could establish a loving bond. We will cherish the bond and the process of its forging.

—Murray Scher
Mark Stevens
Glenn Good
Gregg A. Eichenfield

Preface

This handbook draws together the current knowledge about the counseling of and psychotherapy with men. It is the most inclusive volume to date on the subject. The various authors are expert in their areas and share generously of their expertise.

The underlying assumption of the editors is that gender role issues are integral factors in the therapeutic encounter. As very little has been written that bridges the gap between theoretical knowledge of the sociopsychological issues of male sex-role socialization and therapy with men, this book offers a comprehensive look at men in therapy. A first of its kind, this handbook serves as a reference as well as an introduction to the intricacy of dealing with men in counseling and psychotherapy in a broad range of settings.

The intention of the editors in originating and developing this handbook was to provide a general introduction to the contemporary situation of men in our culture, an understanding of the concerns of a wide array of subpopulations of men, and the most effective manner of dealing with men seeking remediation of their concerns. Aside from examining particular subpopulations of men, the developmental passages of men are also scrutinized. Techniques of working with men, as well as perspectives on men as clients and on therapists' approaches and techniques, are explored. This rich mix of material, it is hoped, will ensure the most efficacious approach to work with men.

Our endeavor is to create a basic understanding of the way in which men come to be what they are: the forces impinging on their lives and the difficulties in aiding them to move from the place of constraint and restraint that gender role dictates for them. It is only with this understanding, plus a source of information on how to aid in the process of moving from the stagnant place in which many men find themselves, that therapists working with men can aid them in changing their lives and achieving a satisfying interaction with their world.

Suggestions, not answers, are provided here. It may be that some of the suggestions are as close to perfect answers as we will achieve, but, at this moment, we cannot know that. We are on the track of discovering how best to work with men, but it would be foolish to assume that we are there yet. Should we claim that, we would be falling into the hypermasculine trap of having to be absolutely sure of the rightness of our judgment. Rather, we would prefer to see our work as always being in progress, to be touched up, improved, amplified, and moved closer to the clearest and most productive answers.

The philosophical posture underlying this book is one of a developmental, profeminist stance that acknowledges the cultural difficulties and constraints inherent in the male role. The authors approach the study of therapy with men from a humanistic, experiential, theoretical base. Our belief is that the greatest part of human behavior is a product of family and culturally based learning. Therefore, we believe that modifications can be made in human behavior. We further believe that the psychotherapeutic encounter, although a significant format for effecting change, is not the only means available. We are committed to the belief that a variety of remediative experiences are available for changing the contemporary situation of men.

The approach in this book is basically practical, although we have paid attention to the theoretical as much as possible. Our purpose has been to provide practitioners and students with information that will enable them to understand the nuances of aiding their male clients as well as having a sufficient repertoire of skills and techniques for implementing that understanding, thus successfully aiding in behavior change.

This work was conceived in a spirit of brotherhood and, because of that, is actively oriented toward the amelioration of the negative affects of male socialization on men, women, and our culture. This dedication results in a work that is oriented toward the fullest expression of individual mental and physical health regardless of gender, sexual preference, ethnic membership, or other individual choice/commitment.

This handbook is intended for all mental health professionals who work with men either as their total responsibility or only as a part of the population with whom they are in contact. It is also intended for those who are not direct caregivers for men but rather are engaged in some institution or enterprise where men are a significant part of the clientele. The book, too, provides an understanding of the difficulties men experience in their lives for even the lay reader. As a whole, the book is a comprehensive exploration of the paths men travel in their development on the way to becoming integrated although often not syntonic members of society.

Those working with men who are experienced in this area and those who are very new to work with this population or some subpopulation thereof will benefit from the accrued insight and experience of the authors of the handbook. The book is written in such a manner as to offer all readers, regardless of speciality, gender, and level of experience, insight into and techniques for the amelioration of men's concerns and difficulties. Because the editors believe that all subpopulations of men are men first and members of their particular group second, it is our belief that the material contained will enable the reader to assist those with whose care they are charged.

The Contemporary Man

Joseph H. Pleck

Critical analyses of the limitations of the male role, for both men and women, began appearing a little over 15 years ago (Berkeley Men's Center, 1971; Sawyer, 1970). Men developing this critical perspective were at first dismissed as inadequate in their masculinity, guilt-ridden dupes of feminism, or discontented homosexuals. (This statement is based on personal experience.) In spite of this initial response, a growing number of books, articles, media reports, conferences, courses, and organizations over the last 15 years have continued the development of this new awareness about and among men.

Today, the examination of male roles has become established, even fashionable. There is now so much being written and said about men that the problem for one interested in the subject is no longer finding relevant material, but determining what is important and true in all that is available. This chapter addresses this need by first presenting three findings from current resarch that appear especially helpful in identifying key parameters of contemporary male experience: men's increasing time in family roles, men's increasing rates of psychological distress relative to women, and the nature and correlates of traditional attitudes about men's roles. The chapter concludes by analyzing the current cultural debate about the extent and nature of change in men, examining in particular Barbara Ehrenreich's *The Hearts of Men* (1983).

Men's Increasing Time in Family Roles

In *Women's Two Roles: Home and Work* (1956), Alva Myrdal argued that women in industrial societies were, to an increasing degree, adding a new role in paid work to their traditional family role. The phrase "women's two roles" caught on as a description of this change in women's lives. A decade later, Myrdal developed her argument a step further: Women having two roles could not succeed in the long run unless men developed two roles as well. For men, having two roles meant adding a greatly enlarged family role to their customary responsibility as family economic breadwinners (Myrdal, 1967).

From this perspective, data on trends in time spent by men in their family roles provide a key social indicator of change in men. By examining data on this variable, one can objectively determine whether men are really changing. Time in the family is, in effect, the social indicator for men analogous to labor force participation for women. A surprisingly large number of studies have investigated how men's participation in family life has changed in the United States over the twentieth century (see detailed review in Pleck, 1985). This research in fact documents that men's family role has increased. Two analyses provide particularly valuable evidence.

In one of the classic American community studies, Robert and Helen Merrill Lynd investigated "Middletown"(Muncie, Indiana) in the mid-20s. Caplow and Chadwick (1979; Caplow, Bahr, Chadwick, Hill, & Williamson, 1982) replicated the study in 1978 with a similarly drawn sample from the same city. About 10% of all fathers were reported by their wives to spend *no* time with their children in 1924; in 1978, the parallel figure was 2%. Thus the proportion of completely uninvolved fathers dropped from 1 in 10 to 1 in 50. (The proportion of fathers spending more than 1 hour per day, the highest reported category of involvement reported by the researchers, rose from 66% to 76%.)

Most who ask whether men are really changing are thinking not of the last 60 years, but of only the last 10 or 20, that is, since the rise of the contemporary women's movement. Juster (1985) provides data on the time spent by adult males in the United States in family work (housework and child care combined) from time diary surveys conducted with national representative samples in 1965 and 1981. Men's time in these activities rose from about 1.6 hours per day in 1965 to slightly under 2.0 hours per day in 1981, an increase of somewhat over 20%. Taking into account women's decreasing time in these activities, men's proportion of all housework and child care (that is, the total performed by the average man and the average woman combined) rose from 20% to 30% over this 16-year period.

Thus, on a key social indicator, men show clear evidence of change in their role, and to more than a trivial degree. This change is not, of course, necessarily occurring to an equal degree among all men. Aggregate figures such as these probably conceal subgroups of men who have not changed or who are doing even less family work than they used to, men who have changed only a little, and men who have changed a great deal. But if an overall generalization is needed, it must be that American men have markedly increased their family participation over the last 60 years. Further, the pace of change over the last two decades (men's proportion of total family work rising from 20% to 30%) seems substantial when one considers that these data describe the U.S. population as a whole, not just the young, the highly educated, residents of college towns, or the large East and West Coast cities. This rate of change is in fact comparable to the increase in the average woman's proportion of the paid work performed by her and the average man combined, which rose from 27% to 35% during this same period (calculated from Juster, 1985).

The most important qualification to be made about these data is that they concern only the amount of time men spend in family roles, and not the degree of responsibility men take. Analyses of how spouses divide family tasks underline the importance of the distinction between simply performing an activity and being responsible for the task being done (Lein, 1984). The extent to which men are *responsible* for family work is much lower than their participation, and has probably not increased as much.

Nonetheless, men's increase in family participation is socially significant. In a similar way, women's increasing labor force participation has had tremendous social consequences, in spite of the fact that women's average earnings relative to men's have not changed. Many would argue today that any woman who aspires to, or actually has, a higher-level job than women have traditionally held (or who has a job, when traditionally she would not have) shows the effects of the changed consciousness among women stimulated by feminism. In the same way, any man who is doing more in the family than he used to, or than his father did, likewise demonstrates the effects of broader cultural change in the male role.

Men's Increasing Rates of Psychological Distress Relative to Women

One of the research results giving impetus to the women's movement during the 1970s was the finding that women have higher rates of mental health disorders, especially depression, than men, and that this gender difference could not be accounted for by biological factors (Chesler, 1972; Guttentag, Salasin, & Belle, 1980). Recent research, however, has documented a significant change over the last three decades in the relationship between gender and psychological distress.

Kessler and McRae (1981; see also McLanahan & Glass, 1985) analyzed five national surveys conducted between 1957 and 1976 that included measures of psychophysiological symptoms such as sleep difficulty, nervousness, headaches, and dizziness. These surveys also included items assessing symptoms such as "times you couldn't take care of things because you just couldn't get going" and "times when personal worries got you down physically." While women reported a higher rate of indicators than did men in all five surveys, the average differer women and men became steadily smaller between 1957 and 19° analyses showed that women's rates of such symptoms increased slightly over these two decades (about four-tenths of a point on the symptom scale, which had a standard deviation of about 5.5). But men's rates increased about three times more (1.1 points). As a result, the "gender gap" in symptoms was 38% smaller at the end of the period than it was at the beginning. Over these two decades, men's mental health deteriorated relative to women's.

It is possible that men's increased reports of psychological distress may not reflect an increase in its acutal frequency, only an increasing willingness to acknowledge it. Undoubtedly, this factor contributes to some degree. However, it cannot be the only explanation, since exactly the same trend is evident in data on attempted suicide from 1960 to the present: Women still do it more, but men are catching up. Generalizing across a large group of studies, the ratio of females to males attempting suicide dropped from about 2.3 to 1 in 1960, to about 1.3 to 1 in 1980 (Kessler & McRae, 1983). (Men show substantially higher rates of successful suicide than women.)

Kessler and McRae (1982) further analyzed the 1976 survey (the Americans View Their Mental Health Re-Study) to identify factors associated with greater psychological distress in men that might account for the decline in men's mental health relative to women since the late 1950s. One of the main changes since the 1950s is, of course, that today more men have employed wives. The increase in wives' employment did account for some of the change in men's psychological symptoms. In the 1976 data, men with employed wives reported significantly more depression and lower self-esteem than sole-breadwinning husbands, though the size of the difference was not great. It is interesting to note that this pattern did not hold true for the youngest group, men in their twenties.

Several factors that the investigator thought might explain exactly *how* wives's employment diminished husband's mental health were not validated. For example, husbands of employed wives did not appear to experience more symptoms because the money their wives made rendered their own breadwinner role less important. In fact, among husbands with employed wives, those with higher-earning wives reported less distress. Likewise, the problem did not seem to be that husbands of employed wives performed more housework and child care. In fact, among husbands with employed wives, those who performed more family tasks showed less, not more, distress.

Pleck (1985) found parallel results in a study focusing specifically on the impact of men performing more family work on their family satisfaction and overall well-being. Pleck's interpretation of this latter, initially puzzling finding is that husbands whose wives are employed, but who do *not* contribute significantly to household and family tasks, exhibit "learned helplessness" behavior (Seligman, 1974). Most two-earner families face considerable demands in maintaining the household and arranging for child care. If housework needs doing and the children need to be cared for, but the husband does not have any behavior in his repertoire that will help meet these needs, he will experience low control and increased stress.

It is sometimes asked whether men actually show signs of hurting as a result of the limitations of the traditional male role, or because relationships between the sexes are changing. The question is sometimes put more pointedly: What is the evidence that men today are actually feeling pain, and are not simply happily enjoying their male privilege? Kessler and McRae's data in fact show that men as a group are experiencing more psychological distress than they did three decades ago, both absolutely and relative to women.

From one point of view, the research discussed earlier about men's increased family participation is the "good news" about contemporary men, while the data about men's increasing psychological symptoms is the "bad news." Some might interpret the two trends together as suggesting that men experience increased stress *because* of the ways they are changing their role. Actually, the data suggest the exact opposite: The increased discomfort occurs predominantly among the men whose own role (as reflected by their family behavior) is *not* changing. Current research suggests that having a nontraditional role, in the sense of an enlarged family role, is good for men's mental health.

Traditional Attitudes
Toward Men's Roles

Recent research has made considerable progress in understanding the nature of traditional attitudes about the gender role behavior appropriate for men. Further, in male samples, studies demonstrate that these attitudes are correlated with other traditional male characteristics. A brief overview of how research on "sex roles" has evolved helps put this research in context.

When contemporary research on gender began in the late 1960s, one of its first topics was sex-role attitudes. This term referred to attitudes about women, and attitudes about differences and relationships between the sexes. Many new scales were developed, documenting how prevalent traditional attitudes were (see Pleck, 1978, for a review). A large volume of research on sex-role "stereotypes" developed at the same time. Stereotype studies investigated exactly the same phenomenon, but with a slightly different questionnaire format: Subjects rated the "typical [or ideal] man" and woman on various adjective dimensions (e.g., strong-weak), rather than responding to attitude statements on agree-disagree scales.

By the early 1970s, research interest in sex-role attitudes and stereotypes declined. Earlier attitude research was in effect supplanted by studies of a related but quite different phenomenon, sex *typing*. While sex-role *attitudes* denote the perceptions an individual has about women and men in general, or as groups, sex *typing* refers to the extent to which a particular individual himself or herself actually has characteristics culturally perceived as masculine or feminine. In measures administered to individuals, sex-role attitudes are reflected by responses to third-person statements ("women are . . . "), while sex typing is assessed by responses to first-person statements ("I am . . . "). (*Sex typing* has long been the dominant term for the first-person construct in developmental psychology, but other disciplines have also used a variety of other terms for it.)

The concepts of sex-role attitudes and sex typing imply two different ways of thinking about the "traditional" male. Conceptualized in terms of sex-role attitudes, the traditional male is one who holds traditional views about the actual and desired characteristics of women and men. Defined in terms of sex typing, however, he is a male who himself has highly masculine characteristics. Both formulations are plausible, but they are clearly quite different.

From the mid-1970s to the present, sex typing and its correlates in women and men became an extremely popular research topic. Much of this research has been theoretically guided by the concept of androgyny, whose fundamental insight is that masculinity and femininity are independent dimensions of personality (rather than opposite ends of the same continuum), so that individuals can theoretically be high on both. This research also employs new measures to assess sex typing, such as the Bem Sex Role Inventory (BSRI) (Bem, 1974) and Spence and Helmreich's (1978) Personal Attributes Questionnaire (PAQ). An initial group of studies appeared to demonstrate that androgyny (being high in both masculine and feminine characteristics) has positive correlates for both sexes. Research on the correlates of being traditionally sex-typed versus androgynous, and on the correlates of the masculinity and femininity subscales of the BSRI and PAQ, continues to be conducted. Recently, this line of research has become increasingly technical and complex, with many reviewers finding considerable ambiguity about what it actually shows (see analysis and reviews cited in Pleck, 1981).

In this context, recent studies of the nature and correlates of attitudes specifically about *male* roles represent a return to the earlier line of research on sex-role attitudes and stereotypes, but with a new focus. One key insight underlying these recent studies is that earlier sex-role attitude research did not distinguish, either theoretically or empirically, traditional attitudes toward women's roles from traditional views of men's roles. While there is probably some relationship between the two, individuals can, for example, have nontraditional attitudes about the roles of women, but continue to hold traditional views about the appropriate roles of men.

Earlier research did not foresee such a possibility. Rather, it simply assumed that gender-related attitudes were either attitudes specifically about women, or attitudes about sex roles in general. In addition, most items in the attitude scales labeled as measuring attitudes specifically about women in fact explicitly or implicitly compare the sexes [e.g., "the father should have greater authority than the mother in the bringing up of children" and "intoxication among women is worse than intoxication among men," from Spence, Helmreich, and Stapp's (1973) Attitudes Toward Women Scale]. Whatever the scales are labeled, the preponderance of such items means that these instruments actually tap attitudes about sex roles in general (in the sense of beliefs about how the sexes should differ from each other), and do not in fact assess attitudes about women differentially from attitudes about men.

Several new scales have been developed to measure traditional attitudes specifically about men, and to do so as independently of attitudes about women as possible (Brannon, 1985; Fiebert, 1983; Mosher & Sirkin, 1984; Snell, 1986). The Brannon Masculinity Scale (BMS), for example, assesses four components of traditional attitudes (or norms) about masculinity: that men should not be feminine (labeled by Brannon "no sissy stuff"); that men should strive to be respected and admired for successful achievement ("the big wheel"); that men should never show weakness or uncertainty ("the sturdy oak"); and that men should seek adventure and risk even accepting violence if necessary ("give 'em hell"). Although the BMS was not necessarily designed for this purpose, it and other male role-attitude scales can be used to document the nature of gender-role norms for males, and the correlates of endorsing or not endorsing these norms.

In a recent study with a sample of 233 male undergraduates from two New England colleges, traditional attitudes about masculinity showed only weak relationships to traditional beliefs concerning women, such as opposing the ERA and insisting that one's wife must be a virgin (Thompson & Pleck, 1986). That is, holding traditional or liberal attitudes about the appropriate behavior of men did *not* necessarily predict whether a male held traditional or liberal attitudes about women. This demonstration that traditionalism in attitudes about the two sexes can be independent empirically makes clear that the two attitudes should also be distinguished theoretically.

In other analyses of these data (Thompson, Grisanti, & Pleck, 1985), college males neither fully endorsed nor rejected traditional norms for masculinity. On the average, subjects gave slight overall endorsement to the norms concerning adventure seeking and not showing weakness (i.e., the sample's mean score was slightly on the "agree" side of the scale midpoint), and weakly rejected the norms of antifemininity and respect through achievement.

This pattern of most and least endorsed male role norms calls for some interpretation. Recent cultural trends may have to some extent undermined the traditional norms regarding antifemininity and respect through achievement. Role prescriptions to conceal weakness and to take adventurous risks, on the other hand, seem to have been affected much less. The relatively high endorsement of the "adventurous risk" factor in an elite college male sample may at first seem surprising. However, though elite, college males are still adolescents, among whom the idea of validating masculinity through adventurous risk-taking appears to still have a considerable hold. The data on teen male drunk driving provide corroborative evidence, as does the popularity of films of the *Rocky* and *Rambo* genre, which enjoy their greatest following among adolescent males.

The Thompson et al. (1985) study found in addition that college males who endorse traditional male role norms also report other characteristics theoretically identified as aspects of the traditional male role. Specifically, they show higher than average levels of homophobia (fear and negative stereotyping of homosexuals, and fear of homosexuality in oneself); higher rates of the "type A behavior pattern" (the constellation of competitive preoccupation with work, impatience, rapid speech, and so forth that has been implicated as a risk factor in coronary heart disease); lower self-disclosure; and greater dominance over their partners in intimate relationships.

The relative endorsement of these (and other) dimensions of traditional attitudes about masculinity will of course not necessarily be the same in other samples of different age, ethnicity, or social class, nor will their correlates always be identical. The nature, correlates, and consequences of traditional attitudes toward masculinity need to be delineated in other social groups and subcultures. By identifying the specific pattern of male role norms and their correlates in this particular sample, the Thompson et al. study contributes to the understanding that the set of expectations for men constituting the "male role" are not fixed and unalterable, but are in fact likely to vary in different social groups.

Such research helps reinforce some simple, but still fundamental points about contemporary men's roles: There are a variety of different expectations inherent in traditional masculinity; the relative strength of these expectations may vary in different groups; and these expectations are in fact associated with other phenomena that have been identified as problems or issues in the male role.

Broader Social Trends Among Men

Today, there is a cultural debate going on about what is happening among men. Are men not changing at all? Are men changing only superficially, or even getting worse? Or are men actually getting better? The answer to each of these questions is yes, for at least some men. That is to say, three broad social trends are evident among American men: continued traditionalism; superficial or negative change; and genuine, positive change. Current cultural debate about men is thus largely about these trends' relative strength. The debate also focuses in part on whether particular phenomena (e.g., men's new family role, men's search for their own fathers, and the men's movement) are examples of genuine, positive change or illustrate only superficial, even negative change.

The statement on these matters that more than any other has come to frame today's debate in feminist and intellectual circles is Barbara Ehrenreich's *The Hearts of Men: American Dreams and the Flight from Commitment* (1983; see also Ehrenreich, 1984). Ehrenreich develops a variant of the "superficial/negative change" argument. She first analyzes the instability in the husband-wife relationship inherent in the husband being the sole or primary breadwinner. She then notes several cultural phenomena, beginning in the 1950s, that encouraged male abdication of the family breadwinner role: *Playboy's* philosophy and advertising, the beatnik movement, and the "counterculture" of the 1960s. Ehrenreich then concludes that men are indeed changing, but only in that (1) men are fleeing the breadwinner role, often abandoning ex-wives and children to poverty, and (2) they are increasingly pursuing narcissistic consumer gratification.

While some evidence supports Ehrenreich's interpretation, parts of it are overstated, and contrary evidence is ignored. As an example of the former, Ehrenreich (1983, p. 11) cites a study finding that only 25% of the women who are awarded child support by the courts actually receive it, and 60% of these receive less than $1500 a year. However, national data (for 1981) actually show that 72% of mothers awarded child-support orders receive child support. Roughly two-thirds of these are receiving the full amount awarded, and the average support received was $2220 a year (U.S. Bureau of the Census, 1983).

While some men fit Ehrenreich's portrait of men fleeing the breadwinner role to pursue consumer gradification, the breadwinner still has a strong hold on the majority. The *Wall Street Journal*, for example, analyzed the impact of Pittsburgh's loss of 100,000 jobs in steel and related industries (equivalent to 60% of its current manufacturing workforce) in the last five years. Faced with imminent foreclosure on his home after six months of unemployment, a 39-year-old man killed himself by jumping in the Monongahela River. "'I knew we needed help, but Henry was too proud to ask for it.' says his widow, Betty, who paid off the mortgage with $9,000 in insurance benefits" (Hymowitz & O'Boyle, 1984, p. 1).[1] These male "breadwinner suicides" did not occur only during the Great Depression; they are still happening today.

Another article portrays the despair resulting from the loss of unionized jobs in the "Rust Belt" industries of the Midwest (Richards, 1986). Loss of these jobs has meant the loss of what male workers called "the ladder," the progression of increasing seniority and wages that traditionally provided advancement into the middle class for generations of blue-collar workers. Even when alternative jobs are available, they are dead ends. Men's occupational suffering is not unique or worse than women's (women, of course, never had access to "the ladder"). But it does reveal the continuing hold of a male breadwinner ideology that Ehrenreich seems too ready to believe has largely disappeared among men.

Yet other reports show that, contrary to the popular stereotype of the consumption-oriented, "yuppie" baby-boomers, this generation is actually less well-off economically and has less discretionary income than the generation before it, particularly when increased income and social security taxes are taken into account (Levy & Michel, 1984). While the narcissistic male consumption patterns Ehrenreich describes may exist among an elite group, they do not seem accurate as a description of the dominant trend among adult males today.

In light of today's economic and labor market dislocations, it seems likely that far more men are being pushed out of the breadwinner role involuntarily than are fleeing it for selfish reasons. Even if rejected by some, fulfillment of the family breadwinner role remains a central objective for the majority of adult men in the United States. Future social historians may well conclude that economic changes undermining the male breadwinner role had an equal or even greater impact on men during the last half of the twentieth century than did feminism.

What Ehrenreich argues is that the dominant change among contemporary men is probably better regarded as only one of several trends of relatively equal importance. While men today are changing in some ways that are superficial or potentially negative for women, contemporary males are also manifesting continued traditionalism in other respects, and demonstrating authentic, positive change in yet others. The challenge facing those who wish to foster positive change is to acknowledge and support it where it exists, and to respond creatively to the forms of traditionalism and only superficial change also so apparent today.

Note

1. Reprinted by permission of the *Wall Street Journal*, copyright Dow Jones & Company, Inc. (1984). All Rights Reserved.

References

Bem, S. (1974). The measurement of psychological androgyny. *Journal of Clinical and Consulting Psychology, 31,* 634-643.

Berkeley Men's Center Manifesto. (1971). [Reprinted 1974 in J. H. Pleck & J. Sawyer (Eds.), *Men and masculinity* (pp. 173-174). Englewood Cliffs, NJ: Prentice-Hall].

Brannon, R. (1985). A scale for measuring attitudes about masculinity. In A. Sargent (Ed.), *Beyond sex roles* (pp. 110-116). St. Paul, MN: West.

Caplow, T., Bahr, H., Chadwick, B., Hill, R., & Williamson, M. H. (1982). *Middletown families: Fifty years of change and continuity.* Minneapolis: University of Minnesota Press.

Caplow, T., & Chadwick, B. (1979). Inequality and life-styles in Middletown, 1920-1978. *Social Science Quarterly, 60,* 367-390.

Chesler, P. (1972). *Women and madness.* Garden City, NY: Doubleday.

Ehrenreich, B. (1983). *The hearts of men: American dreams and the flight from commitment.* Garden City, NY: Anchor Press/Doubleday.

Ehrenreich, B. (1984, May 20). A feminist's view of the new man. *New York Times Sunday Magazine,* pp. 36-39.

Fiebert, M. (1983). Measuring traditional and liberated males' attitudes. *Perceptual and Motor Skills, 56,* 83-86.

Guttentag, M., Salasin, S., & Belle, D. (Eds.). (1980). *The mental health of women.* New York: Academic Press.

Hymowitz, C., & O'Boyle, T. F. (1984, Aug. 21). Pittsburgh's evolution from steel to services sparks a culture clash. *Wall Street Journal,* p. 1.

Juster, F. T. (1985). A note on recent changes in time use. In F. T. Juster and F. Stafford (Eds.), *Time, goods, and well-being* (pp. 313-332). Ann Arbor, MI: Institute for Social Research.

Kessler, R., & McRae, J. (1981). Trends in the relationship between sex and psychological distress: 1957-1976. *American Sociological Review, 46,* 443-452.

Kessler, R., & McRae, J. (1982). The effect of wives' employment on the mental health of married men and women. *American Sociological Review, 47,* 216-227.

Kessler, R., & McRae, J. (1983). Trends in the relationship between sex and attempted suicide. *Journal of Health and Social Behavior, 24,* 98-110.

Lein, L. (1984). *Families without villains.* Lexington, MA: D. C. Heath.

Levy, F., & Michel, R. C. (1984). *Are baby-boomers selfish?* Washington, DC: Urban Institute.

McLanahan, S. S., & Glass, J. L. (1985). A note on the trend in sex differences in psychological distress. *Journal of Health and Social Behavior, 26,* 328-335.

Mosher, D., & Sirkin, M. (1984). Measuring a macho personality constellation. *Journal of Research in Personality, 18,* 150-163.

Myrdal, A. (1967). Foreword. In E. Dahlstrom & E. Liljestrom (Eds.), *The changing roles of men and women* (pp. 9-15). London: Duckworth.

Myrdal, A., & Klein, V. (1956). *Women's two roles: Home and work.* London: Routledge & Kegan Paul.

Pleck, J. H. (1978). Men's traditional attitudes toward women: Conceptual issues in research. In J. Sherman & F. Denmark (Eds.), *The psychology of women: Future directions in research* (pp. 619-644). New York: Psychological Dimensions.

Pleck, J. H. (1981). *The myth of masculinity.* Cambridge, MA: MIT Press.

Pleck, J. H. (1985). *Working Wives, Working Husbands.* Newbury Park, CA: Sage.

Richards, B. (1986, March 12). Down the ladder: They have jobs again in LaPorte, but work doesn't pay so well. *Wall Street Journal,* p. 1

Sawyer, J. (1970). On male liberation. [Reprinted 1974 in J. H. Pleck & J. Sawyer (Eds.), *Men and masculinity* (pp. 171-172). Englewood Cliffs, NJ: Prentice-Hall.]

Seligman, M. (1974). Depression and learned helplessness. In R. Friedman & L. Katz (Eds.), *The psychology of depression: Contemporary theory and research* (pp. 218-239). Washington, DC: Winston.

Snell, W. J. (1986). The masculine role inventory: Components and correlates. *Sex Roles, 15*, 443-456.

Spence, J., & Helmreich, R. (1978). *Masculinity and femininity: Their psychological dimensions, correlates and antecedents.* Austin: University of Texas Press.

Spence, J., Helmreich, R., & Stapp, J. (1973). A short version of the attitudes to women scales (AWS). *Bulletin of the Psychonomic Society, 2*, 21-22.

Thompson, E. H., Jr., Grisanti, C., & Pleck, J. H. (1985). Attitudes toward the male role and their correlates. *Sex Roles, 13*, 413-427.

Thompson, E. H., Jr., & Pleck, J. H. (1986). The structure of male role norms. *American Behavioral Scientist, 29*, 531-544.

U. S. Bureau of the Census. (1983). *Current population reports* (Series P-23, No. 124). *Child support and alimony: 1981* (Advance Report). Washington, DC: Government Printing Office.

I

Techniques and Perspectives

The counseling of any psychotherapy with men at first glance, from what we know historically, appears to be a relatively simple matter. After all, is not the entire corpus of writing about therapy based on men? That is what we were initially taught and what the writers on feminist therapy railed against. However, as the interest in the restrictive character of male gender role socialization has been explored, it has become abundantly clear that the remediation of psychological difficulty in men is far more complex than at first assumed. This section on techniques and perspectives in the psychotherapy of men initiates the examination of how best to ameliorate the problems engendered by the cultural, intrapsychic, and interpersonal context in which contemporary men find themselves.

It is interesting to note that psychotherapy is a feminine endeavor praticed by men, usually on women. Therapy has traditionally supported stereotypic behavior in males and initially did the same for females. The rise of feminist therapy has caused that situation to change for women.

Feminist therapists have sought to empower women instrumentally by releasing their personal and institutional power. Women already had the personal power gained through relationships and through a relational manner of dealing with the world.

Masculist therapy—that is, psychotherapy with men grounded in an understanding of the constrictions created by the male role, strives to empower men relationally through the desensitizing to and teaching of intimacy, as men have already gained power through an instrumental manner of dealing with the world.

There is a paucity of published resources available for studying the process of and techniques with male clients. The work available, however, is generally of good quality. In the dozen or so years that specific attention has been paid to male gender roles and their effect on the psyches of men, there has been a gradual proliferation of writing on men. Attention to the psychotherapy of men, specifically, has been with us for about six years. As with a general resistance to considering males as a special subgroup of the population, so there has been a reluctance to examine males as a special population in the therapeutic encounter. This reluctance is compounded by a resistance to acknowledging the importance of socialization and cultural factors in the emotional difficulties of therapy clients.

Interest in issues of concern to men grew out of the attention to issues of concern to women. It was the women's movement that gave birth to the scrutiny directed at gender-related issues in the socialization and life of men. The historical roots of examining the therapeutic process with men lie in the work of feminist therapists, although the conclusions of that body of work are far different from those derived in scrutinizing the therapy of men. The historical roots are there, however, because it was the innovative idea of considering gender issues in psychotherapy that initiated the examination of such determiners in the psychotherapeutic encounter involving males.

There has been a dearth of writing on psychotherapy with men. Several books, three special issues of journals, and a dozen or two articles have specifically addressed men in therapy. The major thrust of these writings has been to draw attention to the strains of male roles in our culture, to the price exacted for the rewards of living in a man's world, and to the manner in which these costs determine who the male patients are that are worked with as well as how these qualities influence the therapeutic process.

Men are restrained and constrained because of the male role. The expectations of that role cause men to be emotionally flat or repressed, imbued with a competitive spirit, fearful of intimacy, untutored in emotional responsiveness, homophobic, self-annihilating, and remote from human contact. Therapists working with men must be aware of these qualities, understand their effect on therapy, be patient, and respect the integrity of their clients.

In this section, the authors will address general qualities of those who are therapists for men as well as modalities for working with those men. The intention is to inform the reader of the necessary characteristics and training of therapists to optimize performance. A variety of methods for working with men as well as a variety of significant issues for men will be addressed.

1

Men Counseling Men

P. Paul Heppner
Daniel S. Gonzales

The positive and negative effects of gender-role conflicts for both males and females in the United States is well documented (e.g., Deaux, 1976; Maccoby & Jacklin, 1974; O'Leary, 1977; Pleck, 1981). The purpose of this chapter is to discuss some of the implications of the male socialization process within a specific context, the psychotherapy process. In general, the process of male therapists counseling male clients is essentially the same as any counseling relationship; however, special dynamics of the male-male relationship increase the probability that certain events may occur that can either facilitate or hinder the therapeutic process. This is not to imply that the male-male dynamics will always affect the therapeutic process. Rather, the authors conceptualize the specific male-male dynamics as an additional set of variables (among many others) that can affect both the interpersonal and intrapersonal processes in psychotherapy.

We believe that gender issues may affect therapy through the manner in which the client and therapist process information about the therapeutic experience. A male client, for example, might perceive therapy as overfocusing on his weaknesses or as being too revealing and shameful. Or the counselor might become confused by the intimacy in the counseling relationship, and have homophobic reactions. Therefore, to discuss the special dynamics of the male-male therapy relationship the chapter will focus on male issues specifically with regard to the client and counseling. Finally, this chapter will be concluded by briefly discussing implications for research and training.

Author's Note: We would like to express appreciation to Helen J. Roehlke, Walter Cal Johnson, and Bernie R. Hershberger for their comments on previous drafts of this chapter.

Client Issues

Various male concerns have been identified by a number of writers, some of which include achievement (e.g., Crites & Fitzgerald, 1978), power and control (e.g., Komarovsky, 1976), competition (e.g., Lewis, 1978), restrictive emotionality (Skovholt, 1978), homophobia (e.g., Fasteau, 1974), sexual performance (e.g., Goldberg, 1976), career performance and development (e.g., Pleck & Sawyer, 1974), interpersonal relationships (e.g., Lewis, 1978; Zuckerman, 1975), changing male and female gender roles (e.g., David & Brannon, 1976; Dubbert, 1979; Scher, 1979), physical and psychological health (e.g., Goldberg, 1976), and intimacy (e.g., Lewis, 1978; Morgan, 1976). These and other problem areas play a role in bringing men into counseling; however, it is the permutations or combinations of various issues that most adequately describe the complex presenting concerns of most men. Parenthetically, it is the range of permutations of male issues that not only make generalizations about men difficult (Scher, 1979), but also complicate assessment and intervention strategies.

Many times a man will not seek therapy because it is very difficult for him to *admit to himself* that he has a problem. This seems to be more difficult for men than women because the typical male conditioning engenders feelings of self-reliance, dominance, competition, power, control, and high needs for achievement (see O'Neil, 1981). The denial and repression can be so strong that the man is largely unaware of his problems, or it is too aversive to think much about them. Sometimes only after getting very intoxicated, his defenses will temporarily drop and he will disclose his inner worries and feelings, often leaving his comrade very surprised.

When men do seek therapy, a number of gender issues may affect the therapeutic process. Asking for help in our culture often leads men to feel inadequate. Not only is it unacceptable to have problems, but it is also "unmanly" to seek help from anyone, and especially from other men. Scher (1979) notes the cost to self-esteem of the man who is forced to admit that he cannot solve a life problem; it can be doubly embarrassing to reveal one's perceived inadequacies to another man. In fact, to "be a man" often necessitates the importance of being masculine with other men. Thus it is not uncommon for male clients to seek female therapists because women are also perceived by men as able to be nurturing. Male clients working with male therapists may feel shamed and embarrassed, and be hesitant or downright resistant to disclose their inner world, especially their insecurities and doubts to another man. The client's anxiety might be so high that he terminates therapy prematurely. One 45-year-old man "excused" himself from therapy by deciding he "was too old" rather than to allow the therapist to understand his inner world.

It may or may not be useful to examine the male client's need to "save face," perhaps depending on the skills of the counselor, client, and depth of the therapeutic alliance. It is imperative for the counselor to be sensitive to and understanding of the pride of the male (Scher, 1979), as well as his masculine fears. The counselor needs to be cognizant of the male client's anxiety, especially early in therapy, being careful not to push too much too fast. It can be quite helpful for the male therapist to acknowledge the fears of "being known," especially by another man. In fact, male therapists' sensitivity, disclosure, and modeling can impart very powerful messages to the male client. Whatever interventions are used (e.g., self-disclosure, encouragement, verbal reinforcement), it is important to empathize with the male client's anxieties and hesitancies about disclosing his relevant experiences.

Another likely barrier for many male clients is their difficulty in identifying and expressing their affective reactions and processes. Many men have been conditioned "not to feel," to deny or to repress their affective responses. One man recalls the tragedy he felt in seeing the bloody and lifeless body of the first gopher he killed as a boy. His male friend, seeing the boy's emotional reactions, told him to "just think about all the grain they eat." Thus it is not uncommon for men to repress their feelings beyond the reach of consciousness. For example, a hard-driving business executive entered counseling complaining of being "stressed out" at work. As counseling progressed, it was discovered that his father died a year ago at this time and that he never was able to address his emotional reactions to the death of his father. It was only after an extended exploration of the situation that the client began to understand his emotional reactions and could express sadness over his loss.

It is important to realize that while men may consciously withhold information, more often they are genuinely unaware of their affective reactions. In fact, some male clients manifest this in highly sophisticated intellectualization of their psychological processes. Since they are largely unaware of how they feel, they try to logically deduce how they *should* feel, which is often inaccurate. Because of this overutilization of their cognition, it is not uncommon for the male client to complain that "I don't know what I'm feeling." It is therapeutic to understand these men's frustration. One man mournfully acknowledged in a men's group, "I can't cry. I wish I could. I envy those who can get that emotional release."

For many men it is easier to allow themselves to experience emotions such as anger or rage. In fact, a wide range of emotions may be funneled into anger, rage, and violence (Gondolf, 1985) because these feelings are more "acceptable" to the male. For example, a young man was recently facially disfigured in an automobile accident and entered counseling because of "anger" with women. When in counseling, the most important work was to identify his deeper feelings of being hurt and his fears of rejection, especially from women.

In short, a man's lack of emotional awareness may dramatically affect progress in therapy. A primary goal of the therapist is to enhance the man's awareness of his emotional reactions, as well as to increase his understanding of his psychological processes. Sometimes the male client will perceive this affective exploration as "looking for what's wrong." One young man who had difficulties dating women repeatedly interpreted emotional explanations as validation of his incompetence, and subsequently refused to discuss his problems except in an intellectual manner. Because exploring this affect can be quite threatening, the counselor may find that emphasizing the client's strengths during this time may stabilize the client's experience. By highlighting the client's strengths and resources, he may then feel safer to explore and experience his affective world. Again, the sensitivity, disclosure, and modeling of the male therapist can be very reassuring as well as educational for the client. It is essential for the male therapist to communicate both cognitively and affectively "I *understand. I* have been there, too. It *is* hard. I won't *punish* you." It is imperative that the therapist check how the male client is experiencing the therapy process. For example, the counselor might explicitly ask, "How do you feel about what we talked about today? Or, "How do you feel about what you are learning about yourself and who you are?" Or even, "How do you think (fear) I am reacting to the things you said today?" If the client acknowledges some fears, or the counselor suspects the client is experiencing something in the session negatively, it becomes necessary to reframe the event or to educate the client about counseling and/or human psychological processes.

If therapy is effective, sometimes the male client might become more aware of his aggressive experiences. For example, as therapy progressed, a man in his thirties became more acutely aware of feeling so angry that he was shocked by his aggressive impulses. Another man became deeply disturbed by his violent and destructive behavior. A veteran was "horrified" as he reflected on what he had done as a "professional soldier." While many men are socialized to be aggressive and competitive, often men will still be shocked, disturbed, or horrified at what they do or think about doing. Along these lines, Marin (1981) cogently portrays how many Vietnam veterans are now living in moral pain. Such feelings are difficult for men to discuss. Sometimes male clients prematurely leave counseling because the therapist effectively uncovered these feelings, but perhaps too quickly. The male client might believe it is better to repress and avoid such aggression rather than to examine it further. A male counselor who understands the impact of these feelings can be extremely therapeutic in helping the male client understand his psychological world and perhaps aspects of the human condition.

As therapy progresses, and especially as more personal material is disclosed, often a feeling of intimacy and closeness will develop between the counselor and client. Sometimes intimacy occurs when men talk about their deeper feelings of hurt, fear, and anxiety that may lie beneath their anger and hostility. While the deeper levels of intimacy may be a positive indicator of therapeutic effectiveness, the intimate feelings may be simultaneously gratifying and horrifying (see Lewis, 1978; Scher, 1980). To be understood can be validating and highly therapeutic. The intimacy, however, may be confused with sexuality because these two issues are often interrelated for men; thus for a man to feel psychologically close to another man often leads to a range of homophobic reactions. Along with the satisfaction of heightened intimacy with another, the client may also react with fear, disgust, or question his sexuality as well as the therapist and the therapy process. The client may again withdraw from the relationship in various ways (including termination) because the feelings may seem inappropriate or confusing.

It is incumbent upon the therapist to check with the client about such feelings, and help the client separate the feelings of intimacy and sexuality in their relationships. This task is in one sense an educational one, helping the male client identify and recognize the emotional closeness that results from an intimate interpersonal relationship, apart from sexual feelings. If sexual feelings are indeed present, it is our opinion that the counselor should then facilitate an examination of these feelings and clarify the boundaries of the therapeutic relationship. This can be a highly charged issue for most men, and thus necessitates caution. It is imperative not only that the client *is* safe, but also that he *feels* safe in the therapeutic relationship.

Counselor Issues

The counselor, the other half of this dyad, also enters the counseling relationship with his own set of values and assumptions about what a man is and should be. Since most male counselors have also been socialized in the American culture, their values and assumptions, particularly about the male role, can facilitate or inhibit the male client's coping processes and growth.

The male counselor might have sexist attitudes about men and convey this to the male client in varying degrees of subtlety. The counselor might convey a lack of acceptance, perhaps by suggesting that the man is weak, that he should be able to handle this type of problem. Or the counselor may unconsciously convey contempt or disgust for the male client because "men aren't supposed to act like that."

The male counselor, due to his own socialization, may be unable to offer the needed therapeutic interventions. For example, if the counselor is uncomfortable accepting and expressing his own emotions, he may inhibit, consciously or unconsciously, the client's expression of emotion. This can manifest itself in many forms, overt as well as subtle. For example, a young male counselor became frightened by a male client's emotions because he was afraid of "losing control"; as a result the counselor would consistently change the focus of therapy to avoid his own emotional reactions. Another male counselor, in an attempt to compensate for deeply ingrained feelings of inadequacy, developed an aloof and "cool" interpersonal style. In therapy his nonchalant and detached style often made it difficult for clients in general, but men in particular, to confide in and trust him. Yet another male counselor had difficulty in being emotionally supportive and tender with other men. He was afraid of being "too feminine" and thus had difficulty communicating concern and warmth. Another male counselor had difficulty working with male homosexual clients because his feelings of warmth and regard were confused with his homophobic reactions. In short, sometimes male therapists because of their own gender issues are impaired in providing therapeutic conditions for other men; they thus have difficulty touching their male clients psychologically.

Sometimes male counselors can actually harm their male clients. One danger is that the counselor's therapeutic style might actually enhance the dysfunctional patterns in a male client. For example, a male therapist might implicitly reinforce a male client's tendency to intellectualize by attending primarily to the client's cognitions. If a male client was ineffectively coping with his inability to relate with women by intellectualizing and distancing himself from women, the counselor's own issues with women may interfere with his ability to provide effective interventions. The counselor may perpetuate the client's maladaptive patterns by focusing on his rationalizations, rather than the anxiety and discomfort that he experiences with women. The counselor's emphasis on the client's cognitive processes (to the exclusion of his affective processes) can seriously hamper successful therapeutic interventions, especially if it reinforces the client's defenses and maladaptive patterns.

It is not uncommon for male therapists to have needs to exercise control within therapy. The counselor may have a strong desire to control therapy, not for therapeutic reasons, but simply for the sake of control. Again, the effectiveness of therapy is reduced as the counselor works harder to maintain control than to be therapeutic. One male counselor felt a strong need to perform in therapy because a particular male client seemed "critical of the therapy process." A male client began therapy with another male counselor by questioning and doubting the counselor's competence and quality of training. Instead of addressing the client's need for reassurance, the counselor responded defensively, justifying his ability and occupation. The counselor's desire for competence and achievement, coupled with the perceived threat from the client, sometimes influenced the counselor to be less than therapeutic.

Sometimes male counselors have difficulty physically touching male clients as well. Fears of homosexuality can be a major barrier to intimacy. Sometimes a simple hug can communicate much needed concern. A male client who has just made a major disclosure of his emotions, for example, may be especially in need of affirmation and support. If the counselor is hesitant about physical contact, the client may interpret it as inappropriate and not be as likely to share such admissions in the future. If a male counselor feels overly anxious and uncomfortable about touching, he may be less than effective because some touching interventions are unavailable to him.

In contrast, the male-male counseling dyad offers the counselor some unique therapeutic opportunities. The counselor may be able to serve as a role model, demonstrating a range of interpersonal skills (e.g., self-disclosure, owning his feelings) and particularly as a transparent, genuine, fully human, effective man. If a male client was unable to express the pain about the death of a parent, the counselor's self-disclosure of his own parent's death and his reactions to it may serve to widen the phenomenal field of the client so that issues may be addressed through sharing a common emotional experience. Through his interpersonal behaviors and self-disclosures, the male counselor can help the male client to become more aware of his own psychological dynamics.

As the therapy process becomes more intimate, the counselor can reflect the feelings of camaraderie, the sense of partnership and belonging that many people, and men in particular, have learned to value through team sports and male-oriented institutions such as fraternities and the military. For example, a male counselor reflected the sense of camaraderie between the counselor and client, indicating that it was "rewarding to be a part of the therapeutic team." Another therapist who was conducting a men's group found it quite helpful to conceptualize the group as a "team" and that the work accomplished in it was "a team effort." By doing so he was able to elicit a stronger sense of cooperation and alliance from the members. These examples stimulated each male client to examine his feelings about the therapist and, most important, the client's desire for emotional closeness in his primary relationships.

The counselor can also affirm the client's masculinity by explicitly indicating respect for the client as a man. For example, a male client entered counseling; the presenting problem was a deep sense of inadequacy in part resulting from a small penis. He felt that he was not capable of sexually satisfying a woman, which resulted in him becoming distant and isolated from others. He also regarded himself as inferior to most other men and their apparent successes with women; this engendered feelings of resentment and cynicism. As therapy progressed, the male counselor communicated how much he was impressed with the client's courage and his respect for the client as a fully human man. This almost paradoxical intervention was important to the client in restoring his sense of masculinity.

Conclusions

A central assumption of this chapter has been that the male socialization process affects both male clients and counselors so that certain difficulties or opportunities might be encountered in the therapy process. Whereas a wide range of theapeutic benefits are available for male clients, the male-male counseling dyad presents unique opportunities for genuine masculine validation. We believe that knowledge of the male socialization process is critical information for the counseling process, to facilitate understanding of male clients as well as to enhance the awareness of male counselors. Thus it is important that counselors are aware of the male socialization process, and especially that male counselors become aware of the effects of their own socialization process in their professional training and their own therapy.

More and more attention is being given to the gender socialization process of both men and women in American culture as well as other parts of the world. More recently, therapists have begun to examine the implications of the socialization process for the therapy process (e.g., Gilbert, 1985). This body of literature, while important, is still at a very early stage of development; much more attention is needed. For example, women typically seek mental health services more than men. What events take place that cause the reduced frequency for males? What characteristics of male therapists are more (or less) facilitative of change in male clients?

Likewise, much more attention is needed within master's and doctoral-level training programs about the implications of trainees' gender socialization. How both the counselor and client view themselves as men in our culture will affect how both people interact and process information in the therapy experience. We believe that it is critical to understand the cognitive, affective, and behavioral coping processes that men bring into the counseling context to understand more fully how men can benefit from therapy.

References

Crites, J. O., & Fitzgerald, L. F. (1978). The competent male. *The Counseling Psychologist, 7,* 10-14.

David, D. S., & Brannon, R. (Eds.) (1976). *The forty-nine percent majority: The male sex-role.* Reading, MA: Addison-Wesley.

Deaux, K. (1976). *The behavior of women and men.* Monterey, CA: Brooks/Cole.

Dubbert, J. (1979). *A man's place: Masculinity in transition.* Englewood Cliffs, NJ: Prentice-Hall.

Fasteau, M. F. (1974). *The male machine.* New York: McGraw-Hill.

Franks, V., & Burtle, V. (Eds.). (1974). *Women in therapy.* New York: Brunner/Mazel.

Gilbert, L. A. (1985). Educating about gender and sexuality issues in graduate training.

Symposium presented at the annual meeting of the American Psychological Association, Los Angeles.

Goldberg, H. (1976). *The hazards of being male: Surviving the myth of masculine privilege.* New York: Nash.

Gondolf, E. W. (1985). *Men who batter: An integrated approach to stopping wife abuse.* Holmes Beach, FL: Learning Publications.

Komarovsky, M. (1976). *Dilemmas of masculinity: A study of college youth.* New York: W. W. Norton.

Lewis, R. A. (1978). Emotional intimacy among men. *Journal of Social Issues, 34,* 108-121.

Maccoby, E., & Jacklin, C. (1974). *The psychology of sex differences.* Palo Alto, CA: Stanford University Press.

Marin, P. (1981). Living in moral pain. *Psychology Today, 15,* 68-80.

Morgan, B. (1976). Intimacy of disclosure topics and sex differences in self-disclosure. *Sex Roles, 2,* 161-165.

O'Leary, V. (1977). *Toward understanding women.* Monterey, CA: Brooks/Cole.

O'Neil, J. M. (1981). Male sex-role conflicts, sexism, and masculinity: Psychological implications for men, women, and the counseling psychologist. *The Counseling Psychologist, 9,* 61-80.

Pleck, J. H. (1981). *The myth of masculinity.* Cambridge, MA: MIT Press.

Pleck, J. H., & Sawyer, J. (1974). *Men and masculinity.* Englewood Cliffs, NJ: Prentice-Hall.

Scher, M. (1979). On counseling men. *Personnel and Guidance Journal, 58,* 252-254.

Scher, M. (1980). Men and intimacy. *Counseling and Values, 25,* 62-68.

Skovholt, T. (1978). Feminism and men's lives. *Counseling Psychologist, 7,* 3-10.

Zuckerman, E. L. (Ed.). (1975). *Women and men: Roles, attitudes, and power relationships.* New York: Radcliffe Club of New York.

2

Woman Therapist: Male Client

Nancy L. Carlson

An explosion in awareness of the restrictiveness of sex-role expectations for both women and men has occurred over the past few years, a change that was largely precipitated by the women's movement. As women have changed their behavior and self-perceptions through what has been a difficult and painful process, the men in their lives have felt the impact. Many have begun to listen and to examine their own behavior and their perceptions of the male role and its attendant limitations and entitlements.

One effect is a developing men's movement that has spawned some effective support groups and some men have modeled new behaviors in parenting children, in supporting women in their careers, and in relating more openly with each other. Most males, however, still remain largely uncommunicative about their needs and feelings, avoid intimacy except through sex, and remain isolated, competitive, and separate. With concerns being voiced that the world is in danger from male-dominated systems that rely on competition, aggressiveness, and power over people and nature, many men are beginning to seek therapeutic assistance for the growing uneasiness they experience in their lives.

The Development of
Role Identity

Until the late 1970s the model of health for both men and women was the white, middle-class male sex role. Male identity was defined as a series of developmental stages that generally described health as independence, separation, aggression, and unemotional interaction. Conclusions about research utilizing only men as subjects were applied to women even though researchers sometimes, according to Gilligan, dropped women subjects from the studies because their responses were complicating the data (Van Gelder, 1984).

By 1978, Nancy Chodorow had suggested that the development of gender identity for males and for females was quite different and that early parent-child interaction, especially with the mother, set the stage for those differences. Female children, she found in her research, were experienced by the mother as like her and tended to remain in this primary relationship. Attachment and separation, as a result, became the major issues of growth for daughters.

Sons, however, were experienced as different from the mother, and were pushed out (or pushed themselves out) of that relationship with a consequent identification with a distant father and a loss of empathy with the mother. Male issues of growth thus became independence and intimacy. While females know themselves through attachments, males know themselves through separation. Carol Gilligan has argued on the basis of her research on the development of moral values that women see the world in terms of connectedness and are threatened by isolation, and men see the world in terms of autonomy and are threatened by intimacy (Gilligan, 1982).

Males also, according to Jean Baker Miller (1983), often feel abandoned by their fathers, many of whom have developed no basis for the exchange of emotion with their children. Men encourage and even stimulate little boys to anger by sparring physically or verbally with them, then redirect the anger into aggressive behavior by refusing to let it be expressed directly at themselves by punishing it if that occurs. The more hurt, vulnerable, or frightened the boy, the more aggressive he may become. Disconfirmed by his father, the male thus is often unable to experience directly emotions such as fear, hurt, anger or sadness.

Resistance to Therapy

Denied the opportunity of a rich relationship with his mother and feeling emotionally abandoned by his father, the male has little choice but to become part of the membership of the larger group that is dominant in the culture. With male gender identity being based on dominance, separation, and "individuation and a more defensive firming of ego boundaries" (Chodorow, 1978, p. 166), it is unlikely that he will select therapy as a way to solve problems. Therapy threatens that identity with its inherent intimacy and relatedness, and it is often viewed therefore as feminine, something the male must "not be." The expression of vulnerability, emotional needs, pain, and confusion are the antithesis of maleness and may inspire a sense of danger in males who have been taught that to explore their emotional selves will lead to humiliation and rejection, especially by other males. This may be one of the reasons that males often prefer female therapists.

Another may be the belief that there is greater emotional safety with a woman since females are expected to be caregivers. Safety is, of course, crucial to the process of self-exploration in relationships, and it may allow the male to experience intimacy without losing his identity as a male. In a controlled situation, he can reclaim the emotional life he has been unable to live. He can drop his defensive boundaries, explore his fears, sorrows and needs, and reexperience the losses of both parents. Integrating and balancing what Jung (1959) has called the animus (male) and anima (female) parts of himself may be more possible with a female therapist because of her history of intimacy, relationships, and emotional attachment and because she is his "opposite" or counterpart, representing his own anima.

Therapeutic Issues for Males

Therapy with men is complicated by issues that are directly affected by separateness and fear of intimacy. In order to be independent the male has had to reject a relational life and he very early, as a colleague of Janet Surrey's (1983, p. 4) described, learns "not to listen, to shut out my mother's voice so that I would not be distracted from pursuing my own interests." Any effort to reverse the process in order to learn to respond to self and others' feeling states requires a giving up of control and dominance. Such a process may require radical trust and initially inspire terror and anger, then a confrontation with his rejected feminine self, which may be unconscious and completely out of his awareness. The assumption of male entitlement is in direct conflict with the desire for intimacy in which the needs of his emotional self may be met. Such a process may be very confusing to the client and require that the therapist be firm, understanding, and patient. Since some males are more aggressive when frightened or hurt, the female therapist may find him returning to efforts to control and dominate as he struggles with his confusion about himself.

Precipitants for Seeking Therapy

Because seeking help is anathema to the male sex-role stereotype, those males who do request therapy are often in more serious difficulty than females (Kirschner, 1978; Rice, 1969). A colleague recently described working with a young man who was unable to talk about himself; he just sat there in evident pain and responded to questions by nodding or shaking his head. Eventually it became clear that he had just lost a relationship, the first one in his life beyond a deprived existence with his parents, and he felt emotionally incapacitated. Loss or threat of loss often propels males into therapy. Since relationships, especially with females, are so crucial to the expression of any kind of emotional life for some men, the loss is devastating. He may feel emptied of any sense of emotional selfhood, connectedness, aliveness, the half of himself he has relegated to women. Any relationship loss, however, including that of a parent, child, friend, or colleague, may be traumatic. In addition, with the male's investment in work as his life, the loss of a job, college major, or career goal may have the same effect. Incidents of males losing their jobs and continuing their patterns of arising and dressing for work as usual, then returning at the usual hour at the end of the day are heard often enough. These men cannot bear to tell their families that they are out of work. Their very identity is at stake.

In periods of major life change, including divorce, death, or developmental transitions, men often experience a feeling of incompetence and lose a sense of self-worth. The extreme need to achieve and fear of failure, the excessive need to be in control (DuBois, 1978), and terror when things are not in their control make men vulnerable to seeing themselves as "wimps," weak and unable to do what they "should" do. "Masculinity," as Jung (1928) indicated, "means to know one's goal and to do what is necessary to achieve it." This accomplishment-focused lifestyle for men often leaves them susceptible to a collapse of self-esteem when it is based rigidly on external expectations rather than internal flexibility and self-knowledge through relationship to others.

Some men seek therapy because their friends, spouses, or lovers have threatened to leave them unless they begin to change their behavior. Unable to share their dilemma with friends and unable to change through force of will, they accept therapy as a last resort in hopes of averting the loss. A number of young college males on one campus recently requested help for themselves to avoid hitting their girlfriends after being told that if it happened again their girlfriends would leave. Each of the males had been raised in a home where their fathers felt free to hit their mothers to assure control and these young males were experiencing frustration with their girlfriends' demand for equality, respect, and freedom in the relationship.

Sometimes the development of intimacy in a new or continuing relationship is so threatening that it drives the male into therapy. The conflict experienced in desiring the closeness and fearing it precipitates confusion and avoidance of the very person to whom he is attracted. As difficult as it may be if the person is female, the problem is confounded much more by another male, as fears of homosexuality may surface and overwhelm him. Males have received strong societal sanctions for experiencing intimacy only through sex and only with women, and when the desire for emotional intimacy that goes beyond sex surfaces in a relationship, males often assume that sex and intimacy are the same. There are few models from which males can learn to differentiate the two. Fears of homosexuality may occur for the male with either gender when the desire for closeness is felt, as the lack of a wish for sex with a female in a situation of intimacy may be interpreted by him to mean that he must prefer men. Therapy may be one of the best ways to explore and resolve that fear, and to clarify the meanings of both sex and intimacy for the male client.

Therapeutic Process Issues

With male development being grounded in separation there is very little preparation for the first stage of adulthood defined by Erikson as intimacy (1968). His charting of life cycle stages of development holds that identity precedes intimacy, a process that is different for women in that it may be either fused or reversed (Gilligan, 1979). Male identity development presumes individuation and independence, and for males who are confronting the issue of intimacy through attachment to another person, there may be a feeling of a loss of self, a feeling of being smothered as the rigid "boundary between self and world" (Levinson, 1978) lessens, and he becomes threatened by the experience of engulfment. Since males often identify this experience with females, the female therapist may find that he is projecting onto her the feminine side of himself, so long denied and often so primitive and frightening to him. (It will, of course, be important for her to understand that his projections are his and not descriptive of her as she patiently works through these unfamiliar and suppressed feelings of his.) What a man needs to learn in this process is that he can become intimate with another human being without losing his self and without being engulfed. In the safety of the structured therapeutic setting, with its clear limits and boundaries, it becomes possible to try out this feeling side of self with someone who understands the struggle from her greater experience with intimacy. Once he lets go of the control he has had to utilize to protect himself from his own needs, he may reexperience his hurt and anger with both parents and release himself and them from that burden. He may also reexperience those feelings about other losses in his life. Then he can move on to adulthood with its attendant intimacies and struggles as a more whole person, not so dependent on the rules for being a man.

In the therapeutic relationship there is a sharing of the self with another person who does not violate that self. There is, therefore, an opportunity to experience one's deepest fears, hopes, hates, joys, sorrows, and loves. For example, one male client feared that chaos would reign in his life if he let go of the control he felt he had to use to handle life and another feared that he was not worthy as a human being. Still another felt he was incompetent as a person. All felt vulnerable to the desire to be dependent on someone who cared for them, and loved them for who they were, not what they did.

As a male experiences these conflicts and enters a therapeutic relationship with a woman therapist he is likely to want early assurances of his worth. He may be wanting to test his capacity to control the interaction and ensure protection from his own fears. He may become disappointed or angry if he does not receive easy assurance from a woman who understands that shoring up rigid defenses in that manner will only serve to support the sex-role stereotype that is so destructive. In addition, if he controls the interaction, he may in effect sabotage his own growth and undermine the therapist's attempts to be helpful.

These power dynamics in the relationship of the male client with a female counselor appear early and demand recognition if there is to be resolution during the process. For a male to enter therapy and abdicate power to a woman, with whom he is usually expected to be dominant, is very stressful (Downing, 1981)—that is, unless he is experiencing extreme emotional discomfort, at which time alleviating the pain is his primary concern. The power dynamics may become an issue, however, as the pain diminishes. The power issues tend to dissipate with an explanation that he is in charge of defining the direction of the therapy and for educating the therapist about who he is. Once one client heard that from his therapist, he stopped disagreeing with every interpretation she offered and began to express his concerns about his pattern of problems. Her responsibility is to work with him on these issues, including those revolving around power and control, and to assist him toward creating a more rewarding life. A collaborative relationship is one of equals working together toward a mutual goal, and developing a relationship of collaboration and trust usually involves identifying issues of power so that they do not block the process.

There may also be an expectation on the part of the male client that the female therapist will defer to his perceptions of the situation rather than to question them or consider alternative views. Deference to male thinking, as inexperienced female therapists often discover, precipitates neither movement for the client nor a sense of competence in the therapist. The reinforcement of the sex-role stereotype for both people diminishes the potential for developing a rewarding relationship that produces a commitment to his personal growth and change. The tendency to avoid problems by behaving as one always has as a way to avoid painful confrontation with one's self is what brings people to therapy. Necessary to changing that process is learning how to experience what Peck (1978) calls "legitimate suffering" that results from dealing with problems. Acceptance and support, which are essential on the part of the therapist, produce little change without confrontation. To alter any behavior pattern that is self-destructive requires exposing that pattern in a clear, direct, and caring way. It also requires trusting the client's courage and resources for dealing with the pain of recognition of the behavior and the consequences of it for himself and others.

One therapist found that it was not uncommon for males to tell her that she did not know what she was talking about when she said she sensed fear in them in the first few sessions. They would reassure her that they were not afraid of her, only concerned about getting a change accomplished soon. One male said he wasn't sure he could trust her to care about him without involvement outside the office, something she felt was a control issue. She explained why that was not possible. Then he began to share his grief over an impending divorce. She knew he needed the security of clear limits on the relationship with her in order to feel he could be vulnerable. He became anxious again when she explored the depth of the grief with him and often tried to intellectualize it, blaming his wife for not caring and himself for not seeing the divorce coming. Eventually the anxiety became overwhelming and he was unable to sit still. He paced the office until she suggested that he was afraid of being understood at a deep level. He angrily said yes and sat down, realizing how little he had been understood and known for who he was, how much he had missed all his life. Then he cried and told her that his family had always expected him as the only male to take care of them, to be strong and successful, and the provider of advice and action when they were in difficulty. He was never able to receive or be vulnerable because he had to be strong for them; even his wife did not know who he was. The therapist gently suggested that now he could begin to be himself and allow others to take care of him at times. He angrily said he didn't know if he could do that, and she proposed that he would be withholding a gift, that others wanted to take care of him but did not believe he would let them. He relaxed and said he would try.

The male client may not be prepared initially for confrontation from a woman and may become aggressive, defensive, or even threatening, sometimes even terminating therapy. Men often accuse women of being "castrating bitches" when they feel angry at being confronted with something that is painful or feels in some way attacking. Firmness in clarifying what the therapist has observed without judging him negatively and without becoming in turn defensive or hurt by his anger is most often helpful. In addition, the therapist may need to indicate that she understands his pain and that such labels do not apply to her. Remaining centered, consistent, and nondefensive in the face of his aggressiveness is often crucial to his developing trust for her and a commitment to his own therapy.

Defenses that limit the man's capacity to be naturally spontaneous and expressive need to be pointed out and recognized as limiting. While he may refuse to lend any credibility to her interpretation of his defenses, refuse to focus on his feelings, accuse her of being angry at all men, and suggest that she is not meeting his needs nor is she a good therapist, he will still need tact, patience, persistence, and sensitivity from her to move beyond them. As he recognizes these as defenses that are destructive to living a full life, he will gradually give them up and replace them with more healthy and productive behaviors.

Once he begins to see that he has a trustworthy, sensitive, direct and firm collaborator in his therapist, the fear of being out of control and no longer dominant will begin to diminish. He may then begin to experience a desire to be dependent on her, which in turn often produces a fear of dependency as well as a fear of eventual loss of the therapist. Becoming vulnerable to the child subpersonality in himself, which fears being hurt or abandoned by anyone he is beginning to trust and need, and admitting it can be a profound threat for a male who has been separate all his life. Such a crisis sometimes results in sudden termination, renewed efforts to control the interaction, or a sabotaging of the therapy in any number of ways. It is important that the woman therapist recognize both his need and his fear of it and invite him to approach it slowly while she reassures him of her commitment to continue to work with him. He is at his most vulnerable at that time and will instantly move to protect himself if she is not clear and sensitive to it. His greatest fears will be projected onto her then, and she will need to clarify for him the differences between his projections, which are reflections of his own rejected feminine side, and herself.

A male client indicated to his therapist not long ago that he was afraid to continue in counseling because he was becoming frightened of being dependent and feared that he would be judged as weak. When he was assured that he was seen as quite courageous he visibly relaxed and did not mention it again. He, of course, had judged himself as weak, and his fear inhibited his natural expression of need.

As the male client becomes more able to experience his emotions, including those that are painful and associated with his early life and its attendant disappointments, he may continue to need encouragement to share them. Since he may have few skills at expressing feelings, he will require a very sensitive and perceptive confidante who is unafraid of strong emotions. The issues of dependency, need, and sexual attraction between the client and therapist will then have to be talked about. Encouraging the male client to differentiate sex from intimacy by expressing emotional attractions and intimate thoughts and feelings in words, rather than through sexual contact, presents another kind of threat to a man who expresses himself through action. A man who is at ease in making sexual overtures may feel quite inept and embarrassed at speaking about his fear of surrendering control or his need to be cared for. The therapist will need to be comfortable with both her sexuality and being desired by the client so that she can explore the sexual feelings between them *without ever acting on them*. Safety is essential in therapy for the person to grow, and safety from sexual activity helps to assure moving toward healthy intimacy in other relationships. The development of and expression of intimacy in therapy may move the male to adulthood and wholeness, and it may also release the man to own the feminine side of himself for greater balance.

Sharing deep emotions may also permit him to see his separateness, the denial of his needs, his inability to express feelings, and his sense of shame for his vulnerabilities as uncaring of himself and limiting of his ability to give and receive love in his relationships. He may learn to stop evaluating himself so harshly and begin to drop some of the assumptions that he has held about himself and others in favor of new ones that are more empathic. Each of the values he gives up will of course precipitate a period of grieving until he can accept the loss and replace it with a value that is more rewarding and offers him a more positive and deeper sense of self.

As he moves toward the termination of his therapy he may once again begin to experience discomfort, this time with separation from the therapist. Leaving an intimate relationship is painful, and he may try to do it abruptly, thus aborting what some have called the most important part of the process. If aborted, sharing the sadness, appreciating the process, and building anticipation for a healthier life leaves both people with a sense of being unfulfilled, unfinished. To share saying goodbye with an honest expression of feelings about what the relationship means to both is crucial to completing the therapeutic relationship. Then the separation can be complete and fulfilled, and he can move on to assimilate his growth into a healthier life with others.

Special Problems for
the Female Therapist

Therapists cannot move clients past the point where they are in their development. The female therapist therefore, has an obligation to grow beyond the sex role that traps women into limiting behavior that in turn does not challenge the male client and presumes a power imbalance in his favor and a caregiver role for her. One of the earliest learnings for one inexperienced therapist was to let a male client cry. Neither counselor or client had been willing for him to be vulnerable despite his need to be. Once her male supervisor said, "Let him cry," she had permission to challenge him, and he took the opportunity to express feelings he had denied for years. It released him from a great deal of tension and allowed for unanticipated change. Caregiving in that situation was protecting him from his own freedom. Subsequently, the female therapist may need to learn many times to use the power she has as a therapist and woman to free clients from constrictions rather than to collude with maintaining them. Therapists must move beyond limiting sex roles in order for their clients to do so.

Female therapists, like a large percentage of females in this culture, have experienced mistreatment by males because of the power imbalance. The abuse could be in the form of harassment or job discrimination or incest or rape, and if not explored and resolved could have an unconscious effect on the male client. Awareness of one's anger and hurt over previous abuses is crucial in assuring that a male client is not in turn abused for the "sins" of other men. The vulnerable male client cannot be forced to suffer for something he did not do.

Since women have not been offered much opportunity to participate in male-male interactions, it may be difficult to understand male competition and threat, male bonding, and male friendship (which is very different from female friendships), and women will have to spend time learning from their clients what that experience is like without judging it. It is important both for appreciating the man's life experience and for recognizing the anima in herself so that she does not project what may be her own suppressed masculine side on her client.

Depending on its nature, attraction to a male client may present a difficult problem for a woman therapist. If it is toward the male as a son, she may have a tendency to be a mother-caregiver who does not challenge him to grow in significant ways. If it is toward the man as a lover, she may be unable to see him realistically and may precipitate a strong transference by being more unconsciously seductive than consciously helpful. If it is toward the man as a father, she may relate to him as an authority and support a power imbalance by either deferring to him or fighting him. Either deferring or fighting undermines the equality required for his growth in therapy. As attractions are often projections, they need to be recognized and dealt with so that genuine attractiveness of two human beings working in collaboration for the growth of the client is accomplished. Caring for a client and seeing him for who he is provides the greatest opportunity for that growth.

Repulsion for a male client may be the experience of some therapists and such a feeling needs recognition before it has a negative effect on the client. Continuing to work with any client one does not like is neither ethical nor humane. An honest disclosure regarding the therapist's inability to provide what the client may need and suggesting an appropriate referral may be the best service the client can receive. This may occur when a female therapist who has been abused is asked for example to work with a rapist, or she may be offended when asked to work with someone who seems to be a bigot, racist, or sexist. She may be frightened to work with someone who is extremely aggressive, in which case the referral should be immediate. Fear of a client prevents any real possibility of openness and understanding.

All therapists who are able to be gentle and strong, open and aware, grow because of the relationships with their clients. As clients change they have an impact on their change agents as therapists allow themselves to be deeply involved in what Seguin (1965) calls the "psychotherapeutic Eros," the unique and unconditioned love a therapist has for a client, the love that frees another human being to love.

It is an unselfish and undemanding gift to free a man from hiding, disguising, denying, and avoiding his feelings because of an expectation of rejection by both other males, where his self-esteem is at stake, and females, where his dominance is at stake. No less can be given in a world where time appears to be short and fears for our collective future are great. Women therapists who have the opportunity to work with male clients must accept the full responsibility for helping to create a different consciousness of life, one where balance is achieved.

McClelland, (1975, p. 96), found that the characteristic of the power motivation of the mature feminine style was that of "independence, building up resources, and giving." When this is added to an achievement-oriented masculine style in one person, a perspective is possible that is not inherent in either alone. To do this effectively the female therapist must become balanced herself. She must have experienced difficult separations in her life that resulted in individuation and firmer ego boundaries and an integration of risk taking and power into her sense of self. She must be more comfortable with her own anima, her power to confront and create, to change inside and to affect the world. Assuming an emotional, physical, and spiritual responsibility for ourselves and each other may be essential to our survival. Flexibility and personal strength arising from interdependence and the realization of a connectedness to all of life are the building blocks for both men and women to assure an individual and collective future for this earth.

References

Chodorow, N. (1978). *The reproduction of mothering*. Berkeley: University of California Press.

Downing, N. (1981, March). *Counseling men: Issues for female counselors*. Paper presented at the American College Personnel Association Convention, Cincinnati, OH.

DuBois, T. (1978). Male therapists' fears of the feminist movement. *Social Change, 8*, 1-3.

Erikson, R. (1968). *Identity, youth and crisis*. New York: W. W. Norton.

Gilligan, C. (1982). *In a different voice*. Cambridge, MA: Harvard University Press.

Jung, C. G. (1928). *Contributions to analytical psychology*. London: Routledge & Kegan Paul.

Jung, C. G. (1959). *Aion*. London: Routledge & Kegan Paul.

Kirschner, L. A. (1978). Effects of gender on psychotherapy. *Comprehensive Psychiatry, 19*, 79-82.

Levinson, D. (1978). *The seasons of a man's life.* New York: Knopf.

McClelland, D. (1975). *Power: The inner experience.* New York: Irvington.

Miller, J. B. (1983). *The construction of anger in men and women.* Work in progress (No. 83-01). Wellesley, MA: Stone Center.

Peck, S. (1978). *The road less traveled.* New York: Simon & Schuster.

Rice, D. G. (1969). Patient sex differences and selection for individual therapy. *Journal of Nervous and Mental Disease, 148*, 124-133.

Seguin, C. A. (1965). *Love and psychotherapy.* New York: Libra.

Surrey, J. (1983, November). *Self in relation: A theory of women's development.* Paper presented at the Stone Center Colloquium Series, Wellesley, MA.

Van Gelder, L. (1984, January). Carol Gilligan: *Leader for a Different Kind of Future,* pp. 37-40.

3

Counseling Men
in Groups

Frederic E. Rabinowitz
Sam V. Cochran

Over the past decade a number of approaches to working with men in all-male groups have been described. Some of these approaches include consciousness-raising groups (Bradley, Danchik, Foger, & Wodetzki, 1971), structured and unstructured groups for increasing male awareness (Cochran & Rabinowitz, 1983; Washington, 1979), self-help and support groups (Wong, 1978), and all-male psychotherapy groups (Stein, 1982). The identification of issues unique to men has become more important as men initially reacted to the impact of feminism on their lives and later began to articulate issues related to gender-role strain and conflict. Many of these gender-role issues are described in the literature (Fasteau, 1974; Goldberg, 1976; O'Neill, 1981, 1982; Pleck & Sawyer, 1974) and provide some useful topics for men to address in their process of self-discovery. Since many of these issues are interpersonal in nature (e.g., intimacy, competition, anger, restrictive emotionality, power) the usefulness of all-male groups as an environment in which to address them has become increasingly apparent. The group becomes an interpersonal microcosm in which various male issues become manifest and available for study and modification (Yalom, 1975).

Stein (1982) has delineated the values, assumptions, and outcomes that membership in all-male groups represents. Some of these include representing a statement about nontraditional masculine values, providing an opportunity for men to relate to other men in an interpersonal setting without women, providing a setting in which to discuss topics that are usually difficult for men to discuss, such as dependency and sexuality (sexual identity, homosexuality, and early childhood sexual experiences), and increasing the political awareness of men as a means for addressing individual and institutional sexism. The all-male group has become an ideal vehicle for facilitation of these tasks as more men perceive the value of self-discovery and self-change. The practitioner who is forming an all-male group designed to address these issues has many variables and tasks to consider.

The purpose of this chapter is to identify these variables and tasks, specify their dimensions, and suggest various responses for the practitioner. The format parallels the same process the practitioner will follow in addressing the issues that arise in the establishment and facilitation of an all-male group. The reader who is considering facilitating an all-male group is encouraged to consult the references cited within the text of this chapter for further information.

Forming the Group

Prior to the group's first meeting the facilitator needs to consider a number of important issues related to goals, structure, setting, screening, and other variables of an adminsitrative nature. Many of these issues interact and mutually affect one another. However, an attempt will be made to separate them as clearly as possible and raise the questions that need to be considered for each.

GOALS

Specification of the goals of the group is one of the first issues that the group facilitator must address. Will the group be a consciousness-raising group, a psychotherapy group, a growth group, a support group, or a group designed to address a discrete problem or issue?

Consciousness raising groups have the following goals: to increase awareness of the impact of gender-role strain and conflict, to discuss this impact as it relates to the individual group members, and to share personal support in the process of exploration of these issues. Some issues discussed in consciousness raising groups include restrictive emotionality, lack of self-care, conflict concerning issues of competition and power, difficulties with intimacy, individual reactions to feminism and the women's movement, and concerns with male-male and male-female relationships. Growth groups and support groups such as those described by Cochran and Rabinowitz (1983) and Washington (1979) also have goals that converge with the goals for consciousness raising groups yet differ by the amount and type of structure provided by the facilitator.

Stein (1982) has described the content and process of all-male psychotherapy groups. He suggests the following goals for these groups: to decrease current emotional distress, to identify and remediate significant disturbances in interpersonal relationships, and to address concerns about gender identity and gender-role performance as they relate specifically to the group members. These goals are addressed within a context that includes an explicit psychotherapy contract between the members of the group and the facilitator (group psychotherapist) and an expectation that participation in the group will lead to significant interpersonal and intrapsychic change.

Purdy and Nickle (1981), Currie (1983), Buckley, Miller, and Rolfe (1983), and Bern and Bern (1984) all describe groups designed for men who commit acts of violence. The goals of these groups include the following: to increase the awareness of the group members' violent acts, to increase group members' sense of responsibility for their behavior, and to teach group members other avenues for expression of anger and hostility. Additional examples include groups designed to develop intimacy in isolated men (Bresler, 1982) and to explore sexual experiences and issues (Timmers & Drescher, 1979).

STRUCTURE

Consideration of the goals of any group intersects with questions about the dimensions of structure to be provided by the facilitator. In this context, structure refers to the introduction of procedures, agendas, and specific group exercises by the facilitator. Structure usually varies with the type of group. Interpersonal process-oriented psychotherapy groups with an open-ended format typically require relatively more structure (see Rose, 1977; Washington, 1979). Amount of structure may also vary depending on whether the group is time limited (e.g., 8 or 16 sessions) or ongoing (no specific ending date identified in advance). Other aspects of the group that have a bearing on the amount of structure provided by the facilitator include screening, orientation to the group at a member's first meeting, introduction of exercises at the beginning of the group or as part of the ongoing process of the group, and provision of a structured means for terminating the group. Various authors have written about the kinds of structure they provide in their groups (e.g., Croteau & Burda, 1983; Heppner, 1983; Kaufman & Timmers, 1983; Lewis, 1978; Washington, 1979).

SOLO OR COFACILITATION

Assuming that the group to be formed is one that requires leadership (some groups are specifically designed to be leaderless) the question of whether to lead the group solo or to collaborate with a cofacilitator requires careful consideration. Pfeiffer and Jones (1975) outline some of the advantages and disadvantages of cofacilitating groups. The advantages include being able to facilitate group development more easily as well as provide focus for individual development within the group, modeling appropriate interpersonal behavior, providing a cushion or safety net for dealing with heightened affect that may emerge within the group, deflecting member dependency issues onto both facilitators rather than one, and heightening focus and pacing of the group. Some of the disadvantages include the extra investment of energy required, issues of threat and competition that may emerge between the facilitators, overwhelming the group with interventions, different pacing and rhythm, and the presence of mutual blind spots for both facilitators.

The solo facilitator assumes all responsibility for securing the physical setting, advertising the group if needed, screening the prospective members and of course leading the group during the group sessions. For the solo facilitator self-assessment that takes into account comfort with responsibility, leadership style, and knowledge about the proposed group is needed. In addition, Heppner (1981) suggests that men's group facilitators be familiar with their own issues of sexism and countertransference as well as knowledgeable about the particular constellation of issues that males typically bring into counseling.

Cofacilitation requires that the facilitators agree regarding the type of group to be formed, the goals of the group, and the type and nature of structure to be provided. They must be knowledgeable of each others' leadership styles as well as how each responds to typical incidents such as a demanding group member, a member who either monopolizes the conversation or who is silent during meetings, or a member who is absent or tardy on a regular basis. It is important for the facilitators to reach some consensus regarding how these and other potentially disruptive events will be managed. Cofacilitators can plan for structuring time outside the group for discussing both the group as well as each individual member and his progress or lack of progress in the group, need for outside consultation or supervision of their work, and how they each conceptualize their role in the group. Pfeiffer and Jones (1975) provide a cofacilitating inventory that serves as a stimulus as well as a structured instrument for mutual exploration of issues relevant to cofacilitators.

SETTING

The optimal setting for the group will depend on group goals, type of facilitation, and amount and type of structure to be provided. Psychotherapy groups may require a comfortable meeting room that is free from interruptions and that provides privacy and assurance of confidentiality for the members. Comfortable chairs or pillows on the floor serve to increase physical comfort for the members and may increase the likelihood of risk taking. Educational groups may require chairs arranged around a table, a blackboard for various activities, and good lighting. If the group is to be observed for any reason (e.g., training of other group facilitators, supervision of the facilitator, research and so on) there must be a one-way window in the room as well as adequate sound transmission to the observation room. Some facilitators choose to audio- and/or videotape their group sessions. For taped sessions, equipment must be present in the room but not intrude in such a way that it hinders open discussion among group members. Boone and Reid (1978) address these and other considerations in selecting sites for group sessions and work- shops, and provide a checklist to guide facilitators in evaluating and selecting appropriate settings for their groups.

SCREENING

The use of a screening interview for prospective group members prior to entering a group has been widely supported in the literature on group counseling and psychotherapy (Bednar, Weet, Evenson, Lanier, & Melnick, 1974; Van Dyck, 1980). The screening interview serves several purposes. First, it enables the group facilitator to meet with a prospective group member, explain the purpose and goals of the group, and answer any questions regarding the group. Second, it enables the facilitator to assure an optimal "match" between the group goals and the prospective member's goals for the group. Third, it allows the facilitator to refer elsewhere prospective members for whom the group is deemed inappropriate. Finally, it enables the group facilitator to begin to share expectations and shape the norms of the group by discussing the nature of the group and the types of behavior expected in the group.

The group facilitator must specify the questions to explore with the prospective member prior to the screening interview as well as provide a setting for the interview. The following are some suggested questions that may be used as a guide in conducting a screening interview for a growth group or support group. The questions may also be applicable to screening for psychotherapy groups in that they elicit information that can contribute to personality assessment and diagnosis if so desired by the facilitator.

(1) How did you hear about this group?
(2) What do you expect to learn as a member of this group?
(3) Do you have any previous group experience? If so, what was it and what was it like for you?
(4) Are you currently in counseling or psychotherapy for any reason?
(5) What is a typical day like for you?
(6) Have you experienced any significant life events recently such as the loss of a significant person, a change in career, etc.?

(7) What makes you different from other men?
(8) Do you have any questions that relate to this group?

During the course of such an interview the facilitator can articulate expectations regarding attendance, commitment, self-disclosure, confidentiality, outside readings, and willingness to participate in structured exercises. As the interview progresses, the fit or lack of fit of the prospective member's goals with the goals of the group will begin to become clear. In the event of a fit with the group goals, the facilitator will end the interview by informing the prospective member about the first meeting, time, date, and place. If a significant discrepancy with the goals of the group is apparent, the facilitator may note such discrepancy and discuss this with the prospective member. The facilitator will suggest that the prospective member might be better served through a different group, other service, or perhaps no service at all. It is important that the prospective member understand this discrepancy and recognize the need for referral to some other service modality without feeling personally rejected by the facilitator. Two case examples will help clarify some of these issues.

THE CASE OF JIM K.

Jim K. responded to an advertisement in the local newspaper for an all-male group titled "The Male Experience." He had recently been separated from his spouse and was living on his own in a small efficiency apartment for the first time since his undergraduate college days. He had been married for seven years and reported that the current conflict he experienced with his spouse was the first in their marriage. At the screening interview he reported feeling confused and angry and requested a setting in which he could get some answers to the many questions about himself that this recent separation had raised. He also reported an increase in his alcohol intake, difficulty sleeping, and increasing difficulty concentrating on his work as a computer programmer. He had recently been confronted by his supervisor about his declining work performance.

The group facilitator explained that the group was designed to be a support group for men that had chosen to live a nontraditional lifestyle. Discussion of the benefits as well as the strains of these choices, relationships with both men and women, and the impact of feminism on the lives of the members was planned in a group that would be limited to 10 sessions. The facilitator understood that Jim was experiencing a significant amount of distress relative to his current situation, was reporting confusion as well as anger regarding this situation, and was also trying to decide if perhaps some individual psychotherapy might also be helpful. The facilitator explained that the group would be composed of men who had mostly answered many of the questions that Jim was asking for himself and suggested that they might not be of much help to him in his situation. In addition, Jim's significant depressive symptoms, increased drinking, and anger as a predominant affective state led the facilitator to offer Jim a referral for individual psychotherapy rather than a place in the group. Jim agreed with this assessment and accepted the referral with great hope and relief.

THE CASE OF ALAN H.

Alan H. responded to the same advertisement. He reported he had been cohabiting with a woman for the past four years and that their relationship was a good one for him. He described himself as a feminist and was active as a volunteer in a local crisis center. He was employed as a nurse in a large hospital and viewed his career as a nontraditional one with both political and personal implications. He reported an interest in discussing some of the difficulties he experienced in balancing his chosen values with those he had learned as a boy in a conservative midwestern town. He also desired to meet some other men who shared similar values. He had been a member of a similar group several years ago and reported it was a very positive experience for him.

The facilitator explained that the purpose of the group was to discuss these issues, provide support for men that had chosen nontraditional lifestyles and values, and offer an opportunity for men of similar values orientations to meet one another. He noted the congruence of the group goals with Alan's goals for the group, and also understood that Alan had affirmatively chosen these values as an important statement about his lifestyle. He offered Alan a place in the group and informed him of the time, date, and place of the first meeting as well as the planned group activities and time limit. Both agreed that the group would be a good idea for Alan.

SUMMARY

A number of issues regarding group goals, structure, facilitation, setting, and pregroup screening have been raised. The prospective facilitator of all-male groups must consider these issues in shaping a group that will be a useful vehicle for males to explore their own unique concerns. The reader is advised to consult the references cited in each specific section for further clarification and elaboration as well as the various ethical statements of the American Association for Counseling and Development (1981), the National Association of Social Workers (1980), the American College Personnel Association (1981), the Association for Specialists in Group Work (1980), and the American Psychological Association (1981) regarding advertisement, recruitment, and facilitation of personal growth and encounter groups as they might be relevant to the planned group.

The Working Group: Learning Through Conflict and Discovery

The following sections outline the process of a men's consciousness-raising/growth group based on our experience in facilitating these types of groups. Although the conflicts, issues, and stages may not always appear in the order presented, we will describe the group as it unfolds to give the reader a sense of its dynamic quality. While variations in group structure and purpose may alter the depth and intensity of the process, the issues raised and interventions suggested will be useful to the practitioner who is considering facilitating any type of all-male group.

INITIAL GROUP SESSIONS: SETTING THE TONE FOR LEARNING

The initial group session is important in setting the tone for the remainder of the life of the all-male group. The group members, anxious and hopeful, will be looking to the facilitator for structure and leadership. There may be an initial press from the members to get the facilitator to define the situation by introducing an exercise that will relieve their increasing levels of anxiety. The facilitator, based on personal orientation and the expected length of the group, may choose to rescue the group from its initial floundering or allow the natural group process to take its course.

Heppner (1983), Lewis (1978), and Washington (1979) suggest specific exercises to serve as icebreakers to facilitate introductory interactions among group participants. These exercises ask the group members to pair up, respond to a stimulus that elicits feelings about being male, and to share these feelings with a partner and then with the group as a whole. This procedure helps the group members get to know each other more rapidly. The structured approach has been shown to reduce initial levels of interpersonal anxiety (Washington, 1979), provide specific direction in the form of planned topics for discussion (Wong, 1978), and increase initial self-disclosure (Crews & Melnick, 1976).

Negative effects of early structure have also been documented (Lieberman, Yalom, & Miles, 1973). Group members may come to rely on the facilitator to rescue them from uncomfortable silences and conflicts that arise, leading to passivity and a lack of initiative in later stages of the group. The use of structure also seems to protect the male members from dealing with the interpersonal discomfort generated by being in an atypical all-male group that is not related to business, sports, or a specific task (Stein, 1982).

It has been our experience that if the group is to be longer than six sessions, the early role of the facilitator is best served by clarifying and supporting members in their initial discomfort while refraining from becoming too directive. This forces the members to confront the ambiguity of the situation and to take responsibility for their participation in the group. Following an awkward silence, one of the members usually suggests an icebreaker exercise that allows for the learning of names, occupation, and reasons for being in the group. This exercise will temporarily decrease anxiety and permit group members to communicate in familiar socially stereotyped conversational modes—taking turns speaking about past experiences in an intellectual and nonemotional manner. In the open-ended ongoing men's group, it is advised that new members be told in the screening interview that they will be expected to talk about themselves in the first meeting. This permits the new member to become involved in the group from the beginning and resensitizes the old members to the anxiety of being new to the group situation.

It is important for the facilitator to pay attention to the nonverbal components of early group communication. Arms folded across the body, minimal eye contact when speaking, and noticeable physical distance between group members should tip off the facilitator to underlying discomfort. By expressing feelings of anxiety and discomfort the facilitator can model nondefensive self-disclosure and a willingness to be vulnerable. The expression of flexible sex-role qualities by a male facilitator provides support and motivation to members attempting to make changes in their own lives through their participation in the group (Stein, 1982).

As the group becomes used to its members' and facilitator's characteristic styles of interacting, normative behavior patterns will come to be expected. This may take the form of taking turns speaking, waiting for the facilitator to intervene in interactions, and encouraging quiet members to be more expressive. At the root of this group behavior is a need for security and inclusion that is necessary before members risk experimenting with new behavior (Schutz, 1967; Yalom, 1975).

EARLY GROUP SESSIONS:
ENCOUNTERING RESISTANCE

One of the earliest communication problems encountered in the all-male group is that of self-listening (Farrell, 1975). Rather than listening to others to genuinely appreciate what is being expressed, group members tend to listen only long enough to prepare for what they are going to say in response. This prototypical form of relating reflects the aggressive and competitive nature of male communication (Lewis, 1978; Solomon, 1982). While being aware of their own tendency to engage in this type of communication, male facilitators need to be able to respond to the group members' attempts at self-expression by displaying high levels of empathic understanding. Exercises that incorporate communication skills with self-disclosure (Egan, 1986) may also be useful in improving listening ability among the men in the group.

Aside from poor communication, the early group process is also hampered by ambivalence about change (Stein, 1982). Although the group members will talk about their desire to integrate masculine and feminine qualities and have a less rigid sex-role style, the difficulty lies in translating these ideals into actual behavior. The facilitator role becomes one of drawing attention to discrepancies between what is being discussed and the accompanying here-and-now behavior of members. It can be expected that the men will become frustrated when confronted with this discrepancy. Some will find refuge in rationalizations about the positive aspects of the male role and blame women for their plight, while others will express guilt and self-blame for having unwanted male characteristics. The group "depression" that permeates this stage seems to be indicative of the male resistance to letting go of years of sex-role training despite the intellectual awareness of its harm (Silverberg, 1986).

A common pitfall of men's group facilitators dealing with male resistance is the overuse of interpretation as a form of intervention. Stein (1982) suggests that it is more helpful to male group members for facilitators to emphasize affective interventions because of the male tendency to use intellectual insights as a means of avoiding the expression of feelings. It is useful to have group members use "I" statements when describing their experience; to focus on the feelings being expressed rather than the content; to be aware of the discrepancies between verbal and nonverbal behavior; and to confront the resistances blocking emotional awareness through gestalt and psychodrama exercises (see Fedder & Ronall, 1980; Perls, 1969; Polster & Polster, 1973). Techniques that clarify and deepen the affective component of communication serve to help individual members feel understood, assist in modeling effective interaction among the members and promote the establishment of a trusting relationship between members and the facilitator (Cochran & Rabinowitz, 1983; Lewis, 1978).

MIDDLE GROUP SESSIONS: CHANGING THROUGH CONFLICT

Interpersonal conflict occurring between group members and toward the facilitator provides the opportunity for changing long-term patterns of behavior (Bion, 1961; Corey & Corey, 1982; Yalom, 1975). As members come to feel more secure in the group setting, individual differences in attitudes, cultural backgrounds, power needs, competitiveness and interpersonal style become sources of tension and hostility. Because many men have learned to deal with their anger in maladaptive ways (violent acting-out, self-destruction, denial/explosion, passive-aggression), the facilitator must closely monitor how aggression is being expressed in the group. It is important that facilitators be cognizant of their own style of handling angry feelings and aware of possible countertransference issues that might interfere with helping members to deal with their anger (Corey & Corey, 1982; Heppner, 1981; Stein, 1982).

In our experience, hostility and aggression is usually expressed indirectly in the form of ignoring a member's comment, the off-hand sexist remark, intellectual debating, absenteeism, interpersonal withdrawal, or generalized angry statements about individuals not present in the group. If not addressed, these indirect statements can undermine the trust and safety of the group situation and lead to an escalation of unproductive interaction. The following interchange from one of our groups illustrates how facilitator intervention following an indirect expression of hostility can provide the group with an opportunity to explore the emotional and interpersonal impact of the comments on the individuals involved as well as stimulate discussion on male hostility and aggression.

> *Jim:* I hate women who always tell you what to do, especially in bed. . . . You're damned if you want sex and damned if you don't. How could anyone be happy with that?
>
> *Jack:* You don't know what you're talking about. . . . Love is a two-way street where both people have to communicate their needs.
>
> *Facilitator:* Jim, You seem pretty angry. It sounds like you have had a personal experience with this type of woman.
>
> *Jim:* Yea, I still get pissed whenever I hear about a man who is letting a woman run his life. I was in a one-sided relationship for a long time and I almost went crazy.
>
> *Facilitator:* Jack, you responded fairly strongly to Jim's comment.
>
> *Jack:* It just pissed me off that he was generalizing so much. I like my wife to be assertive. I'm in this group to learn more about myself so I can be better in relationships, not to bash women.
>
> *Facilitator:* Can you tell Jim this directly?
>
> *Jack:* Look Jim . . . It pissed me off when you talked about women that way.
>
> *Jim:* Hey, I'm sorry. All I meant was that my experience with Julie was horrible for me. I really felt like shit after being with her.
>
> *Facilitator:* Jim, what are you experiencing now?
>
> *Jim:* I feel like I made a fool of myself in front of everyone.
>
> *Bob:* Jim, I admire your willingness to say how you felt about Julie. I can't seem to get the nerve up to talk to my partner about how I feel.
>
> *Rick:* I wish I could be more straightforward when my girlfriend ticks me off. I usually just walk away feeling sorry for myself.

The conflict that arises in the group at this point represents an occasion for growth and understanding among members. By owning the affective component of the remarks each individual learns about himself and how he affects others. Other group members who are watching the exchange also feel moved to comment about their own feelings, increasing the communication to the rest of the group. The member who reveals that he feels foolish is quickly supported by another member who admires his ability to talk so bluntly about these issues. The facilitator's role in dealing with conflict is to assist in the identification of underlying feelings, to encourage members to be responsible for their statements, to direct members to speak directly to each other, and to maintain a present-centered orientation toward the individual and the group.

Absenteeism, withdrawal from participation, and boredom may be indications that the group is not meeting the needs of certain members (Yalom, 1975). It is important that the facilitator use these events as springboards for discussion about what is occurring in the group. It is not unusual for members to reveal feelings of being controlled or manipulated by the facilitator's interventions. Some may feel they are changing to be more like the facilitator and resent the loss of identity they are experiencing. Others, harboring alternative viewpoints about the direction of the group, have difficulty expressing their disagreement with the leadership. While these observations have face validity, they also seem to reflect the nature of the transference relationship that develops between members and facilitator (Corey & Corey, 1982).

In many cases, the facilitator or older group member comes to represent a significant authority figure to individuals in the group. Many men have strong feelings about their fathers or male caretakers that have been suppressed for much of their adult lives (Bly, 1986; Osherson, 1986). The facilitator, without becoming defensive, needs to be able to encourage the men to encounter the images of their fathers. Appropriate interventions might include empty-chair gestalt work, psychodrama with members playing various roles, and guided imagery. With the potential to experience the anger, hurt, and despair at having had to deny natural aspects of themselves in order to be men in our culture, male group members can use the group setting to have a dialogue with their fathers and themselves about their true feelings.

Often, the breakthrough of strong emotion by one of the members leads to an increased sense of closeness within the group. It is not unusual for members to identify with the feelings and experience of that individual in a way that seems deeper and more involved than previous encounters in the group. There is a sense that the grip of control so important to the male identity has been temporarily abandoned and that responding is occurring without intellectual processing. This may allow for uncensored displays of caring and support that include physical embracing and emotional expressivity. Because of the overwhelming nature of these feelings, it is essential that the facilitator use a gentle and accepting manner to encourage members experiencing discomfort to talk about what they are feeling.

The interpersonal closeness and intimacy that develops after some deep work in the men's group has occurred may raise the issue of underlying homophobia (Fasteau, 1974; Lewis, 1978; O'Neil, 1981). Based on the premise that men are only supposed to feel closeness, affection, and sexual feelings toward women, the urge to give a hug to show caring and support to another man outside of the athletic field may lead to panic about sexual identity. It is important for facilitators to help the group address the issue of touching other males through discussion or experiential exercises (Washington, 1979). Sexual identity concerns of a more serious nature may require the facilitator to meet individually with a group member in order to discuss arrangements for more intensive individual therapy outside of the group.

The presence of homosexual or bisexual group members raises fears for the strictly heterosexual members (Beane, 1981). Although initially accepted out of politeness by the straight men, the homosexual group members may feel that they are not being fully incorporated into the group because of their sexual identity. Heterosexual members will often avoid making interpersonal contact with homosexual members and tend to ask questions that reflect their own fears of being homosexual. The facilitator should anticipate this division and encourage the subgroups to discuss their stereotypes and prejudices toward each other openly. Although this may be difficult initially, the dialogue that ensues will often bring the groups to appreciate their similarities and differences.

Once members expect to wrestle with conflicts during the group sessions, there will be a marked change in role for the facilitator. The working men's group will function more autonomously, providing its own support and challenge to its members. A sustained level of trust often emerges between the men that allows for spontaneous humor, disagreement, confrontation, and displays of caring and support. Unlike earlier stages of the group process, outside issues brought into the group are more likely to be dealt with in the present rather than as distractions from current dynamics. Conflicts that have been brought up earlier will typically recycle and be addressed in a manner that allows for greater awareness and growth among the members.

FINAL GROUP SESSIONS: TERMINATION

The final sessions of the men's group are often devoted to consolidating the learning that has occurred throughout the group experience as well as dealing with issues of separation and loss. As termination nears, members tend to distance themselves from each other and are often reluctant to risk bringing up new concerns. There is also the danger that unresolved conflict may go unchallenged because of the withdrawal of emotional investment in the group. There may be a tendency for members to deny the importance of their learning, to question its applicability in the real world, and to downplay the emotional attachment to one another. It is therefore necessary that the facilitator directly address the issue of termination and the feelings that are involved in the process of letting go of the group as a source of support and interpersonal learning.

The amount of time spent on termination issues will depend on the length of the group and the cohesiveness that has developed. A group that has met for 10 sessions may devote the last 2 to this process, while one that has met for a year may need 5 or more sessions to fully deal with the ending. Corey and Corey (1982) suggest that the members' tasks in the final stage of group are: (a) dealing with feelings of separation; (b) preparing to generalize in-group learning to everyday life; (c) giving and receiving feedback; (d) completing unfinished issues brought to the group; (e) evaluating the impact of the group; and (f) making decisions as to what changes to make and how these can be implemented.

The role of the facilitator is to encourage the expression of grief and sadness as it relates to the separation process and gently to confront member attempts at minimization and denial of these feelings. It is not uncommon for participants to wish they had gotten to know the facilitator and/or quiet members better and to express anxiety about applying their learning to an outside world they perceive as less than accepting of the values learned within the group. It is important to include time for the giving and receiving of feedback among members and facilitator. This gives members a chance to work through unfinished interpersonal conflict, to acknowledge changing perceptions of each other across the life of the group, to give constructive appraisals of areas of strengths and those needing improvement and to provide support for the changes that each individual has made within the group.

A final goal for the termination sessions is assisting group members to consolidate their experience in a conceptual framework that allows them to recall and encode personally significant gender-role learning. Corey and Corey (1982) suggest that the consolidation process is assisted by reviewing the history of the group and evaluating the progress that individuals have made on their personal goals. Exercises that encourage imagining the maintenance of gender-role freedom in the future, setting personal and institutional goals for life after the group, and thinking about ways one might avoid discounting the group experience are helpful in preparing members for the challenges of continued growth following its dissolution.

Summary

This chapter has considered in detail the issues involved in forming and facilitating an all-male group. Group goals, screening, structure, and management of the ongoing process of the group have been discussed. Clearly, many of these issues are issues in common with any group intervention. Several dimensions of the all-male group differentiate it from other general psychotherapy, growth, or educational groups. These include an opportunity to discuss issues of special relevance to men in an all-male setting, the opportunity to acquire necessary interpersonal skills related to intimacy and self-disclosure, and an opportunity to reflect on and examine the values learned in being raised in a predominantly male-dominated culture. It is hoped that the humanizing experience of participation in an all-male growth group, consciousness raising group, or psychotherapy group will have impact beyond the group experience itself and will contribute in some way to the reshaping of our culture into one where cooperation, support, and expressivity as well as individuality are valued.

References

American Association for Counseling and Development. (1981). *Ethical standards.* Alexandria, VA: Author.

American College Personnel Association. (1981). American College Personnel Association Statement of Ethical and Professional Standards. *Journal of College Student Personnel, 22,* 184-189.

American Psychological Association. (1981). Ethical principles of psychologists. *American Psychologist, 36,* 633-638.

Association for Specialists in Group Work. (1980). *Ethical guidelines for group leaders.* Alexandria, VA: Author.

Beane, J. (1981). "I'd rather be dead than gay": Counseling gay men who are coming out. *Personnel and Guidance Journal, 60,* 222-225.

Bednar, R. A., Weet, C., Evenson, P., Lanier, D., & Melnick, J. (1974). Empirical guidelines for group therapy: pretraining, cohesion, and modeling. *Journal of Applied Behavioral Science, 10,* 149-165.

Bern, E. H., & Bern, L. L. (1984). A group program for men who commit violence towards their wives. *Social Work with Groups, 7,* 63-77.

Bion, W. R. (1961). *Experiences in groups.* New York: Basic Books.

Bly, R. (1986). Men's initiation rights. *Utne Reader, 15,* 42-49.

Boone, T. A., & Reid, R. A. (1978). Selecting workshop sites. In J. W. Pfeiffer & J. E. Jones (Eds.). *The 1978 annual handbook for group facilitators.* La Jolla, CA: University Associates.

Bradley, M., Danchik, L., Foger, M., & Wodetzki, T. (1971). *Unbecoming men.* New York: Times Change Press.

Bresler, E. (1982). Filling an empty universe: Poetry therapy with a group of emotionally isolated men. *Social Work with Groups, 5,* 65-70.

Buckley, L. B., Miller, D., & Rolfe, T. A. (1983). Treatment groups for violent men: two approaches. A Windsor model. *Social Work with Groups, 6,* 189-195.

Cochran, S. V., & Rabinowitz, F. E. (1983). An experiential men's group for the university community. *Journal of College Student Personnel, 24,* 163-164.

Corey, G., & Corey, M. S. (1982). *Groups: Process and practice.* Monterey, CA: Brooks/Cole.

Crews, C. Y., & Melnick, J. (1976). Use of initial and delayed structure in facilitating group development. *Journal of Counseling Psychology, 23,* 92-98.

Croteau, J. M., & Burda, P. C. (1983). Structured group programming on men's roles: A creative approach to change. *Personnel and Guidance Journal, 62,* 243-245.

Currie, D. W. (1983). Treatment groups for violent men: two approaches. A Toronto model. *Social Work with Groups, 6,* 179-188.

Egan, G. (1986). *The skilled helper* (3rd ed.). Monterey, CA: Brooks/Cole.

Farrell, W. T. (1975). *The liberated man.* New York: Random House.

Fasteau, M. E. (1974). *The male machine.* New York: McGraw-Hill.

Fedder, B., & Ronall, R. (1980). *Beyond the hot seat: Gestalt approaches to group work.* New York: Brunner-Mazel.

Goldberg, H. (1976). *The hazards of being male: Surviving the myth of masculine privilege.* New York: Nash.

Heppner, P. P. (1981). Counseling men in groups. *Personnel and Guidance Journal, 60,* 249-252.

Heppner, P. P. (1983). Structured group activities for counseling men. *Journal of College Student Personnel, 24,* 275-277.

Kaufman, J., & Timmers, R. L. (1983). Searching for the hairy man. *Social Work with Groups, 6,* 163-175.

Lewis, R. A. (1978). Emotional intimacy among men. *Journal of Social Issues, 34,* 108-121.

Lieberman, M. A., Yalom, I. D., & Miles, M. B. (1973). *Encounter groups: First facts.* New York: Basic Books.

National Association of Social Workers. (1980). The NASW Code of Ethics. *Social Work, 25,* 184-188.

O'Neil, J. M. (1981). Patterns of gender role conflict and strain: Sexism and fear of femininity in men's lives. *Personnel and Guidance Journal, 59,* 203-210.

O'Neil, J. M. (1982). Gender role conflict and strain in men's lives: Implications for psychiatrists, psychologists, and other human service providers. In K. L. Solomon & N. B. Levy (Eds.). *Men in transition: Theory and therapy.* New York: Plenum.

Osherson, S. (1986). Finding our fathers. *Utne Reader, 15,* 36-39.

Perls, F. (1969). *Gestalt therapy verbatim.* Moab, UT: Real People Press.

Pfeiffer, J. W., & Jones, J. E. (1975). Co-facilitating. In J. W. Pfeiffer & J. E. Jones (Eds.). *The 1975 annual handbook for group facilitators.* La Jolla, CA: University Associates.

Pleck, J. H., & Sawyer, J. S. (1974). *Men and masculinity.* New Jersey: Prentice-Hall.

Polster, E., & Polster, M. (1973). *Gestalt therapy integrated: Contours of theory and practice.* New York: Brunner-Mazel.

Purdy, F., & Nickle, N. (1981). Practice principles for working with groups of men who batter. *Social Work with Groups, 4,* 111-122.

Rose, S. D. (1977). *Group therapy: A behavioral approach.* Englewood Cliffs, NJ: Prentice-Hall.

Schutz, W. C. (1967). *The FIRO scales.* Palo Alto, CA: Consulting Psychologists Press.

Silverberg, R. A. (1986). *Psychotherapy for men.* Springfield, IL: Charles C Thomas.

Solomon, K. L. (1982). The masculine gender role: Description. In K. L. Solomon & N. B. Levy (Eds.). *Men in transition: Theory and therapy.* New York: Plenum.

Stein, T. S. (1982). Men's groups. In K. L. Solomon & N. B. Levy (Eds.). *Men in transition: Theory and therapy.* New York: Plenum.

Timmers, R. L., & Drescher, E. L. (1979). A group approach to male sexual awareness. *Social Work with Groups, 2,* 247-257.

Van Dyck, B. J. (1980). Analysis of selection criteria for short-term group counseling clients. *Personnel and Guidance Journal, 60,* 226-230.

Washington, C. S. (1979). Men counseling men: Redefining the male machine. *Personnel and Guidance Journal, 57,* 462-463.

Wong, M. R. (1978). Males in transition and the self-help group. *The Counseling Psychologist, 7,* 46-50.

Yalom, I. D. (1975). *The theory and practice of group psychotherapy* (2nd ed.). New York: Basic Books.

4

Career Counseling
with Men

Thomas E. Dubois
Thomas M. Marino

A man would never get the notion of writing a book on the peculiar situations of the human male. (de Beauvior, 1953/1976, p. xv)

Ms. Beauvior was correct . . . in 1953. Let's face it, one only writes about the plight of people who are recognized as suffering or discriminated against in some way. Although male writers have certainly portrayed individual men in painful, tragic situations, from Job in the Bible to Willie Loman in "Death of a Salesman," there has been until recently almost nothing written about the "peculiar situation of the human male."

Feminism and the women's movement have forced males to notice that there *is* a male condition. Women's issues have received so much press and exposure that all but only the most unaware males could help reflecting on their place in the world and/or the quality of their lives. In the past men did not think much about such things. They were faced with issues related to surviving and getting ahead. Today, most men come from traditional families where fathers were breadwinners and mothers were homemakers and part-time workers.

The traditional male models of work that most men have introjected are now colliding with other societal realities of the 1980s such as the demands and conflicts of dual-career marriages; the integration of women into traditional male occupations; changes in technology; new expectations about balancing work with family relationships; and the stress of maintaining the traditional male belief that occupational success equals high self-esteem.

This collision of traditional male values with these new forces is a source of great intrapersonal and interpersonal conflict for men as well as women. As others have pointed out (Berger & Wright, 1978; O'Neil, 1981; Pleck, 1981; Skovholt & Morgan, 1981), male socialization has taught men that work is primary. Men have learned that they are known by what they do, how much they earn, and how much status they have. The bottom line is that they must work and support their family. All other roles are considered secondary.

The challenge of these traditional male paradigms and values strikes at the heart of masculinity. The result is that men are anxious and confused. It is a time of action and reaction: Often they are asked, told, even mandated to make changes instigated by women.

These "forced" changes can generate anger and fear in men because there is so much at stake. With most of their identity tied up in career, they feel that they have more to lose. In addition, they are being asked by women to make changes that are not traditionally male or valued by other men. Essentially they have to learn about living more intimately and cooperatively with their wives and children.

Since more counselors are increasingly confronted with male clients who are affected by these societal changes, it is important that they appreciate these male dilemmas and refrain from focusing entirely on the intrapsychic world of their clients. This chapter is aimed at developing an understanding of both the internal and external forces that shape and influence men's work-related lives, so that counselors can more comprehensively treat men with career-related concerns.

Self-Esteem, Status, and Upward Mobility

If self-esteem is connected with respecting oneself, feeling positively toward oneself, and thinking that one is worthy and useful, then it would follow logically that those people whose definition of success is the most narrow are at the greatest risk of becoming anxious, disillusioned, and unfulfilled. Many men fall into this category. For most men, work success accounts for most of their sense of self-worth/esteem (Goldberg, 1977; Morgan, Skovholt and Orr, 1979; Pleck, 1981).

Since much of men's self-esteem and gender identification is measured in terms of what they do, it is understandable that men are obsessed with achievement and success (O'Neil, 1981). Although the degree to which these male values affect men's career and personal development varies depending on age, social class, ethnic background, and gender-role socialization, few men escape the strain and conflict of pursuing "manliness."

Besides the narrowness of the success formula, the king-of-the-hill aspect of the pursuit is stressful and exhausting. No one is or can be really secure in a competitively based world. In Alan Sillitoe's short story, "The Loneliness of the Long Distance Runner," the main protagonist, a cross-country runner, states, "All I knew was that you had to run, run, run, without knowing why you were running, but on you went . . . and the winning post was no end to it . . . because on you had to go" (Sillitoe, 1971, pp. 37-38).

This short quote contains much of what constitutes gender-role strain and conflict in men. Since men's sense of maleness is so dependent upon getting somewhere without being allowed to stop and savor what they have achieved, it is no wonder that men with one eye on the winning post and the other looking over their shoulder, are more emotionally distant and anxious than women.

This seems to be a pretty grim picture of how men live. One might wonder why most men don't recognize their condition and become more proactive about changing it. But the fact is that much of manliness is associated with enduring pain and suffering. As Osherson in his work *Finding Our Fathers* (1986, p. 64) states, "Many men learn from their fathers that to be in the work world means to suffer, indeed that manhood itself is a kind of dreadful obligation."

Paradoxically, men have felt a sense of masculine pride in their suffering as breadwinners. In the past, even if their jobs were unheroic and uninteresting, they could at least feel that supporting the family was man's work. Essentially, men have been united by sharing perseverance and sweat. However, with the large influx of women in the workplace, this "privilege" of the breadwinner's role has been reduced. There are fewer and fewer domains that men can label as "man's."

As tenuous as it might have been, maintaining and keeping women at home enhanced men's sense of self-worth and made them feel like more of a man because it made them unlike women. This aspect of male socialization is critical to men's sense of self-esteem: Much of what passes for masculinity is a reaction to femininity. Being a man means being unlike a woman. Much of being male is based upon *not* being certain things, that is, avoiding feelings, behaviors, awarenesses, and activities that might evoke unmanly responses (Gerzon, 1982; Jourard, 1971; Liss-Levinson, 1981; O'Neil, 1981; Skovholt & Hansen, 1980).

The constriction of the male role makes men even more vulnerable concerning their work. In this adult variation of king-of-the-hill, the real truth is that few men ever "make it." Those who do get there live in dull fear and apprehension and those who are looking upward feel a sense of failure because they can't get there. The truth is that there are only so many spots at the top. As Harris (1986, p. 8) has noted, "Most [men] work in jobs where they cannot live out the 'American Dream' as portrayed by the media. The number of individuals in professional white collar occupations account for only 15% of all employed men, or 8% of the total male population. Indeed only twenty-nine percent of men in the U.S. make $25,000 or more." Harris (1986, p. 9) adds that most men will never get status jobs. He notes that 45% of working men are in blue-collar jobs, many without college educations. These vast numbers of men in the working class are in jobs that are often dull, dangerous, and repetitive. Even if they are making a decent income, they often feel inadequate when faced with the "failure" to live up to the media's image of the successful male.

Even highly educated men have aspirations that don't fit with the reality of available top level positions. There are only so many prestigious schools, organizations, and firms; consequently, these men are forever struggling for the limited positions available. This highly competitive struggle is not only stressful and unhealthy, it is more often than not discouraging and dispiriting. Furthermore, without support and communication from other men, men will continue to feel inadequate, internalizing their "failure," assuming they must be at fault or that someone else is to blame.

Failing to see the Horatio Alger myth for what it is, men will continue to work harder and experience fatigue, stress, illness, and ongoing disillusionment. The blind circuitousness of this process perpetuates a demoralizing sense in men that life is meaningless and empty.

Although most men don't literally think that winning and getting ahead are a matter of life and death, the fact is that most men *behave* that way. The tendency to compete and push so strongly and doggedly comes from a view that one is either a winner or a loser. This strong focus on winning is not only the result of connecting masculinity with competing, but is linked with men's fear of being feminine. As Tooley (1977, p. 191) has stated, "Fear of emasculation, whether expressed as the boyhood fear of castration or the grownup male fear of impotence, remains the core organizer of adult male life experience."

The interaction of these two forces is very potent. The key phrase "core organizer," stresses that much of this behavior is unconsciously embedded in the male psyche so that men are driven by the fear of not being potent. Their lives revolve around avoiding the feminine sides of themselves because they associate feminine behaviors with weakness—that is, impotence.

This obsession with winning and upward mobility also means that men cannot feel good about themselves if they choose to stay where they are. They cannot appreciate who they are or what they are doing. A part of the need to achieve is the drive to accumulate visible symbols of success in the form of prestigious positions, beautiful homes, expensive cars, and other wordly goods. These are symbols to him and the world that he is successful and moving forward.

Since much of masculinity is predicated on accumulating these symbols, rather than on feeling intrinsically rewarded, it is almost a cliche to note that competent, satisfied workers "advance" to positions of greater prestige and authority. Teachers become principals; competent researchers are pushed into administration; and skilled workers become supervisors and foremen. This process is fueled by both the success orientation of the individuals and the organizational norms that demand it.

These career-related binds are costly and complex, colliding in men's psyches, rendering them frightened, confused, and threatened. O'Neil (1981) notes that this constant male role conflict and overload often causes men to implode at work and explode at home, resulting in family violence and discord. The opposite may also be true. Unable to feel competent at home, a man brings his discontent to work. Other writers (Crites & Fitzgerald, 1980; Harrison, 1978; Korzman, 1986) have documented and discussed the extent to which men's health is threatened by these work-related conflicts and demands, showing that men greatly exceed women in stress-related deaths and illnesses.

Balancing Work and Other Priorities

As previously stated, the male paradigm emphasizes invulnerability and independence to such an extent that men are often isolated from friends and family; consequently, males often ignore learning and caring about intimacy. They continue to look toward work and career to fulfill personal needs. But turning toward work doesn't meet most men's needs for intimacy and it further distances them from significant others simply because they are not around enough to relate.

Unable to rectify their discontent and to understand their predicament, they often seek solace and pride in their suffering. Although much of this suffering is real, it is also a shield from the demands of others for intimacy, a way to legitimize distance and noninvolvement (Druck & Simmons, 1985). A wife and children can hardly criticize a man for supporting them and making their lives more comfortable.

One of the most difficult questions men have to deal with is whether they can be both ambitious at work and successful as a father and partner. For men who are trying to "make it" at work, the job usually comes first, family second. Several authors have discussed the conflicts men have between work and family, and how the need for task completion can be a detriment to relationship maintenance and really "being there" for one's children (Berger & Wright, 1978; Goldberg, 1977; Nichols, 1975; Osherson, 1986; Pleck & Sawyer, 1974).

Male socialization and role conflicts aside, it is important to understand how hard most people must work just to make ends meet. Work for many men often leaves them too tired to manage a social life, unless it's handed to them when they get home. Some men consider it a luxury to be able to focus on things *other* than work. As a result of this stress, many men adopt the belief that if they become successful they will be able to stop work and enjoy themselves. Few make this belief a reality; for others it is often too late.

Many men are secretly or unconsciously angry and depressed by the traditional bargain they have made with their wives; having been consigned to the world of work and primary economic responsibility and thus being cut off from their families. Having made this bargain, as the "natural" order of things, they feel trapped and powerless to make changes in their role. Some experience a great sense of loss. Further, many men agree in principle with equal parental leave but cannot see themselves taking time off to care for a child for fear that taking a paternity leave would negatively affect their careers.

How much has the traditional pattern given way to more equal roles for men and women? Bell (1982) suggested that more men today give relationships greater precedence over work. Skovholt and Morgan (1981) felt that there had been a shift in the conceptualization of roles for men and women with (1) biological differences in sex being deemphasized and the (2) work achievement role for women and the personal affiliation role for men being stressed more. It is still a question as to how far most men in today's world have actually broadened their lives to make relationships and personal issues more important. Certainly some men have made these changes.

The significant problem facing men is adjusting to a different image of what a man is. Can men learn to live in situations of less control and greater dependence? It is likely that men fear not only being overshadowed by the capability of the women they are with but, more important, also losing status and therefore control of their life situations. The feeling that women should not support men or be the primary breadwinner is deeply ingrained in both sexes. Most men feel either guilty or threatened in situations of less pay or no pay, even when income is no problem. Many men are not able to handle the "opportunity" of not working—for example, to follow a woman who goes on paid leave for a year. Basically it is a problem of having less control. A common response for men in such situations is consciously to suppress feelings of fear and anger, in order not to appear vulnerable or nonsupportive. These unacknowledged feelings, however, often surface as resentment, a kind of backlash that undermines intimacy. Ambiguous feelings such as these are common in relationships in the midst of change. Counseling at these times can help unravel these hidden agendas and conflicts, helping couples to discuss their feelings more honestly and openly.

Developmental Issues

A number of authors have discussed career issues from a developmental perspective (Brim, 1976; Bookneck,

1976; Cohen, 1979; Levinson, 1978; Sheehy, 1977; Thomas, 1981). Levinson (1978) argued that we all live through the same developmental periods in adulthood, and that for men in particular life passages revolve around work. The adult life cycle theorists generally describe a more or less regular and predictable life work pattern for men who are "successful," from first career choice to retirement. The pattern involves: (1) career choice; (2) education and preparation; (3) getting ahead, playing the game, workaholic, absent from family, spouse's goals subordinated; (4) midlife crisis—facing limits or failure, change in career—may "return to family," who may be leaving; (5) retirement.

These authors have generally emphasized the turmoil and stagnation that can occur at different stages in men's career development along with the possibility of renewal and adjustment to a new stage. Possible alternatives to the more traditional life-work developmental pattern might involve the integration of work and family responsibilities, as in a dual-career marriage, part-time employment, or even as house-husband. It seems true, however, that these alternatives often do not really arise as conscious possibilities for men until about midlife, a time when many men seek counseling.

The so-called midlife period, usually occurring around the time when men approach 40, can be a particularly stressful time. For many men divorce catapults them into doubt and confusion at midlife. For other men it may be a forced career change, illness, or the loss of a loved one. By the time men are fortyish, they have spent a number of years "getting somewhere" and many are "lost" in their work. By this time, however, many begin to know, or at least suspect, that wealth, status, fame or power cannot be a shield from life's realities. Midlife is often a time when men start to realize that they are vulnerable to age, illness, and death; many have experienced the death or illness of parents. It can be a time for them to consider renegotiating the contract, for asking themselves if they want to continue jeopardizing their health and relationships in exchange for more money and status. At the heart of this assessment is the issue of self-respect. Taking the risk at this time of life to confront these existential questions exposes men to deep feelings of vulnerability. For many it can be easier to rush back to work and avoid the awkwardness of these strange feelings. Excessive work may be hard and costly to a degree, but it is familiar and predictable.

Erikson (1963) described midlife as potentially offering ways of becoming interpersonally "generative," an opportunity to nurture and actualize untapped resources in oneself. Unfortunately, in one study, Farrell and Rosenberg (1981) found only one-third of a broad sample of normal men at midlife achieved a positive "generative solution" at midlife.

Other problems often compound the difficulties men experience in attempting to reevaluate their priorities. Very often a man's family depends upon his continued financial/economic productivity in order to maintain a given level of status and to remain financially solvent and responsible. While women at midlife are often encouraged to emerge from the home and to find new vocations and interests in life, men are often not given the same encouragement. Society has a vested interest in keeping the midlife male locked into his traditional roles and responsibilities. Osherson (1986) discussed the problem that many men face at midlife when the wife and kids are off into exciting new work and experiences, while he feels a leveling off or decline in his career. For some men it seems like everyone in the family is going onto something bigger and better except him.

Similar conflicts and questions are often raised at the time of retirement. Most men are not prepared for retirement and its impact on their self-concept and emotions. Many men have still at this time defined themselves almost entirely in relation to their work. Self-esteem and control issues can become particularly acute.

Skovholt and Morgan (1981) discussed a number of retirement issues, including the importance of physical health, financial security, and positive interpersonal relationships. They also described at length the problems of men who have had too much of their self-esteem connected with work. Others have described the traumas men experience in moving from significant activity in male-dominated places to inactivity in places dominated by wives; for most men the workplace has been their place of control in their adult lives (Skovholt & Hansen, 1980). Again, there are opportunities for growth and renewal as well as problems facing men at retirement. Counselors need to encourage men to find these opportunities. For those men who continue "too long" at any life stage to try and find all of their meaning through work there is usually a growing sense of emptiness coupled with a sense that one has never done enough. Those men who finally discover that work isn't everything have to struggle with the question of, "Now what?"

Counseling Issues and Approaches

During this time of rapid changes, an increasing number of men are experiencing career shifts, unemployment, midlife issues, retirement, and other identity crises. Some men want to change their jobs because of boredom or frustration. Corporate people often want out of the bottom-line-only mentality. Technical people sometimes want more contact with people. Some men want to change jobs out of a feeling of being unable to be assertive enough to get what they need from their present job or they may feel themselves losing out in a competitive struggle. Lack of status or insufficient income motivates many men to seek change. People in human service occupations talk about burnout or about being at a dead end. Many men leave jobs they like in teaching or human service work to go to higher-paying jobs in business and industry, sometimes because of status, but often because they cannot afford to remain.

Generally, those who make the most successful job switches are motivated not only to escape a particular job but also by positive attraction to something else. However, seeking career change can also be an attempt to avoid dealing with the real problem. The increasing complexity of career and life decisions, often involving difficult choices and compromises, means that men will increasingly turn to counselors for help.

Career counseling is often initiated at a time of performance failure. Male issues may for the first time become relevant as men are faced with crises and difficult times. A man seeking career counseling might really be searching for legitimacy for the sides of himself that have been lost (O'Neil, 1981). Some men are looking for outlets for expression of feelings from conflicts and other stresses on the job.

Traditional career counseling has consisted mainly of discovering individual traits, analyzing occupational requirements, and matching the individual to the job (Weinrach, 1979). Increasingly, computer programs such as the *System of Interactive Guidance and Information* (1974), better known as "SIGI," are being developed and used for matching interests and values to available jobs. A common adjunct to traditional career counseling has been the teaching of job searching skills, such as interviewing techniques, application, and resume writing skills.

Although providing accurate information to clients about their interests, skills, and employment possibilities and helping them to find work are important, it is not enough. Much of a man's personal identity and sense of worth is connected to his work; therefore, career counseling must encompass examining many psychological factors and issues that go beyond aptitude, intelligence, and interest. An increased awareness and sensitivity to needs and feelings surrounding work increases the potential for making sound career choices.

Counseling may sometimes best be focused on enhancing the current work situation. A man may need greater self-knowledge or greater acceptance of his fears and other feelings he has while on the job. Osherson (1986) described how at work a man may unconsciously repeat his own father-son relationship through mentor-mentee relationships, with all the same problems and unresolved issues.

Skovholt and Morgan (1981) noted that it is sometimes important to teach clients how to focus their energy productively. This might involve teaching new work attitudes, stress or time management skills, or long-range planning skills. These skills are often best learned in structured workshops or experience-oriented classroom situations; therefore, it is important for the counselor to be aware of these opportunities in the local community. Some men may also need decision-making skills, interpersonal communication skills, and/or assertiveness training.

Increasingly the industrial sector is recognizing the need for such training and is offering programs for employees in these areas. Often men need help in learning how to deal with conflict and cooperation and how to discriminate between productive conflict and conflict that is excessive or dysfunctional. For this issue, group training sessions are often more useful than individual counseling.

Skovholt and Morgan (1981, p. 234), while observing that the work of the career counselor has been centered primarily on facilitating movement from powerlessness to power, noted that "facilitating upward mobility and increased consumption may no longer be totally virtuous work for career counselors." It is at least important to ask how career counselors can intervene to help men understand and deal with power and competition issues, problems of control, and career and family conflicts. How can counselors help men to clarify their values concerning their roles as breadwinner, husband, and father?

To begin with, it is important that counselors provide a great deal of active support for men and encourage them to express their feelings. Open questioning can help a man define how he sees the masculine role and its alternatives.

Providing readings may also be helpful. There is an ever growing number of useful books on men's issues concerning work, which can be recommended as an adjunct to counseling. Books such as Levinson's *The Seasons of a Man's Life* (1978), Sheehy's *Passages* (1977), and LaBier's *Modern Madness* (1986) have helped some men achieve a better sense of their experiences while going through the emotional turmoil brought about by major life and occupational changes. Osherson's book *Finding our Fathers* (1986) offers a useful understanding of men's feelings about their work in the context of upbringing and family relationships. Bowles's *What Color Is Your Parachute* (1987), which is revised yearly, provides concrete information about changing careers and applying for jobs.

Of particular importance in career counseling is helping men examine how gender-role conflicts influence their emotional, physical, and inter-personal lives. Sometimes men need counseling where deeper feelings may be explored and encouraged, where other potential sides can be exposed and developed, and where fears can be confronted. Counseling should work toward heightened awareness and understanding of feelings, offering a man expanded choices.

Counselors should encourage men to explore the limitations of the traditional male role, particularly needs for status and control. Many men are "workaholics" or are caught up in the seduction of money and power. Although counselors cannot deny the importance of social status, which is usually based on job and money, they can help a man to try and find a balance between this comparative type of status and other sources of meaning. Is it possible to lower work output (even to medium levels) in order to avoid self-destructiveness or to find other goals, such as establishing or enhancing personal relationships? Many men who would like to find greater balance in their lives have to confront fears of the "social demotion" involved in the reduction of their status as breadwinner. Career counseling should include examining ambitions and desires for achievement and wrestling with one's limitations.

As women take on traditional male work roles, denying the male-only association of these patterns, men need help dealing with losses of gender privilege and with confronting their fears about women moving into jobs that were once men's exclusive territory. The percentage of males entering traditional female occupations is smaller. This may be due to economic and desirability factors, as "women's jobs" traditionally pay less; however, studies suggest that there is also a larger stigma attached to men who do "women's work" (Yanico, 1978). Counseling can provide support for men who are considering or working in nontraditional work roles.

Most men experience gaps between their aspirations and their occupational realities. Their unhappiness at not "being something" often distracts them from the reality of what is now. For the unemployed man whose self-esteem is based primarily on comparative performance, these conflicts are particularly unbearable.

A typical example is David, who unexpectedly lost his job. He felt a devastating loss of face, but he was reluctant to acknowledge his major fear—that of not being able to support his family. As David mostly got encouragement and understanding from family and friends, he felt his fears were inexcusable. Although he did not admit to others his loss of self-confidence, thoughts of failure and self-incrimination gradually took over. David tried to find another job, but the possibilities were below his standards for income and prestige; for other positions he lacked the necessary training or credentials.

Gradually, David removed himself emotionally from family and friends, and his marriage deteriorated. He drank more and more. He felt no desire for sexual or other intimate contact with his wife. His wife's ultimatum that he see a therapist or she would leave finally convinced him to seek professional help. He was depressed, at times angry, and feeling increasingly hopeless.

When David began counseling sessions he did not admit that he wanted help. He continued, however, and gradually began to let go of some of his pride. As he began to see himself more objectively, he looked at the images he had carried of what a man should be. He learned that his expectations had been projected as absolute male standards.

Later David joined a men's group and talked more openly about his feelings than ever before in his life. He also took a part-time job and went back to school in a field he had been interested in for a long time. Being in a classroom was an uncomfortable experience at first. This time David was able to talk about his anxiety with some of the older students. He found that others felt similarly. He began to develop a sense of himself, based on concrete experiences and feelings. He recognized that his previous sense of self had been based on his perception of his relative status amongst his working peers.

During this time, David's wife had begun working part-time, which at first made him anxious and uncertain. By talking with his group, he saw that his feelings stemmed from his fear of not being dominant in his family. Recognizing this fear, he gradually became more comfortable with the situation.

As David prepared himself for a new way of fitting into the work world, he realized that status had been the largest factor in his first career choice. Though status is still important to David, he no longer feels that it is running his life.

Counselor Variables

In addition to effective counseling skills, counselors need an awareness of how technical and personal skills and interests relate to the actual world of work. Further, career counselors working with men must understand how work for men fits into the broader cultural milieu.

Career counselors also need to have an awareness of their own gender-role issues, and to understand in particular their own level of commitment to the status quo. Even counselors' subtle adherence to traditional masculine and feminine stereotypes can be restricting. Men exploring career questions or nontraditional lifestyles deserve a counselor who is accepting of nontraditional ways of thinking about work, marriage, and family life. Such a counselor will be able to support men effectively in dealing with their changing roles and facilitate more innovative solutions.

For males in our society, work is still primary; all other roles are secondary. This is certainly also true for most professional counselors. It is not uncommon to encounter male counselors who, while espousing feminist values, either deny, overlook, or are unconscious of their own male issues. Many counselors, even those with nontraditional values, still live more or less traditional lifestyles, and they often carry some combination of these factors or influences into their counseling work. Male counselors often fear feminism and in particular feminist therapists who make claims that women clients should see a woman (Dubois, 1978). This is partly a male economic and status issue, in which the breadwinner-provider role is threatened.

A number of authors who discuss traditional and nontraditional occupations have noted that it is often easier for counselors to support a female client in espousing values seen as traditionally male than to support a male client living in accord with values seen as traditionally reserved for women (Berger & Wright, 1978; Skovholt & Morgan, 1981). It has been shown (Broverman, Broverman, Clarkson, Rosencrantz, & Vogel, 1970) that many counselors—male and female—tend to share traditional male success values both privately and professionally; therefore, they are more able to support women in new roles because they are aspiring to male goals and attributes. Now counselors are confronted with male clients who are affected by these societal changes. Counselors can help men by supporting nontraditional/"deviant" roles that their clients are considering or have chosen. Support will come primarily from counselors who have examined their own value systems and who can support nontraditional behavior.

Another variable to consider here is the openness of the counselor and the use of self-disclosure. In working with men concerning career issues, it is often appropriate and useful for counselors to share some of their own discomforts that parallel the client's presenting problems or struggles. Particularly coming from male counselors, such disclosure can help by giving permission and by modeling the expression of emotions. It can also promote a feeling of acceptance and collaboration. In addition, a therapists's self-disclosure usually helps a client to open up or admit to deeper fears and anxieties since he sees that others have the same fears or concerns. Sharing concerns may also be a way of modeling a willingness to explore and take risks while attempting to grow and understand one's own life more fully. Here again, a counselor's unexamined life can serve as a role model of avoidance.

Another counselor variable of prime importance has to do with social class differences. Most men and women in the helping professions were raised in the middle class and are largely ignorant of the problems facing working-class men. It is undoubtedly difficult for some counselors to understand being consigned to low status and feeling trapped with few choices. Therefore, it is especially important for counselors to have respect for and to try to understand men with problems of economic and class insecurity. Although it is not possible within the limited scope of this chapter to deal with the impact of such issues as race and sexual orientation on career choices and problems, it is important to acknowledge and draw attention to their importance in career counseling.

References

Bell, D. H. (1981). Up from patriarchy: The male role in historical perspective. In R. A. Lewis (Ed.), *Men in difficult times.* Englewood Cliffs, NJ: Prentice-Hall.

Bell, D. H. (1982). *Being a man: The paradox of masculinity*. New York: Harcourt, Brace, Jovanovich.

Berger, M., & Wright, L. (1978). Divided allegiance: Men, work and family. *The Counseling Psychologist, 7*, 50-52.

Bookneck, G. A. (1976). A developmental approach to counseling adults. *The Counseling Psychologist, 6*, 37-40.

Bowles, R. N. (1987). *What color is your parachute? A practical manual for job-hunters and career changers*. Berkeley, CA: Ten Speed Press.

Brim, O. G. (1976). Theories of the male mid-life crisis. *The Counseling Psychologist, 6*, 2-9.

Broverman, I. K., Broverman, D. M., Clarkson, F. E., Rosencrantz, P. S., & Vogel, S. R. (1970). Sex role stereotypes and clinical judgements of mental health. *Journal of Clinical and Consulting Psychology, 34*, 1-7.

Cohen, J. F. (1979). Male roles in mid-life. *Family Coordinator, 28*, 465-471.

Crites, J. O. (1976). Career counseling: A comprehensive approach. *The Counseling Psychologist, 6*, 2-12.

Crites, J. O., & Fitzgerald, L. F. (1980). The competent male. In Skovholt et al. (Eds.), *Counseling men*. Belmont, CA: Wadsworth.

de Beauvoir, S. (1976). *The second sex*. (H. M. Parshley, trans.). New York: Alfred Knopf.

Druck, K., & Simmons, J. (1985). *The secrets men keep*. Garden City, NY: Doubleday.

Dubois, T. E. (1978). Male therapists' fears of the feminist movement: Bringing the new consciousness into their experience. *Social Change, 8*, 1-3.

Educational Testing Services. (1974). *System of interactive guidance and information*. Princeton, NJ: Author.

Erikson, E. (1983). *Childhood and society*. New York: W. W. Norton.

Farrell, M., & Rosenberg, S. (1981). *Men at midlife*. Dover, MA: Auburn House.

Gerzon, M. (1982). *A choice of heroes: The changing face of American manhood*. Boston: Houghton Mifflin.

Goldberg, H. (1977). *The hazards of being male*. New York: New American Library.

Gottfredson, L. S. (1979). Aspiration-job match: Age trends in a large nationally representative sample of young white men. *Journal of Counseling Psychology, 26*, 319-328.

Harris, I. (1986, Summer). Media myths and the reality of men's work. *Changing Men*.

Harrison, J. (1978). Warning: The male sex role may be dangerous to your health. *Journal of Social Issues, 34*, 65-86.

Jourard, S. (1971). *The transparent self* (rev. ed.). Princeton, NJ: Van Nostrand.

Korzman, P. (1986, Summer). Hazards in the workplace. *Changing Men*, pp. 11-12.

LaBier, D. (1986). *Modern madness: The emotional fallout of success*. Reading, MA: Addison-Wesley.

Levinson, D. J. (1978). *The seasons of a man's life*. New York: Knopf.

Liss-Levinson, W. (1981). Men without playfulness. In R. A. Lewis (Ed.), *Men in difficult times: A book of original readings* (pp. 24-25). Englewood Cliffs, NJ: Prentice-Hall.

Mitchell, J. S. (1981). Difficult times for the family: Social change hurts. In R. A. Lewis (Ed.) *Men in difficult times: A book of original readings*. Englewood Cliffs, NJ: Prentice-Hall.

Morgan, J. I., Skovholt, T. M., & Orr J. M. (1979). Career counseling with men: The shifting focus. In S. G. Weinrach (Ed.), *Career counseling: Theoretical and practical perspectives*. New York: McGraw-Hill.

Nichols, J. (1975). *Men's liberation: A new definition of masculinity*. New York: Penguin.

O'Neil, J. M. (1981). Male sex-role conflicts, sexism and masculinity: Psychological implications for men, women and the counseling psychologist. *The Counseling Psychologist, 9*, 61-80.

Osherson, S. (1986). *Finding our fathers: The unfinished business of manhood*. New York: Macmillan.

Pleck, J. H. (1981). Men's power with women, other men, and society: A men's movement analysis. In R. A. Lewis (Ed.), *Men in difficult times: A book of original readings* (pp. 242-243). Englewood Cliffs, NJ: Prentice-Hall.

Pleck, J. H., & Sawyer, J. (1974). *Men and masculinity.* Englewood Cliffs, NJ: Prentice-Hall.

Sheehy, G. (1977). *Passages.* New York: Bantam.

Sillitoe, A. (1971). *The loneliness of the long distance runner.* New York: Signet.

Skovholt, T. M., & Hansen, A. (1980). Men's development: A perspective and some themes. In Skovholt et al. (Eds.), *Counseling Men* (pp. 1-39). Belmont, CA: Wadsworth.

Skovholt, T. M., & Morgan, J. I. (1981, December). Career development: An outline of issues for men. *Personnel & Guidance Journal.*

Thomas, L. E. (1981). A typology of mid-life career changes. *J. of Vocational Behavior, 16,* 173-182.

Tooley, K. M. (1977). Johnny, I hardly know ye: Toward revision of the theory of male psychosexual development. *American Journal of Orthopsychiatry, 47,* 184-195.

Weinrach, S. G. (1979). *Career counseling: Theoretical and practical perspectives,* New York: McGraw-Hill.

Yanico, B. J. (1978). Sex bias in career information: Effects of language attitudes. *Journal of Vocational Behavior, 13,* 26-34.

5

Hard Issues and Soft Spots: Counseling Men About Sexuality

Jeffrey C. Fracher
Michael S. Kimmel

> Nothing shows more clearly the extent to which modern society has atomized itself than the isolation in sexual ignorance which exists among us. . . . Many cultures, the most primitive and the most complex, have entertained sexual fears of an irrational sort, but probably our culture is unique in strictly isolating the individual in the fears that society has devised. (Trilling, 1954)

Sam is a 28-year-old white, single factory worker. He lives alone in a two-family home that he owns, and attends night school at a community college.[1] The third of six sons in a blue-collar, Eastern European Catholic family, Sam is a conscientious, hard-working, and responsible man with very traditional values. He describes himself as a sexual late-bloomer, having begun dating only after graduation from an all-male Catholic high school. Although strong and handsome, he has always lacked confidence with women, and describes himself as male peer-oriented, actively involved in sports, and spending much of his leisure time with "the boys."

Prior to his first sexual intercourse, two years ago at age 26, Sam had fabricated stories to tell his friends so as not to appear inadequate. He felt a great deal of shame and embarrassment that his public presentation of his

---

Authors' Note: This chapter represents a full collaboration, and our names appear in alphabetical order for convenience. Critical reactions from John Gagnon, Murray Scher, and Mark Stevens have been very helpful.

sexual exploits had no basis in reality. His limited sexual knowledge caused him great anxiety and difficulty, especially since the woman with whom he was involved had had previous sexual encounters. Upon completion of intercourse, she reported that he "came too fast" (i.e., less than one minute, or after several thrusts), a statement that he reported, "hit me between the eyes." His second attempt at intercourse was no more successful, despite his use of a condom to reduce sensation, and he subsequently broke off this relationship because of the shame and embarrassment about his sexual incompetence, and the fear that word would leak out to his friends. He subsequently developed a secondary pattern of sexual avoidance, and when he first came to treatment, indicating that he was "not a real man because I can't satisfy a woman," he had not had sex for two years, and was reluctant to resume dating until his premature ejaculation was vastly improved.

Joe is a 34-year-old CPA who has been married for three years. The youngest of five children and the only male in a middle-class Irish-American family, Joe feels his father had high expectations for him, and exhibited only neutrality or criticism. Joe was without a male role model who conveyed that it was OK to fail. In fact, he portrayed men as strong, competent, without feelings, and without problems or failings, and believes he can never live up to the image his father had for him. Consequently, Joe is terrified that failure to please a woman sexually may result in criticism that will challenge his masculinity; he will not be a "real man." Anticipating this criticism from his wife, his sexual interest is reduced.

When first seen in therapy, Joe evidenced a total lack of sexual interest in his wife, but a high degree of sexual interest involving sexual fantasies, pornography, and masturbation. He said "lust is an obsession with me," indicating a high sex drive when sex is anonymous, and though he felt sexually inadequate with his wife, he felt sexually potent with women he devalues, such as prostitutes. He could not understand his almost total lack of sexual interest in his wife.

Bill is a 52-year-old engineer, who has been married for 25 years. From a white, middle-class Protestant background, he has one grown child, and initially came to treatment upon referral from a urologist. He had seen numerous physicians after experiencing erectile dysfunction three years ago, and has actively sought a physical explanation for it.

Bill's wife, Ann, was quite vocal about her disappointment in his failure to perform sexually. Bill had always been the sexual initiator, and Ann had come to expect that he should be in charge. Both believed that the only "real sex" is intercourse with an erect penis. Ann frequently commented that she felt "emotionally empty" without intercourse, thereby adding to his sense of inadequacy. The loss of his capacity for erection, Bill told the therapist, meant that he had lost his masculinity, and he worried openly about displeasing Ann and her possibly leaving him.

His fear of lost masculinity spilled over into his job performance, and he became depressed and withdrew from social activities. Bill was unaware that as an older man, he required more direct penile stimulation for an erection, since he had never required it in the past, and was unable to ask for it from Ann. He felt that a "real man never has to ask his wife for anything sexually," and should be able to perform without her help. The pattern of erectile dysfunction was part of a broader pattern of inability to tolerate failure, and he had begun to lose self-confidence since his masculinity was almost entirely predicated upon erectile functioning. "Nothing else matters," he confided, if his masculinity (evidenced by a functional erection) was not present. Everything was suddenly on the line— his self-worth, his marriage, and his career—if he proved unable to correct his problem.

Sam, Joe, and Bill manifest the three most common sexual complaints of men seeking therapy. But underlying premature ejaculation, inhibited sexual desire, and erectile dysfunction is a common thread, binding these and other sexual problems together. Each fears that his sexual problem damages his sense of masculinity, makes him less of a "real man." In a sense, we might say that all three men "suffer" from masculinity.

This chapter will explore how gender becomes one of the key organizing principles of male sexuality, informing and structuring men's sexual experiences. It will discuss how both gender and sexuality are socially constructed, and how therapeutic strategies to help men deal with sexual problems can raise issues of gender identity. This is especially important, of course, since so many therapeutic interventions rely on a diagnostic model that is simultaneously overly individualistic (in that it locates the source of the problem entirely within the individual) and transhistorical (in that it assumes that all cultures exhibit similar patterns at all times). The chapter combines a comparative and historical understanding of how both gender and sexuality are socially constructed with a psychoanalytic understanding of the transformative possibilities contained within the therapeutic relationship. This combination will lead us to discuss both social and therapeutic interventions that might facilitate healthier sexual expression for men.

The Social Construction of Sexuality and Masculinity

Sexuality is socially constructed, a learned set of both behaviors and cognitive interpretations of those behaviors. Sexuality is less the product of biological drives than of a socialization process, and this socialization process is specific to any culture at any particular time. This means that "social roles are not vehicles for the expression of sexual impulse but that sexuality becomes a vehicle for expressing the needs of social roles" (Gagnon & Simon, 1973, p. 45). *That* we are sexual is determined by a biological imperative toward reproduction, but *how* we are sexual—where, when, how often, with whom, and why—has to do with cultural learning, with meanings transmitted in a cultural setting. Sexuality varies from culture to culture; it changes in any one culture over time; it changes over the course of each of our lives. Sexual beings are made and not born; we make ourselves into sexual beings within a cultural framework. While it may appear counterintuitive, this perspective suggests that the elusive quality commonly called "desire" is actually a relatively unimportant part of sexual conduct. As Gagnon and Simon argue (1973, p. 103), "the availability of sexual partners, their ages, their incomes, their point in the economic process, their time commitments . . . shape their sexual careers far more than the minor influence of sexual desire." Sexuality is learned in roughly the same way as anything else is learned in our culture. As Gagnon writes (1977, p. 2):

> In any given society, at any given moment, people become sexual in the same way as they become everything else. Without much reflection, they pick up directions from their social environment. They acquire and assemble meanings, skills and values from the people around them. Their critical choices are often made by going along and drifting. People learn when they are quite young a few of the things that they are expected to be, and continue slowly to accumulate a belief in who they are and ought to be through the rest of childhood, adolescence, and adulthood. Sexual conduct is learned in the same ways and through the same processes; it is acquired and assembled in human interaction, judged and performed in specific cultural and historical worlds.

If sexuality is socially constructed, perhaps the most significant element of the construction—the foundation upon which we construct our sexuality—is gender. For men, the notion of masculinity, the cultural definition of manhood, serves as the primary building block of sexuality. It is through our understanding of masculinity that we construct a sexuality, and it is through our sexualities that we confirm the successful construction of our gender identity. Gender informs sexuality; sexuality confirms gender. Thus men have much at stake when they confront a sexual problem: They risk their self-image as men.

Like sexuality, gender in general, and masculinity in particular, is socially constructed; that is, what we understand to be masculine varies from culture to culture, over historical time within any one culture, and over the course of any one person's life within any culture. What we consider masculine or feminine in our culture is also not the result of some biological imperative, not some religious requirement, but a socially organized mode of behavior. What is masculine is not set in stone, but historically fluid. The pioneering research on gender by anthropologist Margaret Mead (1934) and others has specified how widely the cultural requirements of masculinity—what it takes to be a "real man" in any particular culture—vary. And these gender categories also shift in any one culture over time. Who would suggest, for example, that what was prescribed among upper-class Frenchmen in the eighteenth century—rare silk stockings and red patent leather high heels, prolific amounts of perfume and facial powder, powdered wigs and very long hair, and a rather precious preoccupation with love poems, dainty furniture, and roses— resembles our contemporary version of masculinity?

The assertion of the social construction of sexuality and gender leads naturally to two related questions. First, we need to specify precisely the dimensions of masculinity within contemporary American culture. How is masculinity organized as a normative set of behaviors and attitudes? Second, we need to specify precisely the ways in which this socially constructed gender identity informs male sexual development. How is masculinity expressed through sexuality?

Brannon and David's (1976, p. 12) summary of the normative structure of contemporary American masculinity is relevant here. Masculinity requires the avoidance and repudiation of all behaviors that are even remotely associated with femininity ("no sissy stuff"); this requires a ceaseless patrolling of one's boundaries, an incessant surveillance of one's performances to ensure that one is sufficiently male. Men must be "big wheels" since success and status are key determinants of masculinity, and they must be "sturdy oaks," exuding a manly air of self-confidence, toughness, and self-reliance, as well as reliability. Men must "give 'em hell," presenting an aura of aggression and daring, and attitude of constantly "going for it."

The normative organization of masculinity has been verified empirically (see Thompson & Pleck, 1986) and has obviously important implications for male sexuality. In a sense, sexuality is the location of the enactment of masculinity; sexuality allows the expression of masculinity. Male sexual socialization informs men that sexuality is the proving ground of adequate gender identity, and provides the script that men will adopt, with individual modification, as the foundation for sexual activity.

In a sense, when we examine the normative sexuality that is constructed from the typical organization of masculinity, it is not so much sexual problems that are of interest, but the problematization of "normal" sexuality, understanding perhaps the pathological elements within normal sexual functioning. This allows us to bridge the chasm between men who experience sexual dysfunction and those who, ostensibly, do not, and explore how men array themselves along a continuum of sexual expressions. Because masculinity provides the basic framework of sexual organization, and because masculinity requires adherence to certain rules that may retard or constrain emotional expression, we might fruitfully explore how even "normal" male sexuality evidences specific pathological symptoms, so that men who present exaggerated versions of these symptoms in therapy may better perceive their problems in a larger, sociological context of gender relations in contemporary society.[2]

The social construction of male sexuality raises a crucial theoretical issue. In the past, both social science research and clinical practice were informed by a model of discrete dichotomies. Categories for analysis implied a dualistic worldview in which a phenomenon was classified as either X or Y. Thus one was either male or female, heterosexual or homosexual, normal or pathological. Since the pioneering studies of Alfred Kinsey and his associates (see Kinsey, Pomeroy, & Martin, 1948; Kinsey & Gebhard, 1954), however, this traditional model of mutually exclusive dichotomous variables has given way to a model of a continuum of behaviors along which individuals array themselves. The continuum model allows individuals to reposition themselves at different moments in the life course, and it allows the researcher or clinician a point of entry into a relationship with the behaviors being discussed. The people we study and the people we counsel are less some curious "other" and more a variation on a set of behaviors that we ourselves embody as well. The articulation of the continuum model also requires that the level of analysis of any behavior include a social analysis of the context for behavior and the social construction of definitions of normality. It thus permits a truly *social* psychology.

The Male Sexual Script

Male sexual socialization teaches young men that sex is secret, morally wrong, and pleasurable. The association of sexual pleasure with feelings of guilt and shame is articulated early in the young boy's development, and reinforced throughout the life course by family, school, religion, and media images of sexuality. Young males are instructed, in locker rooms and playgrounds, to detach their emotions from sexual expression. In early masturbatory experience, the logic of detachment accommodates the twin demands of sexual pleasuring and guilt and shame. Later, detachment serves the "healthy" heterosexual male by permitting delay of orgasm in order to please his sexual partner, and serves the "healthy" homosexual male by permitting numerous sexual partners without cluttering up the scene with unpleasant emotional connection. (We will return to an exploration of the similarities between heterosexual and homosexual male sexuality below.)

Detachment requires a self-objectification, a distancing from one's self, and the development of a "secret sexual self" that performs sexual acts according to culturally derived scripts (Gagnon & Simon, 1973, p. 64). That men use the language of work as metaphors for sexual conduct—"getting the job done," "performing well," "achieving orgasm"—illustrates more than a passing interest in turning everything into a job whose performance can be evaluated; it reinforces detachment so that the body becomes a sexual machine, a performer instead of an authentic actor. The penis is transformed from an organ of sexual pleasure into a "tool," an instrument by which the performance is carried out, a thing, separate from the self. Many men report that they have conversations with their penises, and often cajole, plead with, or demand that they become and remain erect without orgasmic release. The penis can become the man's enemy, ready to engage in the most shameful conspiracy possible: performance failure. Is it any wonder that "performance anxiety" is a normative experience for male sexual behavior?

Men's earliest forays into sexuality, especially masturbation, are the first location of sexual anxiety. Masturbation teaches young men that sexuality is about the detachment of emotions from sex, that sex is important in itself. Second, men learn that sex is something covert, to be hidden; that is, men learn to privatize sexual experience, without skills to share the experience. And masturbation also teaches men that sexuality is phallocentric, that the penis is the center of the sexual universe. Finally, the tools of masturbation, especially sexual fantasy, teach men to objectify the self, to separate the self from the body, to focus on parts of bodies and not whole beings, often to speak of one's self in the third person.

Adolescent sexual socialization reinforces these behavioral demands that govern male sexuality. Passivity is absolutely forbidden, and the young male must attempt to escalate the sexual element at all times. To do otherwise is to avoid "giving 'em hell" and expose potential feminine behaviors. This constant pressure for escalation derives from the phallocentric component to male sexuality—"it only counts if I put it in," a student told one of us. Since normative heterosexuality assigns to men the role of "doer" and women the role of "gatekeeper," determining the level of sexual experience appropriate to any specific situation, this relentless pressure to escalate prevents either the male or the female from experiencing the sexual pleasure of any point along the continuum. No sooner does he "arrive" at a particular sexual experience—touching her breast, for example, than he begins strategizing the ways in which he can escalate, go further. To do less would expose him as less than manly. The female instantly must determine the limits of the encounter and devise the logistics that will prevent escalation if those limits have been reached. Since both male and female maintain a persistent orientation to the future (how to escalate and how to prevent escalation), neither can experience the pleasure of the points en route to full sexual intercourse. In fact, what men learn is that intercourse is the appropriate end-point of any sexual encounter, and that only intercourse "counts" in the tabulation of sexual encounters.

Since the focus is entirely phallocentric and intercourse is the goal to be achieved in adolescent sexual encounters, the stakes regarding sexual performance are extremely high, and consequently so is the anxiety about performance failure. Big wheels and sturdy oaks do not experience sexual dysfunction.

This continuum of male sexual dysfunction—ranging from what we might call the "normatively operative dysfunctional" to the cases of extreme distress of men who present themselves for therapeutic intervention—is reinforced in adult heterosexual relations as well. How do men maintain the sexual distancing and objectification that they perceive is required for healthy functioning? American comedian Woody Allen described, in his night-club routines, a rather typical male strategy. After describing himself as "a stud," Allen comments:

> While making love, in an effort [pause] to prolong [pause] the moment of ecstacy, I think of baseball players. All right, now you know. So the two of us are making love violently, and she's digging it, so I figure I better start thinking of baseball players pretty quickly. So I figure it's one out, and the Giants are up. Mays lines a single to right. He takes second on a wild pitch. Now she's digging her nails into my neck. I decide to pinch-hit for McCovey. [pause for laughter] Alou pops out. Haller singles, Mays takes third. Now I've got a first and third situation. Two outs and the Giants are behind by one run. I don't know whether to squeeze or to steal. [pause for laughter] She's been in the shower for ten minutes already. [pause] I can't tell you anymore, this is too personal. [pause] The Giants won.[3]

Readers may be struck by several themes—the imputation of violence, how her pleasure leads to his decision to think of baseball players, the requirement of victory in the baseball game, and the sexual innuendo contained within the baseball language—but the text provides a startlingly honest revelation of male sexual distancing. Here is a device that is so successful at delaying ejaculation that the narrator is rendered utterly unaware of his partner. "She's been in the shower for ten minutes already," Allen remarks, as if he's just noticed.

Much of peer sexual socialization consists of the conveying of these strategic actions that the male can perform to make himself a more adequate sexual partner. Men are often told to think of sports, work, or some other nonsexual event, or to repeat multiplication tables or mathematical formulas in order to avoid premature ejaculation. It's as if sexual adequacy could be measured by time elapsed between penetration and orgasm, and the sexual experience itself is transformed into an endurance test in which pleasure, if present at all, is almost accidental.

The contemporary male sexual script—the normative construction of sexuality—provides a continuum along which men array themselves for the script's enactment. The script contains dicta for sexual distancing, objectification, phallocentrism, a pressure to become and remain erect without ejaculation for as long as possible, all of which serve as indicators of masculinity as well as sexual potency. Adequate sexual functioning is seen as the proof of masculinity, so sexual problems will inevitably damage male gender identity. This is what makes treatment of sexual disorders a treatment of gender-identity issues.

Although this chapter has concentrated on sexual disorders for heterosexual men, this is not for analytic reasons, or from a sense of how these problems might manifest differently for gay men. Quite the contrary, in fact. Since gender identity is the key variable in understanding sexual behaviors, we would argue that heterosexual and homosexual men have more in common in regard to their sexuality than they evidence differences. This is especially true since 1969, when the Stonewall riots in New York and the subsequent emergence of the gay liberation movement led to the possibility for gay men to recover and repair their "damaged" sense of masculinity. Earlier gay men had been seen as "failed men," but the emergence of the gay male "clone" particularly has dispelled that notion. In the nation's gay "ghettos," gay men often enact a hypermasculine ethic, complete with its attendant sexual scripting of distancing, phallocentrism, objectification, and separation of emotion from physical sensation. Another reason that heterosexual and homosexual men exhibit similar gender-based sexual behaviors is that all boys are subject to an anticipatory socialization toward heterosexuality, regardless of their eventual sexual preference. There is no anticipatory socialization toward homosexuality in this culture, so male gender socialization will be enacted with both male and female sexual partners. Finally, we have not focused on gay men as a specific group because to do so would require the marginalization of gay men as a group separate from the normative script of male sexuality. Both gay and straight men are men first, and both have "male sex."

Therapeutic interventions

Our analysis of the social context of men's sexual problems makes it essential that therapeutic strategies remain aware of a context larger than simple symptom remission. Treatment must also challenge the myths, assumptions, and expectations that create the dysfunctional context for male sexual behavior (see Kaplan, 1974, 1983; LoPiccolo & LoPiccolo, 1978; Tollison & Adams, 1979).

Men seeking treatment for sexual difficulties will most often present with a symptom such as erectile failure, premature ejaculation, or inhibited desire. However, the *response* to this symptom, such as anxiety, depression, or low self-esteem is usually what brings the man into treatment, and this response derives from the man's relationship to an ideal vision of masculinity. The construction of this masculine ideal therefore needs to be addressed since it often creates the imperative command—to be in a constant state of potential sexual arousal, to achieve and maintain perfectly potent erections on command, and to delay ejaculation for a long time—which results in the performance anxiety that creates the symptom in the first place.

Sex therapy exercises, such as those developed by William Masters and Virginia Johnson and others, are usually effective only when the social context of gender ideals has also been addressed. This is accomplished by exploring and challenging the myths of male sexuality, modeling by the therapist of a different version of masculinity, giving permission to the patient to fail, and self-disclosure by the therapist of the doubts, fears of inadequacy, and other anxieties that all men experience. These will significantly reduce the isolation that the patient may experience, the fear that he is the only man who experiences such sexually-linked problems. These methods may be used to reorient men's assumptions about what constitutes masculinity, even though the therapist will be unable to change the entire social edifice that has been constructed upon these gender assumptions. Both the cognitive as well as the physical script must be addressed in treating sexual dysfunction; the cognitive script is perhaps the more important.

Recall these specific examples drawn from case materials. Sam's sexual performance was charged with anxiety and shame regarding both female partners and male peers. He was adamant that no one know he was seeking therapy, and went to great lengths to assure that confidentiality be preserved. He revealed significant embarrassment and shame with the therapist in early sessions, which subsided once the condition was normalized by the therapist.

Sam had grown up with exaggerated expectations of male sexual performance—that men must perform sexually on cue and never experience any sexual difficulty—that were consistent with the social milieu in which he was raised. He held women on a pedestal and believed that a man must please a woman or risk losing her. The stakes were thus quite high. Sam was also terrified of appearing "unmanly" with women, which resulted in a high degree of performance anxiety, which in turn prompted the premature ejaculation. The cycle of anxiety and failure finally brought Sam to treatment. Finally, Sam was detached from his own sexuality, his own body both sexually and emotionally. His objectification of his penis made it impossible for him to monitor impending ejaculation, and he was therefore unable to moderate the intensity of sensation prior to the point of ejaculatory inevitability. This common pattern among men who experience premature ejaculation suggests that such a response comes not from hypersensitivity but rather an atrophied sensitivity, based on objectification of the phallus.

Sam's treatment consisted of permission from another man—the therapist—to experience this problem and the attempt by the therapist to normalize the situation and reframe it as a problem any man might encounter. The problem was redefined as a sign of virility rather than an indication of its absence; Sam came to understand his sexual drive as quite high, which led to high levels of excitement that he had not yet learned to control. The therapist presented suggestions to control ejaculation that helped him moderate the intensity of arousal in order to better control his ejaculation. The important work, however, challenged the myths and cognitive script that Sam maintained regarding his sexuality. The attention given to his sexual performance, what he demanded of himself and what he believed women demanded of him, helped him reorient his sexuality into a less performance-oriented style.

Joe, the 34-year-old CPA, experienced low sexual desire with his wife though he masturbated regularly. Masturbatory fantasies involving images of women wanting him, finding him highly desirable, populated his fantasy world. When his self-esteem was low, as when he lost his job, for example, his sexual fantasies increased markedly. These fantasies of prowess with devalued women restored, he felt, his worth as a man. Interest in pornography included a script in which women were passive and men in control, very unlike the situation he perceives with his wife. He complained that he is caught in a vicious cycle, since without sexual interest in his wife he's not a "real man," and if he's not a "real man" then he has no sexual desire for her. He suggested that if he could only master a masculine challenge that was not sexual, such as finding another job or another competitive situation, he believed his sexual interest in his wife would increase. He felt he needed the mastery of a masculine challenge to confirm his sense of self as a man, which would then find further confirmation in the sexual arena. This adds an empirical confirmation of Gagnon and Simon's argument (1973) that genital sexuality contains many nonsexual motives, including the desire for achievement, power, and peer approval. Joe came to therapy with a great deal of shame at having to be there, and was especially ashamed at having to tell another man about his failures as a man. He was greatly relieved by the therapist's understanding, self-disclosure, and nonjudgmental stance, which enhanced the therapist's credibility and Joe's commitment to treatment.

One cognitive script that Joe challenged in counseling was his embrace of the "madonna/whore" ideology. In this formulation, any woman worth having (the madonna—mother or wife) was perceived as both asexual and as sexually rejecting of him, since his failures rendered him less of a real man. A "whore," on the other hand, would be both sexually available and interested in him, so she is consequently devalued and avoided. He could be sexual with her because the stakes are so low. This reinforces the cultural equation between sexual pleasure and cultural guilt and shame, since Joe would only want to be sexual with those who would not want to be sexual with him. This common motif in male sexual socialization frequently emerges in descriptions of "good girls" and "bad girls" in high school.

Joe's therapy included individual short-term counseling with the goal of helping him see the relationship between his self-esteem and his inhibited sexual desire. Traditional masculine definitions of success were the sole basis for Joe's self-esteem, and these were challenged in the context of a supportive therapeutic environment. The failure of childhood male role models was contrasted with new role models who provide permission to fail, helping Joe view sexuality as noncompetitive and non-achievement-oriented activity. Joe began to experience a return of sexual desire for his wife, as he became less phallocentric and more able to see sex as a vehicle for expressing intimacy and caring rather than a performance for an objectified self and other.

Bill, the 52-year-old married engineer, presented with erectile failure, which is part of a larger pattern of intolerance of failure in himself. The failure of his penis to function properly symbolized to him the ultimate collapse of his manhood. Not surprisingly, he had searched for physiological etiologies before seeking psychological counseling, and had been referred by an urologist. It is estimated that less than 50% of all men who present themselves for penile implant surgery have a physiological basis for their problem; if so, the percentage of all men who experience erectile disorders whose etiology is physiological is less than 5%. Yet the pressure to salvage a sense of masculinity that might be damaged by a psychological problem leads thousands of men to request surgical prosthesis every year (see, for example, Tiefer, 1986).

Bill and his wife, Ann, confronted in therapy the myths of male sexuality that they embraced, including such dicta as "a real man always wants sex," "the only real sex is intercourse," and "the man must always be in charge of sex" (see Zilbergeld, 1978). The therapist gave Bill permission to fail by telling him that all men at some time experience erectile dysfunction. Further, Bill was counseled that the real problem is not the erectile failure, but his reaction to this event. Exercises were assigned in which Bill obtained an erection through manual stimulation and then purposely lost the erection to desensitize himself to his terrible fear of failure. This helped him overcome the "what if" fear of losing the erection. Bill was counseled to "slow down" his sexual activity, and to focus on the sensations rather than the physical response, both of which were designed to further remove the performance aspects from his sexual activity. Finally, the therapist helped Bill and Ann redefine the notion of masculinity by stating that "a real man is strong enough to take risks, eschew stereotypes, to ask for what he needs sexually from a partner, and, most of all, to tolerate failure."

As Bill and Ann's cognitive script changed, his ability to function sexually improved. Though Bill still does not get full erections on a consistent basis, this fact is no longer catastrophic for him. He and Ann now have a broader script both physically and cognitively, which allows them to have other sexual play and the shared intimacy that it provides.

As one can see from these case studies, several themes run consistently through therapeutic strategies in counseling men about sexual problems, and many of these themes also relate directly to issues of social analysis as well as clinical practice. For example, the therapeutic environment must be experienced as supportive, and care must be taken so that the therapist not appear too threatening or too "successful" to the patient. The gender of the therapist with the male patient will raise different issues at this point. A male therapist can empathize with the patient, and greatly reduce his sense of isolation, while a female therapist can provide positive reactions to fears of masculine inadequacy, and thereby provide a positive experience with a woman they may translate to nontherapeutic situations.

Second, the presenting symptom should be "normalized," that is, it should be cast within the wider frame of male socialization to sexuality. It is not so much that the patient is "bad," "wrong," or "abnormal" but that he has experienced some of the contradictory demands of masculinity in ways that have become dysfunctional for his sexual experiences. It is often crucial to help the patient realize that he is not the only man who experiences these problems, and that these problems are only problems seen from within a certain construct of masculinity.

In this way, the therapist can help the patient to dissociate sexuality from his sense of masculinity, to break the facile identification between sexual performance and masculinity. Masculinity can be confirmed by more than erectile capacity, constant sexual interest, and a long duration of intercourse; in fact, as we have argued, normal male sexuality often requires the dissociation of emotional intimacy and connectedness for adequate sexual functioning. Raising the level of analysis from the treatment of individual symptoms to a social construction of gender and sexuality does not mean abandoning the treatment of the presenting symptoms, but rather retaining their embeddedness in the social context from which they emerge. Counseling men about sexuality involves, along with individualized treatment, the redefinition of what it means to be a man in contemporary American society. Therapeutic treatments pitched at both the social and the individual levels can help men become more expressive lovers and friends and fathers, as well as more "functional" sexual partners. That a man's most important sexual organ is his mind is as true today as ever.

Notes

1. The names of the individual patients have been changed.

2. To assert a pathological element to what is culturally defined as "normal" is a contentious argument. But such an argument derives logically from assertions about the

social construction of gender and sexuality. Perhaps an analogy would prove helpful. One might also argue that given the cultural definition of femininity in our culture, especially the normative prescriptions for how women are supposed to look to be most attractive, *all* women manifest a problematic relationship to food. Even the most "normal" woman, having been socialized in a culture stressing unnatural thinness, will experience some pathological symptoms around eating. This assertion will surely shed a very different light on the treatment of women presenting eating disorders, such as bulimia or anorexia nervosa. Instead of treating them in their *difference* from other women, by contextualizing their symptoms within the larger frame of the construction of femininity in American culture, they can be seen as exaggerating an already culturally prescribed problematic relationship to eating. This position has the additional benefit, as it would in the treatment of male sexual disorders, of resisting the temptation to "blame the victim" for her or his acting out an exaggerated version of a traditional script.

3. Woody Allen, *the Nightclub Years,* United Artists Records (1971). Used by permission.

References

David, D., & Brannon, R. (1976). *The forty-nine percent majority.* Reading, MA: Addison-Wesley.

Gagnon, J. (1977). *Human sexualities.* Chicago: Scott, Foresman.

Gagnon, J., & Simon, W. (1973). *Sexual conduct.* Chicago: Aldine.

Kaplan, H. S., (1974). *The new sex therapy.* New York: Brunner-Mazel.

Kimmel, M. (Ed.). (in press). *Changing men: New directions in research on men and masculinity.* Newbury Park, CA: Sage.

Kinsey, A. C., & Pomeroy, W. (1948). *Sexual behavior in the human male.* Philadelphia: Saunders.

LoPiccolo, J., & LoPiccolo, L. (1978). *Handbook of sex therapy.* New York: Plenum.

Mead, M. (1935). *Sex and temperament in three primitive societies.* New York: William Morrow.

Thompson, E. H., Jr., & Pleck, J. H. (1986). The structure of male role norms. *American Behavioral Scientist, 29,* 531-543.

Tiefer, L. (1986). In pursuit of the perfect penis: The medicalization of male sexuality. *American Behavioral Scientist, 29,* 579-599.

Tollison, C. D., & Adams, H. (1979). *Sexual disorders: Treatment, theory, and research.* New York: Gardner.

Trilling, L. (1954). *The liberal imagination.* New York: Knopf.

Wagner, G., & Green, R. (1984). *Impotence: Physiological, psychological, surgical diagnosis and treatment.* New York: Plenum.

Zilbergeld, B. (1978). *Male sexuality.* New York: Simon & Schuster.

6

Grief Work with Men

J. Eugene Knott

This chapter will first synthesize the pertinent sociocultural influences on men's experiences of loss and grief, dealing particularly with reactions to loss due to death. This will be followed by a short summary of the available research on men and bereavement. Then, some technical and philosophical bases for treatment of men with "grief work" needs will be sketched, followed by an examination of the variations in format, approach, and setting for such therapies.

Loss in general, and death loss in particular, with its immutability, lies at the core of man's complex relationship with himself. To deal with a man's grief, in all likelihood, one needs to begin with that initial step—for both therapist and bereaved counselee—of coming to terms with one's own mortality. Further, the inexpressiveness characteristic of Western males confronts the therapist with a truly formidable task regardless of the presenting issue (Balswick & Peek, 1971). A cartoon from the "Peanuts" comic strip illustrated this with a slight twist. In it, Lucy says to Charlie Brown, "Women shouldn't be the only ones to cry . . . men should realize that it's all right for them to cry, too." Whereupon, Charlie proceeds to shed a tear. But, this only causes Lucy, in disgust, to challenge him, saying, "First, you have to have something happen!"

When someone dies or is dying, something obviously does happen. But it may be an overwhelming conflict for many men simultaneously to express their feelings, maintain their self-image, and contend with deeper psychological meanings of a particular death loss. Another of the symbolic and linguistic ironies of men in grief may be found in the phrase "grief work." The term was first used by Erich Lindemann (1944) to connote the energy-depleting demands of mourning and dealing with one's inner experience of loss. The stereotype of a male being unable to "work," to intentionally abandon (social and psychic) "business as usual" in order to cope with the conflictive reactions he's experiencing may be too taxing a demand. Thus, for reasons more learned by the gender than innate to the species, the process of "grief work" may be approached by most men in today's world with great misgiving, confusion, and at too great an estimated cost, if at all. Not only is it out of character for the male, and probably out of the realm of comfortable reference to his prior experience, it is un-American and unsupported in his work culture. There is far too much importance relative to survivorship following other losses to do even summary justice to each, let alone the combination, in these few pages. Thus this chapter will address men's losses through death and some approaches to facilitating the aforementioned "grief work" for and with them. This focus will not, however, include one's own death per se, or the small deaths that are incurred via losses in more commonplace events that fall short of irreversibility due to death. Several complementary chapters in this section will suffice for those topics. Nor will the "dying trajectory" and "death surround," as sociologists have called the phenomena of the dying process itself, be addressed. That too has been the subject of much scrutiny in all forms of media, especially in the last decade or so. An excellent recent source on the subject of anticipatory grief is Rando's *Loss and Anticipatory Grief* (1986). The balance of this chapter will deal with those men who are attempting to come to terms with (including the avoidance thereof) the realized physical death of persons significant to their lives.

Whither Grief?

First, I provide some operational definitions to simplify subsequent discussion. The terminology adopted includes a definition of *bereavement* as "the perception of loss." More pointedly, it involves the recognition that *I* am the loser! I am the one who has been left behind to suffer someone's loss. It is a self-reference that is critical to the "grief work" to follow, and yet has the feature of often rendering a man psychosocially impotent to help himself with this unplanned, unwanted change in his life. *Grief*, then, is the syndrome of reactions one engages in as a response to bereavement. It is at once automatic and controlled, anabolic and catabolic as well as physiological and psychological in combination, entails approach and avoidance in thought and behavior, and is universal as well as idiosyncratic in expression. It encompasses all one does, with and without fully conscious intent, to "cope" with the finality of this loss and its meanings. While these responses are not unique to men, they do often manifest in sex-role specific ways. Hoffman (1977), a decade ago, reviewed the research on sex differences in empathy and related behaviors and found support for the cultural stereotype of men being less empathic, less expressive, and more instrumental in their ameliorative responses than women. If anything, this seems to have intensified in the decade since. Thus the range of allowable expressions of grief may be no more expanded or available than for our fathers and theirs.

Mourning is the "shared process of grieving," even if that sharing is unintentional or limited to but a single other empathic soul. It is grief gone public, and includes the private and open social occasions and rituals chosen to affirm one's connection to the dead person, and the tacit appeal for acknowledgment of one's bereavement. For increasing numbers of men, it is an acceptance of the need for finishing some unfinished business having to do with the recently dead relative, and an emancipating yet integrating dynamic whereby a man can acquire a suitable perspective on his survivorship and his unique co-history with the dead person. A short summary of the scant but growing research literature on men's bereavement might be useful at this point.

The Effects of Bereavement

Men who are bereaved can be observed from several vantage points. Research findings typically have categorized bereavement outcomes according to role relationship to the deceased. The roles for men are primarily five: son, spouse, brother, father, and friend or colleague. There are also generational and in-law extensions of these for family relatives, but the chapter will focus only on the first five.

SON

Childhood bereavement studies offer somewhat equivocal findings for boys and girls who lose a parent to death, citing greater risk for children under five and for adolescents, and for boys whose father dies in their teen years. Other than that, there are no noteworthy sex differences. The outcome factors of most importance relate to preexisting systemic difficulties in the family. In that light, boys' so-called acting out behaviors are traditionally less acceptable in polite society, as they frequently are more threatening to persons and property. Otherwise, the nature of the death event itself contains the only serious influences on satisfactory grief work by children. These include unanticipated and violent deaths, and, to a lesser extent, unreconciled negative feelings toward the dead person (Osterweis, Solomon, & Green, 1984). Conceptual and therapeutic approaches for working with adolescents who are bereaved can be found in a number of helpful chapters in a recent book edited by Coor and McNeil (1986).

SPOUSE

Spousal or conjugal bereavement is the most researched area of all the problems of bereavement. Compared to widows, widowers seem to reattach to new women in relationships more often and sooner, and also show higher risk for both morbidity and mortality, particularly men between 35 and 75. This latter finding has been a fairly stable one over the past 20 years and across several cultures (Vachon, 1976; Osterweis et al., 1984). It suggests the adverse consequences of a typical masculine lifestyle extend over the life span and may intensify with life-threatening potential during early bereavement (Rees, 1972; Rees & Lutkins, 1967). There appear, however, to be few sex differences in experienced distress following conjugal loss, but less expressiveness is exhibited by males.

The literature further attests to greater difficulty for bereaved males who cannot function independently, or who had highly ambivalent marital relationships (Helsing, Szklo, & Comstock, 1981). Particular problems occur with health and survival when bereaved men use maladaptive approaches like heavy medication and alcohol abuse, or do not heed their own health care needs.

Parkes and Weiss (1983) noted higher chronic illness death rates, especially for vascular and coronary diseases, and for younger bereaved males, while those over 65 years had increased mortality from infectious disease, accidents, and suicides. In summary of male spousal bereavement, Jacobs and Ostfeld (1977) suggest that these morbidity and mortality excesses may be mediated by behavioral changes following widowhood that compromise good self-care habits or management needs.

FATHER

If, as Cook (1983) asserts, the nature of mourning depends on the relationship the bereaved had with the deceased, then the expectation that parental bereavement might be different and probably more troublesome than the loss of other relationships may be well founded. Indeed, many authors argue that such is the case. Research in recent longitudinal studies supports that assertion, and even hints at a totally different pattern of bereavement over time following the death of one's child.

Rando (1983) gave testimony to the intensity of grief felt by parents whose child dies before adulthood, and offers the not-so-consoling prospect of a worsening of emotional reaction for some over the first several years. This is in direct opposition to the pattern of gradual decrease of emotional intensity in grieving over adult losses after the initial months (Glick, Parkes, & Weiss, 1975).

Some (Berardo, 1970; Charmaz, 1980) have suggested that gender not only mediates reaction to the death of a family member, but, in the case of losing a child, the father is further victimized by the hypermasculine ethic (Schiff, 1977) and the easier, more comfortable sympathizing mothers experience from supportive others (Gyulay & Miles, 1973). Cook's (1983) findings underscore these latter points, noting that fathers were likelier to cite nonfamily as helpful to them. They also reported less comfort with discussing their child's loss, and a greater emphasis on managing and controlling emotional behavior rather than sharing their wife's grief. Unfortunately, no published accounts of studies on the differential effects of separation and divorce on this form of grief exist at this time. The need for research on this topic increases weekly. Generally speaking, the death of a child can be and often is the final strain that leads to a marital breakup— an immense stressor to even a solid, mutually supportive couple.

ADULT SIBLING

Very little has been written about adult sibling bereavement, which is usually classified under adult bereavement. A pair of unpublished studies (Knott, Kirkpatrick, & Scala, 1982; Knott & Scala, 1981), however, suggest that siblings too may be at greater risk for premature death in the two years following a brother's or sister's death. This effect does appear to worsen with increasing survivor age, although this does not seem to affect men more harshly than women.

ADULT CHILD

The death of a parent occurs annually to 1 in every 20 adults in this country, yet little research on this exists. While no sex differences in bereavement reaction or risk have been noted (Sanders, 1979-1980; Horowitz, Weiss, & Kaltreider, 1981) since Freud's (1917/1957) early writings on the subject, the male adult child's reaction, and the father's death in particular have been the frequent focus of much literature, both empirical and popular. The symbolism may be influenced in part by the fact that 75% of the time the first parent to die is the father. Grief work in these circumstances often seems to be involved with the meanings of loss of one's developmental buffer against being next in line to face mortality. Also, the unfinished agenda with parents that most children carry into adulthood can take on new significance in their psychic economy upon a parent's death (Malinak, Hoyt, & Patterson, 1979).

NONFAMILY

Practically nothing has been published to suggest that men who lose non-kin relationships due to death are at greater risk for poor grief resolution. No empirical work has been found to suggest it has even been a subject of research scrutiny. The category of friend or colleague, which could encompass a variety of other more specific role relationships such as teacher-student, mentor-protegé, partners, supervisor-supervisee, and so on, is still wide open to investigation. Neither the particular cultural and ethnic influences on the grieving process nor the matters of intentioned death through suicide or homicide will be in focus here, although these are special situations and variables of significance in the mourning process. Three recent publications have provided clinicians with excellent source materials and are strongly recommended as supplemental reading. They are Rando's *Grief, Dying and Death* (1984), Raphael's *The Anatomy of Bereavement* (1983), and *Bereavement* by Osterweis et al. (1984).

Influencing Variables

In addition to determining the nature and importance of the relationship that has been lost through this death, the felt appropriateness of the loss developmentally, and whether there was anticipation of the death are also critical features. Moreover, the family and social supports that are available is a pivotal factor, as are both the person's previous successful coping with losses and his abilities to deal with the way in which the relative died.

Before presenting some models for helping men with grief work, two key points should be noted:

(1) Most people resolve their issues over death loss, and accomplish their grief work over time without undue complications, and without professional help.
(2) The parameters of normal grief expression are exceedingly broad. They include somatic symptoms, reminiscences both sad and affirming, extreme irritability, depression, self-doubt, inertia, and withdrawal. These manifest idiosyncratically, and pose genuinely worrisome challenges only when they get in the way of usual patterns of conduct, are protracted for months without change, and represent risks to healthy functioning.

In those situations where counseling or therapy seem called for, most avenues of help lead in one or a combination of three ways: one-to-one, self-help, or group modalities. The chapter will examine some key considerations for each.

One-to-One

Individual treatment should include address of each of the following in loosely sequential phases:
(1) *Determine the nature of the bereavement.* This means gathering data

about how the man has been feeling, thinking, and behaving since the death. It includes learning who has died, under what circumstances, and the general view of the acceptibility of this death at this time for your client. While some fairly universal and predictable details will emerge, it is important for both the helper *and* the bereaved individual to experience the expression of that information both verbally and nonverbally. This sets the stage for an initial appraisal and determination of the person's needs and affective states. Besides, there will always be some very personal, unique features to that presentation.

(2) *Familiarize oneself with the personal loss history.* This line of inquiry serves to provide three things: a context for understanding this particular loss and death; a framework for assaying the client's approaches to coping; and an expression of self-assessment by the man relative to being "loser" and victim, and how he views his/her general role toward the dead person and their dying.

(3) *Convey a sense of the "normalcy" of the grief.* Often, the biggest need for the recently bereaved is to be assured that their range of behaviors, thoughts, and feelings is quite common for what has happened to them. Once they can grasp the notion that they're not "losing it," and their confusing, even sometimes negative emotions, such as anger, are both allowable and normal consequences of bereavement, the fuller range of topics to be examined becomes more approachable. Anxiety-reduction is often the necessary beginning to our therapeutic encounters, and is especially needed here.

(4) *Identify the meanings of the loss.* In addition to the death of a person important to them, clients are encouraged repeatedly to explore the other roles that person played so centrally for them, and of which they are feeling deprived now. For example, a spouse may have been also a best friend, a lover and sex partner, a confidante, and have served any number of more mundane but easily missed roles in his life. A fuller appreciation of these meanings—real and symbolic—is pivotal to the healing needed. As another instance, a father's or son's death may have significant personal meaning beyond the tangible, beyond the absence, and may be particularly poignant for males who subscribe to some fairly stereotypical views of manliness and posterity, as described earlier in this chapter.

(5) *Enable expression of the gamut of feelings held by the bereaved.* This has to do particularly with the felt injunctions against speaking ill of the dead and defenseless. It is quite common and reasonable for a man to hold some measure of both guilt and anger over another's death. The guilt can be over things said and done, as over acts of omission. The "unfinished business" often brought forcefully to one's awareness by an unexpected death usually is colored deeply by such feelings. Even an unspoken "goodbye" can evoke these powerful emotions. Anger also comes with the baggage of incomplete plans, thwarted hopes, and outrage at the uncontrol-

lable poor timing and unavoidable sense of injustice that accompanies most deaths. The descriptor "untimely" has always struck me as a needless truism that describes nearly all deaths as experienced by most, though not all, survivors. Not to be lost here either is the need for the bereaved man to give vent to his positive and intimate views of how he felt attached to his dead relative or friend.

(6) *Examine aspects of secondary loss and gain.* Of particular importance at this juncture of treatment is an examination of the redemptive irony of loss experience in life—there is always "gain" to be found accompanying every loss. With bereavement in this culture, finding that gain is not an easy task, for there are too many prohibitions against such admissions. But a healing perspective comes more surely through seeing the gains in survivorship—the strengths commanded by the psychosocial legacies of it, the relief, the new appreciation of what matters—death is the ultimate values clarification experience. This comes gradually over time with some tactful framing by the therapist, and is an essential benchmark of grief resolution and healing the wounds of loss.

(7) *Explore life without . . .* A needed transition to looking ahead eventually arises, and signals a willingness to deal with the analysts' task of "emancipation from bondage to the deceased" (Lindemann, 1944). This shift to living in the absence of the dead relative entails a fascinating set of adaptations by the bereaved male. It is a form of psychosocial homeostasis, a seeking to assume and/or reassign roles, as well as to divorce oneself from some that are not replaceable, not wanted or needed in the dead person's absence. Finally, this process involves formulating some concrete plans, contemplating future wants and needs with an intentional self-centeredness that is characteristically free of external motivation. It is action undertaken for himself. A final gesture takes the process full circle: terminating therapy, saying goodbye and sustaining loss once more, but in a planned, willful, controllable way.

One can note the phasic shift in the temporal focus of this model from reconciliation of the past to the more existential matters of bereavement and, finally, to concerns over one's future. This general pattern also characterizes the nonindividual approaches that follow as well.

The amount of time for such facilitated grief work can vary greatly, as the many variables of influence cited earlier alter the course of treatment according to their depth and perturbing effects. Significant dates, sights, events, music, and so on all can further provide important opportunities and even rituals for working through one's agenda with the death loss and dead person. Further, grief work often will begin with a singular focus, and stimulate needed recourse to finish incomplete or arrested mourning over previous other losses.

Self-Help

This movement of the past 30 years has strong roots in assisting widowed people with Phyllis Silverman's (1966) programs in Boston. Lately, the self-help modalities are strong, often overlapping ways of abetting grief work. They are mainly bibliotherapy, and mutual aid or self-help groups. The many first-person and survivor narrations of dying and grief in recent years, telephone tapes, and the many talk shows in the media, along with popular magazines having rediscovered "grief," afford men opportunities to tap into bereavement issues in private without having to uncover their facades of stoicism. Readings and films can augment group-based self-help approaches, as well.

Mutual Aid/Self-Help Groups

As Levy (1979) points out, groups of people banding together for psychosocial improvement

> focus the major portion of their efforts on fostering communication between their members, providing them with social support, and responding to their needs on both cognitive and social levels. (p. 264)

The specific processes he found to be operative in these groups, which make self-help approaches particularly powerful and effective formats with potentially great merit for males are these:

BEHAVIORALLY ORIENTED PROCESSES

(1) both direct and vicarious social reinforcement for the development of desirable behaviors and the elimination or control of problematic behaviors;
(2) training, indoctrination, and support in the use of various kinds of self-control behaviors;
(3) model of methods of coping with stresses and changing behavior; and
(4) providing members with an agenda of actions they can engage in to change their social environment.

COGNITIVELY ORIENTED PROCESSES

(1) removing members' mystification over their experiences and increasing their expectancy for change and help by providing them with a rationale for their problems or distress and for the group's way of dealing with it;
(2) provision of normative and instrumental information and advice;

(3) expansion of the range of alternative perceptions of members' problems and circumstances and of the actions they might take to cope with their problems;

(4) enhancement of members' discriminative abilities regarding the stimulus and event contingencies in their lives;

(5) support for changes in attitudes toward oneself, one's own behavior, and society;

(6) social comparison and consensual validation leading to a reduction or elimination of members' uncertainty and sense of isolation or uniqueness regarding their problems and experiences; and

(7) the emergence of an alternative or substitute culture and social structure within which members can develop new definitions of their personal identities and new norms upon which they can base their self-esteem.

The Compassionate Friends, Theos, Share, Make Today Count and numerous other self-help groups, including hundreds of hospice-sponsored bereavement groups nationwide, offer witness to the widespread appeal, need, and utility of bereavement self-help or mutual aid groups. Male-only groups would not seem necessary, but could be successfully implemented. Sherman (1979) offered an analysis of the ideology and dynamics in a bereaved parents group that provides useful background for this topic in a self-help group. Also, combinations of media and mutual aid group activities also afford a very effective approach as well. Yet, some time probably needs to pass after the death before a self-help group can be entered. A format for one such group approach to resolving personal death loss can be found in Drum and Knott (1977).

Group

Bridging over into more traditional therapy groups, one finds a good deal of theory and little useful research reported. The first focus of conceptual writings has been on enabling bereaved people to come to grips with their loss. This may not be mediated solely or predictably by the intervening time since a death, but is more often affected by a number of the variables mentioned earlier. Delayed grief, for instance, may be due to a rapid and fully preoccupying assumption of caretaker duties upon the death of a spouse or parent. Absent grief, where typical outward manifestations of bereavement are not visible, may reflect a loose attachment to the dead person, while sometimes also masking a deeper-seated co-history of conflict. Treatment often is prescribed, also, for dealing with the anxiety and depression aspects of loss that are most common.

Typically, group configurations will overtly enable the bereaved members to work through the "unfinished business" with the dead relative, while simultaneously providing a social support network for them. For too many men, social support is a minimal or altogether deprived facet of their lives, so group work—and especially men-only membership—may prove quite useful and can have great worth even beyond the group's ostensible purpose. Getting men to convene in same-sex groups for talk therapies, however, frequently is quite difficult, with the notable exceptions of some bereaved fathers' experiences recently, and, of course, the larger number of less therapy-like postaddiction self-help groups.

Final Word

Getting men in need of counseling to come for help is often the biggest challenge to their benefiting from therapeutic assistance. It is even more difficult to enable them to avail themselves of professional assistance if the need was occasioned by a death loss. Working to loosen the bonds of masculinity may be the major impediment to helping them loosen the bonds of unreconciled grief. Unfortunately, that may have never been harder for Western males than at the present time.

References

Balswick, J. O., & Peek, C. W. (1971). The inexpressive male: A tragedy of American society. *The Family Coordinator, 20*, 363-368.

Charmaz, K. (1980). *The social reality of death*. Reading, MA: Addison-Wesley.

Cook, J. A. (1983). A death in the family: Parental bereavement in the first year. *Suicide and Life-Threatening Behavior, 13*, 42-61.

Corr, C. A., & McNeil, J. N. (1986). *Adolescence and death*. New York: Springer.

Drum, D. J., & Knott, J. E. (1977). *Structured groups for facilitating development*. New York: Human Sciences Press.

Freud, S. (1957). *Mourning and melancholia. The standard edition of the complete psychological works of Sigmund Freud* (Vol. 14; originally published 1917). (J. Strachey ed.). London: Hogarth Press.

Glick, I. O., Parkes, C. M., & Weiss, R. (1975). *The first year of bereavement*. New York: Basic Books.

Gyulay, J., & Miles, M. S. (1973). The family with a terminally ill child. In B. Hymovich and C. Barnard (Eds.), *Family health care*. New York: McGraw-Hill.

Helsing, K. J., Szklo, M., & Comstock, G. W. (1981). Factors associated with mortality after widowhood. *American Journal of Public Health, 71*, 802-809.

Hoffman, M. L. (1977). Sex differences in empathy and related behaviors. *Psychological Bulletin, 84*, 712-722.

Horowitz, M. J., Weiss, D., Kaltreider, N., Wilner, N., Leong, A., & Marmar, C. (1981). Initial psychological response to parental death. *Archives of General Psychiatry, 38*, 316-323.

Jacobs, S., & Ostfeld, A. (1977). An epidemiological review of the mortality of bereavement. *Psychosomatic Medicine, 39*, 344-357.

Knott, J. E., Kirkpatrick, H., & Scala, M. E. (1982). Sympathetic death: fact or fiction. Paper presented at FDEC Conference, San Diego.

Knott, J. E., & Scala, M. E. (1981). Bereaved to death: Taking me with you. Paper presented at FDEC Conference, Kansas City.

Levy, L. H. (1979). Processes and activities in groups. In M. A. Lieberman & G. Bond (Eds.), *Self-help groups for coping with crisis.* San Francisco: Jossey-Bass.

Lindemann, E. (1944). Symptomatology and management of acute grief. *American Journal of Psychiatry, 101,* 141-148.

Malinak, D. P., Hoyt, M. F., & Patterson, V. (1979). Adult's reactions to the death of a parent: A preliminary study. *American Journal of Psychiatry, 136,* 1152-1156.

Osterweis, M., Solomon, F., & Green, M. (Eds.). (1984). *Bereavement: Reactions, consequences, and care.* Washington, DC: National Academy Press.

Parkes, C. M., & Weiss, R. S. (1983). *Recovery from bereavement.* New York: Basic Books.

Rando, T. A. (1983). An investigation of grief and adaptation in parents whose children have died from cancer. *Journal of Pediatric Psychology, 8,* 3-20.

Rando, T. A. (1984). *Grief, dying, and death.* Champaign, IL: Research Press.

Raphael, B. (1983). *The anatomy of bereavement.* New York: Basic Books.

Rees, W. D. (1972). Bereavement and illness. *Journal of Thanatology, 2,* 814.

Rees, W. D., & Lutkins, S. G. (1967). Mortality of bereavement. *British Medical Journal, 4,* 13.

Sanders, C. A. (1979-1980). A comparison of adult bereavement in the death of a spouse, child, and parent. *Omega, 10,* 303-322.

Schiff, H. S. (1977). *The bereaved parent.* New York: Penguin Books.

Sherman, B. (1979). Emergence of ideology in a bereaved parents group. In M. A. Lieberman & G. Bond (Eds.), *Self-help groups for coping with crisis.* San Francisco: Jossey-Bass.

Silverman, P. R. (1966). Services to the widowed during the period of bereavement. In *Social work practice: Proceedings.* New York: Columbia University Press.

Vachon, M.L.S. (1976). Grief and bereavement following the death of a spouse. *Canadian Psychiatric Association Journal, 21,* 35-44.

7

Body-Focused Psychotherapy with Men

Edward W. L. Smith

Balanced living is found in the intermediate zone, in the territory lying between the poles of the extremes. Our attention is called to this truth in Aristotelian philosophy by the "doctrine of the mean," known more popularly as the "golden mean." Often it is easier to walk the path of the extreme. "All or nothing," "always or never." These are easier to recognize than "not too much, not too little," and "sometimes." It is easier to lean on the pole of an extreme than to find one's balance on the middle path, not wandering too far to either side. Extreme behavior lacks such balance, and is therefore the symptom and the portent of a life uncentered. This is not to say that a person who lives creatively stays on a very narrow path, never tending toward one pole or the other. Rather, it means that the person who lives creatively makes mini-swings within the middle territory, but does not swing all the way to one extreme or the other. Being centered is a flexible, dynamic process of balancing by means of such mini-swings. Polar positions are not free, but rather are rigid and static.

To make this more concrete, and specific to the psychological dynamics of males, this chapter will explore the dimension of male rigidity. This requires some basic understanding of the male rigid character structure. Character structure, as presented in the psychoanalytic and Reichian tradition (Smith, 1985), is seen as developing from early life experiences. Character development depends on the degree of fixation at the various erogenous levels, as result of certain traumatic experiences. The result, which manifests both psychologically and physically, is a relatively fixed pattern of behavior. Although "character" is a hypothetical syndrome, and no one is a pure character type, what therapists look for is which character type is dominant and which other types may play a secondary role in the person's dynamics.

The five character types recognized in the neo-Reichian school of bioenergetics are in a development sequence. The earliest type is the schizoid, then the oral, the psychopath, the masochist, and then the rigid types. If the etiological trauma is relatively early, the probability is that the person will have difficulty developing through the successive stages as well. This makes sense, in that some of the developmental tasks of the stage of the trauma will not be mastered, leaving the child to enter the next developmental stage with a deficit. Therefore, the character types are in a descending order of complexity, as there is a partial adding of type to type, the earlier the initial trauma. In addition, as one moves higher in the developmental sequence of the character types, there is greater variety in the syndrome, since there has been more personality differentiation prior to the trauma.

Psychological issues having their etiology in a developmental stage prior to clear gender differentiation tend to manifest in quite similar ways in men and women. The several issues are the same for all children before the time they see themselves as boys and girls. The general themes are maternal rejection and schizoid character formation, maternal deprivation and oral character, parental overpowering and psychopathic character, the over-bearing mother and submissive father (who stifle the child's spontaneity and leave him or her feeling pushed, nagged, and guilty) and masochistic character formation. As these characterological styles are set before children see themselves as boys or girls, the gender issue is of only secondary influence in the formation of the pathological patterns of the adult.

With the arrival of gender identity, one's "boyness" or "girlness" becomes an integral factor in further character formation. The rigid female character, or histrionic character, is differentiated from the rigid male character even though the trauma is the same—rejection of love by the father. When the father rejects the child's love, he is rejecting an aspect of his daughter or his son. The girl is having her female love turned away by her opposite-sex parent. This means the father's rejection of her budding female sexuality, and sets the pattern for subsequent dealings with men. And so the hystrionic sets upon a life-long quest for male affirmation of her childlike sexuality. This is her unfinished business, her incomplete gestalt creating tension for closure.

For the young boy, the rejection of his love is a statement that he is not good enough. Since he experiences himself as a boy, this means he is not a good enough male, as judged by his same-sex parent. His rejection is not sexualized, but is clearly "genderized." His unfinished business is to prove himself as a boy/man.

The key element in the rigid male is the father's rejection of the son's affection and the pushing away of the boy. By being pushed away the boy feels "not good enough." At the same time the father makes the expression of his love for his son, to whatever degree he feels such, contingent on the son's performance. But, whatever his son does, it is never quite good enough. The boy never measures up to his father's standard. So, the boy grows up always believing that he has to perform. And, since his own love for his father was rejected, he gives up on reaching out with love in order not to feel frustrated and hurt anymore.

So, what is a boy to do? Residing in a man's body, and destined to live out the existential decisions come to in response to a father's rejection, how is one to live? The existential decisions become the guides. "Dad let me know that I am not good enough for him to love me. Therefore, *I must constantly try to prove myself.* 'I will!' is my call to action, my determined declaration. I am ambitious and competitive. Under stress I am prone to take action, attending to details. I work hard, even overwork, and will keep at the job until it is done, and done perfectly. Often, therefore, I will be seen as self-confident, perhaps even arrogant, and impressive in my penchant for action. In order to reach high levels of achievement and strive for perfection I demand structure. Some would call me obsessive or compulsive.

"Dad spurned my affection, my expressions of love for him. Therefore, *I must protect myself from hurt by never reaching out, never being soft or too warm.* So, I am hard and cold. I will not surrender to soft and tender feelings.

"Perhaps you recognize me by the way I hold back in my body. You may see that I am stiff with pride. My body reflects the rigidity that my inflexible existential choices demand. Sometimes, as I walk or otherwise move about, it becomes painfully obvious that I am all too literally 'tight-assed.'

"In my relationships I can offer several appealing qualities. I will get fairly close, and bring a lot of energy to a relationship. I will be strong and active, quite dependable, and one to rely on to solve external problems. But, be warned. I will not relate on an emotional level. In fact, I will actively oppose the expression of feelings. As I denigrate feelings, you may find me emotionally insensitive and unavailable. My pattern of overwork, and obsessive compulsive task orientation bespeak my subordination of personhood to the attainment of goals. You will find my beliefs, opinions, and values as inflexible and unyielding as the postural muscles of my body" (Smith, 1984, 1985).

What has been described is the man who is "too hard." This is the hypermasculine man—active, forceful, arrogantly competitive, and un-feeling. If this man is "too hard," there must be a polar opposite who is "too soft."

The man who is "too soft" is interesting characterologically in that he represents a mixed type. Ironically, he too is rigid. However, that characterological rigidity is mixed with oral character structure. Therefore, he shows many of the characteristics that follow from pregenital oral deprivation. *The outstanding characteristic of the "too soft" male is his passive-receptive attitude.*

"Having a passive-receptive way of being in the world, how am I to behave? I lack aggressiveness, and find self-assertion very difficult. My tendency is to be gentle and humble, perhaps overly polite and considerate. I am fearful. Life is scary to me, so I avoid risks and conflicts. At times I am paralyzed with fear. Since my aggression is blocked, I often feel helpless and hopeless.

"My way of being in the world is clearly reflected in my body structure and bodily movements. My voice is soft and modulated, lacking in resonance and sharpness. Not only does my voice sound boyish, but I have a boyish look to my face. My face is soft, as is my whole body, on the surface. My hands are soft and have a weak quality about them. My muscles stay underdeveloped. My shoulders and hips are narrow. So, overall, I may remind you of a preadolescent boy. My movements are not brusque or forceful. Instead, my actions have a quality of caution and softness, perhaps even weakness. At times people label my movements and gestures as effeminate. What they don't understand is that I am masculine, but passive, paralyzed with fear. My maternal deprivation is reflected in my underdeveloped, boyish body. Orally deprived, as I was, I carry the scar, and am terrified of abandonment. So, I must tread lightly and move softly. My deeper muscles are tense. This severe tension reflects my response to my father's rejection, as surely as my surface softness reflects my mother's unavailability. So, here I am, 'undernourished' and 'not good enough.'

"Relating to women is difficult for me. I find myself being dependent and mothered when the woman is inclined toward such a role. At times I can play father to a younger woman. But, a man to woman peer relationship eludes me."

In contrast to the hypermasculine man described earlier, his opposite on the dimension of rigidity is the man who is "too soft." The latter is overly sensitive, fearful, and passive, a caricature of what has traditionally been described as the hysterical woman. He has, indeed, been identified in the clinical literature as the male hysteric.

In the idiom of the East, the too-soft male is too yin and too-hard male is too yang. The soft male embodies an excess of yin force and tends to lack a balancing yang energy. This leaves him vulnerable to being hurt through his overly sensitive nature. It also means he will shy away from much of life, lacking the healthy aggressiveness necessary to reach out and take hold of life. His opposite, the too-hard male, embodies an excess of yang force, and lacks the yin energy necessary for balance. Through his forcefulness and willfulness he may hurt others and be unfeeling. In addition, this rigid stance prevents him from an openness to receiving tenderness and finding the joy of soft emotions.

The Eastern symbol for unity, the T'ai gi, better known as the yin-yang, graphically illustrates the balanced composition of the yin and the yang forces. The circle is equally divided by a smoothly flowing "S" curve, forming a white half and black half. Within the white half is a dot of black, and within the black half is a dot of white. Unity, wholeness, balance. The marriage of yin and yang. This is not a blend, a mixing of black and white into a uniform gray. Rather it is black space and white space within the whole, each interpenetrated by its contrasting opposite.

The T'ai gi is a suitable symbol to aid in the understanding of the problem and the resolution of the problem of the too-soft and too-hard male. The idea is to introduce yin energy or yang energy where it is deficient. This task is guided by an insight emphasized by Jung (1963). To shift now to the language of Jungian theory, the too-soft male is denying his animus, while the too-hard male is repressing his anima. Animus and anima, as masculine and feminine principles, respectively, can be allowed to manifest or not. The too-soft male denies his animus its manifestation, holding back with fear. The too-hard male represses his anima, allowing only the masculine principle to guide his thoughts and actions. But as Jung instructed us, the energy repressed is present in the unconscious, and will press for expression. Our therapeutic task, then, for the too-soft male is to support his expression of his latent masculine hardness. In the case of the too-hard male, our task is to facilitate the uncovering of his repressed anima or soft feminine principle.

In Figure 7.1 I have summarized the characteristics of the too-soft and the too-hard male. These form the two poles within the dimension of male rigidity.

The too-soft male and the too-hard male are incomplete in their manifest being. In both cases their way of being in the world is out of balance. Rather than creatively living in the intermediate zone of the "golden mean," making mini-swings toward one pole at times, the other at times, each tends to stay at one pole. Therapy for each can be thought of as an Hegelian dialectical process. The pole at which the client is rigidly in place forms a manitestly lived "thesis," the opposite pole the "antithesis." By supporting the living of the antithesis the therapist may facilitate a creative "synthesis."

Examing the specifics of the therapeutic task first, consider the too-soft male. The task is to toughen the man who is too soft. Since this client is fearful, he must not be pushed too fast, but rather he is to be given adequate support and encouragement in his movements toward toughness.

Since the too-soft male's tendency is to be passive, shy, and quiet, emphasize with him experiencing in the therapy room what it is like to be active, bold, and loud. To this end, Smith (1985) suggested body postures, movements, and sounds. Such exercises allow a dramatic enactment of emotionally laden material. These exercises must be graded so that they match the growing edge of the client. In other words, if the exercise is not

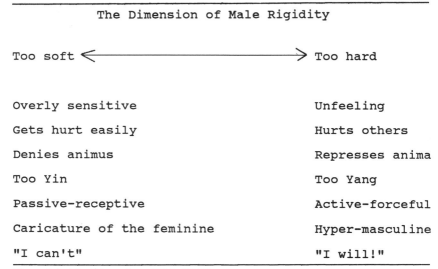

Figure 7.1   The Dimension of Male Rigidity

advanced enough for the client, little or nothing of value will be gained. If, on the other hand, the exercise is too advanced, the client will not feel safe enough to enter into it fully, and will again gain little or nothing. Worse still, he may scare himself, reinforcing his timid, passive style. This is the "boomerang effect" that occurs when the exercise is graded too high. *The idea is to provide a psychodramatic experience through which the client successfully transports himself beyond his previously assumed limits.* The too-soft male is living out a script that prohibits his masculine-assertive expression. Each time he is able to break his script he weakens its power and relaxes his rigid adherence to that way of being.

A good way to move into the psychodramatic exercise is to listen to the client's story as he tells it. Watch and listen for manifestations of the "be soft" script. Notice the lack of animation, the cautious, inhibited gesture, the effeminate mannerism, the shy posture. Hear the guarded, soft voice, and hear the language designed to avoid confrontation. Any of these can be noted and pointed out to the client. Any characterological manifestation can be productively used in this way.

The therapist's two tools are "support" and "frustration." His job is one of supporting any of the client's honest attempts at expression of his best self, and frustrating the client's attempts to continue his characterological script. Pointing out characterological manifestations, as mentioned above, is a way of frustrating the client's unchallenged continuation of his script. In order to support his expressions of his best self, encouragement can be offered and acknowledgment given when such expression is in evidence. The psychodramatic exercise is an event, designed from the story material given by the client and for the purpose of giving him the opportunity to break from his script there in the counseling room. The consulting room is a safe place to experiment with new behavior.

There is much artistry that goes into the creation of the psychodramatic experiment. It is learned through practice and, most important, apprenticeship with a skilled practitioner. All that can be offered here are some guidelines. Once a characterological manifestation is noted and commented on, the client can be invited to experiment with it, transforming it into a harder, more forceful, bolder expression. This may mean changing a constricted posture into a more open, expansive one. It may mean speaking more loudly and breathing more deeply. And it may mean to imagine someone is present and to speak directly *to* that person with clearly assertive language, rather than only to talk *about* her or him.

The idea is to recognize the "soft scenario" and invite the client to redo it as a "hard scenario." It is these excursions into bold expression that bring forth the heretofore denied animus. On the way to these more active, forceful expressions, the client may get scared. It is as if the original authors of the "be soft" script (various parenting figures) come forth with their greatest force to stop the client from extricating himself from their life-long grip. When this happens, those voices are to be identified and confronted psychodramatically, with the therapist's support.

Since the purpose is not to practice a performance that is to be presented at a later time but rather to facilitate a characterological shift, the expressions to be worked toward are extreme. Remember, the synthesis comes about only after the thesis is opposed by its *anti*-thesis. This is the law of the human dialectical process. Years of dwelling at one extreme requires many excursions to the other extreme before the golden mean can be recognized. So, in working with the too-soft male, we need to persist in the psychodrama of the "hard scenario" over time, session after session, until the client has grown comfortable with stomping his feet, waving his fists, kicking the cushions, screaming, laughing from his belly until the room echoes. He has known shyness; now he must know boldness.

In addition to this therapy work in the consulting room, carefully assigned homework is useful in working with the too-soft male. This falls into two categories. First, the client can be invited to practice more assertive, active, forceful ways of being in his social life. Sometimes specific anticipated events can be discussed and a particular course of action can be decided upon in the therapy session. The carrying out of that course of action is then the homework assignment. Just as the psychodramatic work done in the counseling room needs to be graded to the client's level, so it is too with the homework to be carried out in the literal world.

The second type of homework involves some ongoing activity outside therapy that brings forth the expression of the animus energy. The therapist may suggest that the client find such an activity, but it is usually better if the client himself shops around and chooses the particular one. Any martial art, outdoor survival training, or vigorous physical discipline will potentially be of value for the too-soft male in his growth toward freeing his animus. The key, once again, is in the activity's being graded to the client's progressing level. Unfortunately, many too-soft men have had their characterological position only reinforced when they have been discouraged or even humiliated by an activity beyond their level or an instructor who was "too hard."

Consider now the treatment of that instructor, or one of his cohorts in the Society of the Too Hard, assuming that he comes for therapy. And that is quite an assumption; as numerous as the "too hard" men are in our culture, they are among the least likely to approach psychotherapy willingly. They may be coerced or ordered into therapy with some frequency, but are not so frequent volunteers, and this makes sense. After all, the hypermasculine image does not find peace with asking for help with one's life, let alone one's emotions. What is addressed here is the body-oriented psychotherapy of the too-hard male who has come to the point of voluntary participation. The task question, of course, is how does the therapist soften the male who is too hard?

Whereas the task of toughening the too-soft male is one of disinhibiting his pent-up animus energies, the task of softening the too-hard male is one of inviting out a repressed anima. In the former case the technique, as discussed above, is to exaggerate the shy animus expressions into their full-blown form. The technique is different in the case of bringing forth latent anima energy.

The too-hard male is likely to exhibit considerable muscular tension throughout his body. Stiff with pride, and ready for action, his back side, including hips, back, neck, and shoulders, may be tight and hard. At the same time, his front side, including chest and abdomen, will be tense in order to protect his vulnerability to soft feelings.

The major focus of body work with the too-hard male is on his front side, since this is the major body locus of tender emotion. This psycho-biological fact is reflected in our lived language by such phrases as "letting your heart melt," being "broken hearted," being "love sick," which includes loss of appetite and "butterflies in my stomach," and feeling deep feelings in the "pit of my stomach." In the kinesic communication of some animals, submission is shown by the animal's exposing its "soft underbelly." In yoga, the chest region is known as the "heart chakra," and is associated with the experience of love.

Before entering into this body work designed to melt the body armor of the chest and abdomen, it is usually necessary to do some cognitive framing for the client. The too-hard male is a "thinking type," in contrast with a "feeling type," to use a distinction from Jung. This means that he leads with his thinking, and wants to understand. Once the client has committed himself to therapy and understands the rationale for this body work, it can be undertaken.

The specific procedure is to have the client lie on his back. If he is not too threatened by this, it is preferable for him to be unclothed from the waist up. The skin to skin contact is more powerful. Then offer the following instructions:

> Relax as much as you can. I want you to breathe deeply, through your mouth, and make an "aaahhh" sound as you exhale. I am going to place my hand on your chest and leave it there for awhile. Let whatever wants to happen, happen. Allow any body sensations, memories, or emotions that want to come, come. Let me know when something important happens.

Maintain this static contact for up to 10 or 15 minutes, unless something important happens sooner. Break the silence only to restate part of the instructions, if needed, or ask what he is aware of, if you see something happen (a tear, a change in posture, a tremble, or such) and he does not speak of it within a reasonable amount of time.

Over a series of therapy sessions one might try hand placements on the client's upper chest, along the sternum, upper abdomen (between rib cage and navel), and lower abdomen (between navel and pubic bone). One might work in this way to invite a softening or letting go of the muscular tension by which the client binds his tender feelings. As he allows his armor to melt, he will begin to get in touch with his softer emotions. As he allows the therapist *to touch* his tender parts, the touch invites him *to get in touch* with his tender feelings. (Demonstration and supervised practice are strongly advised before undertaking hands-on body work.)

As memories and feelings emerge, that material can then be processed using a variety of therapeutic procedures. One particular way of processing this body-accessed material is to set up a dramatic enactment, the basics of which were presented earlier while discussing the treatment of the too-soft man. In the case of the too-hard man, the emphasis will be on his psychodramatic expression of his tender feelings—sadness, hurt, disappointment, love, caring. From his feelings and memories brought forward by the body work, a scenario can be envisioned that can then be acted out in the here-and-now context, allowing the client to express fully his feelings to the imagined appropriate target.

When this work is far enough along and when the client has reached a point of significantly reduced armoring in his chest and abdomen, work on his back armoring can begin. If the work on his back is undertaken prior to the chest and abdominal softening, the client will resist mightily, presenting a concrete-like back, almost impermeable to any touch.

When the client is ready for body work on his back, two procedures can be used—soft technique and hard technique (Smith, 1985). Soft technique has been described, the only change now being that the therapist would place his hands on various points of the back, wherever he can find tension or where the client reports tension. The instructions are the same as before, but obviously the client needs to be lying face down. A variation in the work is to have the client lie on his back while the therapist simultaneously contacts a point on the client's front and back. This usually works best if the touch is applied to points directly opposite each other on the chest or abdomen and the back. An exception is the holding of the nape of the neck and some chest or abdominal point.

Some of the hard techniques absolutely require demonstration and supervised practice, so they will not be described here. A hard technique is deep muscle massage on the back. Instructions similar to those used with the soft technique can be used, substituting "I am going to massage the muscles of your back," where appropriate. Again, emergent feelings and memories can then be processed through a mutually created psychodrama.

Difficult as it is to capture the richness of psychotherapy by writing about it, it is even more difficult when part of the therapeutic technique is nonverbal. Body work needs to be studied experientially in order to get a real feel for it. This chapter describes the basics of working with too-soft and too-hard men. It provides information for recognizing the too-soft and the too-hard male, understanding their core dynamics, and understanding some of the basic guidelines of a body-oriented psychotherapeutic treatment. Elaboration of this material can be found in *The Body in Psychotherapy* (Smith, 1985). So, in either case, therapy seeks attainment of a dynamic balance for the client. The more extreme the client's skew toward too soft or too hard, the more extreme his experience of the opposite needs to be. The more extreme the poles, the more powerful their synthesis. The more powerful the synthesis, the more powerfully whole the man.

References

Jung, C. (1963). *Aion: researches into the phenomenology of the self.* Princeton, NJ: Princeton University Press.

Smith, E. (1984). Characterological styles of emotional plague behavior. *Energy and Character, 15,* 1, 38-44.

Smith, E. (1985). *The body in psychotherapy.* Jefferson, NC: McFarland.

8

Training Others to Counsel Men

Gregg A. Eichenfield
Mark Stevens

Within the last 10 years there has been a steady increase of articles written in the area of male socialization and the male experience (Doyle, 1986; Fasteau, 1974; O'Neil, 1981; Pleck, 1981; Pleck & Sawyer, 1974; Solomon & Levy, 1982). How this information has been utilized in terms of training psychotherapists to counsel men has not been documented in the literature. This chapter will attempt to incorporate some of the existing literature on men into a multifaceted training program utilizing both experiential and didactic training approaches. The didactic information is drawn from various academic disciplines such as social psychology, feminist therapy, and clinical/counseling psychology; the experiential component of the training program is designed to increase personal awareness and professional competency.

We recognize that training others to counsel men can occur over a variety of time frames and using different methods. For the purpose of discussion the format used here will be a full-day (e.g., eight hours) training program. We believe that this format can serve as an excellent beginning— to be expanded (or reduced) depending on the training needs and resources of the training system.

There are many ways to train individuals to improve their counseling skills. One such method is to immerse trainees in a certain therapeutic style or theoretical orientation. Another method is to look at presenting problems as the issue of focus (e.g., depression, bulimia, chemical dependency) and provide materials and training seminars on the specific issue. A third method is to look at specific populations (e.g., blacks, Asians, gay/Lesbian, male/female) and focus on specific therapeutic issues that

TABLE 8.1
Workshop Outline: Training Others to Counsel Men

1. Review of expectations, goals, and norms of the day	Time:	15 minutes
2. Getting to know men or "Our Learned Myths of Masculinity"		
a. Experiential exercise	Time:	60 minutes
b. Didactic integration	Time:	60 minutes
3. How male clients "do" therapy; or dealing with process and countertransference issues		
a. Brief didactic presentation about the process of men entering therapy	Time:	10 minutes
b. Experiential exercise about experiences of doing therapy with men	Time:	90 minutes
c. Didactic integration of above material	Time:	30-60 minutes
4. Working with male clients on a feeling level		
a. Didactic background	Time:	10 minutes
b. Experiential exercises	Time:	30 minutes
c. Observing a trainer work with a male client or trainee	Time:	60 minutes
d. Didactic integration of above material	Time:	30 minutes
5. Case presentation by the trainees Experiential and Didactic	Time:	60 minutes
6. Evaluation of the program	Time:	20 minutes

may involve the subpopulation. The particular model presented in this chapter will not focus on theoretical orientation or presenting problems but rather on the population of men, and will look at the trainee's prejudices and levels of awareness of men's issues. Specifically, this chapter will concentrate on a training program that seeks to increase awareness and knowledge of gender as a factor affecting treatment and thus seeks to increase competency in counseling skills.

We recognize that training others to counsel men happens in both formal and informal modes. Supervision (group and individual), seminars, and workshops are all formal ways to do this training. Equally important are the informal modes of training such as modeling agency behavior for dealing with women's and men's issues, and personal growth groups or support groups that emphasize men's and women's roles. These areas will be discussed in the latter part of the chapter.

There are several variables and approaches that must be considered when designing a training program intended to increase counseling skills. These variables include: current level of counseling skill, theoretical orientation, number of trainees, previous knowledge of subject matter, expected training opportunities in the future (e.g., opportunities to work with male clients), expectations as to the method of training (e.g., didactic versus experiential) and trust level of trainees.

This particular training program/workshop is designed for advanced students and practicing professionals in psychology, social work, or marriage and family counseling. It can also be adapted for paraprofessionals. Because of the content of the program, it is recommended that there be a near even distribution of men and women. If that is not possible, process attention should be given to the underrepresented group (e.g., five male trainees and one female trainee). It is also strongly recommended that at least one of the trainers be a male. Experiential exercises are a major factor in this particular training program; therefore, the trust level among those involved should be considered an important variable and promoted. The facilitator/trainer skill level is also important. In this type of program we have found that trainers who are flexible, nondefensive, self-disclosing, encouraging of dialogue, knowledgeable about men's and women's issues, and are not stuck on a "right" way to do therapy help make this program/workshop on counseling men most useful.

Table 8.1 provides the outline of the workshop.

Description of the Workshop

REVIEW OF GOALS AND EXPECTATIONS FOR THE PROGRAM

Goals

(1) Increase awareness of male socialization and men's issues as it relates to their socialization.
(2) Increase knowledge of why men seek counseling and their expectations of counseling.
(3) Increase knowledge of how men are as clients and ways to best deal with the therapeutic process of men in counseling.
(4) Increase self-understanding related to male socialization and counseling males.

Norms

(1) Participate at your own pace.
(2) Listen nondefensively.
(3) Be open to new ideas.

GETTING TO KNOW MEN, OR
"OUR LEARNED MYTHS
OF MASCULINITY"

After reviewing the agenda for the day, we recommend that the initial introduction to counseling men be done through an experiential exercise that focuses on male socialization. A few examples of experiential exercises that can serve as a catalyst to talk about male socialization will subsequently be presented.

Option 1. Listening to music by Geof Morgan (Morgan, 1984), who writes in a clear, thought-provoking and humorous manner about the male experience. Songs such as "American Male," "Good-bye John Wayne," "It Comes with the Plumbing," "Homophobia," "Penis Song," and "Stop It" address different men's issues such as male violence, male role models, men's health, male competition, male sexuality, and male relationships with women. The music/lyrics allow the participants to relate their experiences of growing up male or watching other males grow up. Small group discussion can be helpful to increase self-disclosure. (We suggest passing out lyric sheets in advance to assist in the discussion.)

Option 2. Much of male socialization is learned through the models or male heroes that men seek to live up to (Gerzon, 1982). Ask the trainees to brainstorm a list of male heroes that influenced their conceptualization of what a "real man" is like. The list usually includes athletes, movie stars, and movie roles. Ask the trainees to list beside each hero/model attributes (physical and psychological) that they associate with that person.

Option 3. A more personal and self-revealing exercise includes a reflection of how and from whom in their family trainees learned about the roles of masculinity. Discussion usually will focus on fathers, grandfathers, and the patriarchy of their family.

Option 4. There are several excellent (and short!) films about men that serve as a starting point to discuss male socialization. These films include: *Stale Images and Tight Buns* (1984), and *Like Men* (1986). Given more time, the full-length movie *Stand By Me* (1986) can also serve as a discussion catalyst.

With each of these exercises, the task of the trainer will be to keep the discussion on a personal level, encouraging the trainees to share their own stories and powerful memories about childhood and how they learned about their concept of masculinity. Trainees' powerful feelings about significant men in their lives are frequently revealed. Integrating the experiential exercise into a working theoretical and conceptual framework of male socialization can now be accomplished. Stevens and Hershberger (1985) outline a framework of how male socialization affects the behavior and attitudes of men. In this work, which has been influenced by O'Neill (1981), Pleck (1981), and Scher (1981), Stevens and Hershberger first identify basic sex-role stereotypes of how men have learned to conceptualize masculinity and femininity. This framework then identifies attitudes toward self and others that may have been introjected by this sex-role stereotyping. Based on those introjected attitudes, behavior outcomes for men are highlighted. Finally the framework identifies symptoms (presenting problems) that men bring to therapy that are extensions of their introjected attitudes and subsequent behaviors.

HOW MEN "DO" THERAPY: PROCESS AND COUNTERTRANSFERENCE

Using the conceptual material of the previous section as background information, trainees will have the opportunity to learn about the expectations and feelings that men have about entering therapy. Also discussed or highlighted will be the process issues involved while counseling men.

One important way to understand how men "do" therapy is to allow the trainees to share their feelings and thoughts about working with men. There will be obvious differences between how men feel/think about counseling men versus how women feel/think about counseling men. Issues for male counselors usually center on competition, power struggles, and homophobia. Issues for women usually involve feeling objectified, stereotyped, and sexualized.

Asking the following open-ended questions may help facilitate this discussion: (Trainees can choose two or three to answer)

(1) How do I respond differently to women clients than male clients?
(2) What I like most about working with male clients is . . .
(3) What I like least about working with male clients is . . .
(4) I am most comfortable with male clients who . . .
(5) I am least comfortable with male clients who . . .
(6) I would never work with a male client who . . .
(7) I find myself wanting my male clients to . . .
(8) What most men like best about therapy with me is . . .
(9) What most men like least about therapy with me is . . .

How this portion of the program is facilitated will depend on the size and trust level of the group. We have found that asking the trainees to first write down their responses to the open-ended questions and then to discuss their responses in large or small groups is most productive for processing this experience.

There are several themes that may emerge from the above discussions. Following are themes that occur often:

TABLE 8.2

Stevens and Hershberger's (1985) Framework: How Male Socialization Affects the Behavior and Attitudes of Man

A. Sex-Role Stereotypes

Men[a]	Women[b]
Competitive	Passive
Strong	Dependent
In control	Emotional
In charge	Illogical
Achievement oriented	Naive, gullible
Intelligent	Beautiful
Non-feeling	Sensitive
Don't cry	Nurturing
Mechanical	Neat
Dominant	Patient
Protective	Good mothers
All knowing	Soft, warm
Logical	Fickle
Stud	Romantic
Breadwinner	Seductive
Initiator of sex	Artistic
Independent	Crack under pressure
Authority	Physically weak
Athletic	Sex = love
Sex = accomplishment	

B. Men's Attitudes

Toward Self	Toward Others
Must be on "top" to be O.K.	Homophobic
I'm nothing if I'm not providing.	Homosexist
Things won't be O.K. until I've taken care of . . .	You need to be wrong for me to be right
I need to be right.	Don't show weaknesses to others.
I need to manage (control) myself, my environment, and all the people around me.	Relationships are a lesser priority.
Future goals are more important than present desires.	Relationships are useful for accomplishing tasks.
	Misogynistic

a. If a man is not like this, he is a sissy, queer, or gay.
b. If a woman is not like this, she is a bitch, dyke, or women's libber.

C. Behavioral Outcomes for Men

Emotional restrictedness

Aggression

Isolation

Rape: Confusion of violence with sexuality and sex behaviors

Lower life expectancy

Objectify women

Lack closeness with men, except in socially acceptable ways

Advice givers

Low satisfaction with self

Hard time receiving

Give in the form of protection, money, possessions, and financial security

Lack closeness with women and children

D. Symptoms brought into Therapy

Low self-esteem

Depression

Sexual dysfunction

Alcoholism

Stress related physical problems

Don't feel close to anyone

Relationships don't work

Fear of failure

Performance anxiety

Suicidal because girlfriend broke up with me

Midlife crisis

Confusion about gender-role expectations

Don't experience joy

Suicidal, but don't know why

Don't know who I am

Problems with my anger

NOTE: By presenting this material and soliciting personal anecdotes and examples, trainees gain an understanding of the emotional and physical toll on men who buy into these "myths of masculinity."

(1) Therapy as antithetical to the male experience. Most men are basically resistant to therapy. Many men are in hiding with respect to their feelings (Scher, 1981) and subsequently are intimidated by therpeutic approaches that emphasize feeling awareness. Men are taught to be independent and "fixers"; therefore, going to see a therapist for help can be perceived as being weak (or less powerful than a man "should" be).

(2) Relationship between counselor and client. The way in which the male client has bought into the myths of masculinity can be played out in the therapy relationship. Male socialization issues such as intimacy, power, control, objectification, homophobia, vulnerability, and competition can serve as both *obstacles* to the therapy encounter as well as *opportunities* for interpretation, resolution, and growth.

(3) What men want from counseling. Basically, men want to be taken seriously. They have a need for affection, acceptance and nurturance. Men feel a need for productivity. They want to learn how to be vulnerable while at the same time keeping their sense of dignity, strength, and pride. Men often feel misunderstood and unappreciated, and therefore will respond positively to a genuine, nonjudgmental, and understanding therapist.

(4) Male versus female therapists. Some differences may occur in counseling men when the therapist is male as opposed to female. The male client with a male therapist may want affection, acceptance, and nurturance—and may fear it (e.g., homophobia). The client may also hold an expectation that the male therapist will (or should) " 'fix' what ails him" (see point 1 above). With female therapists, the emphasis in therapy may be nurturance and understanding, thus challenging the man's issue of "independence."

WORKING WITH THE MALE
CLIENT ON A FEELING LEVEL

We have found it helpful to have a section of the training program that specifically addresses working with male clients on a feeling level. Two basic assumptions are made: (1) men who seek help are usually in pain (even if they do not show their pain) and (2) men are (biologically and psychologically) able to feel. At some time in his life, the male client was taught that being a "real man" meant turning off the emotions and turning on the cognitions. This part of a man's socialization has had a negative impact on his psychological and physical well-being. On a relationship level, feelings can serve as a channel for expressing and experiencing intimacy with others. As a man's option to express and experience feelings gets shut off, so does his ability to feel alive and make contact with others. Many people (and therapists, too!) believe that the only emotion that men are comfortable with is anger. From our perspective it is not that men are comfortable with anger but rather they are highly uncomfortable with expressing the "flip side" of anger—that of being hurt and vulnerable (since these are not "manly" emotions). After a brief lecture and discussion on why relearning to feel is important for men in counseling the trainees are asked to write down one feeling they have difficulty experiencing/expressing. They are asked to share with a partner the answers to the following questions:

(1) How did you learn to have trouble with that particular feeling?
(2) What intimidates you about that feeling?
(3) How long have you had trouble with that feeling?
(4) How has the difficulty you have with that feeling gotten in the way of enjoying your life more?

After a brief discussion in a group format about similarities, differences, insights, and so on that trainees had during the above exercise, the trainer asks for a male volunteer who wants to work on experiencing/expressing feelings more. Drawing on the assumption that all men do feel and that meaningful events are accompanied by feelings that may have been stored away, those feelings can be recalled and reexperienced. The trainer may work therapeutically with the trainee for 20-30 minutes, working in a mode that asks the trainee to recall a significant, meaningful event in his life. Events that involve early loss, embarrassment, or fear are powerful stimuli for accessing feelings. The rationale for this portion of the training is that for therapists to work effectively with their feelings, they must be aware of how they resist experiencing/expressing feelings. Training programs and most theoretical schools of psychology talk about the importance of feelings, yet specific training on how to work with feelings is limited. We encourage trainees to follow some of these guidelines when working with men on a feeling level:

(1) Be patient.
(2) Be genuine.
(3) Expect resistance (reluctance).
(4) View men as in pain and wanting relief, yet not wanting to be vulnerable.
(5) Check out *your* comfort level and readiness to deal with a client's feelings that may have been blocked for many years.
(6) Be a good role model: Talk and relate on a feeling level with feeling language when appropriate.

After working with the trainee it is suggested the trainer have time to debrief with the group and share support for the male who volunteered. Didactically it is important to analyze and highlight how feelings were accessed in this particular exercise. Another option to train others to work with male clients on a feeling level is for the trainer to bring a video- or audiotape of a session that shows work with a male client on a feeling/process level.

CASE PRESENTATIONS: INTEGRATION OF MATERIAL

Empowering the trainees to utilize the information presented is a useful way to complete the program/workshop. Ideally the trainees will leave with added insight, confusion, unanswered questions, and enthusiasm to pursue those unanswered questions. Case vignettes of male clients can serve as useful stimulus material for this integration exercise. In groups of three or four, trainees are asked to come up with an assessment of the client based on the male role socialization model presented earlier. They are also asked to design a therapeutic treatment plan. Another option is to have a trainer or trainee present a male client who could be discussed in a group supervision format. If the trainer has video or audiotapes of sessions, these tapes could also be helpful.

EVALUATION

As with any type of training program or workshop, a written and verbal evaluation of the usefulness of the program is strongly recommended.

Creating a Holistic Training Program for Teaching Others to Counsel Men

As discussed earlier in this chapter, there are both formal and informal ways to provide training for counseling men. We have introduced in this chapter a detailed example of a formal method for training. In addition to structured training as detailed earlier, other formal and informal methods of training will be discussed.

FORMAL METHODS

Individual supervision: There are many models for doing individual supervision. We believe that no matter what type of supervision model is used, the issue of gender can be brought into the supervision process. Ideally, the supervisor is knowledgeable of male socialization issues and of counseling men. Individual supervision can be an ideal learning environment for helping the supervisee increase awareness of countertransference issues in counseling men. Feminist therapy supervisors (Rosewater & Walker, 1985; Schaef, 1981) discuss the importance of being aware of the processes that go on among the supervisor, supervisee, and client. In addition, the gender-role dynamics between the supervisor and supervisee can serve as a learning opportunity (especially if one or both are male) in the area of gender-role issues and conflict resolution.

Group supervision: Group supervision can be a learning environment where the gender of the client can be discussed as an important variable in the counseling process. How this is accomplished will depend on the leadership style and the supervisor's awareness of men's issues. In a safe learning environment, process issues among group members as they relate to gender-role differences can be addressed and utilized as a learning opportunity.

SEMINARS

Many training agencies do not address the process of counseling men. An informal survey of counseling training programs reported many seminars on counseling women and few on counseling men. A brief (1-2 hour) introduction to counseling men can serve as a reminder that the gender of a client is an important variable to consider and counseling men is not the opposite of counseling women. Additionally, we recommend that training seminars on such topics as counseling ethnic minorities, incest survivors, substance abusers, gays and lesbians, depression and other populations or clinical issues address gender differences as they relate to the counseling process.

INFORMAL METHODS

Modeling of agency staff: When professional staff members acknowledge and deal with their own gender-role differences, this modeling can serve as a prime training opportunity. Examples include processing differences in communication patterns or decision-making processes among male and female staff members. Competitive and homophobic feelings/behaviors between male staff members may also be opportunities to encourage deeper understanding of male socialization issues. We have found that trainees are acutely aware of gender-role issues among staff members and subsequently can learn a great deal from a staff that does not ignore conflict in the area of gender-role differences.

Personal growth opportunities: Many counseling professionals have reported that participating in consciousness raising (CR) groups was a useful (although secondary) way to increase their understanding of gender-role differences. Men report that these groups helped them come to a greater understanding of their own concerns about homophobia, competition, isolation, control and power needs, and other male socialization issues. Women report their CR experiences helped them work on issues of unexpressed anger toward men, empowerment, and a deeper understanding of male power and control. CR groups are not designed to increase one's counseling skill level, although insight and personal growth in the area of gender-role concerns could positively influence one's ability to counsel men. Most CR groups are formed outside of the working environment; we do know, however, of counseling centers where CR and gender-role support groups have been formed for staff and/or trainees.

Professional literature: There are only a few ongoing periodicals/newsletters that can serve as resources for acquiring knowledge about men's issues. These include *Changing Men, Brother, Nurturing News,* and the *Men's Studies Newsletter.* Having these and other articles on counseling men available to staff and trainees could be helpful.

PROGRAMMING AND OUTREACH FOR MEN

A way to keep current interest in learning about men's issues and counseling men is to have your agency provide psychoeducational programs for men. Many college campuses and communities show a need for men's programming on such issues as fathering, male friendship, date and aquaintance rape, AIDS, dual-career relationships, and so on. As the agency and its staff become more comfortable and experienced with men's programming, so too will this awareness and training become integrated into counseling strategies with men.

Conclusion

Training others to counsel men is developmentally in its infancy. Writing in this area appears not to exist. Psychology and other related disciplines could pay more attention to male gender and male sex-role socialization issues as important variables of the psychotherapy process. The importance of teaching or training others to expand their understanding of how and why male clients feel/think/behave is the basis of this chapter.

References

Bliss, S., Diamond, J., & Doyle, J. (Eds.). *Men's Studies Newsletter,* Newsletter of the Men's Studies Task Group of the National Organization for Changing Men, Watseka, IL.

Brother, Newsletter of the National Organization for Changing Men, Watseka, IL.

Cote, R., & Biernbaum, M. (Eds.). *Changing men: Issues in gender, sex and politics.* Madison, WI.

Doyle, J. (1986). *Sex and gender.* Dubuque, IA: W. C. Brown.

Fasteau, M. F. (1974). *The male machine.* New York: McGraw-Hill.

Gerzon, M. (1982). *A choice of heroes: The changing face of American manhood.* Boston: Houghton Mifflin.

Giveans, D. L. (Ed.). *Nurturing news: A quarterly forum for nurturing men.* San Francisco, CA.

Morgan, G. (1984). *It comes with the plumbing* [Record]. Bellingham, WA: Nexus Records.

Morton, P. (Producer). (1986). *Like men* [Film]. Chicago: UCVideo.

O.A.S.I.S., Inc. (Producers). (1984). State roles and tight buns: Images of men in advertising [Slides/audiotape]. Brighton, MA: Author.

O'Neil, J. M. (1981). Male sex-role conflicts, sexism and masculinity: Psychological implications for men, women and the counseling psychologist. *The Counseling Psychologist, 9,* 61-80.

Pleck, J. H. (1981). Men's power with women, other men, and society: A men's movement analysis. In R. A. Lewis (Ed.), *Men in difficult times* (pp. 242-243). Englewood Cliffs, NJ: Prentice-Hall.

Pleck, J. H., & Sawyer, J. (1974). *Men and masculinity.* Englewood Cliffs, NJ: Prentice-Hall.

Reiner, R. (Director). (1985). *Stand by me* [Film]. Hollywood, CA: TriStar.

Rosewater, L., & Walker, L. (1985). *Handbook of feminist therapy: Women's issues in psychotherapy.* New York: Springer.

Schaef, A. W. (1981). *Women's reality: An emerging female system in the white male society.* Minneapolis, MN: Winston Press.

Scher, M. (1981). Men in hiding: A challenge for the counselor. *Personnel and Guidance Journal, 60,* 199-202.

Solomon, K. L., & Levy, N. B. (1982). *Men in transition: Theory and therapy.* New York: Plenum.

Stevens, M., & Hershberger, B. (1985, October). *Counseling men.* Paper presented at the Ohio College Counselors Conference, Columbus.

II

Developmental Issues

Numerous chapters in this book mention issues related to men's development. Men's development proceeds along a variety of dimensions (e.g., cognitive, gender-role identity, moral, psychosocial). All of these developmental dimensions have the capacity to have an impact on a male client's views of himself, his interactions with his environment, and the therapeutic encounter. This introduction provides a synopsis of the main psychosocial theories of development pertaining to men.

Theories of development have many implications for psychotherapy with men. One aspect of furthering the development of male clients is assisting them to better understand themselves and the demands that the environment places upon them. By viewing clients' concerns within a developmental context, therapists may enhance their understanding of the pertinent issues for their clients. The therapist can more clearly grasp the implications of the client's past experiences, work effectively with his current issues, and provide anticipatory guidance regarding the sequence of stages and feelings that he will likely experience in the future. Therapists who understand the developmental sequences relevant to their client's needs may thus provide a more facilitative blend of challenge and support specifically tailored to promote a client's successful resolution of a given developmental task. More specifically, Knefelkamp, Widick, and Stroad (1975) not only recommend that the current developmental stage of the client be taken into account, but also that therapists make suggestions and engage in interventions that facilitate client movement to a stage one step beyond his or her current stage. These reasonably sized steps are hypothesized to lessen the client's resistance and confusion and to increase the likelihood of a successful resolution of stage-related tasks.

However, before a therapist can hope to provide specific developmental stage-based suggestions to a client, the therapist must be familiar with the relevant models of human development. Carl Jung (1954, 1969, 1971) posited theories about human development over the life span. In synopsis,

Jung saw people's tasks during the first half of life (up to age 40) as that of developing their dominant personality preferences. During the first half of life, Jung saw people as polarized and lacking an integration, balance, harmony, and wholeness. However, it is interesting to note that much of contemporary sex-role literature questions the necessity and, indeed, the advisability of people delaying integration of their masculine and feminine personality aspects.

Another theorist, Erik Erikson (1950, 1968), is particularly well known for his psychosocial stage theory of human development. He posited a sequential eight-stage model, each with associated tasks and crises. Within each stage, the major task is to resolve adequately the polar outcomes presented by that stage. Some of the polar outcomes proposed by Erikson are industry versus inferiority (10-14 years), identity versus role confusion (14-20 years), intimacy versus isolation (20-40 years), generativity versus stagnation (40-65 years), and integrity versus despair (65+ years). Many additional development models have subsequently been hypothesized that build upon Erikson's original work.

Robert Havighurst (Chickering & Havighurst, 1981; Havighurst, 1953) added new definitions and developmental tasks to the literature on human development. Developmental tasks were defined as "the physiological, psychological and social demands a person must satisfy in order to be judged by others and to judge himself or herself to be a reasonably happy and successful person"(Chickering & Havighurst, 1981, p. 25). Havighurst (1953) emphasized the role of external, age-related social pressures and expectations as they interact with one's own preferences and values. Also, social and historical factors such as race and social class were acknowledged to influence the options available to the person. Similar to Erikson's (1950) concept of "readiness," Havighurst defined the term *teachable moment*: a time when the individual has sufficient physical maturity, experiences the demand from social norms, and aspires and values a specific goal. Such moments sometimes occur in the therapy process when clients feel a particularly poignant interest in resolving an issue in their lives.

George Vaillant (1977) conducted a longitudinal study of Harvard males judged to be "the best and the brightest" in their classes. He extensively examined how these men's adaptive and defensive mechanisms influenced their development. Vaillant posited four stages occurring between the ages of 21 and 55 (e.g., age 20-30, intimacy and career consolidation). However, for the men in Vaillant's study, there was great variation in the timing of these stages, with some stages beginning as much as 10 years apart in different individuals.

Daniel Levinson (1978) studied men between the ages of 35 and 45. Levinson hypothesized a man's "life structure" to evolve through an alternating sequence of "transitional" and "stable" stages over the life span. Levinson believed that reassessment and changes in life structure reflected individuals' efforts to resolve incongruence between their perceived sense of the self in a given life structure and aspects of self that were not emphasized or valued in that structure.

One startling observation made by Levinson (1978) was that "close friendship with a man or woman is rarely experienced by American men" (p. 335). Levinson found that most of the American men did not have an intimate male friend after they left college, and never had an intimate, nonsexual friendship with a woman. Levinson thus urged, "We need to understand why friendship is so rare, and what consequences this deprivation has for adult life" (p. 335).

Another important theorist, Roger Gould (1972, 1975, 1978), described the developmental process in terms of shedding of illusions. He hypothesized four age-related transformations between the ages of 16 and 45. An example of one period is the stage called "opening up to what's inside," which occurs between the ages of 28 and 34. The major false assumption to be shed during this period is: "Life is simple and controllable. There is no significant coexisting contradictory force within me." Gould also recommended a seven-step process for people to employ, with or without a therapist, in overcoming these inhibiting childhood assumptions.

Along with the human development literature discussed previously, another body of literature with relevance to male development is the sex-role socialization literature. The recent focus on gender orientation development and sex roles allows the mental health practitioner to begin to conceptualize and intervene with the male client in ways that heretofore have been unavailable. Although the sex-role literature is presently insufficiently developed to have its own formal theory of male development, it does offer a collection of issues that are not currently addressed by the major psychological theories of male development. A likely area of future research is that of alternative male gender consciousness development. While *masculist* may be the term adopted to describe certain men in the future, such men are currently called liberated, sensitive, changing, profeminist, or nontraditional. Just as models of minority identity (Atkinson, Morten, & Sue, 1983) and feminist identity (Downing & Roush, 1985) development have been hypothesized, a model of masculist identity development is also needed. Some of the questions that need to be addressed include: What are the developmental stages by which men develop alternative gender consciousness? What are the precipitating events and moderating variables that facilitate or impede men's "masculist" identity development? Preliminary efforts in this area are appearing in the theoretical literature (Clark, Taylor, & Stevens, 1986), but more research is clearly needed.

Many chapters of this book address men's development during adult life, and through specific life events. This developmental section focuses on therapy with Western males during three potentially salient life periods—

adolescence, college years, and later adult life. The chapters seek to highlight core tasks faced by men during these periods and to explore new intervention possibilities.

References

Atkinson, D. R., Morten, G., & Sue, D. W. (1983). *Counseling American minorities* (2nd ed.). Dubuque, IA: William Brown.

Chickering, A. W., & Havighurst, R. J. (1981). The life cycle. In A. W. Chickering (Ed.), *The modern American college.* San Francisco: Jossey-Bass.

Clark, C. G., Taylor, K. T., & Stevens, M. A. (1986, November). Dealing with sex roles in groups: A developmental approach. *Journal for Specialists in Group Work, 11*(14), 200-208.

Downing, N. E., & Roush, K. L. (1985). From passive acceptance to active commitment: A model of feminist identity development for women. *The Counseling Psychologist, 13*(4), 695-709.

Erikson, E. H. (1950). *Childhood and society.* New York: W. W. Norton.

Erikson, E. H. (1968). *Identity, youth, and crisis.* New York: W. W. Norton.

Gould, R. L. (1972). The phases of adult life: A study in developmental psychology. *American Journal of Psychiatry, 59,* 465-469.

Gould, R. L. (1975, February). Adult life stages: Growth toward self-tolerance. *Psychology Today,* 26-29.

Gould, R. L., (1978). *Transformations: Growth and change in adult life.* New York: Simon & Schuster.

Havighurst, R. J. (1953). *Human development and education.* New York: Longman, Green.

Jung, C. G. (1954). The development of personality. In H. Read, M. Fordham, G. Adler, & W. McGuire (Eds.), *Collected works* (Vol. 17), Bollingen Series, XX (R.F.C. Hull, Trans.). Princeton, NJ: Princeton University Press.

Jung, C. G. (1969). The states of life. In H. Read, M. Fordham, G. Adler, & W. McGuire (Eds.), *Collected works* (Vol. 8), Bollingen Series XX (R.F.C. Hull, Trans.). Princeton, NJ: Princeton University Press.

Jung, C. G. (1971). Psychological types. In H. Read, M. Fordham, G. Adler, & W. McGuire (Eds.), *Collected works* (Vol. 6), Bollingen Series XX (R.F.C. Hull, Trans.). Princeton, NJ: Princeton University Press.

Knefelkamp, L. L., Widick, C. C., & Stroad, B. (1975). Cognitive-developmental theory: A guide to counseling women. In L. Harmon, J. Birk, L. Fitzgerald, & M. Tanney (Eds.), *Counseling women.* Monterey, CA: Brooks/Cole.

Levinson, D. J. (1978). *The seasons of a man's life.* New York: Knopf.

Vaillant, G. E. (1977). *Adaptation to life.* Boston: Little, Brown.

9

Identity Integration: Counseling the Adolescent Male

Richard F. Lazur

Adolescence—a time of change, growth, and discovery—a time when a boy becomes a man. It is a time of physical changes, psychological growth, and the discovery of self and new arenas of life. It's a time of differentiation, of discovering and asserting autonomy, of rebelling, of learning new approaches and stretching the limits. Often this occurs with much conflict, confusion, frustration, and pain. It's not easy being a teenager: One's whole life is in flux, individual identity is unstable, and peer and environmental demands are stressful. Adolescence is a time of gains and losses; it is a time when individuals consolidate their identity structure and come to know and understand who they really are.

For the male, it's a time of integrating his masculine identity, a time when societal expectations and his internal beliefs develop, consolidate, and are incorporated. His thoughts and behaviors as a person, his outlook and his approach to life as transacted through everyday activities are integrated with his perceptions, conceptions, attitudes, and beliefs about what it means to be a man. It is a somewhat turbulent time as his body goes through hormonal changes and the accompanying physiological transformation. Cognitive operations transform the way he perceives and makes meaning of the world around him. It is a time of psychological growth; a time of conflict, pain, and change.

The adolescent no longer listens compliantly to everything the parent-authority says, but seeks to assert his own autonomy, his own personhood. Peers take on new importance: They form the context of the individual's world as reflected in his dress, habits, and social activities. He abandons some former habits, develops new interests, and excels in new areas. It is a time of flux, a time of personal identity confusion from which evolves an integrated adult personality. The developmental task is to form and integrate an identity (Erikson, 1968).

Not all changes that occur during this period evoke a developmental crisis. Many changes occur on their own and can be successfully negotiated without therapeutic intervention. This chapter, however, will focus on those changes in which the adolescent male experiences conflict—either psychological or behavioral—that warrants therapeutic intervention. This may be evidenced by a variety of different behaviors including academic problems, difficulties in relationships with parents and/or peers, depression, suicide, antisocial acting-out, substance abuse, sexual promiscuity, or general malaise and unhappiness. It will address the issues that arise in the therapist's office, be it school, hospital, detention center, or outpatient setting.

This chapter will focus on those areas in which the male sex role influences and determines the adolescent's masculine identity. It will concentrate on how the adolescent male negotiates the developmental task of separation/individuation, autonomy, identity formation (including sexual identity), relationships with male and female peers and adults, work, and social activities including cars, sports, and music. It will address these issues for the adolescent male from the outset of puberty to high school graduation. The older adolescent is preparing for the transition to young adulthood and asserting himself in the real world. The issues he experiences are covered in the following chapter.

Beginning Treatment

An important aspect of working with an adolescent male is engaging him in treatment. More often than not, he doesn't want to be there! It is something that his family, school, or the courts want for him, but that the adolescent does not want for himself. During the initial interview, it is important to know what brings him to counseling, where he would be and what he would be doing if he weren't at the meeting, what he wants and how he thinks counseling can change things, and what difference, if any, that would make in his life. The answers prove quite informative.

It is important to form a working relationship with the adolescent. Get to know him. Find out about his likes, dislikes, how he spends his time, his taste in music, cars, sports. When asking about school, remember that he may feel he is being chided for poor performance; he wants to save face, so pose questions in a way that gives him an out if he needs it. In the early stages, it is important to form a working alliance wherein he can trust, disclose, and explore issues; the facts will unravel as the therapy proceeds.

In working with an adolescent it is useful to appeal to his strength, that part which wants to develop and mature. He wants to take on more responsibilities and make decisions for himself, to become an adult, but he is not quite sure what it entails or how to do it. Although adulthood is appealing, it can also be scary. Like training wheels that aided his learning to ride a bike, counseling helps the adolescent during the developmental transition: It is important to have someone there to provide balance, support, and encouragement until he can gain mastery and balance himself.

There are some guys, however, who remain resistant to counseling. But most often, regardless of the protestations, the adolescent knows why he is there. He may not like or wish to talk about it, but he knows what the problem is, and why he is in counseling. And he holds out the hope that the therapist will know what is going on with him and will help him deal effectively with these life events. This hope is the strength to which the therapist wants to appeal—to work through those issues that the adolescent has been unable to address for himself. By allying with the healthy part of the individual, the therapist is able to help the adolescent start to clarify his own thoughts, feelings, and actions so that he can feel more in control of his life. Therapy doesn't necessarily mean that he will get what he wants—he may never get that—but it provides the means for him to look at the situation, to identify his needs, and to find appropriate means of having them gratified. The therapist's task lies in teaching that the adolescent can gain control over his life situation and not act out his feelings for fear of being overwhelmed.

The therapeutic relationship holds the premise that the adolescent can feel safe, examine issues of conflict, and grow. He may feel that he is the only one in the world who has attempted such a thing; he may feel ashamed, embarrassed, or fearful that he will be locked away in an insane asylum. It is the therapist who must ensure the client's safety. At times, this involves setting limits, and stating that no improprieties will be acted on, at least not in the counseling room. It involves keeping him informed of events that affect him, even if it means commenting about things he doesn't want to hear. It is important to be honest and to state clearly the boundaries of what is acceptable and what is not tolerable. Ensuring his safety involves assuring him that nothing is too bizarre or outrageous. Let him know he is not being judged but is working on his own search.

It is important for the adolescent to learn how to deal with his feelings, frustrations, and disappointments. Fearing that his feelings will overwhelm him, he will do anything to make them go away. He may think he is unable to tolerate psychological pain, so he seeks immediate relief. Drugs and alcohol often serve this self-medicating purpose. He may feel powerless, desperate, or out of control. The goal of treatment is to help him tolerate his experience, to sit with his feelings, to grieve his losses, and to find more adaptive ways to deal with life demands. This is done by sitting with the adolescent, offering safety and reassurance that he is neither abnormal nor alone, and building controls that enable him to endure the discomfort. The controls are built by having him look at the way he thinks about the situation, examining his attitudes, challenging his misperceptions, and offering more suitable alternatives.

> Joshua, 17, was failing two courses and doing poorly in several others. He worked 30 hours per week in a fast food restaurant and played on the school baseball team. He considered dropping out of school and working full-time or enlisting in the Army. He kept himself so busy he didn't have time to think. He came to the school counselor to sort through his options and make some choices for his future. Two years earlier, his older brother drowned in a boating accident leaving Joshua the only child. His parents were desolate; they didn't discuss the accident. Joshua's father, a fire captain, maintained a "stiff upper lip" and wouldn't talk about his feelings or the loss for the entire family. Joshua thought that in order to follow in his father's (and brother's) footsteps, he, too, shouldn't disclose his feelings despite their obvious intrusion in his everyday functioning. Joshua had difficulty tolerating his feelings, and the work in therapy consisted of helping him deal with his loss and build more adaptive ways to go on with his life.

Many adolescents feel overwhelmed by the demands of life. Prompted by peer pressure, the drive to excel, the need to please parents or themselves, or the feeling that no one understands, they believe life just isn't worth living. Suicide is something that many adolescents have considered at one time or another. All adolescents should be asked if they have thought about suicide. The question should be direct, not couched in euphemism, and should include probes about a plan, thoughts about death, religious beliefs, and meaningfulness of life. This information will suggest how much the individual is hurting and in need of help. All discussion of suicide should be considered seriously and not blithely dismissed as a "stage."

> Kevin, 16, had everything going for him. He was the class vice-president, member of the basketball team, and an honor student. In January of his junior year in high school, he ingested 60 Tylenol tablets resulting in his medical and psychiatric hospitalization. Although he had more visitors than other patients, he would talk to his therapist about his loneliness, emptiness, and lack of satisfaction with his life. He wondered "if it's worth it." He wasn't afraid to die. His outpatient treatment, a slow process, focused on his way of thinking about both himself and life, and his lack of a cohesive self.

The role of the therapist is to help the adolescent look at the ways he integrates his masculinity into his everyday life. More often than not, this is subtly done by addressing those issues important to the male: how he interacts with friends, his concerns about dating, his assumptions about work, his thoughts about "male" activities, including cars and sports, as well as talking abut his concerns about his masculinity. Many males present their concerns through non-verbal communication including dress, tatoos, habits (smoking, drinking, fast driving, aggressive or antisocial behaviors) as well as hypermasculinity, aggression, and seeming lack of feeling. These issues can and should be addressed to see how the adolescent thinks about himself, his male sex role, and how it interplays in both his psychology and interactions with the everyday world in which he lives.

Male Sex Roles

The traditional definition of male sex roles suggested that a male internalized his masculinity by becoming aware of his membership in the group, adopting the characteristics of that group, and acting according to the widely shared and accepted beliefs about how that group should act. It was believed that the boy tried on the male sex role by modeling himself after his father and other male role models (Kagan, 1964). The traditional sex-role identity paradigm conceptualized sexual identity in terms of masculine and feminine polarities, and asserted that the development of a masculine identity is a risky, failure-prone process. It maintained that because of an inner psychological need appropriate sex-role identity is necessary for good psychological adjustment. It suggested that problems in sex-role identity account for men's negative attitudes and behaviors toward women. The traditional sex-role paradigm declared that hypermasculinity indicates insecurity; homosexuality, a disturbance of sex-role identity (Pleck, 1981).

This model suggests a standard against which males measure themselves. The standard is not explicit but is somehow "known" by males, and passed through generations in the definition of masculinity. In particular, it is held by those who perpetuate sexism; to them, the standard is power, ability, and not being feminine. Some men feel it is important to hold these myths because it keeps them in power.

Homophobia

Because the traditional sex-role identity paradigm conceptualized sexual identity in terms of masculine and feminine polarities, anything that is feminine is not masculine. This myth restricts males from developing the fullness of their human potential because feelings and the show of emotion, being concerned about others, and expressive characteristics have been identified as not being masculine. Therefore, men who have these qualities are not masculine; they must be like women. To be like a woman is a threat to a male's masculine identity; he somehow failed as a male. To be like a woman suggests that he is homosexual. The logic of this has never been very clear but apparently it is because the choice in partner is the same, a male. Males find being compared to a woman or being called gay very threatening. The fear of homosexuality or being labeled a homosexual is a powerful "social controllant" (Lehne, 1976) of masculine behaviors. It threatens membership in the male group; the myth ostracizes gays from the male group and perceives them as not being masculine. This myth devalues other people, particularly women and men who can openly express the fullness of their feelings regardless of their choice in sexual partner. Adolescents are particularly vulnerable to this myth because they are hyperalert to their environment, especially sensitive to how they think others perceive them, and their wish to belong to a socially acceptable group.

In adhering to the mythical male sex-role identity, an adolescent might adopt a hypermasculine stance to ward off the possibility of being considered homosexual. The adolescent male often explores his emergent sexuality with other males. It is the fear of discovery and possible rejection that prompts him to adopt an antigay or overly masculine stance. It also interferes with his wish to maintain intimacy with childhood friends and separates him from closeness with other males, often leading to distant relationships of adulthood (Bell, 1982).

> Jake, 15, had a tatoo on his arm, wore leather jacket and boots, and walked with a swagger. He prided himself on his ability to bench press 225 lbs. He bragged about his sexual exploits and how he would "beat up on fags." He wore his masculinity like a neon sign. The only feeling of tenderness he could express was about his mother; he didn't want guys to get the wrong idea about him. He attempted to intimidate anyone who got too close.

The adolescent who is gay experiences another kind of problem. Often he feels like a misfit, socially alienated and shut off from peers and others who are important to him. This is particularly true of an adolescent in a small, rural community who does not have access to more tolerant attitudes often found in a metropolitan area. He believes he is carrying a horrible secret that cannot be revealed to anyone. His self-esteem is threatened: His identity as a sexual being, as a person, is at stake. As Beane (1981) stated in the title of his article, "I'd Rather Be Dead than Gay," the gay male, like other males, has adopted the myth that homosexuality is "illegal, immoral, sick, sinful, disgusting, unacceptable and a mental illness" (p. 223). The therapist who understands his patient can be a great advantage here.

In his senior year of high school, Mark found himself thinking about his best friend, David. Whenever they were together, Mark's heart rate increased, he felt the need to impress, and he enjoyed the physical contact that was part of their horseplay. He even found himself masturbating to fantasies of David. He believed he was abnormal, that something was wrong with him because of his attraction to David. He was scared and feared being ridiculed for being gay.

During adolescence, the individual's identity is in flux. He is uncertain about how he feels. His sexual urges rise. He is attracted to both male and female friends. He confuses intimacy and sexuality. He is learning to control his impulses, to share his feelings, and to realize that he need not act on his urges. He also needs to become aware of his needs for nurturance, and his wish for closeness. He should be able to investigate all facets of his personality and their significance to him as a person. He should not close himself from important parts of himself for fear it interferes with his masculinity.

Regardless of the moral stance of the therapist, the goal of treatment is not to project personal beliefs on the individual in therapy but to help the patient look at and explore his own actions, perceptions, and feelings. If the therapist believes there is not a good match and that treatment may possibly be destructive to the individual's health, a referral should be made, especially for the vulnerable adolescent who is not as knowledgeable or experienced as the therapist. He depends on the judgment and experience of the therapist. The first rule is "Do no harm."

Integration of Masculine Identity

If the adolescent adheres to the myth of male sex-role identity, he is bound to have problems integrating his personality in a healthy manner. He is likely to give up many facets of his personhood that up to now he thoroughly enjoyed. Rather than rigidly adhere to the male sex-role identity, if the male derives his identity from a conversation between himself and the world around him he is able to integrate his masculine identity within his total personality without exacting cost to either (Lazur, 1983).

An individual does not act alone but rather in the context of the environment (Sullivan, 1953). There is an interaction between the male and the world in which he lives. Through this interaction, the individual projects an image of himself to the world and in return receives feedback from others. It is a constant give and take between him and those around him; he is "in conversation." While the individual may look to the same-sex group for validation, reassurance, support, and acceptance, he carries on a dialogue with the environment as a way of internalizing his masculine identity. Through this conversation, a male validates both himself and others by comparing himself to others and providing a standard against which others can compare themselves.

Through this interaction, a male can adjust his masculine identity to meet the needs of self and others. He does not need to be restricted in the breadth of definition of his masculine identity but can adapt to the situation and be validated. This allows a freedom and fluidity not available to rigid stereotypic behaviors. It allows a man to express his needs according to the demands of the situation. He makes the choice, it is not prescribed for him nor is he held fast to it by a rigidly defined sex role. For the adolescent, this conversation takes place in his everyday life. He becomes aware of his masculine identity, and integrates it in his identity as a person.

One goal of therapy is to help the adolescent look at and understand his personal constructs about self and other. Although he may fear either his feelings or the discovery of unresolved conflicts about his masculinity, it is important to the adolescent's identity integration to know as much as possible about himself. The therapist can help him by exploring how he thinks about and expresses intimacy in relationships with both the same and opposite sex.

Adolescent Male Relationships

Peer relationships concern the teenage male. He sees himself as different from other guys. They have more than he, whether it be strength, good looks, money, talent, intelligence, ability, or whatever; he doubts himself. He is full of insecurities. And nowhere does this become more apparent than in his relationships with his peers, those with whom he lives his everyday life.

The quality of peer relationships is important in the formation of the individual's identity as well as being a prototype for future significant relationships. Youniss and Smollar (1985) found that adolescent males engaged in recreational or sports activities and often included the use of drugs and alcohol in their interactions. While intimate communication was part of close relationships, it was not the main activity of interpersonal contact; other instrumental activities were. While able to talk about their friendship, future plans, schoolwork, and dating behaviors, close male friends preferred to discuss their problems with females. Opposite-sex friends or parents were selected by the adolescent male to discuss his fears about life, moral standards, or views on society. Problems with other males and personal insecurities were not expressed to another male. Close friends neither tried to understand nor attempted to explain the reason for ideas whether the discussion involved schoolwork, family, or friendships.

It is useful to explore the adolescent's understanding of peer relationships. Discuss with him what the relationship means to him, what he gains, what he gives. Ask about what they do together, what their common interests and common goals are, and how important this other person is. Talk about how they perceive each other, and what makes their relationship "special," and what would happen when a third party—perhaps a female—is introduced. This is important for the adolescent to know and value the aspects of his male relationships.

Camaraderie is an important aspect in male relationships. Helping each other, standing up for each other, and knowing that the other guy will be there when needed are important aspects of friendships. Even though same-sex relationships are not often sought after, males enjoy being with other males and receiving support, validation, and acceptance from the interaction. Through sharing in a conversation, each benefits: They give and receive feedback, validate each other's sense of self, and receive emotional support, even if it is unspoken.

For many adolscents, especially those who have difficulty forming and sustaining relationships, the group is an important means to develop social awareness and interpersonal skills. Not only does the individual have the opportunity to see how others see the same situation, but the structure of the group teaches appropriate ways to interact.

Developing Heterosexual Relationships

With adolescence comes the awareness of sexuality and the opposite sex. There is anxiety, uncertainty, and ignorance, which is expressed in various behaviors ranging from boastful strutting to isolation. Females, who were once ignored or badgered, now become the focus of attention. The myth is that males know "all the right moves"; the reality is that the adolescent male more often than not doesn't know what to do, how to act, or what to say. He feels insecure. He fears rejection, not being liked, not being accepted. He fears making a fool of himself, which he sometimes does. Forming a heterosexual relationship takes time and practice. The adolescent may need to learn social skills: how to start and maintain a conversation, how to state his thoughts and feelings clearly, and how to express his needs appropriately and respect those of another. Postpubertal heterosexual relationships are a new venture for both parties and require education and practice.

Psychologists have found that men look to women for emotional support (Pleck, 1976, 1980) and nurturance (Scher, 1980), and that adolescent males share their intimate insecurities and vulnerabilities with females (Youniss & Smollar, 1985). During these nascent relationships, it is important for the male to look to the female not just as someone who gives to him, but as a person with whom he can share. There should be a genuine give and take in which the male becomes aware of and meets the psychological, emotional, and physical needs of the female. He should also learn that females are not the only ones who nurture and gratify his needs.

Therapists working with adolescents need to be aware of the transference. The female therapist is often perceived as the object of fantasies, sexual desire, or infatuation; the male therapist is perceived as role model: competent, able, secure. The therapist should explore the meaning and significance of the adolescent's feelings, and in the process, come to know and understand the adolescent's psychology. Transference can be both positive and negative; it represents both the wish and the fear. By using the transference, the therapist helps the adolescent recognize areas of conflict that when made conscious, consolidate his identity.

Body Image

The first signs of maturation a boy discovers are with his body: He is changing. He may feel awkward, lanky, uncoordinated, or he may feel he hasn't changed at all. He may think he's too small, worry that his voice hasn't changed, and fear that he won't display muscles. He may be self-conscious, dissatisfied with the way he looks, and feel out of place.

The adolescent male undergoes many changes in puberty and adolescence. There is an awkward spurt of growth when his hands and legs don't work together. He may feel shy and self-conscious about his body; he may not want to show it to anyone. He may feel awkward in gym or at the beach. He might believe that others guys are more developed than he is.

As part of the male myth, guys are supposed to be large, have big muscles, and be able to lift twice their weight. Adolescence is an awkward time of growth and development. The adolescent may have difficulty expressing his awkwardness to anyone, much less to a therapist. Gentle inquiry about sports, muscles, growth, body size, and looks can be enlightening about the teenager's feelings of self-worth and satisfaction with his physical maturation.

Sexual Responsibility

As the adolescent matures sexually, his natural drive is to be sexual. He wants to try out this new found part of himself. He is curious; he wonders how everything works, and if his penis works as it should. He talks with other adolescents, jokes with them, and may even adopt the false bravado that ensures that he is "one of the guys." He is curious about the opposite sex and wants to experiment. He may find himself in a bind: He wants to experiment but his moral upbringing may not condone premarital intercourse. It is a battle of id and superego.

Sorenson (1972) found that 59% of adolescent males have had sexual intercourse. One of the lasting consequences of sexuality is conception. Males are accountable for their actions, and nowhere is this more important than in the creation of new life. Whether he is sexually active or not, it is important to inquire about his attitude toward sexual responsibility—in particular, his becoming a father. When the teenager indicates he is sexually active and might be responsible for new life, it is important to explore the nature of the sexual relationship, his life goals, and how the responsibilities of children fit in with both his and his partner's life plan. Ask if he wants a child, what fathering a child means, and if he wants to get married. Discuss the financial, emotional, and physical responsibilities. Determine if having a child gratifies a wish for closeness, of being wanted by another person, a wish that the adolescent experiences as being ungratified in his own life. Remember that while he is trying to be an adult, he is still in the process of his own psychological growth and development.

Even though they believe they do, adolescents often do not have a clear understanding of biological facts. At times, the role of therapist is to educate. This may involve a discussion of reproduction, birth control, precautions, alternatives, and sexually transmitted diseases. The counseling should not take a moralistic stance but, as with all counseling, remain neutral with the goal of clarification of the individual's needs.

Work

An important part of growing up is the first job, whether it be for the source of revenue, the experience, or filling time, the job is important in the way men conceptualize their masculinity (Lazur, 1983; Tolson, 1977). Work represents power, strength, ability; it is a sign of adult responsibility.

The first job may be a paper route, lawnmowing, or flipping hamburgers; it may be after school or during the summer. It offers an opportunity to learn and master work responsibilities as well as the accompanying financial rewards. Discuss the adolescent's thoughts and feelings about money and job responsibilities. Many parents, especially fathers, express concern that their sons are not motivated. They fear their son will not become much of anything because of his seemingly lackadaisical attitude toward household chores and responsibilities. For the adolescent, work at home is different from, and not quite as exciting as, work outside the home.

Work offers an opportunity for the teenager to meet new and different people, to practice and develop social skills, and to experience the self-gratification that comes from a sense of accomplishment. It also provides a means to greater autonomy.

Males attach a significant importance to work and money. According to the myth, it is how they identify themselves, a clear measure of success and value as a person. It also provides an arena for competition. In discussing the adolescent's thoughts about work, look for his values. Discuss how he perceives job responsibilities, his attitude toward work, and his career plans. How realistic are his expectations? This of course varies with age and realistic perceptions, but it is useful in guiding the adolescent in his identity formation.

The Holding Environment

The task of adolescence is to separate and individuate. Often that is easier said than done. Parents may have a hard time assisting the child in his developmental transition because of their own needs. Those who wish to cling to their children often are reluctant to let go and allow the children to start on their own; they may fear abandonment or rejection. The child may have filled an important role in the marital relationship or for the individual parent, and the adolescent's separation may pose significant threat to the homeostasis. The child may be blamed for the cause of family discord, or any number of familial problems. The role of the therapist is to help both the parents and the adolescent separate so that the child can successfully negotiate the adolescent developmental transition. Sometimes the most difficult part of being a parent is in letting the child leave; it is a leap of trust that the child will follow his good sense and make decisions that are not destructive.

The parents' task is to provide a holding environment to support the child during the transition. The adolescent wants them to be available, provide guidance, support, reassurance, safety, acceptance, as well as financial assistance in helping him make it successfully into adulthood. At the same time, he does not want them encroaching on his individuality. As he asserts his autonomy and separates from the holding environment he had known as a child, he will rebel. He will make his parents angry. He will do things they do not like, things that will test their tolerance and level of frustration. He may appear unmotivated. His parents will worry about him. The parents' task is to be available, consistent, and to provide reasonable limits with clear consequences whenever an infraction occurs. Many parents need help in setting clear, *realistic* limits with appropriate consequences. The adolescent himself looks to those who can provide him with stability and who can help him grow and mature into a functioning adult without running his life.

During this transition time of life, the individual is particularly vulnerable to events occuring in the world around him. If the holding environment fails, he is likely to experience a psychological setback. While not an irretrievable loss, there is an added psychological conflict that the individual will have to resolve. If a divorce is threatened during this time, it may have profound impact on the adolescent: He relies upon his parents for his sense of security. His world is already shaky and full of insecurities; with a divorce, it falls apart. When his parents told him they planned to separate, one teenager smashed expensive living room furniture and bashed in the front door during a psychotic decompensation. It was more stress than he could handle, and it was his way of telling them that his world was falling apart around him. Another withdrew into himself and didn't talk with anyone. He lost interest in school, and his grades plummeted. When another discovered his father's affair, he became boisterous and cocksure, making enemies and pushing people away by his abrasive behaviors. The therapist should help both the adolescent and his parents during this developmental transition; it is not always an easy transition for all concerned.

Conclusion

Counseling the adolescent male can be one of the most rewarding experiences afforded a therapist. It is a time of change, of growth, and discovery. Even with severely impaired youth, the changes are noticeable. The goal is to help the adolescent understand the meaning of his life, make changes in his maladaptive behaviors, and learn more adaptive ways of interacting with the world. If he changes the way he thinks about himself and those around him, is able to feel good about himself and his life as he moves into manhood, then the therapist has had an impact. Adolescence is one of the most dynamic, fluid times in an individual's life, and a time when the therapist can see the fruits of his labors. There is nothing more satisfying to a therapist than an adolescent saying, "Thanks, you've helped me change my life."

References

Beane, J. (1981). "I'd rather be dead than gay": Counseling men who are coming out. *The Personnel and Guidance Journal, 60,* 222-226.

Bell, D. (1982). *Being a man: The paradox of masculinity.* Lexington, MA: Lewis.

Erikson, E. (1968). *Identity, youth and crisis.* New York: W. W. Norton.

Kagan, J. (1964). Acquisition and significance of sex typing and sex role identity. In M. L. Hoffman and L. W. Hoffman (Eds.), *Review of child development research* (Vol. 1). New York: Russell Sage.

Lazur, R. F. (1983). *What it means to be a man: A phenomenological study of masculinity.* Unpublished doctoral dissertation, Massachusetts School of Professional Psychology, Dedham, MA.

Lehne, G. K. (1976). Homophobia among men. In D. David & R. Brannon (Eds.), *The forty-nine percent majority: The male sex role.* Reading, MA: Addison-Wesley.

Pleck, J. (1976). The male sex role: Definitions, problems, and sources of change. *Journal of Social Issues, 32,* 155-164.

Pleck, J. (1980). Men's power with women, other men, and society. In E. H. Pleck & J. H. Pleck (Eds.), *The American man* (pp. 417-433). Englewood Cliffs, NJ: Prentice-Hall.

Pleck, J. (1981). *The myth of masculinity.* Cambridge, MA: MIT Press.

Scher, M. (1980). Men and intimacy. *Counseling and Value, 25,* 62-68.

Sorenson, R. C. (1972). *Adolescent sexuality in contemporary America.* New York: World.

Sullivan, H. S. (1953). *The interpersonal theory of psychiatry.* New York: W. W. Norton.

Tolson, A. (1977). *The limits of masculinity.* New York: Harper & Row.

Youniss, J., & Smollar, J. (1985). *Adolescent relations with mothers, fathers, and friends.* Chicago: University of Chicago Press.

10

Developmental Issues, Environmental Influences, and the Nature of Therapy with College Men

Glenn Good
Ronald May

The college years represent a time of tremendous personal change for college students (Feldman & Newcomb, 1969). As students leave their family of origin for the collegiate world, they embark upon a developmental journey that takes them from adolescence into adulthood. The developmental challenges facing college students include developing a sense of autonomy and identity, exploring intimacy in relationships, and committing to a set of values and lifestyle choices (Chickering, 1969). Throughout this journey the male student inevitably confronts his socialization as a male and encounters opportunities for redefining his masculinity. While the possibilities may be exciting, the process is often confusing, threatening, and painful. This chapter explores the developmental struggles of male college students and the influences of the campus environment as well as counseling approaches for effectively facilitating young men's growth as well-balanced persons.

Psychological Concerns and Help Seeking

The majority of studies on help seeking among college students reveal a pattern of gender-related differences.

Numerous studies (for example, Shueman & Medvene, 1981) have indicated a higher prevalence of mental health concerns and need for assistance being reported by college women compared to their male counterparts. Similarly, other authors (see Tracey et al., 1984) have found college men to be less interested in outreach workshops aimed at personal enrichment than are women. These findings are interesting when considered along with a National Institute of Mental Health Survey (Robins et al., 1984) that reported a relatively proportional rate of emotional concerns among men and women in the general population. Role restrictiveness, as manifested by limited awareness of feelings, difficulty with self-disclosure, and a need to control situations may lead college men to be more hesitant to acknowledge emotional problems, and perhaps even to be less aware of their own internal difficulties (O'Neil, 1981; Warren, 1983).

Along with sex differences in help seeking, some studies (for example, Collins & Sedlacek, 1974) have also reported sex differences in types of presenting concerns. In general, these studies found women reporting intrapsychic concerns and men identifying difficulties in controlling or adapting to external events. For instance, Koplik and DeVito (1986) found women concerned with loneliness, low self-esteem, and depression, while men wanted to be more popular and proficient in securing dates. Furthermore, it seems that while women tend to attribute relationship problems to interactional difficulties, men more frequently attribute conflicts to problems in their partners and to external events (Wood, 1986). It appears that, unlike women, college men are more oriented toward controlling external events and the perceptions and behaviors of others rather than focusing upon their personal involvement in the process (Gilligan, 1982; Wood, 1986).

This line of reasoning seems to be validated by studies exploring college students' expectations of counseling. Again, numerous studies (Harding & Yanico, 1983; Subich, 1983) have reported a consistent pattern of different expectations for college women and men. Women tend to expect a high quality of facilitative conditions such as acceptance, genuineness, and immediacy. On the other hand, men expect a counselor to be directive, analytical, and self-disclosing. Consistent with sex-role socialization, college men appear to have a task-oriented view of counseling in which the counselor provides advice and direction for controlling the external environment. Unlike their female counterparts, college men—at least initially—are more cautious in viewing counseling as a safe opportunity to explore their internal worlds. These different perspectives of counseling might be better understood by examining the developmental journeys traveled by college men and women.

Psychosocial Development

The college years of the traditional-age student witness the developmental issues of late adolescence. Numerous theories have been proposed to describe the psychosocial (Chickering, 1969; Heath, 1965; Keniston, 1971) and cognitive (Kohlberg, 1971; Perry, 1970) development of college students. Chickering (1969) proposed seven vectors (tasks) that constitute identity development in college students, including the first three vectors of developing competence, managing emotions, and developing autonomy. With respect to the task of developing competence, students attempt to develop a sense of competence with intellectual, physical, and social skills. As an example, one sensitive though timid upperclassman who was heavily involved in helping others suffered considerable loneliness and low self-esteem as a result of his inability to ask women out on dates.

In the realm of the management of emotions, students must also attempt to learn to become aware of emotions, control their expression, and learn to interpret these emotions when making decisions. For instance, an inability to accept feelings of loneliness and rejection may contribute to emotional acting out, as in acquaintance rape. Male students are often most conscious of anger but must also learn to identify and differentiate the variety of other emotions. This task may be facilitated as the student begins to perceive his ability to acknowledge and express emotional needs as a personal strength rather than as a weakness.

The third vector of autonomy development involves acquiring emotional independence from the reassurance and approval of others while simultaneously recognizing the need for interdependence. However, the need to prove oneself in a new environment may lead the male student to reject help from family or campus personnel while excessively relying on reassurance from peers. For example, a male student who drinks heavily with his buddies may mistake his rebelliousness for independence from others. The successful completion of this task is signaled when the student develops confidence to risk disapproval from peers and to accept assistance without being overly dependent.

The development of competence, emotional management, and autonomy provide a foundation for the fourth vector, establishing identity. Chickering considered identity development to be the central developmental task. This sense of identity represents an internal consistency of values, emotions, beliefs, and behaviors. The establishment of identity also provides a more stable foundation for pursuing the remaining vectors: freeing interpersonal relationships, clarifying purpose, and developing integrity. Freeing interpersonal relationships involves initially recognizing, then tolerating, and finally appreciating differences between persons.

Purpose development involves formulating plans and priorities necessary for career and lifestyle commitments. Finally, developing integrity involves personalizing a set of values congruent with one's decisions and behaviors.

Chickering's theory can be seen to have clear implications for men's gender identity and role development. The vectors of developing competence, managing emotions, and developing autonomy are laden with sex-role expectations and influences. Further, the successful resolution of gender issues related to competence, managing emotions, and autonomy can facilitate the development of a more androgynous male identity. Additionally, it is clear that successful completion of the tasks related to freeing interpersonal relationships would be essential for considering alternative perspectives of masculinity in oneself and in relationship to others. Also, in resolving the tasks associated with developing purpose, a man who had earlier developed a more androgynous identity would be freer to consider more options than would a man who had not developed an androgynous identity. These broadened choices include: the consideration of nontraditional careers, egalitarian relationships, and noncompetitive and less stressful lifestyles. Clearly, nonsexist value development in men can be seen to be related to Chickering's theory of psychosocial development.

Cognitive Development

In addition to psychosocial changes, college students may also make significant strides in their cognitive development (Widick, Knefelkamp, & Parker, 1980). Perry's (1970) hierarchical, sequential scheme of cognitive development describes four positions through which a student moves from a simplistic, categorical view of reality to a more complex, pluralistic view of knowledge and truth. Entering freshmen most commonly manifest Perry's first position of "dualism." The dualist views the world in distinct categories—good or bad, right or wrong. The dualist believes in absolute truth, relying upon authorities to transmit these answers while relying only minimally upon their own capacities. In considering masculinity, this student would most probably view men as strong or weak, manly or unmanly, heterosexual or homosexual. Further, these students would expect counselors to give direct advice to help them solve concrete problems and to gain social approval.

In the second position, "mulitiplicity," the student considers there to be an unlimited plurality of points of view. The multiplist believes that all people have the right to their opinions, and all opinions are valued equally. No criteria are used to evaluate the validity of a particular perspective. At this phase, the student may begin to analyze the male role and to consider alternative expressions of masculinity. A counselor might facilitate this consideration of alternative views, but the student may still have limited capacities for internalizing the implications of these views.

Greater cognitive complexity emerges with "relativism," the third position. The student begins to consider knowledge as relative and contextual, dependent upon a specific circumstance. Having forsaken their old truths, relativistic students may begin to consider the meaning of their own existence. These students are then ready to assume more personal responsibility and to explore new roles. During this position, students are more able to weigh the various implications of the concept of masculinity and sex roles. A counselor might help these students to consider their own needs in a problem situation and to evaluate the consequences of alternative ways of responding. For instance, a student experiencing a relationship conflict might consider directly sharing his feelings and unmet needs with his friends or mate.

The fourth position, "commitment to relativism," involves choosing values and beliefs that are consistent with an emerging identity. These students recognize diverse, conflicting themes within themselves, which create ambiguity and uncertainty in their lives. However, these students do internalize guiding principles to help them make choices with regard to career, a set of values, and selection of an intimate partner. It is in this position that students are able to commit to a synthesized view of themselves and their concept of masculinity. They are able to explain the various concepts as well as the reasons for their decisions. Counseling becomes more introspective, intuitive, and affective as students take greater risks, develop deeper self-understanding, and clarify their directions in life.

While these four stages appear sequential, a student's progress is rarely steady. Students may remain in a fixed position or possibly even retreat somewhat as they consolidate changes and develop a readiness to move forward. Clearly, in counseling male college students, an awareness of the clients' cognitive level of development is useful in selecting optimal interventions and enhancing therapeutic effectiveness.

Environmental Influences on Development and the Null Environment Regarding Alternative Male Gender Roles

People do not develop in a vacuum. Fortunately, increasing attention has been given in recent years to the impact of the college environment in promoting student development (Delworth & Piel, 1978; Huebner, 1980). Freeman (1975) coined the term *null academic environment* to describe the detrimental impact of a sex-role "neutral" campus environment on women's academic achievement. Similarly, on most college campuses, male students encounter what might be termed *the null environment regarding alternative male gender roles*, an environment that neither differentially encourages nor discourages male students to explore their gender-role socialization. Throughout their precollege lives, however, men are inculcated with the traditional male mystique; they lack an equal exposure to alternative male gender roles. Colleges that assume a "neutral" stance on male sex-role issues fail to acknowledge the impact of precollege learning upon most students. Unfortunately, a campus that fails *actively to promote* male students' exploration of their gender-role identity inherently supports traditional male roles. These roles are often supported via existing campus institutions such as athletic teams and fraternities. In addition to lacking a proactive alternative gender-role presence, many campuses present the following additional environmental barriers to gender-role exploration: patriarchic faculty, peer pressure, homophobia, sexist humor, counseling aimed at "adjustment" to social norms, and academic and career advising leaning toward traditional roles.

Student services offices are given the mission of promoting student growth and development. From our perspective, this includes responsibility for encouraging students' exploration of alternatives to traditional sex roles. While not specifying what type of male role identity is ultimately desirable for each college male, alternatives to traditional male socialization warrant exploration. There are numerous types of interventions that may favorably alter the college climate, the male student's view of himself, and his interactions with others. Campus environmental alterations may also change the nature of the issues with which men struggle, and subsequently change the nature of the issues that men bring to counseling. Environmental influences that promote gender-role growth include: androgynous role models, psychoeducational programs on gender roles, men's/women's studies courses and resource centers, men's groups, community men's networks, and nonsexist personal and career counseling and advising. Some interventions may be designed to reach men who rarely seek out counseling on their own, such as screening disciplinary referrals for personal concerns, providing drug education programs to athletes, and conducting acquaintance rape workshops with fraternities. While much more research is needed, the important task of evaluating different types of psychoeducational programming for promoting college men's development has already begun (Murphy & Archer, 1986).

Several authors (Blocker, 1978; Knefelkamp, Widick, & Stroad, 1975) have described approaches to facilitating students' development through environmental and programmatic interventions. Their suggestions include carefully appraising students' level of development and selecting experiences that provide masterable challenges to students at each developmental level. For instance, freshmen with a dualistic perspective may find the conversations in a men's group too emotionally intense, complex, or abstract for their developmental level. On the other hand, a mixed-sex program on sex-role stereotypes might challenge their perceptions while offering greater comfort and familiarity. It is also important that students have the opportunity to evaluate and process these experiences in a safe environment. Other ways to promote development suggested by Blocker (1978) include: exposure to role models who are slightly more advanced cognitively; exposure to networks of empathic and caring individuals, such as residence hall staff and faculty; and both intrinsic and extrinsic rewards for engaging in developmental struggles. Rewards can include such things as clear, honest feedback during group sessions and the opportunity to participate in volunteer and internship experiences.

In sum, an understanding of person-environment interactions is critical to promoting male development. The college/university environment has been clearly identified as a bastion of sexism (Banning, 1983; Sandler & Hall, 1982, 1984). An ecological perspective can reduce internal and external punishment for men struggling against significant environmental restraints. University personnel can use knowledge of person-environment interactions for shaping campuses into more humane living and learning environments. Although the dynamics of organizational change are complex, models have been developed (Fawcett, Huebner, & Banning, 1978; Kaiser, 1978) and implemented (Conyne, 1975; Daher, Corazzini, & McKinnon, 1977; Huebner, 1979), which offer promise for promoting both individual student growth and social change within institutions of higher education.

The Nature of Counseling College Men

As mentioned earlier, college men frequently experience difficulty entering into counseling since many of the basic elements of counseling are in direct opposition to traditional male socialization (Bruch & Skovholt, 1982; Chamow, 1978). Examples of this conflict include dependence on another person, emphasis on recognition and expression of feelings, and the requirements that one disclose honestly and interact genuinely in counseling. Hence, the very nature of counseling may be antithetical to the traditional male role with its emphasis on independence, rationality, and emotional/interpersonal control. Nonetheless, the risks men experience in entering therapy will be mentioned only briefly here, as they are discussed in greater detail in other chapters.

Regardless of the risks involved there are of course some college men who do seek psychological assistance. Perhaps these men feel so greatly burdened by their difficulties that they are able to overcome the stigma of help seeking. Or, conversely, perhaps men seeking help are less traditional in their sex role and hence are not as affected by the conflict between traditional male roles and help seeking (Voit, 1980). Some common presenting concerns for which college males do seek help include academic performance and major/career choice concerns, substance abuse (alcohol and drugs), anger and behavior problems, alienation, loneliness, shyness, relationship issues, sexuality/sexual identity concerns, and racial/ethnic identity issues. Many of these problems are themselves natural outgrowths of the restricting traditional male role (O'Neil, Helms, Gable, David, & Wrightsman, 1986).

When examining the traditional male role, it becomes clear that common concerns for which men may enter counseling are career-related issues. Traditionally, men are expected to place considerable emphasis on their academic major and career. For men, work equals self-esteem and survival; men very rarely consider the option that they won't need an occupation. Additionally, having a presenting concern related to academic major/occupational choice is frequently a more socially and personally acceptable way to "get one's foot in the door" of a counseling center. Often this also provides a chance to "test the water" and perhaps to discuss more threatening concerns later if indeed counseling appears sufficiently safe to do so.

One concern that may be presented after trust is built, or perhaps even initially, is that of alcohol and drug abuse, a concern that itself is a recognized problem on many college campuses. The traditional male role often encourages reliance upon alcohol and/or drugs to bolster courage, assuage doubts, and numb physical as well as emotional pain. It is not surprising that with the freedom of being away from home, a desire to be accepted by one's peers, and extensive upheaval in one's personal structure many college men experience serious problems with drug and alcohol abuse. For example, one male college student was referred to the counseling center after assaulting his girlfriend and a residence hall staff member while intoxicated. The incident was precipitated by a breakup in the relationship, resulting in strong feelings of abandonment and jealousy. While in a counseling group, the young man explored the modeling he had witnessed with his father, who responded to his own frustrations by punishing others. The student went on to explore the lack of nurturance he felt from his father and committed himself to becoming a more nurturing and tolerant man.

The interpersonal and sexuality issues facing college men are numerous. On the college campus, men often feel conflicting pressure to date, to be outgoing, to compete and excel, to be independent, to be sexually active, to be a skilled lover, and to be sensitive to women. Yet while men are expected to be proficient in these areas, rarely are they taught such skills, nor is there permission to be socially awkward while trying to develop confidence and grace. An illustration of an intervention to address this difficulty was an acquaintance rape workshop in a residence hall, which led to a lively discussion between the men and women participants. A brainstorming of sex-role expectations and games used to initiate sexual contact illuminated the artificiality of traditional dating interactions. While the men and women were able to examine their collusion in perpetuating these interactions, the men also clearly heard the women's desire for more genuineness, sensitivity, and respect from their dating partners.

Likewise, the college environment can have a variety of influences on young men with regard to their race and/or ethnic identity. In addition to both overt and covert discrimination, minority students may also experience stress as a result of out-group/in-group rejection-acceptance phenomena (Smith, 1985). However, individuals who do not identify with a traditional white majority are likely to be additionally mistrustful of seeking help from a counseling center or therapist whom they believe would hold a traditional white majority orientation. Thus a counseling center and/or particular therapist(s) with a reputation for effectively serving members of specific racial/ethnic groups (e.g., Blacks, Hispanics, Asians, Native Americans) or special populations (e.g., gays and lesbians, the physically challenged, religious groups) will be likely to attract a larger proportion of students from those groups than would otherwise seek assistance.

Choice, Change, and Confusion Reduction

In conceputalizing and intervening with the problems that college men bring to counseling, one useful approach is the Choice, Change, and Confusion Reduction Model (Gilmore, 1973; Tyler, 1969). According to this model, counseling can have one or some combination of three overlapping general purposes: choice, change, and/or confusion reduction. This model can be of mutual use to both the counselor and the client in conceptualizing the nature of client's concerns, and in planning for appropriate counseling interventions. These three categories of counseling purposes—choice, change, and confusion reduction—use terms that both the client and the therapist can understand and employ in accurately describing the specific purpose of counseling. Through establishing the specific purpose of counseling, the nature of the *process* of counseling and of the *tasks* faced by the client and counselor in clarifying and resolving concerns become more explicit. Further, for the college man who so often only tentatively seeks professional assistance, providing initial structure to the counseling situation via discussion of these three purposes is often useful in reducing the client's anxiety. Each of these three purposes of counseling will be elaborated subsequently.

Being human means that people must choose, or choose not to choose, their own way of being in the world. A man who is coping effectively with his life acknowledges the ambiguity of life and makes the best decisions possible at that time; he chooses what he will do, how he will do it, and essentially who he will be. Clients who enter counseling seeking to make decisions about their lives are wrestling with "Choice"; they seek counseling to facilitate their use of effective planning and decision-making skills. Some examples of choices that male clients present for counseling include the following:

> My girl friend thinks that we should be monogamous. I really like her a lot and don't want to hurt her, but I don't think I'm ready to settle down yet. I wanted some help figuring out what to do.

> There are lots of interesting courses here, but I've got to stop floating around and figure out my major!

> I've known that I'm gay for a while now. I feel like it's time that I tell my family. I'm just not sure if I should come out to them or not, though.

The counselor assisting each student may recognize the purpose of counseling as assisting the students in utilizing effective decision-making skills. Numerous authors have developed models of rational problem solving (e.g., D'Zurilla & Goldfried, 1971) that are generally effective in assisting clients with choice concerns. In addition to providing the client with a problem-solving/decision-making model, the counselor's tasks also involve helping the client to collect relevant information; working with the client in assimilating and evaluating the data, ensuring that the different pieces of information are adequately summarized and that their relative meaning is emotionally and cognitively understood; assisting the client to predict the implications of the alternatives that they develop; and, finally, to develop contingency plans. Since this rational, logical approach is congruent with male socialization, such an approach may be particularly useful for short-term counseling. However, deeper therapeutic interventions will likely require an exploration of more affective and intuitive capacities that are not likely to have been previously acknowledged or reinforced. These resources may be tapped through the use of visual imagery, dream work, nonverbal observations, music and movement, sculpting, and touching. The reawakening of suppressed wishes and desires can also facilitate choice making.

In contrast to choice as a purpose of counseling, change as a counseling purpose involves a client desiring to modify his emotional response, cognitive pattern, or behavioral reaction. He may seek "to do, think, or feel some specific thing more often or less often, or in some situations, but not in others" (Gilmore, 1973, p. 58). For the therapist, this frequently means supporting a scared young man as he first encounters change while also guiding him through experiences anomalous with and destructive to his previous maladaptive personal constructs (Mahoney, 1980). Utilizing a masculist approach as outlined in the final chapter, the therapist is responsible for talking with the client about the nature of counseling and then sharing responsibility for what occurs in counseling, as much as is possible. Some examples of client concerns based on change include the following:

> Whenever I try and study, I get distracted and do something else. My grades are showing it. If I don't learn to concentrate on my studies more, I won't be around here much longer.

> Because of my disability, my parents sheltered me, and I never had any friends in high school. I want to make friends here, but I feel too shy to ever talk to people.

> Whenever I get in a situation where there's a difference of opinion, I feel like I always *have* to win. Other people are starting to avoid me, and it's really causing some problems with my girlfriend. Besides, I don't feel that good about it myself either.

With these types of concerns, the counselor assists the client in implementing the changes that he desires. Cognitive and behavioral interventions are commonly employed to produce such changes (Ellis & Harper, 1975; Lazarus, 1976; Rimm & Masters, 1979). When employing cognitive and behavioral approaches, the therapist has primary responsibility for designing effective incremental lessons, pacing challenges to the client's level, and reinforcing positive changes.

Client-desired change may also be an indication of the clients' separation and individuation from his family of origin. From this perspective, the desired change may also represent a violation of a parental injunction or family rule. Gestalt, psychodynamic, and/or family systems approaches may be useful for these types of interventions (Fagan & Shepherd, 1970; Lax, Bach, & Burland, 1980; Satir, 1983). From these perspectives, the therapist promotes emotional awareness and insights of childhood experiences and provides opportunities for working through the relevant conflicts from a retrospective and/or here-and-now context.

Confusion reduction is often an initial stage of therapy in which clients present choice and/or change concerns. However, many clients' *primary* purpose in seeking counseling is to reduce the amount of confusion that they are experiencing. That college men would be confused is hardly surprising, given the vast number of factors impinging upon them. Frequently they are "on their own" for the first time and are trying to present themselves as confident, assured, directed, and sexually proficient.

Concurrently, there may be strong expectations from peer groups and/or family to excel in academics, athletics, fraternity life, social life, and/or student government. Furthermore, all of these forces are occurring when college men are typically experiencing tremendous pressure to adopt and conform to the masculine mystique. They are expected to act as men, to "pass for" men, and indeed, to excel as men.

As mentioned earlier, it is theorized that college men pass through developmental stages. As college men wrestle with the pragmatics of their psychosocial, cognitive, and moral development, confusion is a natural product. As a counseling purpose, confusion reduction is likely to occur when an individual has inadequate personal structure with which to perceive and comprehend his daily life. An individual is likely to experience confusion and anxiety—frequently sufficient to interfere with his daily functioning—when the set of assumptions that he uses to interpret his world becomes ineffective. Some client concerns that are likely to result in counseling directed toward confusion reduction are as follows:

> I feel pretty strange about coming here for help, . . . It seems like if I'm not feeling strong and secure, and I dare to tell someone how I feel, I get kidded about it, or they get turned off. Isn't it supposed to be O.K. for guys to have feelings?

> When I was in high school, I didn't give much thought to being black. But at this campus, some white people seem to be really prejudiced against me. It is starting to make me think a lot more about what it means to me to be a black.

> In the little town that I grew up in, everybody was a Christian and followed the Bible. Here at the college, I've met a lot of different people. Well, I'm not sure *what* I really believe about God anymore. I just wanted some help getting my thoughts sorted out.

Perhaps because one's confusion may stem from many sources, a great diversity of therapeutic strategies surround confusion reduction as a counseling purpose. Numerous approaches such as client-centered, gestalt, and psychodynamic may be effective in assisting clients to understand better themselves and their place in the world. In order to be of assistance to the confused client, the therapist must respect the importance of one's personal structure in deriving a sense of meaning from an otherwise chaotic world. Counselors must also appreciate the difficulty men face in unveiling, reconstructing, and developing more adaptive and realistic personal structures.

Since ambiguity is typically antithetical to the male role's call for instrumental action, male clients are likely to be particularly uncomfortable with "hanging in there" while struggling with issues as abstract as values, meaning, and current implications of past learning. Furthermore, they may feel a need to mask any confusion. For this reason, the therapist has particular responsibility for helping the client to anticipate and prepare for often uncomfortable reactions to the examination of one's values and attempts to view oneself and the world in different ways. In addition, confusion can be discussed as a necessary, if not essential part of the change process. The therapist may encourage the client to explore the impact of his gender socialization on his apprehensions about the counseling process. Further, most male college clients benefit from repeated acknowledgment of the strength shown by seeking assistance, the courage shown by exploring the scary world within themselves, and the patience required to tolerate the anxiety that this process produces. In addition to assisting men to reach their self-identified goals, encouraging men to enjoy the self-exploration and growth *process* itself are worthy counseling achievements.

In sum, college men are facing difficult and complex developmental challenges at a time when they frequently feel the least permission to be uncertain or confused. Those individuals and institutions seeking to facilitate male college students' growth have the responsibility to be sensitive to male gender-role issues, create proactive environmental influences, and provide appropriate psychological interventions.

Self-Help Resources

Music

Lapow, Gary. *Tell it from the heart* [Record]. Springhill.
Morgan, Geof. *It comes with the plumbing* [Record]. Bellingham, WA: Nexus.
Morgan, Geof. *Finally letting it go* [Record]. Bellingham, WA: Nexus.

Books

Gambrill, E., & Richey, C. (1985). *Taking charge of your social life.* Belmont, CA: Wadsworth.
Goldberg, H. (1977). *The hazards of being male.* New York: New American Library.
Goldberg, H. (1979). *The new male.* New York: Signet.
Pleck, J., & Sawyer, J. (1974). *Men and masculinity.* Englewood Cliffs, NJ: Prentice-Hall.
Rubin, L. (1983). *Intimate strangers.* New York: Harper & Row.
Zilbergeld, B. (1978). *Male sexuality.* New York: Bantam.

References

Banning, J. H. (1983, October). *The environmental conditions of racism and sexism: A challenge for campus counseling centers.* Paper presented at the meeting of the Association of University and College Center Directors, Colorado Springs, CO.
Blocker, D. H. (1978). Campus learning environments and the ecology of student development. In J. H. Banning (Ed.), *Campus ecology: A perspective for student affairs.* Cincinnati, OH: National Student Personnel Association.

Bruch, M. A., & Skovholt, T. M. (1982). Counseling services and men in need: A problem in person-environment matching. *American Mental Health Counseling Association Journal, 4,* 89-96.

Chamow, L. (1978). Some thoughts on the difficulty men have initiating individual therapy. *Family Therapy, 5*(1), 67-71.

Chickering, A. W. (1969). *Education and identity.* San Francisco: Jossey-Bass.

Collins, A. M., & Sedlacek, W. E. (1974). Counselor ratings of male and female clients. *Journal of the National Association for Women Deans, Adminsitrators, and Counselors, 37,* 128-132.

Conyne, R. K. (1975). Environmental assessment: Mapping for counselor action. *Personnel and Guidance Journal, 54,* 150-155.

Daher, D. M., Corazzini, J. G., & McKinnon, R. D. (1977). An environmental redesign program for residence halls. *Journal of College Student Personnel, 18,* 11-15.

Delworth, U., & Piel, E. (1978). Students and their institutions: An interactive perspective. In C. A. Parker (Ed.), *Encouraging development in students.* Minneapolis: University of Minnesota Press.

D'Zurilla, T. J., & Goldfried, J. M. (1971). Problem solving and behavior modification. *Journal of Abnormal Psychology, 78,* 107-126.

Ellis, A., & Harper, R. A. (1976). *A new guide to rational living.* Hollywood, CA: Wilshire.

Fagan, J., & Shepherd, I. L. (1970). *Gestalt therapy now.* New York: Harper & Row.

Fawcett, G., Huebner, L., & Banning, J. H. (1978). Campus ecology: Implementing the design process. In J. H. Banning (Ed.), *Campus ecology: A perspective for student affairs.* Cincinnati, OH: National Student Personnel Association.

Feldman, K. A., & Newcomb, T. M. (Eds.), (1969). The impact of college on students. San Francisco: Jossey-Bass.

Freeman, J. (1975). How to discriminate against women without really trying. In J. Freeman (Ed.), *Women: A feminist perspective.* Palo Alto, CA: Mayfield.

Gilligan, C. (1982). *In a different voice: Psychological theory and women's development.* Cambridge, MA: Harvard University Press.

Gilmore, S. (1973). *The counselor-in-training.* Englewood Cliffs, NJ: Prentice-Hall.

Harding, S. I., & Yanico, B. J. (1983). Counselor gender, type of problem, and expectations about counseling. *Journal of Counseling Psychology, 30,* 294-297.

Heath, D. (1965). *Explorations of maturity.* New York: Appleton-Century-Crofts.

Huebner, L. (1979). Redesigning campus environments. *New directions in student services* (Vol. 8). San Francisco: Jossey-Bass.

Huebner, L. (1980). Interaction of student and campus. In U. Delworth & G. R. Hanson (Eds.), *Student services: A handbook for the professional.* San Francisco: Jossey-Bass.

Kaiser, L. R. (1978). Campus ecology and campus design. In J. H. Banning (Ed.), *Campus ecology: A perspective for student affairs.* Cincinnati, OH: National Student Personnel Association.

Keniston, K. (1971). *Youth and dissent.* New York: Harcourt, Brace, & Jovanovich.

Knefelkamp, L. L., Widick, C. C., & Stroad, B. (1975). Cognitive-development theory: A guide to counseling women. In L. Harmon, J. Birk, L. Fitzgerald, & M. Tanney (Eds.), *Counseling women.* Monterey, CA: Brooks/Cole.

Kohlberg, L. (1971). Stages of moral development. In C. M. Beck, B. S. Crittenden, & E. V. Sullivan (Eds.), *Moral education.* Toronto: University of Toronto Press.

Koplik, E. K., & Devito, J. A. (1986). Problems of freshmen: Comparison of classes of 1976 and 1986. *Journal of College Student Personnel, 27,*(2), 124-131.

Lazarus, A. A. (1976). *Multimodal behavior therapy.* New York: Springer.

Lax, R. F., Bach, S., & Burland, J. A. (1980). *Rapproachment: the critical subphase of separation-individuation.* New York: Jason Aronson.

Mahoney, M. J. (Ed.). (1980). *Psychotherapy process: Current issues and future directions.* New York: Plenum.

Murphy, M., & Archer, J. (1986). *Role conflict in college males: Implications for preventive mental health.* Paper presented at the 1986 American College Personnel Association, New Orleans.

O'Neil, J. M. (1981). Male sex role conflicts, sexism, and masculinity: Psychological implications for men, women, and the counseling psychologist. *The Counseling Psychologist, 9*(2), 61-80.

O'Neil, J., Helms, B. J., Gable, R. K., David, L., & Wrightsman, L. S. (1986). Gender-role conflict scale: College men's fear of femininity. *Sex Roles, 14*(5/6), 335-350.

Perry, W., Jr. (1970). *Intellectual and ethical development in the college years.* New York: Holt, Rinehart, & Winston.

Rimm, D. C., & Masters, J. C. (1979). *Behavior therapy: Techniques and empirical findings* (2nd ed.). New York: Academic Press.

Robins, L. N., Heltzer, J. E., Weissman, M. M., Orraschel, H., Gruenberg, E., Burke, J. D., & Reiger, D. A. (1984). Lifetime prevalence of specific psychiatric disorders in three sites. *Archives of General Psychiatry, 41,* 949-958.

Sandler, B. R., & Hall, R. M. (1982). *The classroom climate: A chilly one for women?* Washington, DC: Association of American Colleges.

Sandler, B. R., & Hall, R. M. (1984). *Out of the classroom: A chilly campus climate for women?* Washington, DC: Association of Amerian Colleges.

Satir, V. (1983). *Conjoint family therapy.* Palo Alto, CA: Science and Behavior Books.

Shueman, S. A., & Medvene, A. M. (1981). Student perceptions of appropriateness of presenting problems: What's happened to attitudes in 20 years? *Journal of College Student Personnel, 22,* 264-267.

Smith, E.M.J. (1985). Ethnic minorities: Life stress, social support, and mental health issues. *The Counseling Psychologist, 13*(4), 537-579.

Subich, L. M. (1983). Expectations for counselors as a function of counselor gender specification and subject sex. *Journal of Counseling Psychology, 30,* 421-424.

Tracey, T., Sherry, P., Bauer, G. P., Robbins, T. H., Todaro, L., & Briggs, S. (1984). Help-seeking as a function of student characteristics and program description: A logit-loglinear analysis. *Journal of Counseling Psychology, 31,* 54-62.

Tyler, L. E. (1969). *The work of the counselor* (3rd ed.). New York: Appleton-Century-Crofts.

Voit, R. A. (1982). Effects of student sex-role identity and problem type on likelihood of seeking counseling and preference for counselor sex (Doctoral dissertation, University of Virginia, 1980). *Dissertation Abstracts International, 42,* 3022A.

Warren, L. W. (1983). Male intolerance of depression: A review with implications for psychotherapy. *Clinical Psychology Review, 3,* 147-156.

Widick, C., Knefelkamp, L., & Parker, C. A. (1980). Student development. In U. Delworth & G. R. Hanson (Eds.), *Student services: A handbook for the professional.* San Francisco: Jossey-Bass.

Wood, J. T. (1986). Different voices in relationship crises. *American Behavioral Scientist, 29,* 273-301.

11

Counseling Aging Men

Brooke B. Collison

The most critical element in counseling aging men is gaining access to them for counseling purposes. As a group, men avoid counseling or other help-seeking behaviors, and this is not different for aging men: Therefore, much of the counseling of aging men will need to take place in settings other than the therapist's office—the last place that aging men may go for the help that they desperately need in the critical times of their lives. The most effective role for the therapist may be to work with the persons in the adult male's support or contact network in order to (a) reach the older male indirectly through significant others, and (b) broaden the effective helping base in the several areas that are critically important to older men.

Aging men is a term that will be applied to two age groups: those in the age range 45-60, and those 60 and beyond. All men can be defined as "aging" regardless of their age, but the particular themes that drive men to examine their lives and to behave as they do frequently come to a focus in the two age eras defined above. In a sense, the 45-60 period may be the first time that many men sense that they are "aging" and the 60 and beyond era is a time that they know that they are.

A critical issue that men face in either of the defined eras is, "What does aging mean?" Therefore, the most common therapeutic technique suggested for work with aging men is the set of responses that (a) assist men in assessing lives, (b) determine what their lives mean and what aging means for them, and (c) allow them to implement whatever they need to do as a result of the meaning that they define.

It is most important to work with aging men through developmental stages in what would be defined as "normal" transitions. The pathological states that exist for men at all ages have been described elsewhere. It is the large mass of "normal" men who need focus—men who are aging, and who, through that aging, are being forced to deal with inevitable changes in their work, family, and physical lives. In large part, there are few places where they are invited to address the issues that come from those changes, or if they do address the change issues, it is expected that they will handle them in the typically "manly" way of showing no reaction and minimizing the "bother" that they represent.

Developmental Issues— (Ages 45-60)

It has been fortunate for men that writers such as Levinson (1978), Vaillant (1977), Golan (1981), and Neugarten (1968) have described the nature of normal developmental processes for men. As a result, the concepts surrounding "transitions" have become more a part of the public's vocabulary, making it easier than it once was for a few men, as well as those around them, to discuss openly life issues centering on work, personal and family relationships, and physical performance.

The 45- to 60-year-old man will have many life changes that require intense discussion and analysis to clarify their meaning. Consider work situations, for example: It is in the 45-60 era that men will know that they have either reached, exceeded, or fallen short of the major career goals that they set early in life. In either respect, whether men have exceeded or fallen short of goals, they need an opportunity to discuss the significance of goal attainment. The following counselor-client excerpt is illustrative:

Counselor: What is happening for you now in your job situation?
Client: Not a lot.
Counselor: You say that without much feeling.
Client: I suppose so. There isn't much excitement there now.
Counselor: What would it take for it to be exciting?
Client: I don't know. I am doing what I set out to do 15 years ago. I've reached the place I wanted to be, and it's not as exciting now as it was 5 or 10 years ago when I was scrambling to get here. I mean, I've made it and there's—like there is no reward.
Counselor: What does "making it" mean to you?
Client: Just that—I've come as far as I wanted to.
Counselor: And what does that really mean?

The evaluation of life goals for men who have met or exceeded their original expectations is as important as it is for men who have to face the disappointment and resultant meaning attached to falling short. Consider the following excerpt:

Client: I just found out that I am being passed over again.

Counselor: What is that like for you?

Client: It really hurts. They must think I can't read the handwriting on the wall, or something. I know that I haven't done as well as I wanted to, but—it still hurts to get passed over and everyone in the world knows it.

Counselor: Getting passed over again has a strong message in it for you, doesn't it?

Client: Yes. I just have to face the fact that I am never going to be what I thought I'd be.

To reach an achievement point and find that it is empty of satisfaction or to miss an achievement point and realize that who you thought you were—based on work attainment criteria—is not what you wanted, are both issues requiring the kind of processing that counseling affords. Yet neither of these situations are the kind that would, of themselves, force a man into a counseling relationship. They are the kind of issues that may be imbedded in other life events. The ennui that results from finding that goal attainment is empty is not unlike the despair that accompanies the realization of goal failure. Both situations are common—in fact, every man has to deal with them to some extent, since every man can be defined as meeting or missing goals related to work situations. For the man who meets or exceeds expected goals, there is little sympathy among peers or family for men to express disappointment at what appears to be a significant accomplishment. The success orientation of most men (O'Neil, 1981a, 1981b) prohibits open discussion by men of their thoughts about failure, and certainly would inhibit discussion of disappointment associated with success.

Family and personal relationships need to be examined by men in their forties and fifties. In the same way that work goals are either met or exceeded—and have meaning attached to them—relationships have meaning attached. That meaning needs review. The obvious developmental issues of children reaching maturity and leaving home, becoming the father of grown and/or married children, redefining marriage relationships, becoming single by virtue of death or divorce, contemplation of remarriage or different partnering—all require examination.

This is also a period when earlier relationships are examined, especially in terms of their effect on men's lives. Perhaps father relationships are most significant. Consider the following excerpt:

Counselor: What do you recall as a "most significant" event with your father?

Client: That's hard to pick out. [Pause] There was one, though.

Counselor: What was that?

Client: Well, I recall a time, I'm not sure how old I was, that I was sick or something was wrong. Maybe I had been hurt or something. And Dad came in and didn't say anything, but just held me. He just hugged me for a long time.

Counselor: How common was it for him to do that?

Client: That is the only time that I can remember. He just didn't hug or things like that.

Counselor: And that one time has really stuck with you, hasn't it?

Client: Yes, except that I haven't thought about it for years, until you just asked me.

Counselor: What do you want to do with that?

Client: I'd like to do the same for him now, I guess. And I'd like for it to be different for my sons.

The opportunity to examine and evaluate father-son relationships is a critical need for men. The man above went ahead to describe the kind of relationship that he wanted to develop with his own two sons and then returned to a focus on his own father, who had recently retired. The sense of urgency that aging brings to relationship management is marked in the conversations of many men.

Perhaps physical changes or changes in physical performance are among the most frequently discussed age-related changes that men engage in. Often, the discussion may not be particularly helpful or therapeutic. Consider the locker-room discussions that are age-related, with bantering about being beaten by an "old man" or that a loss on the racquetball court must be a sign of old age. A missed ball is followed by an admission that "I must be getting old." And fortieth and fiftieth birthdays have become a common vehicle for morbid gifts at parties, which are poorly organized attempts to find humor in morose activities associated with the despair of aging. Greeting card stores have rack upon rack of cards that describe the perils of becoming 40 or 50.

It is important to be able to talk about physical changes in a nonthreatening environment. Again, meaning is a focus:

Counselor: You talk about being worried that you are slipping.

Client: You bet. I would never admit it in public, but I wake up at times wondering if I am going to make it to sixty.

Counselor: What are the signs that tell you that?

Client: Oh, it's physical—I can feel it a lot longer after I run. I don't know if my knees will hold up. And I can't eat or drink like I used to. It's hell to get old.

Counselor: Is that what it means? You're getting old?

Client: Damn right. And I don't like it.

Counselor: But what does "getting old" mean?

When normal transitions occur out of sequence, or simultaneously, or without preparation, they can become crises. Men in the age of 45-60 should be able to predict certain transitions; however, the combination of relationship change (divorce) with an unexpected work or career change (loss of job) or with a precipitous physical change with accompanying onset of physical limitation is likely to require therapeutic assistance beyond a network of supporting friends.

The time of crisis is not the time to develop the supportive networks of personal relationships within which one can examine a life. Because they tend not to have them, men—perhaps more than women—need to work harder to develop supportive networks early in their lives that they can use at those points of crisis calling for additional therapeutic response. The most likely point for those exchanges is within the social group that the man is a part of; however, most social groups are activity focused and provide little in the way of sustaining interpersonal relationships needed in the midst of transition or crisis. One effective method to deal with this issue would be to bring the discussion of age and aging into the open in social groups and men's clubs. Therapists should use scheduled programs, formal seminars, regular discussions, and the like as methods that can push the topic of "aging" into the fore, thus increasing the likelihood that men would engage each other in the kind of discussion that resembles therapy in another setting.

Therapeutic Responding

Whether it is in a personal support network, in a family setting, or in a therapeutic environment, men need the opportunity to have persons interact with them using the following kinds of responses:

- "What is happening in you life now?"
- "How is what is happening fitting with your life goals?"
- "How do you feel about the relationships in your life?"
- "What is missing that you would like to have?"
- "What are you feeling best about?"
- "How are you different now than you were (10, 20, etc.) years ago?"
- "What are you seeing in your future concerning your job, family and relationships, and your physical well-being?"
- "What meaning do you attach to your life now?"

Age 60 and Beyond—New Developmental Stages

The 60-year-old man has to work harder to avoid being aware of impending decisions and issues that retirement and age-related change brings to him. At 60 he is entitled to discounts in many motel and restaurant chains. The atmosphere at sixtieth birthday parties increases in morbidity and gloom, promoted by "friends" who attend. And employment policies begin to force consideration of retirement, job change, and the like. The 60-year-old man who has worked for the government or the military may already have retired—occasionally to start a second career or job. The 60-year-old man who is in a larger company and who is not at the pinnacle of his career may already have seen himself passed over for promotion or responsibility, and the plethora of younger men and women who abound may be perceived as a direct threat. On the other hand, the 60-year-old man may be in a position to become a mentor to the young, and see himself extending his work life through others.

Relationships change for the 60-year-old man. In all likelihood, there are no more children living at home. Most likely, his children are partnered adults with children of their own and the older man may move into a comfortable role as grandparent, or an isolated role of an older man that people stay away from. In either case, there is a need for men to examine this new role and be able to make the necessary adaptations to the lifestyle that the new role demands.

Physical changes are magnified for the 60-year-old man. The news media and popular press present a great deal of conflicting information to men in this age group about what they are likely to experience concerning heart conditions, prostate problems, exercise limitations, sexual performance expectations, and longevity in general. Some topics related to health and performance that were not discussed a few years ago have moved into the open. The *Today Show* may have a discussion of impotence and show models of penile implants used to enable erections for impotent men. The same discussion may also illustrate the difference between physiological and psychological impotence, thus limiting the man's excuse for his impotence—if he has had to explain it to others. The result of private, taboo topics being pressed into the open may enable discussion, but it may also increase anxiety if the man cannot easily discuss that which is private and personal.

The man who has been able to live his life close to the physical edge with excessive smoking, poor diet, heavy drinking, and little consideration for hours of work or sleep will no doubt find in his sixties and beyond that he cannot do what he has always been accustomed to do. Depending upon the meaning and significance that he has placed on those behaviors as indicators of masculinity, the loss or limitation in any of those behavior areas may take on more significance than might be noticed in others.

Butler and Lewis (1982) have pointed out that old age is the period in life with the greatest number of profound crises, often occurring in multiples and in high frequency. They also state that "individual psychotherapy is *least* available to older persons and yet should be a part of any therapeutic relationship" [italics in original] (p. 320). Availability is more than likely tied to money and earning power, which declines with age and retirement.

The critical psychological events for older men concern their reactions to death and grief, decisions, and disabilities. Butler and Lewis (1982) contend that older persons often exhibit a strong desire to resolve problems, to put their lives in order, and to find satisfactions and a second chance—thus making them prime candidates for therapy, which Butler and Lewis have already said is less likely to be available to them. I take the position that the help for men to work through those situations must occur within the normal relationship channels that they have developed rather than from professional therapy, which is less likely to be available to them. The professional therapist, then, may need to give special or extra help to the older men's caring networks for them to become more therapeutic—defined as open and supportive of critical life topics as well as accepting of the personal concerns that are endemic to older men.

WORK AND RETIREMENT

Men need a place to discuss the significance of their work life and the implications that the termination of that work career have for them and the people who are connected to them. The development in recent years of active associations for retired persons has ameliorated the "retired" status somewhat, but for many men who have defined themselves in terms of their work, retirement still presents a significant trauma that must be processed. I am involved in a group where several retired men nearly always introduce themselves in a disparaging manner: "I'm just one of those retired people you read about—don't pay any attention to us," or "If no one will volunteer to do it, you can always call on some of the old retired persons—they don't have anything to fill their time anyway."

Blau (1981) talks about "role exiting" as a concept describing people who leave an established role. There is less discussion of "role acquisition" as an accompanying part of role exiting. Conversations with 60-year-old men need to focus on both aspects of work-related role, with opportunity for life review and reminiscence. The "retirement party" is not an adequate substitute. Consider the following dialogue:

Counselor: How would you summarize your own work career?
Client: Pretty normal, I guess. I was with [public utility] company for my entire life. There have been a lot of changes over the years—a lot of people have come and gone.
Counselor: You must feel good having stuck it out that long.
Client: I suppose so. Maybe I should have done some other things, but I always had a job.
Counselor: Did you like what you did?
Client: Oh, yes. I always found it interesting.
Counselor: What were you able to accomplish as a person and as a professional in [public utility]? . . .

Counselor: Now that you have retired, what is it that has become as important as your work once was?

Client: That might be the problem—I don't have anything which is important to anyone else. Oh, there is my garden, and I like to give produce to others, but there isn't anything that I do now which is really important to anyone. I guess that I do fix some things up around the church, but that's not much.

Clearly, the man quoted above would be hard pressed to find the same value in his retired life as he found in his active work career. Analysis of his worth in retirement could take place in therapy, but may be more effective within established social or family groups. He cannot be told by a therapist that he is valuable apart from work; he must discover that for himself through dialogue with important others.

To this end, members of the clergy provide the most access to aging men. As professionals, they need the kind of training that would enable them to lead the discussions and conversations that focus on work, retirement, meaning of life, and the subsequent issues that aging men need to discuss. Members of the clergy also have the most frequent access to the partners of older men—their spouses and children. It would be an effective intervention for clergy to work with those persons who in turn become enablers of effective discussions among older men.

CHANGING SEXUAL EXPRESSION

It is not likely that many clergy can enter discussions with older men, their spouses and partners, or their children about inevitable changes in the sexual life and activities of older men, but that is another critical area for dialogue. In addition to the mythology of changing sexual performance, there is the reality of changing sexual opportunity for older men. Through death, divorce, or separation, sexual patterns may likely change for older men. Physical changes need to be discussed, as well. For the older man who experiences severe physical problems—prostate or other urinary or reproductive system complaints—the conversation about sexual change will be forced into the open through medical diagnosis and treatment. For the vast majority of older men, however, the arena for open discussion of changing sexual patterns is as closed as it always has been except for the occasional appearance on a TV talk show or, as previously stated, the discussion on a medical news section of "cures for impotence." A solid referral link must be built between medical personnel and therapists in order to avoid a "medical-only" approach to sexual problems.

Members of the clergy need to confront such issues on hospital and nursing home visits. In that setting, it is also more appropriate to confront the topic with the older man's partner. The difficult part is to start the conversation. The next most difficult part is to get the man to acknowledge the core issue. And the other difficulties are to get the partner to acknowledge the male's dilemma in a facilitating manner rather than to minimize the issue. For example, the following dialogue took place with an older man who had undergone two unsuccessful penile implants following prostate surgery that left him impotent. His wife was also involved, more than he, in the dialogue:

Man: The second operation didn't work either. There was a lot of infection which they couldn't clear up.

Woman: I don't know why he had that done. The first one didn't work and I kept telling him that that wasn't that important to me. It was so painful to him. I didn't want him to do the first one. And he didn't even talk to me about doing the second one.

Man: Well, I just wanted to have it done.

Counselor: It sounds like that was very important to you.

Man: Yes. I thought it was kind of funny, too. I could have walked around with a permanent hard on [laughs].

Woman: Oh, I wish you wouldn't say that. It isn't funny. I keep telling you that I don't need that. Just having you around is what's important.

Man: Well, I haven't decided whether to try it again.

Counselor: What would help you decide?

Neither the man nor the woman would address the issue of how much identity was tied to his ability to have an erection. She may have been satisifed to have a husband who was alive. He was not satisfied to be alive without being able to have an erection. Humor became a focal point in their discussion and she was put off by it. The counselor did not do an effective job of confronting either of them on the real issues at hand. It would have been more appropriate for the counselor to have addressed questions to both of them: "What are you hearing your husband say about the importance and meaning attached to having an erection?" "What will your life be like without being able to have an erection?" If the penile implant would not be successful (which in this case it was not), the counselor should address the speculative issues of what life would be like as a man and as a couple without erections. This could extend into instruction and discussions about alternative forms of sexual satisfaction for both, but it would take a good bit of dialogue to break through the discomfort each faced when confronted with the topic.

RELATIONSHIPS WITH CHILDREN

The 60-year-old male has a wonderful opportunity to repair or to enhance relationships with his children. One of the common complaints of the man in this age category is that his children do not pay as much attention to him as they might. The most therapeutic approach to this situation is to have the man examine the nature of his relationships with his children over the years and see what it is that has caused the rift. In most instances, the older man has not taken on a new set of behaviors that alienate the children; he merely has more time on his hands and notices more keenly that his children are not close. Of course, they also have their own time demands, and may be as close (emotionally or physically) as they can be, but it remains that this is an ideal time for the 60-year-old man to learn new parenting strategies. If work was used as an excuse that kept him from being open and sensitive and responsive as a younger parent, then in retirement he may be able to set aside that excuse and practice behaviors that will bring him closer to his children.

> *Man:* I have two adult children here in the city, but you'd never know it—they don't come around much.
> *Counselor:* When do you see them?
> *Man:* Mostly on holidays and birthdays—things like that.
> *Counselor:* What would you like to have happen?
> *Man:* I'd like to see them once in a while just for the hell of it. There shouldn't have to be some special event that they think they have to visit like an obligation.
> *Counselor:* What was it like before you retired?
> *Man:* I guess not much different. They've never come around much since they married.
> *Counselor:* Things are pretty much the same for them, then. Since you've retired, things are different for you, though. What could you do to make that relationship be different for both of you?
> *Man:* Well, I've thought about going over there, but I'm never sure what they are doing, and I sure as hell don't want to be in the way.
> *Counselor:* How long would you wait for them to know what you want?
> *Man:* I don't know. I guess you're saying that it is up to me in some way.

In some respects, retirement can be used as an opportunity to do something that the man has wanted to do for some time. It can be the catalyst for change. Outside of the formal therapeutic setting, older men can get help for revision and improvement of family relationships from those social systems where they normally interact—again placing the man who does not have such a personal network in place at a decided disadvantage. Church groups and social settings can schedule programs and seminars like "How to Get Reacquainted with your Children After Retirement" or other similar topics in a semihumorous fashion. The same situation occurs with divorce or death of a spouse and the subsequent new situation that the older man finds himself in of being able to define new relationships with adult children.

A focus in therapy needs to center on concepts of adulthood and egalitarianism between older men and adult children. If the older man has always seen his children as children, regardless of age, there is little hope for rich adult-adult relationships. This also does not bode well for life eras that call for children to assume more responsibility for aging parents if the only model for relationship is an adult-child model (even for the adult children), because in a dependent state, the older man will most likely be treated as he treated his children. The therapist can suggest that in his older years the man needs to ensure good adult-adult relationships with children so that they will have a model to work from when his own age or infirmity requires their assistance.

A passive approach to improving father-child relationships in the older years would be to have the fathers wait until their adult children come to them and repair what may have been broken. In the new-found leisure that comes with age, maturity, and retirement, older men may be able to take the assertive upper hand and initiate the kind of contact that will benefit both the older man and the adult child.

Acker (1982) has stated that many men have difficulty making contact with their fathers because they fear them. Moreover, they fear what their own contact would do to their fathers. Somehow, the feared father becomes both a powerful and a very fragile figure. Acker led 26 men through a seminar on male issues. As part of the seminar, each man wrote a letter to his father. Acker summarizes their common comment descriptive of why they could not establish emotional contact with their fathers as a fear that if they told their fathers how they felt, "how I felt as a child in relation to you, . . . that you would not be able to take it" (p. 2). Further, Acker concludes that sons fear that their fathers didn't have the emotional strength to tolerate openness from their sons and that fathers are fragile emotionally and must be protected from emotional distress.

Older men can ease the difficulty of reestablishing relationships with children by demonstrating to them that they are not fragile, that they invite the emotional or intimate contact with children that the children may be afraid to initiate. Some therapy may be needed for older men to accomplish this task since, for many, it may require a new set of communication patterns with those same adult children.

DEATH

If death is one of the critical psychological issues for older men, as Butler and Lewis (1982) indicate, then therapists and others in the helping network must continue to engage older men in dialogue about death issues. The natural state of aging is that same-age peers will decrease in number for several reasons, such as death, divorce, and moving. It is incumbent upon older men to add constantly to the friend network, and therapists can assist them in this process in addition to assisting the social groups in which men are found to recognize and respond to the ever diminishing numbers around older men. Adding friends can be difficult, especially for the man who is single after a long marriage and who had friends because his spouse was the one who developed friend relationships. In that respect, following the death of a spouse, the therapist or someone else needs to help older men do an inventory of functions the spouse performed. This goes beyond the obvious of "cooking and caring"—for the widower may discover too late that all social contacts were spouse initiated and he may lack the skills or knowledge to remedy that situation.

A second critical aspect of death discussions for older men is to think of their own. The list of "unfinished business" that most persons carry with them is magnified as the older man contemplates his own death. The therapist can assist by helping identify the agenda items on that list and then enabling discussion of those items for optimal resolution.

NEW LIFE

Older men need not despair in all respects concerning their years beyond 60. It is frequently the case that older men, acknowledging a satisfactory work life and content with their relationships, are able to move toward retirement years with ease and satisfaction. The image peering out of the retirement magazines of a happy, satisfied older man is not uncommon. For many others, a degree of that happiness can be obtained with the help that a good counselor or therapist can provide. It may require confrontive discussion after the death of a spouse about the feelings surrounding the discovery of new relationships. Those feelings may well be laden with guilt—especially if the older man has "come alive" in his later years and looks with sadness at a less lively life in retrospect. The therapist can assist in shifting the focus to the future and to possibilities rather than to the past and regrets.

Summary

Older men are in need of help. It is also difficult to get the help that they need because of their own resistance to being helped and because of the decline in availability of good helping systems as they age. A concerted effort by therapists and persons in the social networks of older men can assist significantly in helping men examine the lives that they have led, the lives they lead, and the lives that they have yet to live. The consequence of such an examination should be improved relationships. It will be hard for men to do it alone; therefore the professional therapist must play an active role both in working with aging men and in enhancing the supportive elements of their social networks.

References

Acker, M. (1982). *With natural piety: Letters of adult men to their fathers.* (Mimeo.) University of Oregon: Eugene.

Blau, Z. S. (1981). *Aging in a changing society* (2nd ed). New York: Franklin Watts.

Butler, R. N., & Lewis, M. I. (1982). *Aging and mental health: Psychosocial and biomedical approaches.* St. Louis: C. V. Mosby.

Golan, N. (1981). *Passing through transitions: A guide for practitioners.* New York: Free Press.

Levinson, D. (1978). *The seasons of a man's life.* New York: Knopf.

Neugarten, B. L. (1968). *Middle age and aging.* Chicago: University of Chicago Press.

O'Neil, J. (1981a). Male sex role conflicts, sexism, and masculinity: Psychological implications for men, women, and the counseling psychologist. *The Counseling Psychologist, 9*(2), 61-80.

O'Neil, J. (1981b). Patterns of gender role conflict and strain: Sexism and fear of femininity in men's lives. *Personnel and Guidance Journal, 60,* 203-209.

Vaillant, G. E. (1977). *Adaptation to life.* Boston: Little, Brown.

III

Ethnicity

In this section authors will address various therapeutic issues and processes relevant to counseling men from different ethnic backgrounds (Asian, Black, and Hispanic) using psychosocial, cultural, and gender-role perspectives. It is well documented that a clear understanding of ethnicity is a crucial variable for the clinician when treating individuals from different cultural and ethnic backgrounds. This section of the handbook will look at race (men of color) as a particular ethnic variable.

The differences in counseling men of color and counseling men from the majority culture (white middle- to upper-class men) are substantial in both content and process. These differences can be attributed to the following:

(1) Gender-role socialization issues are unique and different for men from the nonmajority culture.
(2) Psychological issues such as locus of control and locus of responsibility will be different for men from the nonmajority culture.
(3) Expectations, values, and feelings about being in counseling/therapy will be different for men from the nonmajority culture.
(4) Cultural values and subsequent experiences and behaviors as they relate to issues of competition, power, and cooperation; expression of feelings; religious orientation; family dynamics; attitudes toward women; sexuality; and fathering roles may also be different for men from the nonmajority culture.
(5) Individuals' experiences and values as they relate to class differences may also be a factor in understanding men from the nonmajority culture.

Awareness, understanding, and appreciation of cultural differences is an essential ingredient in developing an effective therapeutic relationship and a positive treatment outcome. Failure to recognize, understand, and appreciate the differing worldviews, communication styles, and valuing of counseling/therapy may lead to frustration for both the client and therapist and to early termination.

Privilege is privilege. Even though men from the nonmajority culture do not have as much privilege as men from the majority culture, men from most cultural backgrounds are socialized into a system where male privilege will be given to them at their birth. With this as a backdrop, the reader may recognize common conceptual threads as they pertain to therapeutic issues with men, no matter what their ethnic or class background is.

These three chapters offer the reader a rather comprehensive list of resources for developing a finer understanding of how ethnicity influences the psychotherapeutic process.

12

Counseling Asian Men

Daniel Booduck Lee
Tuck Takashi Saul

In this chapter, counseling principles guiding the therapeutic processes in working with Asian men are addressed. Although much has been written and documented regarding generic characteristics of the Asian population in the United States, there has been little written specifically about the effects the impact of gender has on influencing the processes of therapy. It is our hope that future research will validate some of the clinical observations and findings presented in this chapter.

Awareness of Differences

An accurate awareness of differences means voluntarily giving up one's own perceptions temporarily in order to gain access to another person's gestalt. Stereotypically, Asian male figures in the majority white society have been depicted in films and in the public media in less than favorable light. For example, old and not so old war movies often depict Asian men as unfeeling, sadistic, cowardly, more animalistic than human. Old TV series such as *Bonanza, MASH,* and *Happy Days* presented caricatures of Asian men emphasizing and making jest of their use of broken English, their physical stature, and their manners. Therefore, having a basic awareness of one's own bias regarding Asian males is an integral starting point in becoming effective in counseling with this specific population. In order to understand this important process leading to self-awareness, ask yourself these questions: (1) What have my reactions been when I have encountered an Asian-American male, be it in person, in the media, or in movies? (2) How have I come to hold these conclusions? (3) How often do I question the validity of these views? Responding to these questions will make possible opportunities to compare one's beliefs about Asian-American men with the information we provide in this chapter.

Generalizations About Asian Men

Traditionally, in Asia men are perceived to be the favored gender. In the context of Confucian tradition, men are seen as being the carriers of their family names and kinship linkages, as well as carrying the heritage of the family tradition. In addition, the order of birth takes precedence, even among males—old over young, the firstborn over the succeeding—in terms of relative authority and level of responsibility. In countries such as Japan, China, and Korea, where the male is regarded as the culturally more favored gender, such a cultural orientation pervasively affects Asian men's intra- and intergender relationships and interactions.

The gender-role dichotomy is more structurally than functionally defined. Often, the man assumes primary responsibility as the breadwinner, the economic provider, and the decision maker when relating to the broader linkage among family, kinship, and society. For instance, if one had parents in need of ongoing health care, usually it is expected that the sons—particularly the oldest one—will assume primary responsibility in caring for the adult parent. (However, his wife may be the actual person to functionally carry out the responsiblity.) The Asian man may encounter an identity crisis of sorts if he doesn't perform this expected role competently.

Coming from male-dominated societies where social responsibilities are carried out by male members, Asian men tend to relate to other men much more comfortably. In certain important matters, they are discouraged from disclosing themselves to women because it violates the normative expectation of not revealing inner feelings, particularly if they reflect weaknesses. Asian men in general have difficulties in submitting or subjugating themselves to an unknown person unless that person's authority is clearly understood and appropriately negotiated. Knowing one's place in society is imperative in a culture where "saving face" is always of the highest priority in any interaction.

Thus the Asian cultural emphasis on formal interpersonal relationships versus the much more informal and spontaneous nature of Westerners can often make Asian men uncomfortable relating to Westerners, who show by their actions a lack of understanding and therefore respect for the cultural differences.

View of Mental Health

The roles of the clinical psychologist, psychiatric social worker, and nurse in most Asian countries are quite different from those found in the United States. In the United States, individuals from these different professions take active roles in the diagnostic interview, treatment, planning, and psychotherapeutic treatment. In most Asian countries today, the physician continues to be the primary caregiver. As compared to the United States, psychotherapy, or "talk therapy," still barely exists in Asian cultures. For example, what we call group psychotherapy in the United States is described as mass education in China and group dialogue in Japan. Since emotional problems or difficulties still are not culturally acceptable, many psychiatric problems of Asians are often manifested through somatic complaints. The symptoms of anxiety and depression, for example, are often attributed by these patients to a defect in the kidney, hormonal imbalance, or malnutrition (Pedersen, 1981). Therefore, the Asian men's expectation of treatment is often a medical solution.

In times of crisis, Asian men have a tendency to search for or use traditional indigenous means to release their conflictual feelings rather than directing their problems to the mental health professionals. They may choose various social settings such as bars, restaurants, tea houses, or clubhouses where they seek comforting companionships and advice. Group songs, chanting, or regressive behaviors are often elicited to produce catharsis of repressed feelings, resentment, anger, grief, or even erotic excitement. Such intermediary processes serve as a therapeutic approach that facilitates corrective feedback or curative factors without having to fear any personal attack, embarrassment, or the trauma of "loss of face." Other indigenous methods may include massage, herb medicine, tea ceremonies, the martial arts, or meditation.

Another example can be drawn from Japanese management practice, which is currently studied and tested in America. Supervisors/supervisees or executive/professional staff join together in an informal setting where repressed feelings can be released and any distressful matters or interpersonal conflicts are resolved in a familiar atmosphere. Using this kind of informal social contextual approach to problem solving is seldom available to Asian men from the contemporary therapeutic communities. Many recent immigrants or first-generation Asian men often find themselves lost in searching for these customary ways of problem solving or conflict resolution.

Therapy and Asian Men

Therapy with Asian men does not require that a therapist necessarily develop new skills. The fundamental skills in being an effective therapist remain the same, such as being able to hear what the client is trying to communicate, accepting the client's view of distress, communicating this understanding in an acceptable manner, and developing treatment goals that take into account the client's level of functioning, resources, and environmental conditions. What is different is that the problems are presented by Asian men.

It is often postulated that treatment efficacy is dictated by good assessment of the client and his or her presenting concerns. Accurate assessment of the interaction between readiness level and degree of acculturation, which include issues of culture, gender, and social content of the Asian-American male client, is crucial in determining success or an early dropping out of treatment (Kleinman, Eisenburg, & Good, 1978).

Asian-Americans in general are confronted with two important issues that affect their identity development and mode of problem solving. The first is the direct conflict of traditional Asian cultural values, such as filial piety and conformity, with traditional American values, such as individualism and independence (Sue & Kirk, 1973). The second is the impact of racism, which is sometimes overt, sometimes subtle, but ever present and pervasive in American society today (Kitano, 1973; Sue & Kirk, 1973). As a result of these two issues, a number of Asian-American personality types have evolved, ranging from the individual who may reject or deny all aspects of being Asian to a radical individual who may espouse a new Asian consciousness while rejecting the traditional values of both Asian and American cultures (Chen, 1981; Sue & Sue, 1971). With each type comes distinct ways that problems are perceived, addressed, and resolved.

Asian-Americans who have been born and acculturated in the United States are often confronted with an acute conflict between identifying themselves as primarily "Americans" and their appearance to others as primarily "Asian" or "Oriental," curtailing being accepted as belonging to this country. Thus an important variable to assess immediately in working with Asian male clients is ascertaining whether that Asian male is a recent immigrant or first, second, third, or fourth-generation American born, and the degree to which he has acculturated and assimilated into mainstream Anglo values and perceptions. Sue and Sue (1971) have proposed a conceptual acculturation and assimilation model that can be used as a guide to assess where a particular Asian man may be in terms of self-identity, self-worth, and clinical expectations. They label these three patterns as the *traditional,* the *transitional,* and the *Asian-American* ways to adjust to the often conflicting demands of the two different cultural traditions.

First, Asian males may remain loyal to their cultural roots by retaining traditional values and expectations. The traditionalist Asian males are oftentimes the most recent immigrants, having spent their primary developmental years within their native culture. They can also be first-, second-, third-, or fourth-generation-born Asian-American males, who, having been brought up in a predominantly Asian community, have accepted the values of that community as their own.

Second, Asian males may attempt to become over-Westernized as a means of solving the bicultural dilemma. These transitional Asian males define their self-worth by how well they have acculturated into white society. However, in their attempts to find acceptance, they are often forced to reject the Asian side of themselves and thus become rejecting of anything that reminds them of being different, including customs, values, behaviors and even physical appearances.

Third, Asian males may define themselves as Asian-America. Like transitional males, Asian-Americans are also rebelling against the cultural conflict, but the emphasis is on the development of a new identity that will enable them to reconcile viable aspects of their heritage with selected values of the majority white culture.

Therapeutic Implications

Depending on where that Asian-American man may be in terms of self-identification, the therapist will address himself or herself to different presenting problems as manifested by the traditionalist, the transitionalist, or the Asian-American. Generally speaking, the therapist or counselor most often is confronted with addressing the problems of guilt and shame and lack of openness in the case of the traditional Asian male; to problems of independence and self-hate in the transitional Asian male; and to issues regarding racism in society with the Asian-American male (Sue & Sue, 1971). A therapist who works with an Asian man with a strong traditional orientation must be aware that when the traditionalist seeks counseling or therapy, this often indicates the person is experiencing intense feelings of shame and guilt, admitting that problems exist that cannot be handled. Thus therapists working with males from a traditional background will often be called upon to alter their usual style of counseling and therapy.

In American psychotherapy, there has been considerable emphasis on the therapist as a neutral, nonjudgmental, noncritical, relatively passive person. In working with the traditional Asian male, however, therapists need to assume the role of the authority figure in order actively to engage in the therapeutic process (Pedersen, 1977, 1981). The traditional Asian male will often have high expectations of the therapist, in terms of demonstrating immediate understanding and knowledge of the client's problem. The usual conceptualization of treatment is therefore short term, with its emphasis on symptomatic relief (Sue, 1976).

In working with the transitional Asian male, the therapist has an obligation to help the client sort out his identity conflicts. Specifically, the transitional male must be helped to distinguish between positive attempts to acculturate and the rejection of his own cultural values (Sue & Sue, 1971). For the therapist to work effectively with such an individual, he or she must be conversant with the culture, history, and experiences of Asians in America. It would also be erroneous to assume that, with such a person, a therapist of an Asian background would work best, realizing that this client is in the process of rejecting his ethnic identity. There might be the risk that the counseling process would terminate prematurely if that person were to work with an Asian therapist.

As in the case of the traditional Asian male, the presenting concerns of a transitional Asian male may be physical, that is, not "I feel depressed or anxious," but rather the physical symptoms of depression and anxiety such as complaints of frequent headaches or of having stomach problems. Again, it is very important to utilize a concrete, directive type of communication approach and minimize open-ended questions. To go after the underlying constructs initially will probably have a tendency to scare off the client and again lead to premature termination.

It has been found that very few of the men in the Asian-American developmental stage utilize any type of mental health services because of its identification with the status quo (Sue & McKinney, 1975). When they do, they are usually suspicious and hostile toward therapists, especially if they are non-Asian. Before any type of therapy can proceed effectively, the therapist will generally have to deal with certain challenges from these Asian-American males. For such a client, any defense on the therapist's part of white society or any explanation of the value of therapy would certainly arouse greater hostility and mistrust. It would be extremely difficult to establish rapport without some honest agreement on the racist nature of American society. Often it has been shown that there is a parallel between growing pride and self-identity and the notion of accepting having emotional problems (Sue, 1981). The following guide (see Table 12.1) highlights and summarizes these differences, as well as the possible therapeutic approach set to utilize in working with the Asian male population.

TABLE 12.1

A. Comparison of Generic Characteristics Distinguishing
   Traditional Counseling from Asian Male Value System

Traditional Western Counseling Model	Asian Male Belief/Value System
Predicated on the assumption of horizontal relationship, individuation, independence, self-disclosure, and change.	Based on vertical relationship, interdependence, self-control, and acceptance of what is.
Emphasis on "getting in touch with your feelings" as a beneficial treatment.	Trained to internalize and meditate about one's personal conflicts. The concept of relating one's innermost personal conflicts to a stranger is seen as negative.
Value of being verbal, direct, assertive, and individualistic.	Valuing use of will power, solving one's own problems, being non-confrontive, practicing humility and modesty, and avoiding bringing shame to the family.
Utilization of verbal therapies.	Meditation approaches, emphasis on introspection, self-discipline, self-control of negative thoughts and feelings.
Goal of therapy: insight, verbalization, and change.	Self-discipline and self-mastery, acceptance of what is.

B. Suggested Therapeutic Approach Set

Focus on internal conflicts.	Focus on external stress(es).
Process-oriented discussion.	Emphasis on direct problem-solving techniques, active problem-resolution management.
Offering internal resolution(s).	Offering external resolution(s).

As can be seen, one of the major principles in working with Asian-American men, be they in the traditional, marginal, or Asian-American stage of development, is that an approach that is too confrontative or emotionally intense at the onset of therapy can increase the level of shame, and therefore result in premature termination of therapy. It is more effective in establishing a therapeutic alliance if the therapist, guided by some understanding and knowledge of cultural factors, responds to what may be viewed as superficial problems and takes the opportunity to establish rapport and trust. A second principle is the importance of confidentiality between therapist and client. A frequent concern of many Asian men is that their friends, and particularly their parents, will find out that they are seeing a therapist. A third principle is providing adequate therapeutic structure when working with Asian male clients. This can be done by providing sufficient guidelines in the form of explanations and suggestions of expectations of therapy. A fourth principle, because of the Asian men's tendency toward emotional inhibition and lower verbal participation, is for the therapist to be more active throughout the session. A fifth principle is for the therapist to assume the role of the authority figure in order to engage actively in the therapeutic process (Pedersen, 1977, 1981). In assuming authority, the therapist is clarifying the boundaries of the relationship thereby making the process less threatening. A sixth principle is that it often is difficult for Asian men to have therapists who are female or who are men who display/represent symbolically feminine qualities. Additionally, being seen by a therapist not perceived as having greater rank or status as that Asian male may also be a barrier. However, once a strong relationship has been established, the therapist has greater freedom to vary the therapeutic approach.

The following case vignettes illustrate some of the aforementioned cultural implications that arise when working with Asian males.

EXAMPLES

A bright male student of Korean ancestry, majoring in clinical psychology, was thought to be suicidal. He had an outstanding academic background prior to coming to the United States as a graduate student. While studying under a different curriculum structure in the United States than he was used to, he began to exhibit unusual behaviors. His exhibited problems involved alienation, noncommunication, and deterioration in his academic performance. He simply closed up. There was no acting out of the experienced distress. This became a great concern for the faculty members and his peers. They tried to convey this concern to him through written communication, phone calls, and attempted visits but without success. As time went by, he was more and more unconnected to any meaningful social contact, further complicating his situation.

This is a case where potential suicide was conjectured as a very imminent possibility. His most recent problems included: (1) not picking up his paychecks for a couple of months; (2) not submitting his papers on time; and (3) consequently his academic status being in serious jeopardy. Before his professors made any academic decision, they contacted the student counseling service. Because of the cultural ramifications in his situation, the case was referred for consultation.

In the Korean environment, his sense of equilibrium was well maintained and his intellectual and social functioning were never challenged. His entire previous school experience had been one of reward by people at all levels.

Because of the current language barrier, the conceptual differences, and expectational discrepancies, he was hampered by unexpected amounts of stress where new strategies for interacting and adaptation were necessary. He was struggling alone with the difficulties involved in bridging his old reality with his current situation. He became quite disillusioned. This was marked by signs of dysfunction in a number of areas—academic, interpersonal, and in his self-perception. Unless a deeper level of interpersonal relationship was established, he would not feel comfortable sharing his inner feelings. Since no such relationships were available to him, he chose not to reveal any feelings to those he perceived to be superficial.

In establishing a therapeutic relationship, the counselor picked an informal setting where comfortable conversation was possible. The initial focus was on the client's competence, reconstructing his ego sphere from a perspective of his previous life. His sense of current failure in another cultural setting was not customary and had not been easily incorporated because of his heightened anxiety defense system. Thus he was unable to deal with his current reality appropriately.

For the first time, the client had been existentially challenged in his sense of competency, as well as his total outlook on life. He could not handle such a generalized sense of failure, nor could he relate this situation to his own ethnic peers. Because his pride was at stake, he could not relate his feelings to any American peers. He was already determined not to reveal his feelings, as long as the relationship remained superficial. Inhibited in approaching faculty, who are customarily perceived to be authorities, it was almost taboo to unload his own personal difficulties on them. His loyalty and respect for faculty members made it even more difficult for him to engage himself while in the middle of his own internal struggle, causing him to distance himself from establishing mentorship relationships. As a result, he could not communicate his inner feelings and his sense of frustration to anyone, leaving his traditional crisis management and cultural adjustments untouched.

In addition, he chose not to communicate his remorseful feelings and sense of failure to his wife back home. Being separated from his wife and his family for several years, he could not reopen his emotional ties. He felt he had lost control and was reaching the edge in a very dangerous existential journey.

If he had chosen conventional ways of problem solving and conflict resolution, he could have prevented his current crisis by using new coping mechanisms and strategies. Through the use of a therapeutic consultation, he reconstructed his ecological system and he was able to change his distorted perception and generalized anxiety over his sense of failure. He began to realize the simple fact that people conditioned by different cultures do have different behavior manifestations. Differences are neutral, they do not require a value judgment. He also realized the importance of increasing his sense of control by mastering new skills in adapting to new realities (acquiring new sets of behavioral strategies and coping skills).

After he was assured that the faculty was genuinely concerned and was willing to alter the system so he could maximize his talents, he was successful in reestablishing his sense of equilibrium, as well as regaining his former reputation in this new environment. This situation required a reciprocal accommodation process, which was essential for achieving a successful outcome in this consultation. Mutual accommodation released him from his heightened anxiety and sense of failure, allowing the restructuring of his perceptions and a reconnecting with significant others, faculty, peers, as well as his own ethnic group members.

As a result of this consultation, the subject was able to share more freely the difficulties encountered in a foreign country and in mastering a second language. He realized that his competency in formal cultural settings was not readily transferable to his present cultural context and required adjustment on his part and on the part of those assisting him.

In another case, an 18-year-old Asian male attending a large midwestern university was seen at the counseling center at the request of his academic adviser due to a sudden change in his overall academic performance from first to second quarter. He was the oldest of three children, born and raised in a small community in Ohio, where his father worked as an engineer and his mother stayed home to attend to the children. Both parents were first-generation Japanese. The parents had always held high expectations for their oldest son and consequently transmitted these values to him. Ever since he was a little boy, his parents had determined that he would go to college and become a physician, scientist, or engineer—jobs that they held in high regard.

Throughout his early schooling, he was a model student, being constantly praised by his teachers. He displayed stereotypic qualities of being hardworking and obedient, never causing problems for his teachers. Going to a predominantly white school, he quickly used his athletic abilities to find acceptance among his peers and to offset any racial discrimination.

He exhibited a great deal of anxiety at the initial counseling contact. A look of surprise was evident when he discovered that the counselor was also Asian. He found it difficult to talk about himself in a personal way. It became quickly apparent that he felt a great deal of shame about having to come to a therapist, and particularly uncomfortable about being seen by an Asian counselor.

Without directly confronting him about his feelings, the counselor recognized his stage as being transitional and initiated action for him to be seen by a white male counselor. When told of the plan for him to see another counselor for follow-up sessions, he asked how many counselors at the center were Asian. When told that only one was, he appeared relieved.

Further exploration by the second counselor revealed significant sources of conflict. First, he felt his declining grades meant he was letting his parents down. Second, he had always been interested in art and music, but felt these areas to be unacceptable professions to his parents. Third, pressure to graduate as soon as possible to minimize financial drain on the family was constantly emphasized. Fourth, for the first time he had experienced rejection solely based on his ethnicity, when he was turned down by several fraternities, and by several white coeds who would not date him because he was Asian. His resentment and shock at being treated differently and the perceived restrictions about his career choice were originally denied and repressed. When he was able clearly to see his anger and hostility toward his parents, much of his physical complaint of frequent headaches vanished. The recognition of having to deal with issues related to his identity and to the impact of racism initially made him extremely depressed and ashamed. After some initial working through the process of supporting him emotionally and providing a safe environment to present a cognitive map of what was occurring with him, he was able slowly to work out of his depression and guilt. The Asian counselor was gradually reintroduced into the therapeutic process to further bridge the internal split that had formed to create the blind spots. Concurrently, his grades improved as progress was made.

As illustrated in these two cases, the therapist must not only have some sense of understanding and knowledge of the different cultural patterns and perceptions held by Asian male clients, but also must be clear as to differences that exist between traditional Western counseling models and the value/belief orientation system underlying an Asian's model for interpersonal relations and his mode of problem solving. Only then can effective counseling transpire.

References

Chen, C. L. (1981). An Asian-American approach to confronting racism. *East/West: The Chinese-American Journal, 15*(27).

Chien, C., & Yamamoto, J. (1982). Asian-American and Pacific islander patients. In F. X. Acosta, J. Yamamoto, & L. A. Evans (Eds.), *Effective psychotherapy for low-income minority patients.* New York: Plenum.

Gardner, R. W., Robey, B., & Smith, P. C. (1985). *Asian Americans: Growth, change, and diversity,* (Population Bulletin, Vol. 40, No. 4), Washington, DC: Population Reference Bureau.

Kitano, H.H.L. (1973). Passive discrimination: The normal person. In S. Sue & N. W. Wagner (Eds.), *Asian Americans: Psychological Perspectives.* Palo Alto, CA: Science and Behavior Books.

Kleinman, A. M., Eisenberg, C., & Good, B. (1978). Culture illness and care: Clinical lessons from anthropological and cross-cultural research. *Annals of Internal Medicine, 88,* 251-258.

Lee, D. B. (1984). *An epidemiological appraisal of Asian-American students, staff and faculty,* (Research Monograph). Columbus: Ohio State University.

Pedersen, P. (1977). The triad model of cross-cultural counselor training. *Personnel and Guidance Journal, 56,* 94-100.

Pedersen, P. (1978). Four dimensions of cross-cultural skill in counselor training. *Personnel and Guidance Journal, 56,* 480-484.

Pedersen, P. (1981). Asian personality theory. In P. Pedersen, W. J. Lanner, J. G. Drauguns, & J. E. Trimple (Eds.), *Counseling across culture* (pp. 537-582). Honolulu: University of Hawaii.

Root, M. P. (1985). Guidelines for facilitating therapy with Asian-American clients. *Psychotherapy, 22*(2), 349-356.

Sue, D. W. (1981). *Counseling the culturally different: Theory and practice.* New York: John Wiley.

Sue, D. W., & Kirk, B. A. (1972). Differential characteristics of Japanese-American and Chinese-American college students. *Journal of Counseling Psychology, 20,* 142-148.

Sue, D. W., & Kirk, B. A. (1972). Psychological characteristics of Chinese-American college students. *Journal of Counseling Psychology, 6,* 491-498.

Sue, S. (1976). Conceptions of mental illness among Asian and Caucasian-American students. *Psychological Report, 38,* 703-708.

Sue, S., & McKinney, M. (1975). Asian-Americans in the community mental health system. *American Journal of Orthopsychiatry, 45,* 111-118.

Sue, S., & Sue, D. W. (1971). Chinese American personality and mental health. *Amerasia Journal, 1*(2), 36-49.

Sue, S., & Wagner, N. (Eds.). (1973). *Asian-Americans: Psychological perspectives.* Palo Alto, CA: Science and Behavior Books.

Watanobe, C. (1973). Self-expression and the Asian-American experience. *Personnel and Guidance Journal, 51,* 390-396.

13

Counseling Black Men

Craig S. Washington

A Cultural Perspective

Men are leaders. Men are smart. Men are powerful. Men are breadwinners. Men are masters of their fate. Men are privileged. These are common assumptions that describe many white male Americans.

What are the characteristics of black men? Black men are dumb. Black men are lazy and shiftless. Black men lack a business sense. Black men are less motivated and often unemployed. Black men are docile and subservient. The black man's status in America is not envied!

An understanding of the black man's historical presence and his continued disenfranchisement in America is a prerequisite to understanding some of the unique issues the black man faces. Counseling black men requires a special sensitivity and knowledge of the black man's status since he is politically, socially, and economically thwarted from fulfilling his masculine role expectations.

Counseling men is a challenge. The ante is greatly raised however, when counseling black men. There are more walls, blocks, and barriers evident. He struggles not only with the cultural scripts that define manhood but with a true double-edged sword of gender-role constraints plus racism. The latter, racism, being more formidable than the first.

The barriers to the black man's successful interaction and self-fulfillment are intertwined with other's learned racist perceptions and male role expectations that foster myths of assumed deficiencies and stereotypes about black men. These myths and misconceptions about the black man continue to abound with little hope for change. The "male privilege," which assumes certain "rights" of passage for men, at the expense of women, is largely negated for black men. The black man encounters a hostile and oppressive society built on institutionalized racism, which works to maintain his low status and threatens his very existence. The black man is a victim. He, unlike his white male counterpart, has few masculine privileges. He too, like women in America, is oppressed.

This chapter on counseling black men focuses on some of the varied environmental stresses that hinder black men in their struggle to exhibit a positive masculine image and in their determination to realize a positive quality of life. I view the counselor as an agent of social change. The counselor's task includes a review of the client's dilemma with a sociological perspective and a systems understanding of the black man's situation. Systemic counseling (Gunnings & Lipscomb, 1986) is a theory of counseling that emphasizes changing dominant systems in order to meet the psychological and survival needs of black people. Both the sociological and systems approaches to assisting black men in counseling are used in this chapter.

The Stress Connection

Stress, defined as any interference that disturbs the functioning that is natural for the organism to avoid (Howard, 1960), is at such chronic unacceptable levels as to cause a sense of helplessness in the black male. The social and environmental conditions are so hostile that at least one writer questioned whether the black man was an endangered species (Leavy, 1983). Leavy outlined a list of societal conditions that are rapidly removing large numbers of black men from the civilian population. These conditions included homicide, enlistment in the military, imprisonment, suicide, unemployment, inadequate health care, drugs and alcoholism, and infant mortality. At present, accidents and homicide are the leading cause of death, with suicide being the number three cause of death. According to the FBI, the overall homicide rate for black males is 60 per 100,000, a rate higher than that of white males, white females, and black females combined (Leavy, 1983). Enlistment differences during the Vietnam War resulted in a disporportionately higher number of blacks than whites killed; and in state prisons around the country, black men represent 170,453 of the 345,960 total imprisoned (Leavy, 1983). These are indeed very stressful indicators of an oppressed group. Clearly, the American political system has generated and sustained a culture of power and privilege for Anglos and a culture of powerlessness and dependency for black Americans (Cook, 1977).

The social conditions discussed create a host of psychological, sociocultural, and economic stressors that interfere with the black man's ability to function in a natural way. These inhuman conditions of unemployment, limited educational access, high crime, high incarceration, high suicide, and high drug abuse steal the black man's ability to fulfill America's image of a man. These inhuman conditions lead to negative psychosocial behaviors. Some examples of the effects of these unacceptable chronic levels of stress are:

- Psychological stressors that occur on intrapsychic, interpsychic, and inter-personal levels and are often experienced as alienation, powerlessness, helplessness, inadequacy, lack of self-esteem, cultural estrangement, and social isolation.
- Sociocultural expectations can often induce anxiety, guilt, conflict, suppressed aggression, and sexual tension, to the degree that the culture operates to bring about acute needs for adjustment to cultural norms.
- Economic stressors such as unemployment, underemployment, job losses, health catastrophes, loss of personal property, and gross indebtedness also exert an unacceptable level of chronic stress.

The observation that stressful situations are more frequent and more severe for blacks than for their white counterparts seems obvious. Such conditions as poverty, joblessness, and broken families are undoubtedly among the major factors contributing to high levels of stress, and are highly correlated with a range of physical, emotional, and behavioral problems among blacks, both male and female (Taylor, 1981).

The black man's passage to manhood is also filled with problems. Black males typically may create their own stylistic walk or "pimp"; the black male may exhibit sexual prowess, athletic skill, streetwise behavior, break-dancing skill, or their verbal facility by "playing the dozens" or "rapping." These masculine behaviors, which often establish one's self-esteem and confidence, are most often in conflict with white society's cultural expectations of the "normal" way for men to demonstrate their masculinity. White men can and are supported in establishing their masculine rite of achieving in education, sports, science, or joining their fathers in their businesses, or with their father's help, establishing their own businesses.

White men also have access to financial institutions, social clubs, and top organizational power positions. While white men assume the often burdensome role expectations of an Anglo culture, white men can choose to follow these male norms of behavior or to cast them off with minimal concern. In contrast, black men are not supported in establishing masculine strength through education, science, engineering, or establishing their own business. Economic racist practices limit access to financial dollars; limit the establishment of a black financial economic base, and limit access to organizational power positions. In sum, stress is more than just the black man's imagination, it is the black man's reality; his back is "up against a wall" in America.

Therapeutic Issues

Counseling is a change process. Yet there is little expectation that black men will be assisted in a process of change since change must occur on a systemic level rather than an intrapsychic one. Black men are blamed individually for their station in life rather than being seen as victims of institutionalized oppression. "Color-blind" behavior on the part of non-black Americans maintains the power structure and the control with whites. The dynamics of this superior and inferior position have existed for decades in white people's relationship with Indians, Mexicans, Asians, and blacks (Katz, 1978), and it continues to dominate the counseling process today. In this dominant-subordinate relationship, subtle and not so subtle counselor expectations lend favor to the client to assimilate or adjust to the counselor's cultural perspective, or risk being seen as maladjusted, antisocial, or deficient in character. In my opinion, counseling has thus far failed as an avenue of psychic support for black men.

STEREOTYPING

Counselors must be aware of their clients' culture and history to function only adequately in a helping role. Every counselor interaction is a cross-cultural interaction, and as such, counselors who fail to understand their clients' racial, ethnic, and cultural norms can cause psychological damage to their clients. Counselors who limit their awareness of cultural differences to their own are not competent to counsel within a culturally diverse population. Conscious and unconscious stereotypes hinder the counselor's ability to provide effective assistance. If a counselor supports the black male's wish to pursue a career in sports or singing, he or she must also encourage the investigation of fields such as math, science, and engineering. The counselor should direct the client in a systematic exploration of the pros and cons of a career in sports. A counselor's decision only to encourage involvement in sports, based on the client's interest, may reflect the counselor's stereotypes about what black men can reasonably accomplish, or it may reflect the counselor's lack of information and ability to direct the client in making constructive long-term life career choices. Since stereotypes often become the only knowledge base that many non-black counselors operate from, it becomes even more important that counselors recognize their values, prejudices, and racial biases prior to offering counseling assistance to minority clients. If the counseling process is to be successful with black males, counselors must get rid of or check their racial biases, stop their reliance on myths, and move from a subjective to a more objective and functional approach to counseling black men.

COUNSELOR-CLIENT SIMILARITY

One's race is a critical variable in the counseling process. Stereotypic beliefs, counselor encapsulation, and the specter of the black male sets up an almost impenetrable barrier. The counselor's lack of familiarity with the client's cultural background arouses many fears in the black client-counselor relationship. The importance of counselor preference has been related to variables such as counselor expertness, trustworthiness, and similarity. Generally, whether or not the non-black counselor can counsel the black male client hinges on both the client's overall perception of the counselor and the black client's level of racial awareness. The counselor can assume a credible status if characteristics of expertness and trustworthiness are present (Hovland, Janis, & Kelley, 1953). Clients often seek a counselor because they believe the counselor is an expert and possesses the necessary knowledge, skills, experience, training, and tools to help (Sue, 1981). Counselors will maintain credibility only if they can demonstrate proficiency and competence. Likewise, trustworthiness is earned by the counselor. A counselor who is perceived as trustworthy is likely to exert more influence over a client than one who is not (Sue, 1981).

Since counseling tends to be an interpersonal influence process, many black clients are attracted to and prefer counselors who hold similar beliefs, opinions, and world perspectives. Sue (1981) noted that interaction with people who are similar to us tend to be rewarding because it validates our convictions. Black clients seem to have indicated a preference for black counselors as the helpers of choice (Eiben, 1970; Harrison, 1978; Phillips, 1960; Wolkon, Moriwaki, & Williams, 1973). White clients demonstrate a preference, too, for white counselors (Carkhuff & Banks, 1970; Lehman, 1969; Tucker, 1969) which tends to reinforce and support that counselor-client similarity is an important factor in the selection of a counselor.

Men, regardless of race, tend not to seek outside emotional help from strangers. Black men follow this pattern, too, and tend to seek psychological assistance even less frequently than white men. When black men do seek help, they are more likely to choose a black man or a black woman to talk with when there is a choice. Black men also follow the cultural norm of seeking out sources of support in the community with religious leaders, family, close friends, or with the men down at the local barbershop. Most often, when black men are seen in therapy by non-blacks, it is because of referral by teachers, employers, courts, social service agencies, or for crisis-oriented situations, not personal growth. In these instances, a distrustful relationship is intensified and the black male client does not fully participate in the counseling session.

There are additional reasons why black men have not beaten a path to the non-black counselor's door. The black man's experience in working with and trusting non-black people has not been positive. Black men who are attuned to their long-suffering history of slavery, to America's continuing practice of racism, and to their continued oppression in American society are not likely to seek help actively from their oppressors. The non-black counselor, particularly the white counselor, is seen as the enemy. In fact, black men hold a genuine distrust of white people due to past and present injustices. These feelings of distrust have resulted from

- a lack of constructive experiences with white people;
- a lack of primary friendships with white people;
- a lack of understanding of and sensitivity to black people;
- continued employment and housing discrimination; and
- continued economic and political discrimination

The black man is also not likely to seek counseling from a non-black counselor because the goals of black clients are different from the goals of traditional counseling. Such counseling tends to focus on meeting the emotional and psychological needs of clients. The thrust of traditional counseling tends to be one that teaches coping skills and helps the client adjust appropriately to the social order. Black clients' needs are often different. Black clients seek more tangible, goal-oriented, and pragmatic rewards. Black clients are often very skilled at coping with life's hardships and have little desire to learn how better to cope with or adjust to institutionalized oppression. The counseling interaction that follows demonstrates this difference between the goals of counseling and the goals of many black clients.

Brian, age 35, lives with his family and four children. He comes to counseling out of despair and states, "I want you to help me get a job. I do not want my family to be trapped on welfare, and I do not want to do anything illegal to get money to support my family. I could move out and leave my family so that my wife could get aid for the children, but I do not want to do that. . . . Can you help me get a job?"

The counselor's response is likely to be something like:

"You are feeling depressed because you're not able to find a job and support your wife and kids. You want to find a job so your family won't be trapped on welfare and so that you can support them."

This response is probably a good emotional response, but it falls short of a functional response for the client. The counselor is trained to respond to the client's emotional need and to encourage the exploration of the client's feelings. This process falls short for many black clients because their level of need is not satisfied by emotional support or personal achievement.

Their level of need is often basic, with needs for food, shelter, clothing, and employment. The counselor needs to be active in initiating a specific plan to assist the client; or to take direct responsibility for helping the client obtain his goal. This action on the counselor's behalf is often difficult because the counselor is taught not to take responsibility for the client. Counselors tend to be better trained to assist the client in looking inward, for personal or intrapsychic deficiencies. Counselors are generally inadequately prepared to work with clients who have physiological or safety levels of need, or who must confront the sociopolitical barriers of racism. Black counselors are often perceived as more helpful to black clients because there is the identification of similar emotional and physical experiences with racism, and more of a willingness to confront this external barrier. In contrast, white counselors often play the "colorblind" role or even deny that racism exists as a barrier.

The non-black counselor is likely to be more successful in counseling with black men if the counselor

- possesses specific knowledge about black racial and cultural history and norms;
- is willing to explore the potential effect of institutionalized racist practices on client success;
- is astute about oppressive structures that thwart the black man's potential for success;
- is honest with self-disclosures, is goal oriented, and is able to establish credibility; and
- actively intervenes into oppressive systems; calls for changes in unjust policies; and acts on behalf of the client as an agent of social change.

The non-black counselor can also seek out other black professionals or community role models to establish a mentoring or consulting relationship as a check for the counselor who works with the black male client.

The non-black counselor who works with the black male client or any culturally different client must come to recognize the varied, unique stresses not faced by white men or women. The counselor must acknowledge external discriminatory barriers. Counselors are urged to take a proactive stance against discriminatory inequities.

SELF-DISCLOSURE
AND TRUST

And the message was, Be a man! And today, the message is, Be a man! And, men don't cry, and men control their emotions, lest they act and look like sissies! All men learn the cultural script of suppressing their emotions. The public display of emotions is incompatible to the masculine presentation of manly qualities. Disclosing one's feelings or investing emotional trust with another conflicts with masculinity. Sharing feelings and trusting are often seen as feminine traits. Counseling, then, a process with self-disclosure as an outcome indicator of positive mental health, may also be viewed as a feminine process. The counselor's attempt to encourage healthy rapport within a trusting relationship is clearly at odds with manhood training. These odds are heightened for black men. In order to survive, black men learn at an early age to limit emotional expression outside of the black community. Black mothers have reared their children to adapt to a segregated system in which they could physically survive. These children are taught to (a) express aggression indirectly, (b) read the thoughts of others while hiding their own, and (c) engage in ritualized accommodating—subordinating behaviors designed to create as few waves as possible (Willie, Kramer, & Brown, 1973). Self-disclosure also conflicts with the projection of masculine strength and power to one's peer group. These protective behaviors, though often seen as resistance by non-black counselors, are the black male's defensive skills for survival, even though these protective skills leave the black male without an outlet for the healthy expression of suppressed feelings.

Counselor Preparation

The opportunity for all people of color to receive effective mental health counseling depends on the profession's proactive commitment to establishing effective counselor training programs. Counselor preparation programs, however, continue to be part of the problem. The traditional training approach incorporates the biases of Western culture and excludes the life experiences, concerns, theories, and needs of people of color (Washington, 1976). If counselors are to be responsive to the diversity of clients in America, then undergraduate and graduate programs must be designed to include the unique cultural variants of racial-, ethnic-, and gender-specific groups.

Hope

Beyond family, church, community resources, and trusted friends, there are few sources of help available to the black man to reduce chronic levels of stress in his life. Counseling, to a great extent, has failed to meet the black male's mental health needs. Counseling has failed to reduce chronic levels of unemployment; failed to challenge racist institutionalized practices that drive black fathers away from their families; failed to give the black man a sense of personal control or a sense of security; and has failed to inspire hope. With so much frustration and despair, hope becomes an important factor for motivating black men to maintain their continued struggle for a better life. Because their hope has been reduced, large numbers of black men have fallen into the ranks of burnouts and emotional casualties (Gardner, 1985). Hope is a valued asset, which when coupled with socially, culturally, and politically aware counselors, can increase the black man's chance for becoming a valued and important contributor to American society.

Summary

The crisis of the black male is real. There are real political, social and economic issues that must be tackled by astute agents of social change. Counseling can become an effective support system for black men if counselors can learn to become effective cross-cultural helpers and proactive change agents.

Recommendations

Following is an outline that counselors are encouraged to follow for the promotion of mental health for black men.

(1) *Engage in self-examination*
- Become aware of their racial, ethnic, religious, and class factors and how they have an impact on clients.
- Become aware of their values and biases and how they affect the black male client.
- Review their counseling approach and goals as they relate to counseling black males.

(2) *Increase self-education*
- Seek education and training in cross-cultural counseling.
- Learn the cultural heritage and history of blacks.
- Study the impact of racism on the social, educational, economic, and political life of blacks.
- Learn and incorporate culturally relevant theories and sources of knowledge.

(3) *Learn the truth about racism*
- Recognize the institutional barriers of racism that block the achievement of blacks.
- Recognize subtle verbal and nonverbal racist behavior.
- Recognize that the "problem with blacks" is a problem with socioeconomic

and political injustice that is manifested in unemployment, underemployment, drug abuse, crime, poor housing, and inferior schools.
- Recognize that the black man's burden is not his skin color but the burden of systematic and institutionalized racism.

(4) *Be conscious of change agents and initiate institutional changes*

- Learn about racism, sexism, and culturally diverse people in counselor education programs.
- Promote the hiring of black counselors, administrators, scientists, engineers, and other role models.
- Work for the elimination of "tracking" policies in schools that exclude college access for blacks.

(5) *Initiate activities that affect black academic achievement*

- Establish success groups to increase support of academic achievement for black youth.
- Develop groups where black men can discuss issues of black masculinity, black history, black male/female relationships, black esteem, and black values.
- Promote black male leadership in school- and community-related activities.
- Provide relevant black literature in the counseling/work environment.
- Organize periodic workshops or parent involvement groups where blacks can discuss important topics such as depression, suicide, and drug abuse, which will provide a forum for defining the characteristics of a positive black manhood.
- Maintain a resource file for those black men who would prefer to talk with a black professional or need guidance from a black counselor.

References

Carkhuff, R. R., & Banks, G. (1970). Training as a preferred mode of facilitating relations between the races and generations. *Journal of Counseling Psychology, 31,* 412-418.

Cook, S. D. (1977). The black man and the American political system: Obligation, resistance, and hope. *Afro-American Issues, 5,* 228-243.

Eiben, R. E. (1970). *White counselees expressed preference for help in solving different types of problems.* Unpublished manuscript, Illinois University.

Gardner, W. E. (1985). Hope: a factor in actualizing the young adult black male. *Journal of Multicultural Counseling & Development, 13*(3).

Gunnings, T. S., & Lipscomb, W. D. (1986). Psychotherapy for black men: A systemic approach. *Journal of Multicultural Counseling and Development, 14,* 17-24.

Harrison, J. (1978). Warning: The male sex role may be dangerous to your health. *Journal of Social Issues, 34,* 65-86.

Hovland, C. I., Janis, I. L., & Kelley, H. H. (1953). *Communication and persuasion.* New Haven, CT: Yale University Press.

Howard, L. (1960). Psychosocial stress. *British Journal of Medical Psychology, 33,* 185-194.

Katz, J. (1978). *White awareness: Handbook for anti-racism training.* Norman: University of Oklahoma.

Leavy, W. (1983). Is the black male an endangered species? *Ebony, 38*(10), 40-46.

Lehman, L. C. (1969). *Influence of race and dialect of communication on attitude formation.* Unpublished doctoral dissertation, University of Denver.

Phillips, W. (1960). Counseling Negro pupils: An educational dilemma. *Journal of Negro Education, 29,* 504-507.

Sue, D. W. (1981). *Counseling the culturally different.* New York: John Wiley.

Taylor, R. L. (1981). Psychological modes of adaptation. In G. E. Lawrence (Ed.), *Black Men.* Newbury Park, CA: Sage.

Tucker, D. E. (1969). *The effect of counselor experience, ethnic and sex variables upon the development of an interpersonal relationship in counseling.* Unpublished doctoral dissertation, University of New Mexico.

Washington, C. S. (1976). *A method for developing self-esteem and authenticity in para-counselors and counselors.* Unpublished doctoral dissertation, University of Massachusetts.

Willie, C. V., Kramer, B. M., & Brown, B. S. (1973). *Racism and mental health.* Pittsburgh: University of Pittsburgh Press.

Wolkon, G. H., Moriwaki, S., & Williams, K. J. (1973). Race and social class as factors in the orientation toward therapy. *Journal of Counseling Psychology, 20,* 312-316.

14

Counseling
Hispanic Men

Luis F. Valdés
Augustine Barón, Jr.
Francisco Q. Ponce

When the term *Hispanic* is used, it may refer to any one of more than 20 nationalities that can be categorized as Spanish speaking or Latino. Obviously, the diversity among Hispanics is large, and national origin plays a key role in the socialization process. For the purpose of this chapter, we will concentrate on three primary Hispanic groups: Cubans, Mexican-Americans (Chicanos), and Puerto Ricans. Our clinical experience is based primarily on Hispanic college and graduate students. Thus some of the observations will be influenced by work in university settings.

This chapter will highlight major constructs and concepts that are most salient in counseling any Hispanic male regardless of specific nationality or social standing. Chief among these are the concepts of acculturation, ethnic identity development, and machismo. These will be discussed as a backdrop to the presentation of several individual and group therapy cases that illustrate the issues in action. The chapter will conclude with a discussion of specific differences across the three primary groups that are important in the counseling process.

Acculturation

In the social science literature, the attention placed on the construct of acculturation has dramatically increased in the last decade (Cuellar, Harris, & Jasso, 1980; Olmedo, 1979; Padilla, 1980). Implications for counseling and therapy have also been explored. It is becoming clear that the construct of acculturation has direct and significant implications for the provision of effective psychotherapy when working with the Hispanic male client.

In particular, it should be noted that acculturation in reference to the mainstream Anglo-American society has been identified as a moderator variable in a number of important processes. These processes include client dropout rate (Miranda, Andujo, Caballero, Guerrero, & Ramos, 1976), self-disclosure (Castro, 1977), willingness to seek professional help (Ruiz, Casas, & Padilla, 1979), success in psychotherapy (Miranda & Castro, 1977), problems with adjustment and psychopathology (Szapocznik, Scopetta, & Tillman, 1979; Torres-Matrullo, 1976), and preference for an ethnically similar counselor (Sanchez & Atkinson, 1983).

Given the significance of acculturation, it is important to assess and incorporate it into work with male Hispanics. Before expanding on the implications of acculturation for working with Hispanic males, a definition will be provided.

Acculturation is conceptualized as a multidimensional and multidirectional process whereby Hispanics absorb, learn, acquire, and integrate the overt and covert cultural characteristics of the host culture. In other words, acculturation as a process comprises the integration of affective, cognitive, and behavioral cultural traits of the predominant culture (Mendoza & Martinez, 1980).

The overt cultural characteristics of dress, language usage, eating habits, and entertainment are more easily incorporated into a new set of functional traits. The covert and more subtle traits pertaining to attitudes, values, beliefs, and affective reactions take longer to acquire. Also, acculturation occurs at a different rate and depth for each individual, depending on a variety of factors including acceptance by the host culture and the motivation of the new immigrant in becoming an accepted and active participant in the host society. Note that the integration of cognitive, behavioral, and affective components will vary for each individual.

The above description of acculturation may sound intricate; it is a complex process that demands such a description. When working with Hispanic males it may be quite informative to assess the extent and depth of acculturation, especially if the presenting problem involves issues of identity, values dissonance or clarification, conflict with generations, adjusting or making it in the dominant culture, and other related concerns.

This recommendation directly challenges previous depictions of the Hispanic people. For a number of decades in the social science literature, before the civil rights movements, a conceptual error was made in depicting all Hispanics as a homogeneous group. Regardless of such obvious differences as national origin, Spanish language variations, and specific cultural traditions, Hispanics were considered one and the same. That is, differences between the various Hispanics groups were not acknowledged, and variations within each Hispanic group were not even considered.

While the Spanish language may be a common characteristic for the various Hispanic groups, differences exist in terms of dress, foods, language variation, physical traits, values, rituals, religion, and beliefs. The same differences exist in the within-group variation found for each Hispanic group.

As an example of this diversity, differences exist in the labels used by the individuals with a common Mexican ancestry. The various terms that have been used include Spanish American, Hispanic, Latino, Spanish, Raza, Mexican-American, Mexican American (without hyphen), Chicano, and Tex-Mex. Many individuals who identify with the term of *Chicano* are offended when they are assumed to be Mexican-American and vice versa. In many parts of the country the term *Chicano* is not accepted by more traditional Mexican-Americans, while some Anglo-Americans may not have even heard of the term.

In establishing a therapeutic relationship, the therapist would be wise to refrain from labeling the Hispanic client with any of the above labels or any other self-identifying label applicable to the various Hispanic groups. A wise strategy to use would be to ask the Hispanic male client what label, if any, he uses to identify himself.

Via the process of acculturation a major step is taken in acknowledging differences among Hispanics on a number of clinically significant areas. In working with Hispanic males, we suggest that therapists assess the acculturation level of their male clients and incorporate this information into their therapeutic interventions. Specifically, it is important to assess the uniqueness of each Hispanic male along such dimensions as degree of cultural commitment and preference for Hispanic culture versus the Anglo-American culture, language usage, generational level, racial/ethnic group and attitudes toward their own Hispanic group. Most of these dimensions have been incorporated into quantitative measures of acculturation that can help account for the client's degree of acculturation.

Some of these acculturation measurement tools include a Measure of Acculturation for Chicano Adolescents (Olmeda, Martinez, & Martinez, 1978), the Behavioral Acculturation Scale (Szapocznik, Scoppeta, & Tillman, 1979), the inclusive Model of Acculturation (Mendoza & Martinez, 1981), the Bilingualism/Multiculturalism Experience Inventory (Ramirez, 1983), and the Acculturation Rating Scale for Mexican-Americans (Cuellar, Harris, & Jasso, 1980). These scales provide viable alternatives and diminish the guesswork in trying to understand (1) the intragroup diversity found among the various Hispanic groups, (2) the diversity found within each Hispanic group, and (3) the uniqueness of each Hispanic client.

With this information, not only could therapists come to terms with the individuality of the Hispanic client, but they could avoid stereotypes, assumptions, and presuppositions about Hispanic males. Also, this information is invaluable in working with issues pertaining to their bilingual bicultural existence, such as conflicts germane to generational differences and stress associated with adapting to the dominant culture.

Specifically, the client's uniqueness may be captured in terms of how he identifies himself, language familiarity and usage, parents' background, generational level, socioeconomic level, educational level, race and ethnicity of friends, degree of extended family, social functioning in two or more cultures, and degree of cultural commitment to each culture.

During the initial counseling sessions the therapist may formally assess the degree of acculturation by asking the client to complete one of the acculturation questionnaires. Informally, the therapist could simply ask the client questions that would generate the same information generated by the acculturation measurements.

Racial/Ethnic Identity Development

For Hispanic males, the process of coming to terms with their racial/ethnic minority identity is another central process with significant clinical implications. This process refers to the painstaking task Hispanics experience in understanding themselves and their specific Hispanic cultural background in the context of a culturally dominant and oppressive society.

Our personal struggles in embracing an identity and our clinical work with Hispanic males indicate that much diversity exists in terms of how Hispanics identify themselves. This diversity may be best conceptualized through a continuum, one end of which is rejection of Hispanic background and total immersion into the Anglo-American culture; at the other end is rejection of the Anglo-American culture and complete embracing of Hispanic culture.

A model developed by Atkinson, Morten, and Sue (1979) may help therapists understand this diversity along with inherent cognitive, behavioral, and affective changes. The model (see Figure 14.1) defines five stages of development that oppressed people may experience as they struggle to understand themselves in terms of their own minority culture, the dominant culture, and the oppressive relationship between the two cultures (Atkinson et al., 1979, p. 35).

The behaviors, cognitions, and affective reactions of Hispanic males may be a function of their degree of acculturation as well as their placement

Stages of Minority Development Model	Attitude toward self	Attitude toward others of same minority	Attitude toward others of different minority	Attitude toward dominant group
Stage 1 - Conformity	Self-Depreciating	Group-Depreciating	Discriminatory	Group-Appreciating
Stage 2 - Dissonance	Conflict between self-depreciating and appreciating	Conflict between group-depreciating and group-appreciating	Conflict between dominant held views of minority hierarchy and feelings of shared experience	Conflict between group-appreciating and group-depreciating
Stage 3 - Resistance and Immersion	Self-Appreciating	Group-Appreciating	Conflict between feelings of empathy for other minority experiences of culturocentrism	Group-Depreciating
Stage 4 - Introspection	Concern with basis of self-appreciation	Concern with nature of equivocal appreciation	Concern with ethnocentric basis for judging others	Concern with the basis of group depreciation
Stage 5 - Synergetic Articulation and awareness	Self-Appreciating	Group-Appreciating	Group-Appreciating	Selective Appreciation

Figure 14.1   Summary of Minority Identity Development Model

in the Minority Identity Development Model. An assessment of the Hispanic client's racial/ethnic minority identity stage may answer a number of clinically important questions such as the following: To what extent is the client accepting of and comfortable with his ethnicity? Is the client proud, ambivalent, or ashamed of his parents and his background? Is the client alienated from himself and his culture? How comfortable is the client with himself, members of his own cultural background, members of other minority groups, and members of the dominant group? Given a particular stage of identity development, what is the client's self-esteem and self-image?

As the reader may have deduced, each stage of minority identity development has implications for conducting counseling and therapy with

Hispanic males. Due to space limitations, the reader is referred to Atkinson et al. (1979) where the implications for each stage are discussed.

Differences Across Hispanic Groups

As mentioned in the introduction, nationality has a profound influence on the socialization process of human beings. Hispanic populations represent tremendous diversity in nationality since there are more than 20 countries that can be considered Hispanic. The three major Latino groups in this country are Cubans, Mexicans, and Puerto Ricans. Each group has its unique history, which has implications for counseling.

Cubans as a group reflect a distinct migratory history when compared to other Hispanic groups. Three phases of migration have been identified (Bernal, 1982). The first phase, from 1959-1965, had two waves. The first wave, from 1959 to 1961, was composed of persons from the upper and upper-middle classes who had hopes of returning when the political climate had improved. The second wave comprised people from the middle class and professional sector who could not accept the Castro revolution.

The second phase, beginning in 1965 and ending in 1973, included mostly middle- and lower middle-class Cubans such as small business owners and skilled laborers. These first two phases of immigrants were not characteristic of Cuba in general since they were largely white, older, and a majority were female.

The third and most recent phase is predominantly non-white, young (15-35 years of age), and male, and included poorly educated, antisocial elements of Cuban society, along with some political prisoners.

These waves of immigration suggest that it is vital for the counselor to ascertain the migratory history of a Cuban client. Class, racial, and political factors are closely linked to various migratory phases and these can provide a useful backdrop against which to assess a client's presenting concerns.

Puerto Ricans have less discernible movements through history; but a clear link between the island of Puerto Rico and the mainland exists since Puerto Ricans have U.S. citizenship and can thus travel freely (Garcia-Preto, 1982). Just as many Cubans are concerned with the political future of their country, Puerto Ricans often focus their political energies around the question of statehood versus independence for their island. Nationalism is thus a key ingredient in the lives of many Cubans and Puerto Ricans, though the degree will depend on acculturation and ethnic identity factors as outlined in previous sections.

Mexican-Americans (Chicanos) as a group appear to have minimal involvement with the political future of Mexico. This is perhaps due to the fact that Mexico has a history of being a relatively stable, democratic country, though its economic condition at present threatens to undermine that stability. Chicanos, too, have a long history of being woven into the fabric of American society since many of the southwestern states were originally Mexican territories and populated by Mexican settlers.

Because of this long history, it is probably fair to say that variations in acculturation are most numerous for Chicanos because several generations are represented across the history of this country. Cubans and Puerto Ricans have a shorter history of migration so that variation in acculturation is smaller in comparison to Chicanos. Nonetheless, family generational level and migratory status are key factors to assess early on in counseling for all three Hispanic groups.

A final important factor concerns variation in racial characteristics. Hispanics represent a mixture of several racial groupings. Some families trace their bloodlines directly back to Spain and consequently retain Caucasian features. Other families share multiple bloodlines comprising Native-American, African, and Caucasian races. The African influence is especially strong in Cuba and Puerto Rico.

Being a "visible" ethnic minority group member because of physical features often plays a critical role in the emotional life of Hispanics. The degree to which a Hispanic has experienced prejudice and discrimination is related to such "visibility" and this must be calculated into any counseling relationship.

Machismo

No other concept is more closely associated with Hispanic men than is *machismo*. Unfortunately, this term has become quite pejorative in its English usage, whereas in Spanish the word has many positive connotations. Non-Hispanic people have taken the term to mean the equivalent of male chauvinism, exaggerated "hyper-masculinity." As such, machismo embodies brutal, sexist behaviors. The use and meaning of this term among Spanish-speaking peoples is quite different. In a Hispanic context, machismo is closely aligned with the concept of chivalry. The definition of chivalrous behavior includes being gallant, courteous, generous, charitable, and courageous. When a Hispanic male is labeled as *un macho* (a macho man), he is seen as a knight in the best sense of that term.

As Ruiz (1981, pp. 191-192) states:

It [machismo] connotes physical strength, sexual attractiveness, virtue, and potency. In this sense, the label "macho" has many of the same connotations it has in English. . . . At a more subtle level of analysis, "real" masculinity among Hispanics involves dignity in personal conduct, respect for others, love for the family, and affection for children. When applied by non-Hispanics to Hispanic males, however, "macho" often is defined in terms of physical aggression, sexual promiscuity, dominance of women, and excessive use of alcohol. In reaction to this abuse, Hispanic women are assumed to be submissive, nurturant, and virtuous thereby maintaining the unity of the Hispanic family despite all the disruption from their fathers, husbands, and sons.

What has happened over the years is that English has usurped the word and reworked the definition, turning it into the functional equivalent of male chauvinism. The sociological and psychological impact of this has been to stereotype unfairly Hispanic men as being exaggeratedly masculine in their behavior. While there is no doubt that chauvinism and sexism occur among Hispanic men, we doubt that they exist to a greater degree than in other groups. Machismo has become an unhealthy characteristic attributed to Hispanic men due largely to linguistic dynamics rather than to reality itself. Taking a Spanish-language term and reworking the meaning in English has served to promote prejudice toward the male members of Latino societies.

Once again, there is no doubt that sexism and chauvinism exist among Hispanics, but these are not the same thing as machismo in the Latino context. Because machismo, as defined in Spanish, is a prized characteristic, some social scientists have asserted that Hispanics condone alcoholism and wife abuse. This shocking conclusion is arrived at because machismo is redefined by these writers as equivalent to chauvinism in English. This is a translational issue that has had serious sociopsychological consequences.

Machismo should not be used to denote sexism or chauvinism so that its positive definition might be asserted and enhanced. Furthermore, it is important to recognize from a counseling standpoint that the use of the word may unduly influence the counselor to expect chauvinistic behavior in Hispanic males. Assuming a highly sexist orientation on the part of Hispanic male clients is both hazardous and unfair until a full assessment is made.

Sexism and chauvinism, especially in their most abusive forms, are not condoned by Hispanic populations, though the level of tolerance for such may be problematic in some families. In summary, the word *machismo* should not be used when chauvinism or sexism is what is being denoted. And when entering a counseling relationship with a Hispanic male, presumptions about his sexism should not be made. Rather careful assessment is necessary since Hispanic men, like all men, have varying degrees of chauvinistic attitudes and behaviors.

Individual Counseling Case

In this section a brief description of an individual counseling case that highlights some key dynamics will be presented. An extensive analysis of a counseling group for Hispanic men will then be outlined illustrating unique group processes and issues. A brief commentary on Hispanic clients in culturally mixed groups is also included.

Shortly after one of the authors began his career as a psychotherapist, a Chicano first-year graduate student was referred to him for counseling regarding depression and anxiety. This was the first Chicano referred to the therapist, so excitement ran high in anticipation of finally being able to work with a fellow Hispanic. The student appeared to have many misgivings about being in graduate school; and though his anxieties seemed understandable, they were heightened by the fact that he did not feel *entitled* to be at a university. This feeling persisted despite his graduation from college with a bachelor's degree. He minimized this accomplishment by belittling the college that granted his degree. Thus he also belittled his efforts as well.

The key dynamic that emerged early on was the issue of *entitlement*. As a low-income Chicano, he had grown up believing that a blue-collar job was his lot in life and that to strive for anything higher was contrary to his upbringing. He was therefore very ill at ease in graduate school since the environment was "too high class" for his background as he saw it.

Feeling and believing that one is entitled to the various possibilities that life offers is a key concern for many minorities who have experienced oppression. Hispanic men who strive for achievement in various forms often must confront strong beliefs about the possibilities that are "legitimate" for them to pursue.

This counseling case illustrated in a very clear way early on how a person can become limited by perceptions, beliefs, and feelings about the options in life. The concept of entitlement is an important focus in many counseling situations and is particularly salient for ethnic minority group members and other oppressed peoples.

The case also illustrated a second key dynamic, which emerged after the fifth session. As that meeting was drawing to a close, the student indicated he had a major disclosure to make. With tears welling up in his eyes, he admitted that when he had heard he was being referred to a Chicano psychologist he thought the agency was discriminating against him by referring him to "second-class treatment." He could not conceive of such a thing as a Chicano psychologist. And if such a person existed, he (or she) could not be very competent!

All along the therapist had assumed that rapport and trust had been building, and clearly this profound disclosure indicated the client was trusting enough to risk it. Obviously, however, early on the client had serious misgivings that had not come to the therapist's attention.

This incident illustrates the need to be attentive to the prejudices that ethnic minorities incorporate about their own group members. Believing that a professional of your own group could not be competent is an excellent example of prejudice turned inward against one's fellow members. Such toxic effects of discrimination may slowly dissipate as more role models of successful, reputable Hispanics develop across all professional occupations.

The counselor, however, must be sensitive to the client's own ethnic identity development as discussed earlier in this chapter. Variations in ethnic pride and acceptance have serious consequences for counseling dynamics, as this case illustrates. With increasing pride and self-acceptance, issues of entitlement begin to be resolved. Also, negative beliefs about one's ethnic group are also transformed into positive assertions, which help the client gain greater self-efficacy.

Group Counseling

Group psychotherapy has been supported as an appropriate treatment modality for Hispanic individuals by a number of writers in the mental health field (Boulette, 1975; Padilla, Ruiz, & Alvarez, 1975). The rationale for referral to group psychotherapy as treatment of choice has been well documented (Rutan & Stone, 1984; Yalom, 1970). At this point in our discussion, we would like to focus on the particular issues likely to be encountered by group leaders in a group targeted for Hispanic men. The issues discussed here were encountered in a group that two of the authors led at a university counseling center. Care should be taken by the reader not to generalize unduly from this setting.

BEGINNING THE GROUP

It has been suggested that psycho-therapeutic treatment for Hispanic clients should be particularly focused on behavioral, goal-oriented, prescriptive, and structured activities and interventions (Herrera & Sanchez, 1980; Valdes, 1984). Early group activity revolves around the process of using the presenting problems that the individual group members bring to the group to identify and clarify realistic, specific, concrete, workable goals. This process allows group members to develop criteria to monitor their progress and ultimately to determine their readiness to end their involvement in the group.

Group members and leaders spend much time negotiating the group goals as well. Early sessions involve decisions about whether the group would be a "rap group," a political action group, a support group, or a psychotherapy/counseling group. The underlying issue seems to be that how the group was defined had some implications for each individual in the group. It can be quite difficult for a majority of the group members to verbally admit that they need help or "have a problem," though ostensibly their attendance is an obvious indicator that there is a concern. Defining the group as a rap group, political action group, or, to some extent, a support group seems to be less threatening to some of the group members.

Another issue that develops early is commitment to the group. Group members discuss sporadic attendance ("I won't be able to make it to the group all the time"; "Can we come and go as we please?"; "Do we have to be here every week?"), lateness, and how to deal with this issue with other group members. The group members tend to be extremely formal and polite with each other, hesitating to deal directly with each other or confront each other concerning their group behavior. This can continue to be a central theme throughout the duration of the group.

Perhaps the most striking issue that emerges in the initial stage of the group process involves the question, "Quien es el mas Mexicano?" or "Who is the most Mexican in the group?" Group members explore this question by focusing on such topics as each individual's level of fluency in the Spanish language, skin color or pigmentation, and the implications and origins of their given name, surname, and nicknames. These questions and subsequent answers seem to determine a certain hierarchy and dimensionality within the group with regard to just how Mexican each group member is. Group leaders can discuss the implications of this hierarchical structure and often it is revealed that it denotes some rank ordering of entitlement to be in the group.

Some other issues that emerge in the initial stage of the group process involve relationships outside the group: dating behavior with both Hispanic women and non-Hispanic women, friendships with other males, feelings of disappointment and inadequacy in relationships, and how each of those issues contributes to their presenting problem and how each of those issues is being played out in the group.

MIDDLE STAGE OF
THE GROUP PROCESS

As the group develops some cohesion and individuals begin to trust and learn skills in self-disclosure, the group process can begin to move in some quite healthy directions. The group often displays some of the typical characteristics that most psychotherapy groups have in common. In addition, however, groups of Hispanic males take on a very uniquely interesting flavor. The members struggle with what could be described as a lack of knowledge and sophistication of the counseling process: how to use the group and leaders for support, how to interact with others using a full range of intrapersonal skills, how to self-disclose, how to listen, how to confront and challenge each other. Though the group leaders meet each individual in the group during a pregroup interview, it becomes obvious during each session that group leaders should take much time before the group meets to educate each individual member about how to be good group members through a "role induction"-type intervention (Hoehn-Saric et al. 1964). This seems particularly important when dealing with a special population group that may not have much familiarity with the counseling process.

At this middle stage of the group process, it appears that the group begins to focus on external factors that they feel are impinging on their lives. The group often spends a significant time bad-mouthing the majority culture, scapegoating "gringos," expressing feelings of powerlessness within the system, and expressing at least indirectly some self-hatred. This self-hatred manifests itself in statements about an inability to identify with, relate to, or appreciate certain aspects of the Hispanic culture, a lack of pride or respect for their ethnic origins or background, and expressing embarrassment about one's family behavior or traditions.

TERMINATION

Several noteworthy developments occur during the final stage of the group process. In addition to the typical termination issues, such as summary of progress and assessment of the attainment of individual and group goals, future goals, and plan of action beyond therapy, the group members focus on the task of brainstorming ways of networking with other Hispanics in the college milieu, ideas for the next group, and ways to recruit new members. There is much planning about how to use other resources, particularly other counseling resources such as individual therapy, coed psychotherapy groups, specific skill or theme groups, and other support groups. Finally, the group members express feelings of sadness, fear, and disappointment about the termination of the group. Saying goodbye is difficult, particularly for members who had reported a lack of significant, meaningful familial or peer relationships in the past. The group members also often make arrangements to meet in various subgroups and dyads to follow up and support their growth and progress in the group.

Hispanic Men in Heterogeneous Psychotherapy Groups

Hispanic men involved in ethnically heterogeneous psychotherapy groups display some unique characteristics during the course of therapy. In addition to the ambivalent feelings about being in therapy, the difficulty experienced during attempts to self-disclose, and the limited awareness of emotions and feelings that a majority of men in groups exhibit, the Hispanic male often finds himself feeling alienated from the group and having difficulty trusting the other members and the group leaders. Talking about these feelings can often be threatening, especially if the Hispanic male has had little or no previous experience in a group of predominantly non-Hispanic individuals.

Another issue that comes to the forefront of awareness for Hispanic males is the initial denial or ignorance of minority/ethnic membership as a relevant factor in the dynamics of the group. Inevitably, the group members begin to realize that for many individual reasons the group has been and is being affected by the presence of a minority group member and that many of the interactions and disclosures that have taken place have been altered by the internal dialogue and particular stereotypes that each of the group members has carried into the group. Discussion about internal dialogue and preconceived notions, by both the non-Hispanic and Hispanic group members, can be fruitful material to use in the group therapy process. Often, all the group members' feelings of alienation, highlighted by ethnic minority group members, become clear for all group members, allowing feelings of closeness and trust to emerge. There is often a decrease of emotional distance and an increase in cohesion when real feelings about race, culture, and ethnicity are disclosed.

Summary

The concepts presented at the beginning of the chapter—acculturation, ethnic identity development, machismo, and nationality—are central to the assessment and counseling of Hispanic men as well as ethnic minorities in general. These concepts are enormous in scope yet they profoundly affect the being of each client.

Counselors working with Hispanic clients are challenged to be knowledgeable about the diversity of Latino cultures. No counselor, however adept, can have a mastery of such knowledge. What is required is an openness to continual learning and exploring. In this regard, it might well be said that culturally sensitive counseling is not so much a set of specialized knowledge and skills as it is a combination of awareness and attitude.

References

Atkinson, D. R., Morten, G., & Sue, D. W. (1979). *Counseling American minorities: A cross-cultural perspective*. Dubuque, IA: W. C. Brown.

Bernal, G. (1982). Cuban families. In M. McGoldrick, J. Pearce, & J. Giordano (Eds.), *Ethnicity and family therapy* (pp. 187-207). New York: Guilford.

Boullette, T. R. (1975). Group therapy with low-income Mexican-Americans. *Social Work, 20,* 403-405.

Castro, F. G. (1977). *Level of acculturation and related considerations in psychotherapy with Spanish speaking/surnamed clients* (Occasional Paper No. 3). Spanish Speaking Mental Health Research Center, University of California, Los Angeles.

Cuellar, I., Harris, L. C., & Jasso, R. (1980). An acculturation rating scale for Mexican-American normal and clinical populations. *Hispanic Journal of Behavioral Sciences, 2,* 199-217.

Garcia-Preto, N. (1982). Puerto Rican families. In M. McGoldrick, J. Pearce, & J. Giordano (Eds.), *Ethnicity and family therapy* (pp. 164-186). New York: Guilford.

Herrera, A. E., & Sanchez, V. C. (1980). Prescriptive group psychotherapy: A successful application in the treatment of low income Spanish-speaking clients. *Psychotherapy: Theory, Research, and Practice, 17,* 167-174.

Hoehn-Saric, R., Frank, J. D., Imber, S. C., Nash, E. H., Stone, A. R., & Battle, C. C. (1964). Systematic preparation of patients for psychotherapy: 1. Effects of therapy behavior and outcome. *Journal of Psychiatric Research, 2,* 267-281.

Mendoza, R. H., & Martinez, J. L. (1981). The measurement of acculturation. In A. Baron, Jr., (Ed.), *Explorations in Chicano psychology.* New York: Holt.

Miranda, M. R., Andujo, E., Caballero, I. L., Guerrero, C., & Ramos, R. A. (1976). Mexican American dropouts in psychotherapy as related to level of acculturation. In M. R. Miranda (Ed.), *Psychotherapy with the Spanish-speaking: Issues in research and service delivery.* Spanish Speaking Mental Health Research Center, University of California, Los Angeles.

Miranda, M. R., & Castro, F. G. (1977). Culture distance and success in psychotherapy with Spanish-speaking clients. In J. L. Martinez (Ed.), *Chicano psychology* (pp. 249-262). New York: Academic Press.

Olmedo, E. L. (1979). Acculturation: A psychometric perspective. *American Psychologist, 34,* 1061-1070.

Olmedo, E. L., Martinez, J. L., & Martinez, S. R. (1978). Measure of acculturation for Chicano adolescents. *Psychological Reports, 42,* 159-170.

Padilla, A. M. (Ed.). (1980). *Acculturation: Theory, models, and some new findings.* Boulder, CO: Westview.

Padilla, A. M., Ruiz, R. A., & Alvarez, R. (1975). Community mental health services for a Spanish-speaking surnamed population. *American Psychologist, 30,* 892-905.

Ramirez, M. (1983). *Psychology of the Americans: Multicultural perspectives in personality and mental health.* New York: Pergamon.

Ruiz, R. A. (1981). Cultural and historical perspective in counseling Hispanics. In D. W. Sue (Ed.), *Counseling the culturally different: Theory and practice* (pp. 186-214). New York: John Wiley.

Ruiz, R. A., Casas, J. M., & Padilla, A. M. (1977). *Culturally relevant behavioristic counseling.* Spanish Speaking Mental Health Research Center. University of California, Los Angeles.

Rutan, J. S., & Stone, W. N. (1984). *Psychodynamic group psychotherapy.* New York: Macmillan.

Sanchez, A. R., & Atkinson, D. R. (1983). Mexican-American cultural commitment preference for counselor ethnicity, and willingness to use counseling. *Journal of Counseling Psychology, 30,* 215-220.

Sue, D. (Ed.). (1981). *Counseling the culturally different: Theory and practice.* New York: John Wiley.

Szapocznik, J., Scopetta, M. A., & Tillman, W. (1979). What changes, what stays the same and what affects acculturative change? In Szapocznik & M. C. Herrera (Eds.), *Cuban*

Americans: Acculturation adjustment and the family. Washington, DC: COSSMHO.

Torres-Matrullo, C. M. (1976). Acculturation and psychopathology among Puerto Rican women in mainland United States. *Journal of Orthopsychiatry, 46,* 710-719.

Valdes, L. F. (1984). The effects of two types of psychotherapy on the self-disclosure and attitude toward seeking professional help of Mexican-Americans (Doctoral dissertation, Texas Tech University, 1984). *Dissertation Abstracts International, 45,* 1927-B.

Yalom, I. D. (1970). *The theory and practice of group psychotherapy.* New York: Basic Books.

IV

Special Populations

This section has been titled "Special Populations." Perhaps a more accurate title would be "Forgotten Men." In this section the authors attempt to deal with men who exist in, or are a part of, some special set of circumstances that produces a major impact on their lives. The most apparent of these "forgotten" men are veterans and those incarcerated. Other men are also taken for granted: gay men, substance-abusing men, violent men, physically challenged men, men in dual-career relationships, men who are bisexual. The writers in this section attempt to deal not only with recently emerging (and not so recent) issues, but also with the men themselves—their uniqueness and the richness of that diversity. As you read this section, please be reminded of the premise that the men in these circumstances, and living these lifestyles, are not necessarily psychopathological. Rather, their diversity should be viewed as one component of their lives.

As this handbook goes to press, we are confronted with significant and powerful issues that have an impact on our society. A significant issue is AIDS (Acquired Immune Deficiency Syndrome) which affects *all* of our lives. As yet there is no cure, and its spread into the heterosexual community makes this disease much more than a "gay plague." The chapter by Fradkin describes some of the work that has been attempted with persons with AIDS (PWAs) and their loved ones.

A second issue deals with the counseling of gay and bisexual men. Fortunately, some research and writing on treating these men and their concerns already exists. As more and more men continue to emerge, "come out," and choose to live a gay affirmative lifestyle, the need increases for the training of counselors to work effectively with gay and bisexual men. The authors encourage training in this area for all counselors: male, female, gay, straight, bisexual. In spite of the hopes of many (as shown by recent Supreme Court rulings), homosexuality and bisexuality will not go away. Therefore, helping professionals must learn to work more effectively with our homosexual and bisexual brothers.

Another area of serious concern involves the counseling of men who are single fathers. As men continue to struggle to break free of the stereotypical roles of males, they are often confronted with the realities of legal issues (divorce proceedings, visitation, custody, "parental" versus maternity leave). These issues result in frustration, pain, and other strong emotions. As with any single parent, becoming a single father or one with joint custody requires adjustment in lifestyles; helping professionals *can* be effective in facilitating these changes.

Three chapters in this section focus exclusively on men and their intimate relationships with significant others. Barry Graff's chapter provides treatment methods on counseling men in couples, with an emphasis on a systems approach. Lucia Gilbert, in her chapter on men in dual-career relationships, narrows the relationship focus even further as she traces the historical, societal, and cultural components of this rapidly growing area of concern and treatment. Don Long presents an alternative treatment method for helping men who are violent toward women— challenging the premise that these men need to learn more control in their lives.

Finally, counseling men with their most "unmanly" stereotypes— physically challenged men and men in health-care settings—is given sensitive treatment by authors Maxwell, Carlton, Sutkin, and Good.

15

Counseling Gay Men

James Harrison

As recently as the early seventies the majority of mental health professionals would have understood their responsibility toward gay people as assisting them to change their sexual orientation. However, the increasing scientific understanding that has emerged in biology, anthropology, psychology, and sociology has given us a better grasp of human sexuality and has supplanted many of the cultural myths about homosexuals. The scientific data collected found a more receptive audience as Western culture grew more sensitive toward individual differences and the rights of minorities, so that mainstream thinking in the psychotherapeutic professions is now more in line with the facts of life as homosexuals experience it.

Gay men face distinctively different issues in their lives from those of gay women. However, before it is possible to consider these specifically men's issues, it is necessary to consider the misunderstanding, stereotyping, and stigmatization that is commonly experienced by all gay people—both men and women—in our culture. It is essential that counselors understand the oppression that all gay people have experienced. Otherwise, it will be difficult to understand the consequent suppression, repression, and other defense mechanisms that gay people have developed to permit psychological survival (Altman, 1971).

What We Know Scientifically About Homosexuality

Psychological research has consistently replicated Evelyn Hooker's pioneering study (1955), which demonstrated (1) that scientific methodology could be used to study homosexuals,

(2) that there is no essential difference between homosexual and hetero-sexual persons in the distribution of psychological health and pathology (or mental health and illness) (Siegelman, 1972), and (3) that there is no single profile of the gay person (Bell & Weinberg, 1978). Other research has converged to confirm that sexual orientation is established early in life (Money & Ehrhardt, 1972; Money, 1980, 1986; Storms, 1986) and is not readily subject to change.

Anthropologists have shown that homosexuality is prevalent in virtually every culture on earth, and is prescribed in many (Ford & Beach, 1951; Herdt, 1982). Research has documented the universality of homosexual activity in other species, thus undercutting the notion that homosexuality is somehow unnatural or a product of [fill in the blank with "the machine age," "capitalism," "communism," "changing family structure," or any other cultural bugaboo conjured up by demagogues in recent decades] (Paul et al., 1982). It is increasingly clear that our Euro-American culture has manifested a sex-phobic orientation that has denied honest information about sex to heterosexuals and homosexuals alike. This denial has resulted in serious stigma and loss of self-esteem for homosexual persons. Sociologists have demonstrated that individuals will fulfill societal expec-tations in conforming to negative stereotypes about the group in which they hold membership. The resulting self-hating or self-destructive attitudes of too many homosexual people in our culture should be viewed as a result of that role conformity (Levine, 1979).

While much remains to be known about homosexuality, sex researchers today generally recognize that our knowledge about homosexuality must go hand in hand with our knowledge about heterosexuality (Weeks, 1985). The larger issue is understanding sexual orientation and attraction in general. But overcoming our ancient prejudices against sex and the conspiracy of silence surrounding the subject is an ongoing process. Nevertheless, recognition of the developments chronicled above has helped gay people to reject views that stigmatize them as undesirable deviants and has helped them to identify themselves as a politically oppressed sexual minority (Marotta, 1981).

Homophobia as Negative Transference

A generation ago, most American children were taught that blacks were inferior to whites; in many Western cultures suspicion or antagonism toward Jews was taught. Similarly, we all grew up in a society that taught us that homosexuality was somehow (a) wrong or sinful, (b) criminal, or (c) pathological. As members of the medical or psychological professions, dedicated to helping and healing through a scientific understanding of the issues, therapists must be aware that they were also indoctrinated with negative assumptions about homosexuals. Some therapists who have rejected the grosser forms of prejudice nevertheless have a lingering belief that interpersonal love, sensual pleasure, and erotic expressions of intimacy that are unrelated to a biological procreative process are in some way inferior, and that couples of the same sex cannot experience the qualities of personal intimacy and physical pleasure that are possible for couples of different sex (Hancock, 1986).

Therapists unaware of the scientific developments indicated in the first part of this chapter, or those who are uncomfortable with the implications of those developments should be honest and disqualify themselves from therapy with gay patients. There are gay-affirmative therapists who are nonjudgmental about sexual orientation and who can treat gay people with unconditional positive regard. Treating gay clients without examining one's own prejudices is comparable to treating black people with the assumption that they are inferior to whites or assisting Jews to adjust to social prejudice and discrimination.

A good test of our readiness to treat gay clients is whether the questions we ask gay clients about sex and sexual relationships are comparable to those we ask heterosexual clients about their sexual activity, and whether we can ask them in a nonjudgmental and straightforward way that facilitates our clients talking about themselves. When the therapist is confident that homophobic, or heterosexist, values will not be imposed on gay patients, then he or she is prepared to counsel homosexuals. In sum, the essential precondition for therapists working with gay clients is an ongoing analysis of their own prejudices and negative transference; this is equally true of all therapists regardless of their sexual orientation.

As a mental health-care provider, one's responsibility is the reparation of injured and underdeveloped egos, the nurturing of self-esteem, and the creation of the conditions for insight and self-understanding. These processes are similar regardless of the sexual orientation of the client. Since many gay clients themselves believe that they are intrinsically inferior because they believe the cultural myths that have been promulgated about them, the first step for the therapist is the examination of his or her own homophobic attitudes and negative countertransference. There can be no ego reparation in the presence of judgmental and condemnatory attitudes.

Helping Clients Deal with Internalized Homophobia

We must also be aware that every homosexual person also learned the same negative notions about homosexuality as we did. Since sexuality is a core dimension of personality, self-hatred directed toward one's sexuality is certain to have consequences in other aspects of our personalities (Malyon, 1982). Perhaps a clinical example will be helpful.

Morris is a 46-year-old Jewish homosexual man, well spoken and well educated at a prestigious university. His speech is polished and refined—certainly WASP, almost British, but not artificial or pretentious. His clothes suggest law or banking—but they do not fit because he is about 40 pounds overweight. He was referred for counseling because he had developed a cardiac arrythmia that is probably attributable to self-prescribed diet, medications, and a sedentary life. His physician believed that he needed psychotherapy to develop a better sense of himself as a condition for finding a healthful means for weight reduction. He is secretive about his homosexuality, which he shares by innuendo only among a small circle of friends—as though they were all admitting something shameful. He works for Catholic charities but does not earn enough to provide a decent life for himself and a widowed, dependent mother. He contributes almost all his time to Russian Orthodox charities because he derives compensatory self-regard from hobnobbing with the Russian "royalty." He has developed an unrequited love for a young gay businessman. He is almost completely ignorant of the gay world and won't go to gay political and social events for fear people will know he's gay. His sexual expression is almost solely with anonymous partners at public baths. He is desperately lonely, unable to provide for himself in a way he was accustomed to as a young man dependent on his once successful father, and he compensates for his unhappiness by eating constantly. He is so anxious in his therapy that he jumps from topic to topic, never discussing any issue fully, and is incapable of permitting the therapist to complete a sentence for fear that his own faltering construction of reality will be challenged. He fled from therapy after six months, returning after several more to report that he had in fact begun to realize that his therapist's comments about his lifestyle were not demeaning but rather that his social strategies were self-destructive. It has taken nearly a year for him to begin to examine his own internalized homophobia and the way he has shaped his life in almost total denial of who he is—not only sexually but even in his cultural identity. Once therapists would have attributed all his problems to his homosexuality rather than to his difficulty in accepting himself as gay and his fear of self-disclosure in a homophobic society.

The Importance of Information

Therapy cannot be a replacement for the rest of a person's world and the rest of a person's life. Humans need companionship. It is almost impossible to be a healthy human without belonging to a community. In most of our society, gay people cannot openly be themselves and be accepted. When it is not possible for gay people to be fully integrated into the institutions of our society, then it is valuable for them to become participants in gay organizations. In too many communities the only gay institutions are the bars.

How can the therapist help? Usually therapists do not provide information to their clients because it is assumed that information necessary for human well-being is available on TV, from newspapers, at church, at the tennis club, from billboards, and from casual conversations at work. In working with gay clients it may be necessary for the therapist to make an adjustment to traditional parameters. Even therapists whose mode of therapy is analytic or nondirective and who do not ordinarily provide information or advice to their clients, are nevertheless familiar with the communities in which they live, the health care and religious institutions available to them, the social and political networks through which people conduct their everyday lives. Because heterosexual therapists experience with heterosexual clients a shared world, they are able to understand and evaluate the degree of social adjustment clients have achieved. When therapists are not familiar with the social resources of the gay community they are hampered in evaluating, understanding, and adequately assisting gay clients. If gay people are not familiar with these resources, then it is difficult for them to achieve a fully healthy life.

How many therapists are aware that there is an organization called the Institute for the Protection of Lesbian and Gay Youth (IPLGY)? That there is another organization called SAGE, Senior Action in a Gay Environment? Do the names *GCN, RFD, Advocate,* or *Body Politic* mean anything? They are but four of the many newspapers and magazines that serve the gay community, each with its own ideology and editorial policies. What about HRCS, LLD, GRA, or NGLTF? They are civil rights and political organizations for gay and lesbian people. What about Dignity, Integrity, Affirmation, or the Metropolitan Community Churches? They are a few of the religious institutions that serve the gay community.

These institutions and organizations exist because the mainstream organizations actively and openly discriminate against gay people. Until very recently the major newspapers and TV networks consistently reported false information about gay people, or only the lurid and sensational stories that sustained prejudice and bigotry. Even now *The New York Times* will not print the word *gay* unless it is in quotes, whether out of ignorance or bad faith it is difficult to know.[1] Consequently, most New Yorkers do not know that there is a gay news program on cable TV; the regional press can be better or worse. For example, *The Charlotte Observer* took an early creative lead in AIDS reporting and does list the local gay cable video show.

It is essential that gay people be permitted to know about available resources. Therapists need to understand that many closeted gays, unsure of themselves, do not know where to buy a magazine and would be fearful to ask for it even if it were available at a local news outlet. The therapist who is prepared to help gay people may need to provide general information, addresses or other resources, and assure their clients that publishers send these materials in plain, sealed envelopes.

Until it is possible for gay people openly to be members and leaders of social, political, and religious institutions it is necessary that there be alternative organizations within which gay people can fulfill their communal needs and express their social responsibilities. In supporting the fullest development of gay clients it is important that the therapist be prepared to provide information and be an active supporter as well.

Special Concerns of Men

In addition to the issues that must be understood to counsel gay people in general, both men and women, there are issues that have a different impact on men. The remainder of this chapter will focus on those issues of being gay that are distinctive for men.

These issues have to do with the relationship between sexual orientation and sex roles, sex-role expectations and sex-role stereotypes. In fact, sexual orientation is often confused with sexual status and sex roles. In sum, the problems that gay men face are almost always related to the incorrect assumption that they are in some way not quite fully men. These issues can be discussed in a general developmental framework.

PREADOLESCENCE

In retrospective studies many gay people report atypical gender behavior in childhood (Bell & Weinberg, 1978). This behavior is not likely to be of concern to the boy unless it results in stigma and consequent abuse by other children. A boy may be brought to a counselor by concerned parents. In such situations it is not possible for the counselor to know if this boy will grow up to be transsexual, heterosexual, or homosexual. Assessment and treatment must go hand in hand. It is essential that the counselor help the parents manage their anxiety and their relationship to the boy, while helping the boy through play or talk therapy to understand and accept himself, while developing coping strategies to protect himself from persons who cannot tolerate difference.

ADOLESCENCE

Enhanced sexual drive and developed cognitive abilities will enable the teenaged boy to become qualitatively aware of his sexual orientation. Depending on his social location, the boy may think, "I am the only person in the world like this," or he may be aware that he is like other "men who love men" if there are visible role models available for him. Depending on the sexual ethos of his family, community, and religious upbringing he may suppress his sexual desires or engage in same-sex play from a very early age. Depending on the tolerance he experiences in the world around him he may "hide his stigma" or alternatively find ways of expressing himself in the social world.

Young people who are becoming aware of their homosexual orientation may mistakenly assume that they must inevitably emulate the only examples available to them. Alternatively, many adult gay people report that they had difficulty understanding that they were gay even though they knew they did not conform to the stereotypes, as they were aware that their erotic responses were limited to people of their own sex (Morin & Garfinkle, 1978; de Monteflores & Schultz, 1978).

Some boys are brought to a counselor because they have been "caught" or entrapped in sexual activity. Other boys may be confused about managing their sexuality and take the initiative in seeking counsel. An ethical counselor will not become the agent of repression, but rather will help the boy understand himself and responsibly manage his sexuality. A good rule is not to say anything to a boy who believes himself to be gay that one would not similarly say to a heterosexual boy. For example, a counselor would not ordinarily say, "How do you know that you are heterosexual?" Such a question is an implicit criticism of the emerging identity of the adolescent and as such can be an assault on his self-esteem. Rather, the counselor will want to help the client understand his fantasies and desires, and find socially and age appropriate ways of expressing them interpersonally.

COMING OUT

The notion of coming out is dependent on a social world in which homosexuality is stigmatized. Otherwise, adolescents would simply pair off in social activities as they wish and there would be no occasion for comment. The assumption that everyone is heterosexual is protective for the young gay person though it stifles self-expression and the emergence of identity. Giving up the security of anonymity is fraught with anxiety. Every gay man, whatever his age, must decide when to stop asking permission to be himself and to go public about his sexual orientation. "Effeminate" boys often have little choice and may be labeled as gay at a very young age. Some boys are mislabeled, and may consequently mislabel themselves as gay, only realizing at a later time that their erotic desires are largely heterosexual, thus contributing to the perpetuation of the myth that people can voluntarily change their sexual orientation. Most gay men—in spite of possible atypical gender interests—

are not effeminate. Many men do not come out until they have followed the unfortunate advice, "Marry the right woman and . . . " Such counsel displays an enormous disregard for the interests of women who are presumed to have no other role in life than to assist men in finding their "heterosexuality." In addition, it is a prescription for subsequent divorce. The failure of many gay men to understand and affirm their sexuality early in adulthood has resulted in the possibility that the largest single subgroup of gay men are married. Instead, the counselor needs to help each man who presents himself for assistance in understanding his own needs, inner strengths, social resources, and means to develop an affirmative lifestyle. Some people will conclude that it is impossible for them to be public about their sexual orientation. It must be understood that this inevitably involves a sacrifice, as it is not possible to be a fully developed person while suppressing such a central aspect of one's selfhood as sexual orientation (Coleman, 1981).

Coming out involves facing the emotions of guilt and shame. All healthy people want to be "good." Yet our gay clients have been taught that it is bad to be the way they are. Some gay people are devoid of guilt because they realize that they are not responsible for their sexual orientation. Others are plagued because of their inability to achieve the ideal expression of their manhood as defined by their religious tradition. Deep-seated, religiously motivated self-condemnation is often difficult to deal with and requires the greatest care and patience on the part of the therapist. Some clients are helped by participating in the gay affirmative religious activities of their respective traditions, which can have a "normalizing" effect—they can see that gays have the same needs and concerns as all other human beings and thereby hasten their developing self-affirmation. They will discover that even those traditions that most adamantly condemn homosexuality have many gay clergy.

It is not uncommon for gay people to be hypercritical of other gay people and the leadership of the gay rights movements. Any manifested shortcoming or lapse from perfection may be used to discredit the movement. Gradually clients can be helped to understand that heterosexual organizations are not discredited because their leaders are fallible and sometimes exercise bad taste or judgment, and that hypercritical attitudes toward gay institutions are a function of internalized homophobia.

All healthy people usually need a sense of belonging and social approval. Consequently, gay men often fear that they will be judged not to measure up to the community standard of maleness. Here men are confronted with the complex interaction of sexism and sex-role stereotyping. Women have less status in our culture than men. Gay men are stereotypically thought to be not "full" men or somehow like women. This is further complicated by the stereotyped view that gay men do not like women, a view that has even been accepted by a minority of gay men. It is possible for the counselor to help the gay male client carefully work his way through this labyrinth to an understanding that gay men are not less than, but are simply different from, heterosexual men on the single variable of their sexual orientation; that healthy men need not think of themselves as either superior or inferior to the other sex; and that liking and disliking is more reliably based on individual characteristics than on class membership.

INTIMACY

All healthy people need intimacy. It is becoming a commonplace observation among gay social scientists that gay men have difficulties establishing intimacy relationships because they are socialized as men, and men in our culture are not trained to facilitate relationships. Men are more likely than women to seek sexual gratification outside committed relationships. Younger men are more likely to be sexually adventurous than older men. Yet every gay man must work out his own pattern of sexual gratification and friendship development.

Because of its blanket condemnation of homosexuality, our culture has offered no guidance for gay men who wish to be socially responsible. Furthermore, there can be no margin for error subsequent to the emergence of the AIDS health crisis. Consequently, it is the responsibility of the counselor to help the individual man affirm his sexuality and to find ways to express it responsibly and safely. Some need help in understanding and practicing safe sex. Others need help in developing communication and courting skills. Others need help in realizing their goal of establishing a committed monogamous pair bond.

NURTURANCE

Our patriarchal culture has defined men in general as nonnurturant and gay men as potential molesters of children (Finkelhor, 1984). These are myths that die hard. Many gay men are formerly married and are parents. They need help in communicating with their children. They often fear that their children will reject them. Actual experience has taught many gay fathers that their children are relatively indifferent to their sexual orientation. Rather, children's affirmation is given or withheld on the basis of the quality of the relationship between father and children (Miller, 1979a, 1979b; Voeller & Walters, 1978).

Other gay men will experience a sense of loss that their sexual orientation makes it unlikely that they will be biological parents. Producing a next generation and having someone to carry on the family name are culturally endorsed ways in which we are helped to deal with our mortality. Some gay men will be able to sublimate these needs into nurturing relationships with nieces and nephews; others into their work. Others will experience a sense of loss; others a relief that they don't have the responsibility. An increasing minority of gay men and male couples are becoming foster parents, adopting children, and occasionally working out parenting relationships with lesbians.

Counselors should know that children raised by gay parents are no more likely to be gay than children raised by heterosexual parents; that it would be all right for a child raised by gay parents to grow up gay; that individual men often need support in articulating their desire and finding the appropriate ways to be nurturers.

AGING AND DEATH

Another common myth is that gay people are lonely in old age. Limited research suggests the opposite. Since gay people have more life experience coping with unusual circumstances, they are apparently more adept in coping with social needs in later life (Berger, 1982). Nevertheless, facing declining strength, mobility, and independence is not easy for anyone in a society that offers so little social security throughout life. Gay men need help in dealing with their own ageism and many will need support in constructing an alternative social and familial network. In a complex intrapsychic dynamic, some gay men equate "youth," with "femininity" or "passivity," or perhaps an outdated image of themselves and find it impossible to be attracted to men of their own age. Men need to be helped to understand that they can make themselves attractive whatever their age by careful health management and awareness.

Fear of death is most often associated with a lack of meaning and purpose in life. Most of us need to have a sense that our life has mattered; that our existence has made a difference. Gay people are no different, but more often they lack the comfort of knowing that their line will be carried forward by children. Therefore, they may need help in establishing some kind of living memorial through a gay institution that can give them the comfort that they have contributed to a healthier society.

We are accustomed to facing death in old age. AIDS has shaken our complacency (Nichols, 1986). A heretofore unknown and at present incurable disease of central African origin has been communicated into the developed world. Because of their high geographical mobility and sexually affirmative lifestyle, gay men were probably the vector of communication and have definitely become the population at greatest risk for the illness. Simple minded and morally primitive people will quickly "blame the victim." But no one could have known the danger until the disease was identified.

Gay men are necessarily reexaming their lifestyle and means of sexual gratification. Many are fearful. Because of the nature of the disease, it is not possible to know for sure that one is in danger even if one has definitely been exposed to the disease. Counselors must be clearly aware that AIDS is not communicated by casual contact, and must keep abreast of the latest medical developments in order to deal responsibly with their clients (Altman, 1986; U.S. Department of Health, 1986).[2] Everyone at risk is necessarily becoming more fully conscious of matters of life and death. In metropolitan centers many people know someone who has died or is dying of AIDS. Those men who have not fully eradicated their internalized homophobia are vulnerable to the blaming attacks of the morally self-righteous. It is the counselor's responsibility to help gay men find means of gratifying their sexual needs without danger to themselves or others.

The Advantages of Being Gay

This chapter has necessarily focused on the problems men face in being gay. It would be unfortunate to leave the counselor with the impression that it is intrinsically a disadvantage in life in belonging to a sexual minority. There is no question that there are hazards that the psychologically vulnerable may not survive. A careful clinical detective would probably find a high incidence of conflict about sexual orientation among young men who have committed suicide. This is a consequence of social oppression—some cannot cope with the stigma.

Nevertheless, those who survive may have developed resiliency and survival skills that make them able to deal more effectively with many of life's other hurdles. Belonging to a minority is especially difficult for teenagers who want more than anything to be a part of the group. But not fully fitting in can also help people to develop a perspective on reality that may enhance creativity and general adaptability. The counselor who can help his gay male clients realize that in no way is their life necessarily inferior, and that nothing necessary for being fully human is totally denied them, will be making an important contribution to the well-being of gay men and the health of our society as well.

Notes

1. In 1987 the *Times* accepted the common practice of calling a people by their preferred name and has subsequently used the word gay freely.

2. Scientific progress is being rapidly made, and persons should consult with local AIDS hotlines for up-to-date information.

References

Allport, G. (1958). *The nature of prejudice.* Garden City, NY: Doubleday.

Altman, D. (1971). *Homosexual: Oppression and liberation.* New York: Avon.

Altman, D. (1986). *AIDS in the mind of America.* Garden City, NY: Anchor Press.

Bell, A. P., & Weinberg, M. S. (1978). *Homosexualities: A study of diversity among men and women.* New York: Simon & Schuster.

Bell, A. P., Weinberg, M. S., & Hammersmith, S. K. (1981). *Sexual preference: Its development in men and women.* Bloomington: Indiana University Press.

Berger, R. M. (1982). *Gay and gray: The older homosexual man.* Urbana: University of Illinois Press.

Coleman, E. (1981). Developmental stages of the coming out process. *Journal of Homosexuality, 7* (2/3), 31-43.

de Monteflores, C. & Schultz, S. (1978). Coming out: similarities and differences for lesbians and gay men. *Journal of Social Issues, 34* (3) 59-72.

Finkelhor, D. (1984). *Child sexual abuse: New theory and research.* New York: Free Press.

Ford, C. & Beach, F. (1951). *Patterns of sexual behavior.* New York: Harper & Row.

Hancock, K. (1986). *Homophobia.* Washington, DC: American Psychological Association.

Harrison, J. (1988). *Choosing a psychotherapist: A guide for gay and lesbian people.* Washington, DC: American Psychological Association.

Herdt, G. H. (Ed.). (1982). *Rituals of manhood: Male initiation in Papua, New Guinea.* Berkeley: University of California Press.

Hetrick, E. S., & Stein, T. S. (1984). *Psychotherapy with homosexuals.* Washington, DC: American Psychiatric Press.

Hooker, E. (1985). The adjustment of the overt male homosexual. *Journal of Personality Assessment, 21,* 18-31.

Kimmel, D. C. (1978). Adult development and aging: A gay perspective. *Journal of Social Issues, 34*(3), 113-130.

Levine, M. (Ed.). (1979). *Gay: The sociology of male homosexuality.* New York: Harper & Row.

Maylon, A. (1982). Psychotherapeutic implications of internalized homophobia in gay men. *Journal of Homosexuality, 1,* 59-70.

Miller, B. (1979a) Unpromised paternity: lifestyles of gay fathers. Pp. 239-252 in N. M. Levine (Ed.) *Gay Men: Sociology of Male Homosexuality.* New York: Harper & Row.

Miller, B. (1979b). Gay fathers and their children. *The Family Coordinator, 28,* 544-552.

Marotta, T. (1981). *The politics of homosexuality.* Boston: Houghton Mifflin.

Money, J. (1980). *Love and love sickness.* Baltimore, MD: Johns Hopkins University Press.

Money, J. (1986). *Love maps.* Baltimore, MD: Johns Hopkins University Press.

Money, J., & Ehrhardt, A. (1972). *Man & woman, boy & girl.* Baltimore, MD: Johns Hopkins University Press.

Morin, S. & Garfinkle, E. (1978). Male homophobia. *Journal of Social Issues, 34* (3), 29-46.

Nichols, S. E. (1986). Psychotherapy and AIDS. In T. S. Stein, and C. J. Cohen, (Eds.), *Contemporary Perspectives on Psychotherapy with Lesbians and Gay Men.* New York: Plenum.

Paul, W., Weinrich, J. D., Gonsiorek, J. C., & Holvedt, M. E. (Eds.), (1982). *Homosexuality: Social, psychological, and biological issues.* Newbury Park, CA: Sage Publications.

Siegelman, M. (1972). Adjustment of male homosexuals and heterosexuals. *Archives of Sexual Behavior, 2,* 9-25.

Storms, M. (1986). *The development of sexual orientation.* Washington, DC: American Psychological Association.

U.S. Department of Health. (1986). *Coping with AIDS.* Rockville, MD: National Institutes of Mental Health

Voeller, B. & Walters, J. (1978). Gay fathers. *The Family Coordinator, 27,* 149-157.

Weeks, J. (1985). *Sexuality and its discontents.* London: Routledge & Kegan Paul.

Weinberg, G. (1972). *Society and the healthy homosexual.* New York: St. Martin's Press.

Woodman, N. J., & Lenna, H. R. (1980). *Counseling with gay men and women.* San Francisco: Jossey-Bass.

16

Counseling
Bisexual Men

David R. Matteson

Both gays and heterosexuals are likely to categorize sexual orientations as falling into two discrete categories. Heterosexuals—out of homophobia—and gays—because of the oppression they have experienced—are likely to perceive these two orientations as "them" and "us." But for self-affirming bisexuals, this division of human experience makes no personal sense.

Like gays, the bisexual man belongs to an invisible minority. But because of his heterosexual interests, it may be easy for him to "pass"; he can maintain a "public identity" that is heterosexual. Of course, if he does so he feels some incongruity, and it is harder for him to affirm the gay part of his experience if it is kept "in the closet." Thus the bisexual man's sexual identity and his lifestyle are likely to be a bit more complex than the gay man's.

This chapter will begin with a discussion of some ways in which the development of bisexual identity is different from that of either heterosexual or homosexual identities. Particular emphasis will be placed on the role of kinesthetic or visual feedback in sexual arousal (for a fuller discussion see Matteson, in press, b). It is important to recognize that very little research has been done on bisexuality. Essentially no longitudinal research on sexual orientation has been done; this sketch of bisexual development is necessarily based on retrospective data from adults and is very tentative. Most of the research on bisexuality has focused on bisexual men in marriages; therefore, most of the examples in this chapter focus on this lifestyle. However, issues regarding identity formation, grieving lost models, and seeking new ones apply to bisexual men regardless of their marital status and lifestyle.

Author's Note: Portions of this chapter have been previously published in Bozett, F. W., *Gay Parents* (Praeger Publishers, 1987).

Sufficient data and experience exist to dismiss some of the myths and confusions about bisexuality, and these will be reviewed. With this background, attention to the special needs of bisexual men when they seek counseling will be addressed. Finally, some suggestions to counselors will be presented, based on the limited clinical literature to date and my experience and research.

Before he can affirm his identity, the bisexual man must struggle with two social taboos: the taboo against homosexuality and the taboo against extramarital sex or multiple relationships. The pressure to conform to the heterosexual expectations of parents and peers leads many bisexuals into heterosexual marriages before they have explored their sexuality sufficiently to recognize and affirm the gay component of their sexual orientation. As noted in the chapter on gay men, the formation of a gay identity is a difficult process, because it is a stigmatized identity and because the gay person is usually raised by heterosexual parents. Most members of minority groups at least have the experience of learning from their parents (also minorities) how to cope with their minority status. In contrast, the invisible minorities grow up among the majority, and only recognize their own minority status when their inner experience begins to conflict with external expectations. This process is clearer, if not easier, for the gay man who experiences no sexual response to women; eventually he realizes that what comes "naturally" for other men simply doesn't interest him. The adolescent who is bisexual is likely to "go along with the gang" longer, since the heterosexual feelings *are* "natural" to him. In the midst of early identity formation, the bisexual male may genuinely believe that his homosexual feelings are simply a result of being sexually frustrated, and that his homosexual explorations are merely adolescent and will disappear once he has a steady heterosexual partner. Since affirming one's bisexuality requires a tolerance for ambiguity,

> confusion should be seen as a sign of mental health, not an indication of neurosis, a fact which needs to be pointed out to bisexuals, who often blame themselves for being confused. (Lourea, 1985, p. 53)

To understand the development of this more complex sexual orientation, it is useful to clarify the roles of visual and kinesthetic lead systems in sexual arousal. (The concept of lead systems comes from the therapeutic theory of neurolinguistic processing; Cameron-Bandler, 1978.)

Visual fantasies and dreams play an important role in discovering one's sexual orientation for a large portion of the bisexual married men studied (Matteson, 1985). Dan, who was in his late twenties when interviewed, provides a prototype of this visual style. Dan and his wife had good communication; both were sensitive and well-educated persons. But Dan was worried that the majority of his sexual dreams and fantasies were of homosexual relationships. He joined a support group for married bisexual men. Two years later, at the time of the second interviews, Dan had left his wife and was living in the gay community. Though most of his sexual activity was now with men, he reported that many of his fantasies and sexual dreams were now of women. Some strongly visual types, like Dan, do not experience their lives as complete unless their visual expectations are met; that is, unless they have both male and female sexual partners concurrently.

There is some evidence (though far from conclusive) that the privatized nature of masturbation in boys leads to the development of elaborate sexual fantasies (Offer & Simon, 1975); this may contribute to a more visual approach to sexual arousal in boys. Generally, adolescent boys are far more likely than girls to engage in masturbation and to have explicitly sexual fantasies before they actually begin interpersonal sexual activities.

It can be hypothesized that men generally discover their sexual orientation first through visual experience, and women first find themselves sexually (and discover their sexual orientation) through their emotional interaction and physical contact with others. To oversimplify, women generally have a kinesthetic "awakening" and a kinesthetic "arousal pattern." Those whose arousal is primarily kinesthetic have very few sexual fantasies or dreams; sexual feelings emerge from a deep emotional relationship. They find it difficult to understand why someone would feel a need to have sex with anyone except their primary partner. Bisexuals of this type are satisfied if they have one good personal/sexual relationship; it makes very little difference if their lover is male or female. They are often sequentially bisexual, some even tending to alternate between male and female lovers. These persons may experience bisexuality as a "choice": For many bisexual women, the awareness of having a "choice" emerged out of a deep friendship with another woman which became sexual (or some other situation in which physical closeness led to sexuality; see Dixon, 1985). This stands in contrast to most of the bisexual men studied, who were obsessed with fantasies long before they met the persons with whom they first acted on their desires.

For bisexuals in committed heterosexual relationships, AIDS presents a special dilemma. Monogamy as a method of reducing the risk of contacting AIDS is not usually a viable option. For bisexuals who view homosexual sex as purely recreational, and do not desire personal intimacy, there is great risk of contacting AIDS unless they are disciplined to have only "safe sex."

Confusions and Myths

Some common myths regarding bisexuality include the belief that bisexuals "choose" their orientation, that bisexuals are really "gay" but are using heterosexual relations as a cover, and that bisexuals are generally "promiscuous." These myths are addressed in the next section.

BISEXUALS HAVE A CHOICE

With increased knowledge and understanding of the gay experience, many professionals are aware that gay men rarely think of their sexual orientation as something they "chose." However, since bisexuals define themselves as being aroused by members of either gender, it is easy to assume that they "have a choice." And for those for whom arousal is triggered primarily by emotional responses or direct physical contact (kinesthetic), there is some truth to that assumption. For the bisexual man whose sexual arousal is largely visually initiated, however, sexual orientation is unlikely to be experienced as a choice. Instead, he is likely to feel that he needs both heterosexual and homosexual activity to live a full and satisfying life.

HETEROSEXUAL MARRIAGE IS A "COVER"

Studies of bisexual husbands in heteosexual marriages have consistently shown that the men did not "deceive" their wives into marrying them; only a minority of the men believed themselves to be gay or bisexual at the time of the marriages (for a review, see Matteson, in press, b). Certainly homophobia played a role in the difficulty these men had in developing a clear sexual identity. But some of those men who overcame their homophobia and became openly and self-affirmatively gay or bisexual nevertheless chose to remain in their marriages. Because their sexual and emotional relationships with their wives were rich and satisfying, they negotiated open marriage contracts. Many of these couples were able to develop stable, satisfying marriages (Matteson, 1985).

The myth that bisexuality is a "way station" to avoid facing one's homosexuality is so strong in gay culture that men who have affirmed their gay identity and then are surprised to find that a particular women turns them on have great difficulty accepting that they may in fact be bisexual. Reentry into the world of heterosexual relations can create some difficult social problems. The Bi Center in San Francisco has offered support groups specifically for persons who have been exclusively homosexual for an extended period and are now aware of heterosexual attractions (Lourea, 1985).

BISEXUALS CANNOT MAINTAIN A FAITHFUL RELATIONSHIP

Faithfulness has been taken to be synonomous with monogamy in much of our heterosexist culture. This definition of faithfulness is shallow and has been challenged even by religious writers (United Church of Canada, 1977). It may be the case that most visually oriented bisexuals cannot make a lasting commitment to monogamy (although some bisexuals who have fully accepted their bisexuality seem able to do so). In terms of maintaining intimacy, the real issue is faithfulness in the relationship, that is, being honest about and following through on the covenants and commitments the couple have made. For most couples, it is crucial to affirm the primacy of the couple relationship if a committed relationship is to remain viable. That is, each partner must feel that he or she is the most important relationship in the partner's life. Primacy, rather than sexual exclusivity, seems central.

Special Needs of Bisexual Men

OVERCOMING HOMOPHOBIA

Part of becoming a healthy and congruent person is overcoming the judgments and evaluations of others, which we have internalized but which are inconsistent with our own experience. It is nearly impossible to have grown up in Western society and not to have internalized some hatred of homosexuality. It is clear from the research that the most significant event in overcoming homophobia is developing a personal relationship with someone and then learning that person is gay or lesbian. Positive models of being gay are very important to developing a positive gay or bisexual identity. This is one of the advantages for a gay or bisexual client being seen by an openly gay counselor. Whatever the orientation of the counselor, it is important that the counselor does not relate in a way that implies that the bisexual or gay lifestyle is inferior or to be pitied. If the counselor is not gay or bisexual, or is not willing to be open about this, it is probably advisable that the client be encouraged to seek experiences (for example, gay-affirmative coming-out groups) where he can get to know persons who are comfortable with being gay.

Men who are just beginning to face their bisexuality often enter counseling because of their confusion. They may not need intensive counseling; they may only need confirmation that it is O.K. to accept the self that they are discovering. Permission giving is often the first step in work with the bisexual client—and often it is the only "therapy" needed (Gochros, 1978; Lourea, 1985). To quote a client:

I knew what I wanted, but was afraid to get what I wanted. What I got from you [the counselor] was the guts to do what I wanted to do. You got me thinking again about myself and my own needs." (Gochros, 1978, p. 8)

RESPECT FOR THE UNIQUENESS OF EACH INDIVIDUAL'S SEXUAL ORIENTATION[1]

It is important to respect each person's sexual orientation without judging it against either heterosexual or gay standards. There is no harm in professionals admitting areas of ignorance if they are open to learn. Counselors need to be honest about their own lack of knowledge when working with persons of minority groups, without abdicating the leadership role in providing help.

The most obvious lack of respect is the subtle inducement of guilt. It has already been noted that bisexuals have a particularly difficult struggle in finding their sexual identity due to lack of models in either the home or in the gay subculture. On top of this, if they are in a committed heterosexual relationship, they face guilt for breaking the vows of sexual exclusivity. Guilt is, perhaps, the most destructive force in the struggle to come to terms with a sexual identity that doesn't fit the norm (Matteson, in press, a).

RESPECT FOR THE INDIVIDUAL'S ATTEMPT TO MEET HIS INTIMACY AND SEXUAL NEEDS IN A WAY THAT IS AUTHENTIC FOR HIM, WITHOUT MONOGAMOUS ASSUMPTIONS

"As we grow up we are faced with the reality that we cannot simultaneously fit in and be ourselves" (Harrison, 1985, p. 42). This quote was written in regard to lesbians and gays, but it applies to both single and coupled bisexuals. The traditional marriage or couple relationship simply doesn't fit them. When bisexual husbands decide to stay married, it is usually for reasons similar to those of heterosexuals. One's dreams of the ideal partner seldom exactly match the real persons we discover our partners to be, yet there may be enough satisfaction and love to affirm that marriage was a good decision after all. Rarely, however, can these relationships remain traditional monogomous marriages.

Frequently, counselors who have not had the opportunity to know many couples with open sexual relationships mistake the open contract for promiscuity or wild permissiveness. They fail to recognize the deep level of trust, and the letting go of possessiveness and control, that can be involved in a love that is based on the needs of two unique individuals. Another common error is to equate a nonmonogamous contract with a lack of commitment, or even to equate bisexuality itself with indecisiveness or confusion (Erik Erikson, 1968).

RESPECT FOR THE BOUNDARIES AND CONTRACTS THE CLIENT HAS WORKED OUT IN HIS RELATIONSHIPS

Perhaps one of the reasons many people respond negatively to the concept of open marriage is their intuitive awareness of the importance of boundary issues in intense and intimate relationships. Just as any successful couple with children, regardless of how much they love the children, must guard the primacy of the marriage from the children's demands, so the mixed orientation couple, though they may embrace an ideal of unbounded love, in practice must work out times and places in which their couple relationship is not intruded upon by the demands of others lovers.

For bisexuals, the issue of sexual exclusiveness, and the expectation that one partner can meet all the other partner's needs, has to be challenged and negotiated on an individual basis, whether in the context of a mixed-orientation marriage or as a single bisexual in a relationship that is moving toward deeper involvement and commitment. One manifestation of the boundary issue is the agreements about how much the nongay partner is told, or wishes to know. Sometimes this is worked out in careful negotiations between the two parties; in other couples it emerges from a subtle series of nonverbal interactions leading to a conspiracy of silence. Either way, if there are "secrets," they are part of this unique relationship. If they appear to be malfunctioning, the counselor may choose to challenge them in an individual session. It is important not to violate the boundaries between partners. There is accommodation in all committed relationships. However, mixed-orientation partnerships frequently require much more individually tailored forms of contracting and caring. Once both partners have accepted that the norms simply don't fit their personalities and needs, the freedoms and limits, the openness, and the boundaries that are set are unique to each couple. The most important general rule for the counselor is to avoid making any assumptions about what is open and what is secret in a particular couple's communication. It is not necessary to know all of the couple's rules if the counselor is especially careful not to be a message carrier between two partners.

Counselors have the responsibility of explaining their own rules in counseling (if they have a "no secrets" rule) from the beginning, before setting up any individual appointments in which the client may spill secrets with the expectation of confidentiality. Many couple counselors believe strongly in open communication between intimates, and see secrets in areas that affect the relationship as potentially destructive. However, counselors are also aware that effective communication involves sensitive timing, not just openness. It is important to remember that the bisexual partner has spent years trying to overcome his homophobia before finally coming out to himself. The nongay partner may have only recently begun to deal with this issue. Appropriate timing for her is important.

Though the counselor needs to be sensitive to issues of timing and secrets, when it appears that one partner keeps information to himself as a form of power or control, even if it is done with the "good intention" of protection, the counselor should consider challenging it. This "protection" can be particularly destructive when it involves patriarchical assumptions of the woman's dependency.

The unilateral secret may be distinguished from a mutually agreed upon silence, where both partners know the situation but contract not to intrude on the other's privacy by discussing it. There is a clear danger that conspiracies of silence will feed into the downward spiral of mistrust (Bozett, 1982). But there also is the fact that the nongay partner may, verbally or nonverbally, signal that she does not want to know too much. It is difficult to judge when a conspiracy of silence is dysfunctional and when it is in the best interests of both parties; certainly the judgment should not be made solely on the grounds of the counselor's ideology.

RESPECT THE SPECIAL NEED FOR CONFIDENTIALITY IN A HOMOPHOBIC SOCIETY

Though many counselors believe that the personal and political advantages of being "out of the closet" in our professions and in our communities outweigh the risks, they also know that the risks are not simply phobic delusions; they are real. The power to make decisions as to when and where to take these risks belongs to the client and his intimates, not to the professional.

RESPECT THE CLIENT'S CHOICE OF THE ISSUES NEEDING PROFESSIONAL HELP, AND GET ON WITH THE GOALS SET BY THE CLIENT

The most frequently stated criticism concerning professionals' work with mixed-orientation couples is that they get fixated on the uniqueness of the lifestyle and lose sight of the issues for which services are being sought. It appears common for counselors to assume that the lifstyle itself is the problem, regardless of the stated reasons the clients give for coming. One woman, married to a bisexual man, described three months of counseling during which she was trying to resolve an issue with her daughter. After a resolution was achieved, the counselor expressed surprise at the mother's profound relief. "You really *were* that upset over your daughter!" the counselor exclaimed. "That really *was* the problem, not your husband?" The counselor had not believed that the husband-wife relationship could be stable, and had assumed it was the underlying cause of the problem. Fortunately, in this case the counselor realized and admitted her own mistake.

The issues of communication, problem-solving skills, too much criticism, failure to give positive support to each other—common issues in couple counseling—may be overlooked when the counselor is distracted by the uniqueness of the alternative lifestyle that a couple has chosen.

The issue can be compounded if the client himself tends to use bisexuality, or fear of latent homosexuality, as a convenient scapegoat on which to blame the things that go wrong in his life (Lourea, 1985), when in fact personality problems exist that have no direct connection to the issue of bisexuality.

The special needs of bisexuals have been organized in this section around the concept of respect. Respect is an interpersonal phenomenon. Some bisexuals, after years of being open about their lifestyle, and with sensitive and supportive partners, families, friends, and colleagues, can work with homophobic professionals without letting the professionals' prejudices affect them personally. Others, with less experience since coming out, and less security and self-respect concerning the bisexual issue, are more vulnerable. The following suggestions may help counselors guard against their own biases being damaging to these more vulnerable clients.

Suggestions to Counselors

GETTING ACCURATE INFORMATION

Until the mid-1970s, very little accurate and unprejudiced information was available on homosexuality, let alone bisexuality. Even now, some gay-affirmative writings continue to treat bisexuality as a "cover" against accepting one's true (gay) identity. The most useful writing on bisexuality has appeared in a series of issues of the *Journal of Homosexuality* (see DeCecco, 1981; DeCecco & Shively, 1983; Klein & Wolfe, 1985).

FINDING SUPPORT NETWORKS

It is an incredibly "normalizing" experience when a client meets a person who has the same "problem" as he does. Normalizing experiences, and experiences interacting with positive models for gay or bisexual identity, are important factors in the development of a positive self-image. It is extremely useful for the bisexual to be in a situation in which being gay is the norm. A gay affirmative group provides a wonderful balance to the years of heterosexist groups he has already experienced, and is usually the safest setting for sharing thoughts about the gay aspects of one's identity. If the counselor or agency cannot provide these experiences directly, it is a valuable adjunct to the counseling to connect the client with persons or groups who can do so. Assisting bisexual clients in this networking is a legitimate function of the counselor, and helps the client to recognize that much of his "problem" is social, rather than intrapsychic (see Gochros, 1978).

Most of the large metropolitan areas have one or two groups that are specifically for bisexuals, often including a group for bisexual and gay men who are married. The easiest way to locate these groups is by calling the local gay switchboard, which is almost always listed in the phone directory under "gay." One of the special problems about being bisexual is that one is tempted to "pass" as "straight" in the heterosexual community (with the accompanying sense of hiding), and then to "pass" as "gay" in the gay community (not daring to speak of one's heterosexual partner). In neither place is one accepted as a whole person. Since there simply is no bisexual community, involvement in an ongoing bisexual group can be of special significance, particularly during the period of forming a clear and affirmative bisexual identity.

Because most bisexuals live much of their daily lives in the heterosexual world, it is also very freeing if they can come out to some of their closest nongay friends. Suggestions for assessing to whom to come out, and how, can be found elsewhere (Borhek, 1983; Hamilton, 1977; Muchmore & Hansen, 1982).

GRIEVING THE
FALLEN GODS

Besides self-discovery and relief, the coming-out process always involves grief, as the person recognizes that models and dreams that they have honored in the past will no longer work for them. The heterosexist model of the monogamous marriage—two children, picket fence, and all—is so much a part of our culture and our family upbringing that its loss must be acknowledged and grieved. For the bisexual man, the experience may be different than for the gay man, particularly if the former is already in a marriage. He may assume prematurely that the marriage must end. Almost certainly the honest acknowledgement of the gay component of his sexual orientation will mean serious changes in the marriage, but if the marriage has been one of common values and real intimacy, it is possible that once the shock of the disclosure of his homosexuality is dealt with, the couple can work out new contracts and agreements that will allow the marriage to continue (Latham & White, 1978; Matteson, 1985). If this is the case, the major grief work concerns the loss of the view of monogamy as the ideal marriage. This is often a harder loss for the wife than the husband, since women in our culture tend to be more socialized for and invested in monogamy than men. But men, too, experience this as a loss, and often feel guilt at "causing" the death of this more "perfect" form of marriage. If the couple is not willing or able to work out a new form of marriage that honors his homosexual needs as well, and it is decided that the marriage must end, then there are other more concrete losses that must be grieved. Nonetheless, the loss of the "model," and the sense that one is now in unchartered territory, is a profound experience that should not be minimized by the counselor.

SYSTEMS THEORY AND INVOLVEMENT OF "SIGNIFICANT OTHERS"

The therapeutic model presented here is one of affirming the naturalness and appropriateness of living out the sexual orientation that the client discovers as "his own." Gay or bisexual clients are not "sick," per se; they have internalized the cultural sickness of homophobia. The important function of groups and role models has already been indicated. A "family" systems approach is particularly useful in working with these clients because it makes concrete the perspective that the problem is not "inside" the client; the disease is a social disease, and the best cure is a social one. Just as parents of a gay man can best communicate their acceptance by actions (such as encouraging their son to bring home his lover to meet them), so the counselor can best communicate his acceptance of the client's homosexuality by suggesting that the client invite his gay lover into the sessions.

MIXED-ORIENTATION MARRIAGES: AN ILLUSTRATION OF SYSTEMS ISSUES

With married bisexuals, there are special reasons to work with the network of people involved, rather than just the bisexual husband. Typically the first request for help comes when disclosure to the wife is imminent, or when his "secret" has been discovered. The bisexual partner is immersed in an identity struggle, often as part of a "midlife crisis"; like most identity struggles, this results in rather narcissistic behaviors during this phase. Further, frequently the bisexual husband is repeating childhood patterns of "escape." Having felt that a portion of his identity was oppressed throughout his growing up, he unwittingly makes a connection between the sexual inhibitions imposed on him by his mother and the fears and inhibitions expressed by his wife. As children, many of us have had a secret place (real or imaginary) to which we ran to escape the oppression and inhibition we felt, a place where our "child" could run free. When the gay component of one's sexual orientation is first acknowledged, it is very freeing, and the gay world often becomes a "free place" that evokes all the joy and hedonism and exuberance of a childhood escape. The years of suppressing this part of ourselves only intensifies the joy of its release and acceptance. The wife's fears and the secretive quality of the escape resonate with the childhood split between sneaking pleasure and being "responsible." There is a risk that the husband will bolt from the marriage into a gay adolescent lifestyle, without discerning which of his feelings are, at least in part, displaced from childhood, and without carefully negotiating what is possible in the relationship with his wife.

This risk seems particularly high in those husbands who, prior to their marriage commitments, have had little contact with gay-affirmative men and have repressed their gay desires well into adulthood (Matteson, 1985). Their identity crisis may be a part of a midlife crisis in which they reevaluate their life's assumptions. Fatigued by family responsibilities and sex-role expectations, the traditional male entertains fantasies of leaving the marital relationship. The perspective of midlife crisis can be a helpful one in counseling with many of the husbands and their wives. (Lourea, 1985).

Working with the couple rather than just with the bisexual husband brings more of these dynamics into focus, and allows the counselor to respond to some of the needs of the wife in the context of acceptance of the husband's newly acknowledged sexual orientation. When it is clear to the husband that the counselor does affirm his bisexuality, but also is responsive to his wife's emotions, it becomes easier for him to do the same—that is, to stop viewing the wife's fear, pain, and anger as statements about his homosexuality or requests that once again he suppress what he has finally begun to affirm, and hear them simply as her genuine feelings. If the husband has had considerable homosexual experience but hidden it from his wife, she is faced with three hard issues at once: the gay issue, the issue of nonmonogamy, and on top of it, the issue of deceit (Matteson, 1985). The feelings of anger, hurt, betrayal, and mistrust must be dealt with before further progress can be made. While the bisexual partner is partially responsible due to his lack of disclosure, it is also important to look at the verbal and nonverbal communication patterns in the relationship that have hindered open communication in the past (Lourea, 1985). That the counselor, in the presence of the wife, can calmly acknowledge the fact of the husband's homosexual desires, without treating these as catastrophic, not only affirms the husband but reduces the panic of the wife.

When the panic subsides, the husband's identity crisis can be given its place, but by seeing them together and directly working on their communication, the importance of the marital relationship in their lives can also be affirmed. Gochros (1978) saw the exploration of options and decision making as the second phase of (individual) work with bisexual husbands. Certainly each spouse needs to consider his or her own options, but it seems wiser, unless a decision has been made to leave the marriage, to work on this phase with both parties present, at least for the majority of the interviews. In some cases it may be helpful to set reasonable goals and time limits regarding decisions to be made (Gochros, 1978); this may reduce the insecurity of the spouse who is feeling in a "reactive" position. However, the counselor should avoid pushing for reality decisions in a way that distracts from the process of each partner examining her or his own needs and learning to express and negotiate them. Opportunities for personal growth are higher during this "unsettled" stage when some of the usual assumptions and defenses are broken down, and with the counselor's help (focusing on the process, not just the results) important personal changes and insights may occur.

The decisions regarding opening up the marriage and negotiating contracts that respect the needs of both parties precipitate discussion of the insecurities and jealousies that arise. Some wives experience more insecurity when "competing" with a male lover. One wife stated, "I know I can compete with any other woman. If I lose, well, at least it was a fair fight. With a man I don't stand a chance. I've lost before I've even begun." On the other hand, the bisexual husband may wish his wife would experiment with bisexual relationships—yet be threatened when she starts dating other men. The issue of jealousy usually boils down to the question of primacy. If each partner is getting enough love and attention from the other to feel sure of "my special place in your life," the jealousy is manageable. It is when the sense of trust and caring within the relationship is in doubt that the issue of what the partner is "giving away" outside the relationship becomes a battleground. The counselor is wise to recognize the focus on "outside involvements" as a form of scapegoating, and instead to encourage "I" statements owning one's own hurt, loneliness, and vulnerability.

Working on the communication between spouses does not mean, of course, pushing for the continuation of the marriage. It does mean refusing to discount or ignore a relationship that has been of great importance, one that must change in the light of the acknowledged bisexuality. Whether the new relationship is one of divorced coparents, and/or close but nonsexual friends, or of partners in an open marriage (to name some of the more likely positive outcomes), the relationship issues should not simply be stepped over, as unfortunately often occurs in individual counseling. (For a summary of the stages in these couples, see Matteson, in press, b).

Support groups for the bisexual partner have already been discussed;

there is no need for the wife to be a part of all the searching and exploring that he needs to do in the gay world. Similarly, the husband cannot take responsibility for his wife's need to develop more of a life of her own, to the extent that she has accepted a "merged identity" that is dependent on him (see Matteson, in press, c), and a women's group that works on the identity issues that modern women now face can be particularly helpful for her.

Separate work is especially indicated for the husband who has moved beyond "adolescent" exploration of the gay scene to a continued relationship with a gay lover. He may feel frightened over the degree to which he feels bonded to his homosexual lover and thus use his heterosexuality as a shield to guard against developing intimacy with another man (Lourea, 1985). Our culture's homophobia runs much deeper than fear of the sexual interaction between two men, and might more accurately be defined as fear of intimacy between men. Individual work with the husband or work with the gay couple may be indicated at this point.

The developing of support beyond the couple relationship is vital; and support includes support of the couple, support of the husband, and support of the wife. The importance of individual friends often needs to be stressed, because many couples have abandoned separate friendships and reduced their social life to couples.

> Instances arise (in these complex marriages) when it is impossible for the individual (spouses) to be supportive of one another; having other people to turn to can relieve pressure as well as add perspective that can help clarify issues. (Lourea, 1985).

If counseling continues beyond the initial crisis, the work often centers around negotiations and recontracting in the marriage. Some couples can manage the negotiations on their own, and thus can use the counseling hour to enhance their level of emotional communication. Others need to limit negotiations to when the counselor is present. Almost all couples need to be encouraged to have "moratorium" times when they are together purely for recreation, and when a "time out" is declared on the discussion of issues that arouse conflict. A major task of the counseling is to teach both partners to take more control over their own lives and their own happiness, and to stop trying to control the other. Two milestones in the counseling are when the woman partner stops trying to control the bisexual man's activities outside their relationship, and when the man begins to initiate discussions or activities that show that he's taking responsibility in the relationship, rather than leaving it up to the woman to take care of herself *and* the relationship.

After the permission-giving stage, and the ensuing exploration of options and the decision-making stage, the individual or couple move to the problems of settling into a new lifestyle (Gochros, 1978). Issues of relating to the children may come up in this phase (these are dealt with in detail in Matteson, in press, b). In some instances, family counseling is helpful at this point. Counselors can be helpful in dealing with decisions about coming out to children and to extended family, and with "training clients to be effectively gay" (Moses & Hawkins, 1982; p. 216); these are issues that have been well addressed in the literature on counseling gays and lesbians.

Often by this time enough networking has been done so the clients have sufficient support in their lives and no longer need to see the counselor on a regular basis. However, the counselor may remain an important resource, and scattered interviews over several years are not uncommon.

Special Issues

THE COUNSELOR'S SEXUAL ORIENTATION

There are some special issues that concern the sexual orientation of the counselor where couple counseling with mixed-orientation relationships is concerned. Only the couples in which the husband is the bisexual will be addressed here (see Coleman, 1985, and Matteson, in press b, for information on bisexual wives). While in most couple counseling it is the woman who seeks counseling whereas the man is likely to be the reluctant partner, the reverse is often the case in mixed-orientation couples. The bisexual man is in personal crisis, and may initiate counseling for himself, involving the woman only at the advice of the systems-oriented counselor. Since he defines his problem as sexually related, he is likely to seek a male counselor. In this situation, the (male) counselor has several strikes against him when trying to engage the woman in counseling: first, that the bisexual man is not convinced she should be there; second, that the partner is not wanting to face this issue and wishes it would just disappear; and third, that the female partner is likely to see the male counselor as naturally aligned with the man. The attempt to balance the rapport between husband and wife (Broderick, 1983) is further complicated if the counselor is known to be gay or bisexual; the woman is likely to be suspicious that the counselor has a hidden agenda of seducing the bisexual man into the gay world.

One has a far better chance of keeping both partners engaged if one starts out with a cocounseling team. A bisexual male counselor may work with a nongay woman cocounselor; at times the women meet together to discuss the woman's issues, while the men meet to discuss the bisexual issues.

THE SIGNIFICANT OTHER

When one is working with a couple in which one partner is bisexual (whether it is a heterosexual couple or a male couple), there may be a "significant other" who is left out—a gay lover, in the case of the heterosexual couple, or the heterosexual lover in the case of the male couple. When that person is significant, it is frequently helpful to meet with the third person, whether or not that relationship is a committed or long-term one. This allows that person access to the counselor, which not only may be of value to that person, but may decrease the chances that that person will sabotage the counseling.

The usual rule in seeing the third "corner" of a triangle is that the counselor will request that the bisexual man inform his primary partner that the counselor will be seeing the other partner. Of course, what goes on in the session is kept confidential unless explicitly agreed otherwise. This keeps the counselor out of a deceitful triangle and yet doesn't put the counselor in the position of communicating *for* members of the triangle. Often a joint session with the bisexual man and the lover is the most helpful format, both to improve communication between this part of the triangle, and to give the opportunity to the lover to ask the counselor questions about this type of arrangement. It is rare that a session with all three present is appropriate. Usually, this is ill-advised with married couples, even where the wife is agreeable, because it tends to undermine the primacy of the marital relationship. The exception, of course, is the rare case where all three believe the married and the homosexual relationships are "equally primary."

In summary, overcoming the guilt and alienation that result from years in "the closet" is often best accomplished in a counseling setting with more than one client. Support networks need to be developed for the bisexual man, and for significant others in his life who are coping with the news of his bisexuality.

Conclusions

Some have claimed that bisexuals have the best of both worlds. Actually, bisexuals often experience a lack of acceptance in either world. Yet they may feel they need relationships in both worlds. The satisfactions of marriage and family may be very appealing and important to them, yet the limitations of monogamous marriage may be unworkable. Developing intimate relationships with persons who can accept their unique needs and working out mutually satisfying agreements and boundaries are complex challenges in this complex lifestyle. Counselors who can affirm their client's sexual orientation and can appreciate the complexity of the bisexual's search for a satisfying lifestyle may find working with bisexual clients especially enriching and challenging.

Note

1. This section and the following four sections are to be published in 1988 by Alyson Publications, Inc. in a book tentatively titled *A Helping Hand: Assisting Gay and Lesbian Clients*. Reprinted by permission.

References

Borhek, M. V. (1983). *Coming out to parents*. New York: Pilgrim.

Bozett, F. (1982). Heterogeneous couples in heterosexual marriages: Gay men and straight women. *Journal of Marital & Family Therapy, 8*, 81-89.

Broderick, C. B. (1983). *The therapeutic triangle: A sourcebook on marital therapy*. Newbury Park, CA: Sage.

Cameron-Bandler, L. (1978). *They lived happily ever after*. Cupertino, CA: Meta Publications.

Coleman, E. (1985). Bisexual women in marriage. *Journal of Homosexuality, 11*, 87-100.

Constantine, L. L. (1972, July). Counseling implications of comarital and multilateral relations. *Family Coordinator*, pp. 267-273.

De Cecco, J. P. (Ed.). (1981). *Journal of Homosexuality*, 6(3).

De Cecco, J. P., & Shively, M. G. (Eds.). (1983). *Bisexual and homosexual identities: Critical theoretical issues. Journal of Homosexuality 9,*(2 & 3).

Dixon, J. K. (1985). Sexuality and relationship changes in married females following the commencement of bisexual activity. *Journal of Homosexuality, 11*, 115-133.

Erikson, E. H. (1968). *Identity, youth and crisis*. New York: W. W. Norton.

Gochros, H. L. (1978, December). Counseling gay husbands. *Journal of Sex Education and Therapy*, pp. 6-10.

Hamilton, W. (1977) *Coming out*. New York: New American Library.

Harrison, J. (1985) Salmagundi review: Distorting the gay vision. *Changing Men, 14*, 20-21, 42-43.

Klein, F., & Wolf, T. J. (Eds.). (1985). Bisexualities: Theory and research. *Journal of Homosexuality, 11*(1 & 2).

Latham, J. D., & White, G. D. (1978). Coping with homosexual expression within heterosexual marriages: Five case studies. *Journal of Sex and Marital Therapy, 4*, 198-212.

Lourea, D. N. (1985). Psycho-social issues related to counseling bisexuals. *Journal of Homosexuality, 11*, 51-63.

Matteson, D. R. (1985). Bisexual men in marriage: Is a positive homosexual identity and stable marriage possible? *Journal of Homosexuality, 11*, 149-172.

Matteson, D. R. (in press, a). Couples in mixed-orientation marriages. In R. J. Kus (Ed.), *A helping hand: Assisting your gay & lesbian clients* (working title). Boston: Alyson Press.

Matteson, D. R. (in press, b). The heterosexually married gay/lesbian parent. In F. W. Bozett (Ed.), *Gay parents*. New York: Praeger.

Matteson, D. R. (in press, c). Identity: The alienated self, the merged self, and the intimate self. In *Proceedings of the First International Meeting on Psychological Teacher Education*. University of Minho, Braga, Portugal.

Matteson, D. R. (n.d.). Sexual arousal: Two pathways to being "turned on." Unpublished manuscript.

Moses, A. E., & Hawkins, R. O. (1982). *Counseling lesbian women and gay men: A life-issues approach.* St. Louis: C. V. Mosby.

Muchmore, W., & Hansen, W. (1982) *Coming out right.* Boston: Alyson.

Offer, D., & Simon, W. (1975) Stages of sexual development. In A. M. Freedman, H. I. Kaplan, & B. J. Sadock, *Comprehensive textbook of psychiatry, 11* (Vol. 2, 2nd ed.). Baltimore, MD: Williams & Wilkins Co.

Ross, M. W. (1983). *The married homosexual man: A psychological study.* Boston: Routledge & Kegan Paul.

Siegel, P. (1981). Androgyny, sex-role rigidity, and homophobia. In J. Chesebro (Ed.). *GaySpeak: Gay male and lesbian communication.* New York: Pilgrim.

United Church of Canada. (1977). Faithfulness—the broader issue (and subsequent sections). In *Position paper: Task force on marriage.* Canada: Author

17

Counseling Men in the AIDS Crisis

Howard R. Fradkin

The AIDS crisis has affected men in many ways, ranging from massive denial to panic to devastation to death. While many diseases do not discriminate, AIDS is largely a disease of the disenfranchised and outcasts of society. Gay and bisexual men, IV drug users and multiple drug abusers, men of color, and hemophiliacs are the ones singled out for the tragedy of AIDS. This chapter will describe the psychosocial issues these men face as well as issues you may face as a therapist. AIDS has attacked the masculinity of these men and these effects will also be considered.

A Brief History

The AIDS crisis began in 1978 when doctors in large urban areas observed some young gay patients with unusual opportunistic infections. At first, it was believed some factor in the gay lifestyle caused AIDS—AIDS was often called the "gay plague." Doctors hypothesized that the immune systems of gay men had become overloaded by multiple infections caused by having many sexual contacts, using large quantities of drugs, and having irregular eating and sleeping habits. Then in 1983, Dr. Luc Montagnier of the Pasteur Institute obtained a virus that he believed to cause AIDS. He named the virus LAV or Lymphadenopathy-Related Virus. In May 1984, Dr. Robert Gallo of the National Cancer Institute in Bethesda, Maryland, also isolated an AIDS-related virus, HTLV-III or Human T-Cell Lymphotropic Virus. After much scientific and political debate, it was agreed to call the virus Human

Immunodeficiency Virus, or HIV. Since the crisis began, an alarming number of men and some women have come down with AIDS. By 1985, AIDS was the number-one killer of men aged 20-50 in New York City and San Francisco and was announced as the number-one health priority of the U.S. Public Health Service.

Epidemiology of AIDS

Nearly all people with AIDS are in one of the following seven risk groups: (1) homosexual/bisexual male— 66%; (2) intravenous (IV) drug abuser—17%; (3) homosexual male and IV drug abuser—8%; (4) hemophilia/coagulation disorder—1% (5) heterosexual cases—4%; (6) transfusion, blood/components—2%; and (7) none of the above—3% (Centers for Disease Control, 1986). There have been no new risk groups identified since mid-1982. Almost 95% of people who have been diagnosed with AIDS are men. Of the cases, 22% are aged 20-29; 47% are aged 30-39; 21% are aged 40-49; 9% are over 49 years of age; and 1% of AIDS cases are children under the age of 13. In regard to racial/ethnic background, 60% are white; 25% are black; 14% are Hispanic/Latino; 2% are other or unknown. The overall mortality rate (death rate) is 54%, with most men dying within three years of diagnosis (Centers for Disease Control, 1986).

Belonging to one of these groups does not necessarily put a person at high risk for contracting AIDS. It is believed that other risk factors may influence and possibly weaken the immune system, either before or after exposure to the virus. These factors may include having a high number of sexual partners; poor personal and sexual hygiene practices; history of sexually transmitted diseases including parasites and hepatitis B; history of antibiotic use or heavy recreational drug use; persistently high psychological stress; social and emotional isolation; lack of self-acceptance; inability to express feelings and anger; and perhaps even genetic factors (Bahnson & Engelman, 1981; Cecchi, 1983; Guiot, 1984).

What Is AIDS?

AIDS stands for Acquired Immune Deficiency Syndrome. A syndrome is a group of clinical symptoms that make up a disease or abnormal condition. A variety of symptoms are characteristic of the disease; however, not all symptoms appear in any one person. The virus causes breakdowns in the immune system, which then allows frequently occurring germs the opportunity to multiply freely, causing "opportunistic diseases." Infection with HIV has varied body responses. Most people remain healthy but are carriers of the virus. Others with Lymphadenopathy Syndrome have swollen lymph glands but no other symptoms typical of AIDS. Some develop AIDS Related Complex (ARC), while others develop a full-blown case of AIDS.

The symptoms of AIDS include: unexplained fevers; shaking chills or drenching night sweats; persistent diarrhea; unexplained persistent fatigue; unexplained swollen glands; pink to purple flat or raised blotches occurring on or under the skin, inside the mouth, nose, eyelids, or rectum; persistent white spots or unusual blemishes in the mouth; and a persistent dry cough not caused by a common respiratory infection.

The most common opportunistic diseases that occur in men with AIDS are a rare form of cancer called Kaposi's Sarcoma, or KS, and a pneumonia called Pneumocystis Carinnii Pneumonia, or PCP. Both of these diseases are often treatable, as are virtually all opportunistic infections. The difference between AIDS and ARC is that persons with ARC have not yet been diagnosed with an opportunistic disease. With either diagnosis, it is possible to appear apparently well and work, be acutely ill, or be chronically ill and have great difficulties in daily living.

Neurological complications are estimated to occur in at least 30% of persons with AIDS (PWAs), and in 10% of PWAs these complications are the initial clinical problem (Bresden & Messing, 1983; Snider, Smith, & Nielson, 1983). Early symptoms include loss of concentration and recent memory, mental slowing, unsteady gait, uncoordination, social withdrawal, and apathy. Navia (1986) has found some clients may develop AIDS Dementia Complex without developing full-blown AIDS. A detailed neurological history and formal neuropsychological testing are necessary to establish a diagnosis.

Psychosocial Issues

Imagine youself going to your doctor's office and being told that you have a diagnosis of AIDS. Allow yourself to imagine the wide range of feelings you might have. Now consider you're told you have ARC. Think about the tremendous range of feelings and thoughts you might be having. Now imagine being exposed to Human Immunodeficiency Virus. what is this like for you?

This portion of the chapter will deal with how men with AIDS, ARC, HIV Positive, and the rest of the "worried well" are affected by the AIDS crisis. Specific emphasis will be placed on how the disease affects us as men.

PSYCHOSOCIAL ISSUES
OF PERSONS WITH AIDS

The best way to describe the process of counseling and dealing with a diagnosis of AIDS is the analogy of riding a roller coaster. Dealing with a diagnosis of AIDS has such tremendous and unsettling implications for any man that at times he will feel so overwhelmed that complete denial is necessary to function (Treese, 1983). At other times, he will experience deep depression, massive confusion, or great loss. Eight phases of counseling people with AIDS have been described by Lopez and Getzel (1984). This is not a stage model, but rather a descriptive model of the many phases, feelings, and interventions within the process of working with a PWA. As the model indicates, psychosocial intervention by counselors is important throughout this process (Christ & Wiener, 1985; Maylon & Pinka, 1983).

Phase 1: Engagement and assessment. The development of AIDS is totally unpredictable. Some men have been sick for some time before receiving their diagnosis. For others, the warning signs come only a short time before diagnosis. Therefore, it is hard to know what to expect in your initial interactions with a PWA. It is important to allow the client to ride on the roller coaster and just experience whatever feelings he may be having. This is not the time for confrontation, interpretation, or giving advice. Allow the dust to settle as the man begins to deal with the reality of his diagnosis. Denial may be present to a large degree. A man may talk with great bravado about how he is going to be the first one to survive and conquer this disease. Support the denial until your client is ready to face the range of emotions that come with such a devastating diagnosis.

Many issues will come to the surface in this early period. Most PWAs have led a fairly independent life prior to diagnosis, having their own apartments and working in careers or full-time jobs. These men may have to face dependency for the first time in their adult lives. There are often great fears associated with this as well as a loss of pride in being able to take care of oneself.

For men in committed relationships, the fear of becoming more dependent and possibly a burden on their partner is particularly difficult. The couple may face financial problems if the PWA is unable to continue working. The PWA may fear rejection from his lover or have to face the disturbing possibility he has transmitted the disease to his partner.

The issue of disclosure is a major one with regard to friends, family, and work associates. Employer reactions have varied from immediate firing to great compassion. Family reactions also vary from tremendous support to complete rejection. Within the gay community, "gay families" frequently have been extremely supportive, but there are also instances of rejection and stigmatization.

Another immediate reaction to diagnosis may be the belief that they are being punished. Many talk about being a "slut" or drug abuser and therefore deserving of AIDS. Some blame it on being gay or bisexual. Even previously well-adjusted gay men succumb to increased internalized homophobia. It is important to confront this judgment and help these men understand that they have a disease like any other disease. Self-loving, not self-loathing, is an important aspect of healing.

Phase 2: Assisting and supporting autonomy. Typical of men, it is often hard for PWAs to ask for help, whether it be financial, emotional, or to meet basic needs. Depending on the client's physical condition, some PWAs may need a great deal of assistance with basic living skills, while others may be more independent. While it can be tempting for the counselor to preempt the autonomy of the client as a response to our own helplessness, it is important to encourage the client to be as autonomous as possible. Clients can get very angry when their autonomy is taken away.

Phase 3: Explaining the therapeutic relationship and meaning of AIDS. The issue of a PWA's continuing dependence is important to address. The PWA is likely to feel ambivalent; while he may appreciate the counselor being there, he may also resent dependence on the counselor and envy the counselor's health. The counselor may be pulled close and then pushed away. It is often difficult for men with AIDS to believe people could really care about them as human beings because of the stigmatization. In this weakened physical and psychological state, clients may internalize this stigmatization, leading to feelings of powerlessness and helplessness.

It is essential to empower the client in every way possible. Encourage him to confront people who withdraw, affirming his right for support. Encourage assertiveness in hospital settings. Help clients ask for explanations of tests and options, including alternative treatment modalities. Help them recognize and assert their right to be treated with respect, not as a freak or leper. Affirm the client's right to determine his own limits and help him learn to listen to his body. Let him decide how much exercise and sleep he needs.

Empowerment includes letting PWAs know they can survive a diagnosis of AIDS. A New York study (Rothenberg, 1986) found people with AIDS who survive more than three years face a decreasing probability of dying from the disease. During the fourth year, there is a leveling off of the probability of dying, and after that time the probability appears to approach zero. The study also noted optimal survival occurred among young, white gay men with Kaposi's Sarcoma. Another study being promoted by the national PWA organization has found that 20% of people with AIDS live longer than the three years predicted as the average life span for those who are diagnosed (Lorenzini & Reynolds, 1982). The study found a number of characteristics of long-term survivors: the ability to externalize the disease, explore alternatives, take responsibility for their own health, say "no," and focus on making life productive. With this kind of information, some clients are able to mobilize their defense system more effectively.

Phase 4: Supporting the client in talking about death. At first, death may be referred to through indirect comments the client makes. For instance, he may say, "I don't know how much longer I can deal with this pain." Due to male socialization, it may be difficult for the PWA to give up because people would be disappointed in him and as well he would be disappointed in himself. It is hard even at this stage to acknowledge our limitations. Counselors may struggle with the same issue, wanting to support the client's exhaustion and desire to let go, but feel guilty or responsible for quickening the client's death. It is important to recognize that we are not responsible for our client's health or death. Our major function is to support the client wherever he may be in this process. Providing a good listening ear and offering neither optimistic nor fatalistic scenarios can be helpful as the client struggles to determine how he will continue his life.

During this phase, it is common for clients to spend time reminiscing about the past and contrasting the future as being very dim. The roller coaster effect is still noticed as clients range from laughing with friends to being deeply depressed.

Also during this time, clients may take a look at their present and past relationships and determine whether it is still possible to work on any of these relationships and resolve past problems. It has been hypothesized that such therapeutic work may enhance the immune competence of PWAs (Bahnson & Engelman, 1981).

Phase 5: Monitoring and maintaining health status. Regardless of whether a person with AIDS is hospitalized, it is important to monitor and maintain the health care received. Help the PWA advocate for quality care when possible. Lowered self-esteem and increased weakness may inhibit their ability to ask for care they deserve.

Anger is a normal emotion in any of these phases. The PWA may be angry at any number of things, from the injustice of the disease, the lack of governmental response, or concrete frustrations such as the doctor not having answers. It is important to validate the anger while helping the PWA vent it to help decrease anxiety and depression levels. Anger can also be channeled into constructive activities including work in PWA and AIDS organizations.

Phase 6: Supporting close relationships and griefwork. Generally the PWA has a sense of when death is near. Although the PWA may desire support from his closest friends and family, they may feel threatened and scared to come around. They may not want to face his impending death, or understand the PWA's sense of relief that the struggle is almost over. The PWA will also be dealing with much grief and loss, including the loss of respect and dignity, career, friends and lover, and bodily functions or mental functions.

Planning for death may occupy a lot of the PWA's attention. Some PWAs will want to die at home. With community task forces and health care, this often can be arranged. Referrals to lawyers and others who can assist in making final plans may also be needed. It is important to consider ahead of time whether and what kind of emergency life-saving measures are desired. These may be as simple as cardio-pulmonary resuscitation (CPR) or as involved as mechanical ventiliation and drug modalities. Many PWAs prefer to plan their own funeral arrangements, which helps them feel they will die with dignity. Because this phase of illness can linger or be very quick, it is important to encourage the client as he is ready to make these plans.

Phase 7: Caring and advocating for the dying client. It is important to continue to advocate for the PWA in his last days and hours. If the person is at home, assure that adequate care is given. If the person is in the hospital, the therapist can help assure that the PWA will die with dignity. The PWA may be unconscious and unable to communicate directly. However, he may be able to hear and recognize voices. Take this time to say goodbye to the client. This is also a time to care for the significant others in the PWA's life. Frequently these people will have very intense feelings that need to be vented. Some may still be in denial and need assistance in letting go.

Phase 8: Grieving and mourning with the family and significant others. Even after the PWA dies, your role continues to be important as family and significant others grieve the loss. In the case of a gay man who dies, there may be significant issues and problems that arise during the planning of the funeral, the funeral itself, and the mourning time that follows. If the man had a lover, he may be excluded from giving any input regarding the funeral unless he has the power of attorney.

After the funeral, the family may want to blame the lover for the death of their son. It may be important to help the lover to stand up for himself and not allow family members to take advantage of him.

PSYCHOSOCIAL ISSUES OF MEN WITH AIDS-RELATED COMPLEX

A diagnosis of ARC can be just as devastating as a diagnosis of AIDS. For some men diagnosed with ARC, it comes after a longer period of seeing their health go downhill without doctors being able to diagnose them. It may be a relief to receive a diagnosis and know what they are fighting against. Others have confirmed their exposure to the virus through antibody testing and have felt like walking time bombs hoping they would not develop ARC, but expecting to be diagnosed. A diagnosis of ARC means an uncertain future. Some men will develop a full-blown case of AIDS. While some will remain in a very weakened state, others will recover.

One of the most comprehensive studies comparing affective reactions of men with AIDS and ARC found the psychosocial needs of people with ARC (PWARCs) have been greatly underestimated (Mandel, 1985).

PWARCs reported higher mean levels of emotional distress, as well as longer mean delay time in seeking medical treatment than men with AIDS. A total of 60% of PWARCs attributed their symptoms to some other disease and did not seek immediate physician care. The median delay for seeking care was about eight months. In the same study, 46% of PWARCs were unemployed due to severe physical problems.

Other factors contribute to greater emotional distress. Half of PWARCs had not discussed their health problems with one or more family members (Mandel, 1985). This was often associated with a lack of disclosure to their families with regard to their sexual orientation. For men who had disclosed their health, PWARCs reported more negative experiences in the disclosure than PWAs. Consistent with this, PWARCs feared rejection more than PWAs. Increased internalized homophobia was found in 25% of PWARCs (Mandel, 1985).

Working on developing a positive attitude can make a difference in how PWARCs cope with the disease. Hay (1984) talks about the importance of loving and forgiving oneself and working on positive relationships. She encourages her clients to use self-hypnosis, meditation, creative visualization, and "mirror talk" to improve their abilities to love themselves. Men with ARC may believe their chances for intimacy are greatly decreased because no one would want to get close to them. While some men may reject them, others will want to get close and share in the experience of caring for and loving a man with ARC.

The AIDS antibody test. Men can now go to an anonymous, confidential clinic to find out if they have been exposed to HIV. It is important in counseling individuals about taking the test to help them look at the potential consequences both emotionally and behaviorally. For some clients, taking the test may be contraindicated because of the extreme anxiety they already feel without knowing their antibody status. For others, it may help to decrease their anxiety if there is little reason to believe they have been exposed and they find out they are negative. The results of testing have been studied by the San Francisco AIDS Health Project. They found 57% of men tested indicated they had improved risk reduction at least somewhat, while 35% said their behaviors had not changed since taking the test (Dlugosch, Gold, & Dilley, 1986); 1% of the participants said their activities had become somewhat less healthy since taking the test. With regard to mood changes, the authors concluded, "Taking the test has a powerful impact on the emotional state of a person, with the expected outcome of great relief and mood improvement for those receiving negative results and heightened anxiety and depression for those with positive results" (Dlugosch et al., 1986, p. 2).

Ongoing counseling either individually or in groups may help men learn more positive ways of coping with the natural stress of being exposed to AIDS. It is important to help these men establish a positive outlook because of the danger of setting themselves up to get the disease.

Maintaining a positive approach is also a way of keeping the immune system strong and preventing further deterioration of health (Coates, Temoshok, & Mandel, 1984; Hay, 1985). Just as with PWAs and PWARCs, men who are HIV positive often have to deal with other underlying conflicts that have been unresolved from the past, including homophobia, drug addiction, negative self-esteem, poor relationships, and poor coping mechanisms in general. Clinical syndromes reported in this group include panic disorders, insomnia, depression, and hypochondriasis (Forstein, 1984).

While the gay community appears to be responding more positively to safe sex guidelines, the greater concern arises about the spread of the disease in the heterosexual and the IV drug community. These communities have been more difficult to reach and it is important for all men who are sexually active or involved within the drug subculture to recognize the great risks they are taking.

Psychosocial Issues of Special Populations

BISEXUAL MEN

The AIDS crisis has presented some unique issues for bisexual men, particularly those who have ongoing relationships with women. Many bisexual men have lived on the fringes of the gay subculture, resulting in a lack of access to appropriate information, resources, and support for themselves. With the onset of the AIDS crisis, these men may not have appropriate information about safe sex and other precautions that could help them protect themselves and their partners.

Many bisexual men in the past have been able to rationalize their outside relationships by telling themselves they posed no danger to themselves or their partners. But now, facing the reality of possible infection often leads to increased anxiety and guilt. Some bisexual men have chosen to cope by refraining from any further activity with other men, causing them to feel unfulfilled and depressed.

The crisis that bisexual men face when they test positive for the HIV virus or are diagnosed with ARC or AIDS can be quite traumatic. Frequently, many of these men have not been open with their partners about the extent of their homosexual activity. Therefore, they face a dual "coming out" to their partners.

THE WORRIED WELL

As the AIDS crisis progresses, the worried well comprise a greater number of people in the community. The worried well include: (1) people with nonspecific symptomatology or people who have a few symptoms for ARC but not enough to make a diagnosis; (2) people with intimate exposure to someone with AIDS or ARC or a person who is HIV positive; (3) people with no known intimate exposure, but who are at risk because of past or present sexual activity and/or past or present drug usage; (4) gay persons who are just coming out; (5) persons not at risk who incorporate anxiety about AIDS into preexisting psychosomatic disorders or other nervous disorders; (6) people not at risk who have been misinformed about AIDS with regard to means of transmission; and (7) any service provider.

The impact of AIDS crisis on the worried well has been incredibly dramatic. For gay men, it has meant a total reevaluation of the gay lifestyle. For many, the 1970s represented a time when gay liberation was at its height and gay men were beginning to feel positive about themselves for the first time. The AIDS crisis hit at the end of this period, causing many gay men to take a hard look at how they were living their lives. Jim is a typical example.

Jim has been an active man in the New York gay community for many years. In 1978 his physician was one of the first to hear about the incidence of Kaposi's Sarcoma and expressed concern to him. Jim told his friends and they labeled him an alarmist. His physician updated him, but his friends continued to discount him. Several years later, Jim and his friends began to face the reality of AIDS. Some chose to become celibate, while others denied the danger. Jim decreased the number of his sexual partners. A year later, some of Jim's friends were diagnosed with ARC and AIDS. Jim learned about safe sex, but found it difficult to change his behavior. He'd never used condoms before and felt awkward talking to his partners about using condoms. At a seminar, he learned safe sex is equal to caring about yourself and your partner. He began to approach sex with a more positive attitude, and recognized that AIDS was probably going to be a part of his life forever. It is eight years since his doctor's first warning; now when he visits friends who have AIDS, he knows just by looking in their eyes when they are going to die. Some of his friends are just going crazy bouncing back and forth between wanting to take care of themselves and being self-destructive. He ranges from anxiety and panic to feeling like a hypochondriac to depression and severe anger and rage at the government's inability and unwillingness to put all their resources together to fight this disease. He's also frustrated because he really doesn't know who to believe in regard to the facts about AIDS.

MINORITY MEN

AIDS as an issue in the black and Latino communities has been kept in the closet, largely due to the myth that AIDS is a white man's disease (Gerald, 1986). In reality, 39% of people with

AIDS are black or Hispanic even though these two groups only comprise 19% of the U.S. population. Of people with color with AIDS, 53% are gay or bisexual and 42% are IV drug users. The biggest reasons for this myth are the homophobia within the black and Latino communities and the problems with access to proper health care. The existence of homosexuality is often denied, making it difficult for men with AIDS or ARC to identify themselves and ask for services. Because of generally poor and discriminatory health care as well as lack of trust in the health-care system, it is typical for blacks and Latinos to delay seeking treatment until they may be very sick. Whereas the general mortality rate for all people with AIDS is roughly three years after diagnosis, many blacks live only eight months after diagnosis (Gale, 1986).

The most important issue to encourage treatment as soon as symptoms are apparent. Saxon (1986) describes the "post-diagnosis syndrome" in which blacks are very angry about their diagnosis. AIDS is particularly difficult for a professional black man because he may feel "They finally got me." It is important to validate this anger while being compassionate and patient with the PWA. It is typical for minority PWAs to be very confused and frightened, partly due to inadequate explanations from their physicians. It is important to support the PWA in helping him get needed medical information to ease his confusion.

In regard to the reactions of families, Latino families tend to give support once they get over the initial shock (Paniagua, 1986). This family acceptance is true only for Hispanics who are acculturated. Hispanics who are "undocumented" have generally left home to be free and do not contact their family upon diagnosis. In the black family, the PWA may die alone. Frequently the black mother is afraid to let her son come home or feels unable to provide financially for the son because of already strained resources (Paniagua, 1986; Saxon, 1986). It is common with the black PWA to claim to be an IV drug user rather than gay or bisexual because he perceives this may be more acceptable to his family.

In terms of ongoing care and financial support for both black and Hispanic PWAs, it is important for therapists to recognize the likelihood of institutional racism affecting the quality of care. The therapist needs to be an advocate for the PWA when the possibility of such discrimination occurs. State disability is limited by what the person paid into it, and typically blacks and Latinos have paid in less and therefore receive even fewer benefits than the typical white client.

IV DRUG AND MULTIPLE DRUG USERS

There is still a controversy over whether multiple drug abuse is a major causative factor in the development of AIDS. Krieger and Caceres (1985) maintain that at least 79% of PWAs have been drug abusers. They maintain that since drugs damage the immune system, it is drug abusers who are at highest risk for developing AIDS.

CLINICAL ISSUES WITH DRUG ABUSERS

Spiegel (1986) argues it is important for PWAs to have a choice as to how to live their life, including whether to become sober. She sees substance abuse treatment as a quality-of-life issue, and emphasizes that although there are many issues for a PWA to face, the therapist may need to deal with chemical dependency before the client can be helped to deal effectively with other psychosocial stressors. Timing is an important issue, particularly because the PWA at diagnosis may already be in the denial mode and therefore be hard to confront about a chemical dependency problem.

Spiegel also suggests discussing the increased risk that drug abusers face, including the danger of blood-to-blood contact and the immunosuppressant qualities of drugs, particularly amylnitrate (poppers). Heterosexuals need to know the AIDS virus is highly transmissible to unborn children.

AIDS education organizations have been very divided in terms of their approach to reaching the drug abusing community. While Spiegel argues that the number-one priority should be to stop drug abuse, it is important to recognize that drug abuse will continue. Therefore, it is important to provide education about safe needle practices and how to "clean the works." Teaching drug agencies about AIDS is important so that in-house education to clients can be provided.

Issues for Therapists

The therapist who chooses to work in the AIDS crisis will face some of the biggest challenges in his or her career. The ability to remain open to our feelings is extremely important in this work. Difficult feelings such as helplessness, anger, and fear are necessary to work through in order to stay open to our clients (Forstein, 1984; Romano, 1985). Without working through such feelings, it is likely the therapist may tend to smooth over the pain of the client in order to smooth over his or her own pain.

A number of other abilities are desirable for the therapist. It is important to have a comfortable respect for the human spirit and be able to accept and discuss spirituality. It is important to be comfortable with death and dying issues. Regardless of orientation, it is important to be open to the use of medication and alternative treatment approaches. Clients tend to be very needy, requiring the therapist to be clear about issues of dependency. Another area for therapists to explore is their own attitude toward sexuality. Homophobia and sex-negative attitudes may affect a therapist's ability to discuss specific sexual practices with clients without appearing judgmental or motherly, as well as to interface with relationship building. For therapists in a high-risk group, the tendency to identify with clients may lead to minimizing the seriousness of the client's situation or, at the other extreme, lead to depression and feelings of helplessness for the therapist.

Most important for any therapist is the necessity to arrange for some type of supportive therapy or networking in order to assist with the healing process of this work. Therapists often experience the same roller-coaster phenomenon as clients. With supervision, it is possible to determine what may be healthy coping mechanisms and what dynamics may be getting in the way. The need to mourn a number of deaths in a relatively short time can be difficult and painful. When mourning is not successfully completed, the dangers of burnout are very real.

Resources for Counselors

In most larger cities, a counselor will be able to draw on the resources of local AIDS task forces (Furstenberg & Olson, 1984). These task forces, which include both health professionals and laypeople, have organized and trained groups of volunteers and "buddies" to reduce the isolation of people with AIDS and provide basic assistance to them with daily living skills and emotional support. Many task forces have employed social service advocates who have experience and connections with the health-care system and economic assistance programs. Such task forces may also provide groups for people with AIDS, their significant others, and groups for the worried well. A listing of all existing task forces is available through the Shanti Project in San Francisco (1986). The same document also lists a number of groups that have been established for PWAs.

There are several useful guides for people with AIDS as well (Los Angeles AIDS Project, 1985; O'Hara, 1984). These publications provide guidelines for how to live a better-quality life. Most AIDS organizations have also developed pamphlets that can be useful in direct work with PWAs as well as with the community. A number of videotapes have also been developed for training purposes. The Shanti Project has videotaped their entire training program, which is tremendously useful as an adjunct to local trainers. Also recommended is "Aids: Care Beyond the Hospital," developed by the San Francisco AIDS Foundation (1984), and training workshops from the AIDS Health Project (1984).

Many governmental economic assistance programs are available to PWAs and PWARCs. I suggest developing a liaison with professionals within these agencies to assist in getting aid as quickly as possible for clients.

Summary

It has been difficult to present all of the immensely complex issues surrounding this crisis adequately. Clearly, a mutlidisciplinary, multidimensional approach is necessary in order to meet the needs of the many thousands of people who have been and will be affected by this crisis. While there is hope on the horizon that medical progress will be made, the psychosociological aspects of the AIDS crisis will have an impact on our society and particularly on men's lives for many years to come. The AIDS crisis provides an opportunity for men to work through a number of difficult issues. It is hoped that through this process we will increase our ability to relate more openly to all men and women.

References

AIDS Health Project. (1984). Training workshops on AIDS [Available from AHP at 333 Valencia Street, Fourth Floor, San Francisco, CA 94102].

Bahnson, C. B., & Engelman, S. (1981, August). *Questions concerning the psychologic impact and treatment of AIDS.* Paper presented at the meeting of the American Psychological Association, Toronto.

Bresden, D. C., & Messing, R. (1983). Neurological syndromes heralding AIDS. *Annals of Neurology, 14,* 141.

Cecchi, R. L. (1983). *Stress: prodrome to immune deficiency.* Paper presented at the meeting of the New York Academy of Sciences, New York City.

Centers for Disease Control. (1986). AIDS weekly surveillance report. [Available from the CDC, Atlanta, GA 30333].

Christ, G. H., & Wiener, L. S. (1985). Psychosocial issues in AIDS. In V. DeVita, S. Hellman, & S. A. Rosenberg (Eds.), *AIDS: Etiology, diagnosis, treatment, and prevention* (pp. 275-297). Philadelphia: Lippincott.

Coates, T. J., Temoshok, L., & Mandel, J. (1984). Psychosocial research is essential to understanding and treating AIDS. *American Psychologist, 39,* 1309-1314.

Dlugosch, G., Gold, M., & Dilley, J. (1986). *AIDS antibody testing: evaluation and counseling. Focus, 1,* 1-3.

Forstein, M. (1984). The psychosocial impact of the acquired immunodeficiency syndrome. *Seminars in Oncology, 11,* 77-82.

Furstenberg, A. L., & Olson, M. M. (1984). Social work and AIDS. *Social Work in Health Care, 9,* 4.

Gale, J. (1986, August). *AIDS in the black community* [In-service training pamphlet, available from Columbus AIDS Task Force, Columbus, OH].

Gerald, G. (1986, March). *AIDS in the black community.* Speech presented at the Southern Christian Leadership Conference, Atlanta.

Guiot, B. J. (1984, March). *The psychodynamics of illness: Toward an AIDS personality?* Paper presented at the meeting of the First International Gay/Lesbian Health Conference, New York City.

Hay, L. (1985). *Doors opening: A positive approach to AIDS* [Cassette tape, videotape, available from 1242 Berkeley Street #6, Santa Monica, CA 90404].

Krieger, T., & Caceres, C. A. (1985, October 24). Unnoticed link in AIDS cases. *Wall Street Journal.*

Lopez, D. J., & Getzel, G. S. (1984). Helping gay AIDS patients in crisis. *Social Case Work: Journal of Social Work, 65,* 387-394.

Lorenzini, J., & Reynolds, B. (1982, March). *Living with AIDS.* Paper presented at the meeting of the Seventh National Lesbian/Gay Health Conference, Washington, D.C.

Los Angeles AIDS Project. (1985). *Living with AIDS* [Available from 937 North Cole Avenue #3, Los Angeles, CA 90038].

Mandel, J. S. (1985). Affective reactions to a diagnosis of AIDS or AIDS-related complex in gay men. Unpublished doctoral dissertation, Wright Institute.

Maylon, A. K., & Pinka, A. T. (1983). Acquired Immune Deficiency Syndrome: A challenge to psychology. *Professional Psychology, 1,*

Navia, B. A. (1986, June). *AIDS Dementia Complex.* Paper presented at the Second International Conference on AIDS, Paris.

O'Hara, A. (1984). *A guide for people with AIDS.* [Available from P. O. Box 4073, Key West, FL 33041].

Paniagua, B. (1986, March). *AIDS and the black and Hispanic family.* Paper presented at the meeting of the Seventh National Lesbian/Gay Health Conference, Washington, D.C.

Romano, N. (1985, March). *The counselor in the AIDS crisis.* Paper presented at the meeting of the American Association for Counseling and Development, New York City.

San Francisco AIDS Foundation. (1984). *AIDS: Care beyond the hospital.* [Available from 333 Valencia Street, 4th floor, San Francisco, CA 94102].

Saxon, L. (1986, March). *Demystifying AIDS in the black community.* Paper presented at the meeting of the Seventh National Lesbian/Gay Health Conference, Washington, D.C.

Shanti Project. (1986). National and international directory of AIDS-related services. [Available from 890 Hayes Street, San Francisco, CA 94117].

Snider, W. D., Smith, D. M., & Nielson, S. (1983). Neurological complications of AIDS: Analysis of 50 patients. *American Neurology, 14,* 403-418.

Spiegel, J. (1986, March). *AIDS training for alcoholism treatment program professionals.* Paper presented at the Seventh National Lesbian/Gay Health Conference, Washington, D.C.

Treese, G. (1983, November). *Psychosocial issues related to the diagnosis of AIDS.* Paper presented at the meeting of the Baylor College of Medicine, Houston.

18

Counseling Single Fathers

Sandra Tedder
Avraham Scherman

Divorce has become a common phenomenon in our society. According to the report of the Bureau of the Census (1983a; 1983b) about 13.7 million children were living with one parent. This is two-thirds more than the number of children living with a single parent in 1970. About 10%—over 1 million—of these children live with their father.

The increase in single fathers' custody is a result of changing trends in the law. During the era of Roman supremacy and the Middle Ages, men owned the children and therefore had the rights to them (Foster & Freed, 1978; Roman & Haddad, 1978; Vail, 1979). The seventeenth and eighteenth centuries saw women becoming more prominent in the caretaking role and the invention of "maternal instinct" took place (Roman & Haddad, 1978; Vail, 1979). By the early 1900s custody was generally awarded to the mother, particularly for those children of "tender years" (Foster & Freed, 1978; Roman & Haddad, 1978; Vail, 1979; Woody, 1978). Today a custody battle is on in many cases. With the "best interests of the child" as the basic criteria (Child Custody Act, 1970), more men are trying for and receiving custody of minor children through the courts (Orthner, Brown & Ferguson, 1976).

Main areas of concern of single fathers center on having adequate support systems, having enough information in various areas, loneliness, and developing coping skills for unfamiliar situations. The role associated with being a single father is sometimes confusing. "When I go to a party," as one aptly put, "I don't know whether to go to the kitchen and trade recipes and kid stories with the women or go to the living room and talk football with the men!" Services and support are available in most communities through support groups, churches, community agencies, private sources, and friends.

Theoretical and Philosophical Bases for Intervention

Adjustment to divorce is a process. It is developmental in nature, going through several stages before there is disentanglement from the former partner. One analogy used by Bruce Fisher (1981) in his book *Rebuilding* is that of a pyramid made up of building blocks. The first layer of blocks includes very basic issues such as acknowledging the divorce, adjusting to being alone, coping with the guilt and rejection associated with divorce, grieving the loss of the expartner, and dealing with the anger that accompanies a separation. These are some powerful feelings that need to be confronted before going on to the next stage. In the next stage each person works toward getting on with life: letting go of the old relationship, enhancing one's own self-concept, making new friendships as well as developing old ones, and leaving many of the difficulties and pitfalls of past relationships behind. Once this point has been reached, new healthier love relationships can develop leaving one with mutual feelings of trust, responsibility, and freedom. Fisher's idea is to work toward self-fulfillment so that a relationship is developed because one feels good enough about oneself to want the relationship to enhance growth, not because it is needed to exist.

Personal growth through this process of adjustment comes from various sources. Building skills in unfamiliar areas such as cooking, household chores, child-rearing matters, child care, and dating are crucial. Without these skills or the money to pay for them, life can be difficult indeed. Sharing information with others is also a source of growth. In support groups for custodial fathers that we conducted, a great deal of the learning and growth came through the experiences of other members of the group. Each individual sharing his own methods and experiences gave others ideas on how to proceed in different or complementary ways (Tedder, Libbee, & Scherman, 1981; Tedder, Scherman, & Sheridan, 1984).

Most communities have resources available to aid in this process of adjustment and learning. Therapy groups dealing with personal issues are available as well as support groups centering around specific issues. Groups for single parents are growing in number. These groups involve speakers on various topics such as spiritual development, practical skills development, and social activities. Not only are the adult needs addressed by community resources, but those of the children are acknowledged as well. Resources range from child development specialists and child-care facilities to recreational activities through local recreational departments and family Ys. The available resources are often plentiful, but the effort to locate them and the time to utilize them are sometimes problems.

A readily available source of potential growth is in the self-help area. Books abound to give insights and suggestions. These are available at odd hours of the day and night, which may fit a schedule when nothing else will. Some available self-help books include *Rebuilding* (Fisher, 1981), *Fathers Without Partners* (Rosenthal & Keshet, 1981), *Creative Divorce* (Krantzler, 1973), and *The Single Father's Handbook* (Gatley & Koulack, 1979). In addition to reading material, discussions about the material are frequently important to check out perceptions and clarify information and feelings. Directions in which to move can also be identified and implemented.

SPECIFIC NEEDS OF SINGLE FATHERS

Both custodial and noncustodial fathers are extremely concerned with whether their children were affected by the divorce and in what way. In order to know what their children should be doing according to their age, many fathers turn to reading child psychology books describing child development. They want to know the physical, social, and intellectual development of children. In addition, they are concerned with the short- and long-term effects of divorce, and what they as parents can do to help their children cope with this crisis period. What and how to explain to the children is another source of apprehension. Often fathers will ask about books they can read or things they can do in order to educate themselves in this area (Bertin, 1981; Gasser & Taylor, 1976).

Children respond emotionally to the divorce, and some fathers have difficulties finding ways to deal with these responses. Many fathers complain that their children do not want to talk with them about their feelings; therefore, they are unsure how their children feel (Tedder et al., 1984).

Some fathers experience guilt feelings about their children being deprived of one parent and try to compensate by being extra nice, permissive, and attentive to them. Others feel that the children are the source of all their problems and they are very hostile toward them. Maintaining an objective perspective of the situation is a difficult task.

Relationships between custodial fathers and noncustodial mothers are often difficult. For the benefit of the children, it is important to keep a relationship with the mother even though some would prefer to terminate the contact completely. Concerns that might appear here are: "What do I do when my child refuses to see his/her mother who insists on exercising her visitation rights?" "My child wants to live with his/her mother." Some mothers break promises, do not arrive on time to pick up their children or come to visit when it was not agreed upon. Other noncustodial parents play the Santa Claus role and do not exert any discipline when children are visiting. All these instances have ramifications on the children's behavior and expectations.

Immediately following divorce the single custodial father faces severe stress. Work that had been accomplished by two people and took a lot of planning and energy is to be done by only one parent. In addition, this parent is also experiencing a high degree of stress that is not only emotional but sometimes financial; he is raising questions about whether the lifestyle enjoyed during the marriage can continue. Coping with these difficulties might raise questions in the single custodial father's mind about his capabilities for facing and solving all of the problems and continuing, at the same time, to function effectively (Bartz & Witcher, 1978; Mendes, 1979).

In the social domain the new single custodial father faces some problems, too. Most of the social contacts were family contacts that involved an intact family. Suddenly, the single custodial father is either no longer invited to these functions or, when invited, he might feel left out. Even more stressful is the occasion when both the custodial and non-custodial parents are invited to the same function by common friends without being told that their ex-spouse had also been invited (Gasser & Taylor, 1976).

The single custodial father suddenly faces the question of what is acceptable behavior: "Could I go out and visit a friend when my son wants me to go bowling tonight?" "Could I bring home a date when my children are still awake?" "Can a date spend the night in my apartment?" "Should I allow a date to criticize the behavior of my children when it has nothing to do with her?"

The divorce leaves a single custodial father cognitively confused: "Where do I get all the knowledge necessary to manage the house, raise my children and take care of my personal needs?" "Do I take care of my personal needs or my children's needs first?" "How do I deal with all the well-intentioned advice and interference from friends and relatives?" "How do I explain to the children all of the changes that have occurred lately in the family status?" In order to cope with this cognitive confusion, the single custodial father needs support and knowledge so that the task does not become overwhelming.

Questions about oneself appear as a problem only some time after the divorce. This occurs on the average about a year following divorce. The reason for this delay is simple: Immediately after separation the single custodial parent has to cope with pressing problems that need immediate attention and has little time seriously to explore identity and personal characteristics. Concerns of dealing with loneliness and stress are the first emotional concerns the individual has to face. Then appear questions such as, "What am I now that I am no longer a husband?" Later questions to appear in this area are questions of personality, such as "What did I do wrong?" "Do I need to change some of my behaviors or perceptions in order to be more effective in a meaningful relationship?" "What could I do to avoid similar problems in the future?"

Single custodial fathers are very concerned with questions related to dating, remarriage, and their legal ramifications. Some of the questions these men raise are how to deal with children's resistance or encouragement to date. To what extent should children be allowed to interfere and what might happen legally if their personal status changes? It is common knowledge that most of the "motions to modify" custody arrangements are filed in court when a change in the personal status of the custodial parent occurs.

Noncustodial fathers are expected to provide financial and child support. They find themselves burdened with financial obligations when their involvement and input in the everyday life of their children is minimal. Usually they have to leave their household taking very little with them. They, too, go through the process of emotional and social disentanglement but with a higher degree of loneliness since the children are not in the home. In addition, they have to fight the popular image of a carefree, newly freed man setting up a "bachelor pad" from which to launch an exciting new social life. These facts coupled with an absence of services for noncustodial fathers is a great source of stress without the appropriate support systems.

Description of Components Included in Individual and Group Intervention

Fathers adopt different lifestyles in order to cope with the new family structure created by the divorce. They experience a variety of concerns relating to themselves and relating to their children. They also develop a personal style in interacting with their children. Therefore, it is important to take all these factors into consideration when developing an intervention plan or raising the awareness of coping strategies with fathers. Five areas of work with parents have been identified: how to help the parent himself, how to help the child emotionally, how to explain to the child what has happened (the cognitive aspects), how to help the parent benefit from simple therapeutic and intervention strategies, and how to deal with dating and remarriage.

HOW TO HELP THE PARENT

Immediately following divorce, some parents may be so involved with their own problems that they neglect to see the needs of the child. The quicker and more effectivley these parents are helped to deal with their own problems the better it will be for the children.

In support groups that we have offered (Tedder et al., 1981, 1984) emphasis has been on the dissemination of knowledge. Parents were not aware of all the community agencies available to them. Lists were compiled of local agencies dealing with day-care centers, mental health facilities, medical institutions, legal aid sources, and agencies who work with school problems and recreation. Pertinent information was included for each agency. Many parents were not aware of the variety and number of services available in the community and found them very useful. Among professional people, it seemed that pediatricians and social workers working with the courts were the most helpful in making themselves available for consultation.

In groups additional cognitive information may be given to parents in the form of bibliographic references for themselves and for their children. In the selection of books, the emphasis is placed on applied material and not on highly theoretical books. In addition, handouts on the expected behavior of children in the physical, social, and intellectual areas, as well as reactions of children to divorce at different age levels, may be helpful. Parents may feel the need for this information to decide whether their children are developing as might be expected.

Visitation with the noncustodial parent and the arrangements associated with it sometimes caused pain and problems. Most parents prefer a formal visitation arrangement that prevents surprises and minimizes contact with the ex-spouse. Several guidelines that could help make visitation easier and smoother are the following:

- The children should be ready on time, having all their needs packed. Don't pick that time to clarify things with the ex-spouse.
- Noncustodial parents should be given rights and responsibilities in raising the children.
- What happened during the visit is the business of the child and the noncustodial parent.
- Be tolerant when the child is showered with presents and entertainment.
- Inform the ex-spouse about developments that need attention.
- Do not make departure or return from a visit unpleasant.

HOW TO HELP THE CHILD
EMOTIONALLY

It is very important for the parents to understand the emotional impact that the divorce has had on the children (Olds, 1980). The children have gone through some important changes that they might want to explore. They might select very odd times to talk about these changes, such as two minutes before the father planned to leave for a meeting, or when they are being put to bed and he is looking forward to having some time for himself. A child willing to talk should be listened to immediately if at all possible. If this is not possible, select a mutually acceptable time, making sure that as the parent, one follows through and spends this time talking with the child. This creates a feeling of openness and frank communication between the custodial parent and the child.

On the other hand, we find that some children completely avoid the subject. Feelings about the divorce are never mentioned. Parents might feel relieved when this is the case. But it does not mean that the child is not preoccupied with thoughts related to the divorce. Parents should encourage children to talk about it. One father felt that his daughter (age 14) could not communicate with him and therefore left in her room a note mentioning that he noticed his daughter was in low spirits and invited her to discuss this in any mode she preferred. To his surprise, the father found a note in the morning after his daughter had left for school asking him to listen to the enclosed tape, which described in detail some of her fears and feelings. This girl preferred not to interact directly, and for a period of time, the communication between the two continued in this way. With younger children stuffed animals, dolls, play activities, and drawings helped to open discussion on the subject.

If the parent feels unable to discuss matters with the child because of his emotional state or any other reason, it is advisable to identify a person who can serve in this role, for example, a relative, a friend, a teacher, a counselor, or a neighbor. It is important to create the environment and opportunities for the child to discuss his or her feelings.

An additional feeling with which the child is concerned is guilt. Children might remember when they were mad at the parent who left and wished she would go, or the time when they went to the zoo and Dad bought something that Mom had said not to buy and afterward they quarrelled. The child might be sure that these were reasons that caused the divorce and therefore feel guilty. By explaining to the child that sometimes people stop being friends, accompanied with appropriate explanations, the child may be helped to stop seeing himself or herself as the cause for the divorce.

Finally, parents might have to deal with the anger or sadness of their children—anger because "I am different," "I cannot spend as much money as before," and sadness because "I don't get to see my other parent as much as I would like." In all these cases, these feelings should be discussed and dealt with. The parent should either assume the active role and initiate discussion or provide opportunities for the child to discuss feelings by spending time and doing things with the child.

HOW AND WHAT TO EXPLAIN TO THE CHILD (THE COGNITIVE ASPECT)

It is no secret that a large number of parents avoid telling their children about the impending divorce. Single parents find it hard to explain why they live in a single-parent home. The younger the child, the higher the frequency of avoiding the subject with the rationale "I will wait until he/she asks," or "Why upset the child now?" Some say, "We will wait until the child grows up and then tell him/her." Among clinicians, such as Gardner (1970) and Grollman (1975), the message is clear: Tell the children about the divorce. This should be done by both parents at the same time and to all the children involved. Children should understand what is happening so that no unrealistic expectations are developed. Of course, the language used during the explanation should match the intellectual development of the children. When the parents find it hard to discuss the divorce themselves, a third party, close to the children, should discuss it with them.

Once children are told about the divorce they might have several concerns. One question young children ask is "Are you going to stop being my Mommy?" It is important to make sure that children understand that the parents continue to remain their parents. Children need to know in detail the arrangements that have been worked out for the future. In the case that there are difficulties in working out these arrangements, parents could say, "We both love you very much. We are not sure what is the best for you and, therefore, we asked the judge to help us in making the decision."

Sometimes separation occurs when the child is very young. At some point in the future the child might be curious about the other parent. "How did my Mom look?" "What type of things did she like to do?" Forster and Stenhouse (1980) suggest several ideas: Talk about the ex-partner, tell about things done together and keep souvenirs such as photos, letters, and cards that make memories vivid. Children can keep in touch with friends and relatives of the noncustodial parent or encourage and arrange for direct contact.

Visitation arrangements should also be clearly described: how children are going to be picked up, how long they will visit, and how the children are going to be returned. Children should be made aware of these details. Some flexibility, however, should be allowed to account for moods and unexpected events.

An area frequently neglected in explanations to the child is the legal one. "How come one day you go to the court and, suddenly, you are not married any more?" Parents of children interested in this area are encouraged to explain the law to children and, if they feel they are not knowledgeable enough, their attorney should be able to answer some of the children's questions. Parents can take their children to the court where they can explain the functions of the court. This is an area where parents should carefully attempt to assess whether there is a need for knowledge and try to answer this need as best they can.

Children are also interested in the effects of divorce on their daily lives. "Will I still be able to take violin lessons?" "Will we go on vacation this summer?" Older children may ask, "Will I still be able to go to college?" These questions require detailed answers so that children are clear in what ways their everyday functioning and future plans are going to be affected by the divorce.

HOW TO HELP THE FATHER BENEFIT FROM SIMPLE THERAPEUTIC AND INTERVENTION STRATEGIES

The approach taken when working with custodial fathers depends on the therapeutic issues. If the main issues are those associated with single fathering, the most common approach is a cognitive-behavioral one.

One might have the feeling that the children are suffering enough and therefore a permissive attitude toward the child should prevail. Fathers may think that this attitude shows understanding for the needs of the child. The contrary is true. Now, when the child is in a state of confusion, there is a need for a structured environment that will stabilize the child's daily life. Understanding does not mean allowing the child to do everything. Children need to know that there is somebody who loves them so much that he will stop them from doing things that are harmful to themselves (Forster & Stenhouse, 1980).

In this search for stabilizing routine activities, it is important to keep, as much as possible, the same social, physical, and recreational lifestyle as existed in the past. Living in the same school district will enable the child to maintain the same friends and continue with past recreational activities.

A child of the same gender as the noncustodial parent ought not to assume so many responsibilities that most of the child's time is taken up by them. There is a need to find some balance between things the child does around the house and things that are done for himself or herself. Placing a chart in the kitchen or living room that is filled in by the child but that the father is instructed to read every day might facilitate solving this problem.

At the end of the week both the father and the child look over the daily activities and discuss whether it allows enough time for the child to do personal things. Another activity recommended to fathers is to have a box entitled, "I wish I had time to do." Every evening before going to bed, the child is encouraged to think about one thing he or she would have liked to have had time to do. At the end of the week the father and child discuss ways to find the time to do preferred activities.

Children might work very hard to bring the parents back together. This might take the form of inviting the noncustodial parent to school activities without telling the custodial parent, actively to initiate contact for an activity with the other parent and asking the parent at home to make the arrangements. Children should be told repeatedly that parents are not planning to get back together. When the children realize that there is no chance of succeeding in this task, they might proceed to find the parent an ideal mate, such as a teacher, and make sure their parent spends time with this potential mate. Sometimes they invite this person to have coffee or plan a class committee meeting at home. Again, it is important to talk with children and make one's position clear. The explanation should be stern but not degrading.

In most cases with which we have dealt, there was a very close relationship between the children and the custodial fathers. Most of the problems that existed between them were either caused because of lack of communication or because the father was not aware that a problem existed. As soon as that awareness was reached, a solution to the problem followed very soon.

HOW TO DEAL WITH DATING AND REMARRIAGE

It is important to realize that dating is threatening to children because it is destroying the hope that their parents are going to get together again. Therefore, children might use any available way to interfere. Young children might sit between the date and the parent and continuously ask questions so that the adults cannot talk. Others might ask embarrassing questions the first time they meet the date such as, "Are you going to be my new mommy?" Older children might be embarrassed that their parents are doing things that only young people are supposed to do, such as going on dates and thinking about marriage. They might feel confused and rejected by their parent and angry or afraid of the new partner. Noncustodial parents, who are not married and are keeping constant contact with the children, might also encourage these attitudes in the children. Therefore, it is important to prepare the children and to create a trusting environment.

A father could begin by explaining to the children that he cared for the absent parent, but now that she is not around, he feels the need to meet and spend time with people his own age. Dating or spending time with other adults should not rock the regular routine of activities in which the children are engaged, and the relationship with the noncustodial parent should not be threatened by this new development. These precautions will reduce the resistance of the children to dating and, at the same time, will increase the children's awareness of the finality of the divorce. Children should be assured that they are the most important thing in the parent's life. But at the same time, the children should not be allowed to completely control the parent's behavior.

Fathers raise the question of how soon after the divorce one should begin to date. Therapists should emphasize that on the one hand it would be inappropriate to do it too soon because the children need some time to grieve about the broken relationship and adjust behaviorally and cognitively to the new environment. On the other hand, if too much time passes, the children might settle into a new routine of the single-parent family and a change such as dating would be threatening.

Another question fathers might raise is how to deal with some of the problems you encounter when you begin dating again? Some children are very rude with visitors of the opposite sex: "I don't like you," "When will you go home?" The parent's first impulse is to send the child out of the room or to be authoritative and punitive. It might be more helpful to explain that not liking someone is no reason to be impolite. It is especially important to talk with the child and understand his or her reservations. Again, offer assurances that relationships with new adults will not affect the special tie with the child. At all times, parents should keep in mind that they themselves have needs, and in order to build a satisfying relationship with their children, these needs should be satisfied.

Children might not like the looks of the father's new friend. Their concern is that their father is going to change his style in order to adapt to the new partner. Keeping values and behavior constant will cause these concerns to disappear with the passing of time. Some dates can annoy children by taking the role of an "educator" as soon as they enter the home. Children will resent this attitude and ask, "What gives you the right to tell me what to do when I don't even know you?" Some fathers feel caught in the middle. Fathers should be assured that the date, if sensitive, should understand the children's reactions. If this understanding does not happen, the fathers can gently request that criticism or advice the date has about the children should be funneled through them. If the date is offended, this might indicate future problems and the relationship might be reconsidered.

Fathers might report that some children miss the absent parent so much that they immediately become close friends with everyone that they date. The child might suffer from continuous "losses" of adults when these adults disappear. It raises questions about the way adults behave and about the wisdom of getting involved in a relationship. In these instances we would recommend the children be kept out of this process unless things are serious.

Another area where questions arise is entering into sexual relationships as a single father. Should children be fully aware of the parent's sexual activities or should it be a complete secret? Between these two extremes there are many possibilities. Sex in an intact family is generally private. Therefore, sexual behavior of a single parent should also be private. Young children might ask questions such as, "Did she sleep with you in the same bed last night?" Older children might use the parent's behavior as a model. One father realized the effect of his behavior only when his adolescent son brought his girlfriend home one weekend and announced that she was remaining to sleep in his room.

Finally, fathers ask how to deal with the quesion: "Dad, are you getting married?" Children should be reassured that they will be the first to know if and when it will be considered.

Future Trends

As illustrated in the introduction, child custody has gone through various periods when either fathers or mothers almost exclusively received custody. Today the trend is still for the mother to receive custody. However, with the new laws emphasizing the best interests of the child, more men are vying for and receiving custody—if not full custody at least joint custody with shared responsibility. Part of this change is a recognition of the fact that parenting and nurturing are key issues in raising children, not stereotypic ideas of mothering or fathering. Both males and females have these parenting and nurturing instincts and abilities. In 1977 the American Psychological Association approved a resolution supporting this idea, stating that men should not be discriminated against in child custody as well as other child-related issues based on their sex. This statement supports the idea that mothers and fathers can make equally good parents (Salk, 1977).

Another dimension that is beginning to be explored and utilized in divorce is mediation (Haynes, 1981). This entails the partners meeting with a mediator to make property settlements and custody decisions in a less adversarial and more rational and peaceful way. Mediation involves attention to the emotional aspect of the divorce as well as the practical aspects with the interests of both parties being protected by a neutral person. In resolving conflict in this way, relations are often better between former partners, which can evolve into cooperative parenting for the children.

The public awareness and acceptance of fathers as custodial parents has had an impact on more fathers seeking and receiving custody. This has resulted in a need for new and/or modified information and services to facilitate coping with this population. This also involves the awareness of special issues with which single fathers have to deal. In this chapter, we have attempted to give some theoretical perspectives as well as some practical interventions that work with this special population.

References

Bartz, K. W., & Witcher, W. C. (1978). When father gets custody. *Children Today, 7,* 2-6.

Bertin, E. A. (1981). The father as mother. *Family Advocate, 2,* 24-26, 48.

Cantor, D. W. (1977). School-based groups for children of divorce. *Journal of Divorce, 1,* 183-187.

Child Custody Act of 1970. (new) P.A. 1970, No. 91, *Compiled Laws Annotated,* 73-84.

Fisher, B. (1981). *Rebuilding: When your relationship ends.* San Luis Obispo, CA: Impact Publishers.

Forster, J., & Stenhouse, C. (1980). *Take one parent.* Edinburg: Scottish Council for Single Parents.

Foster, H. H., & Freed, D. J. (1978). Life with fathers. In S. N. Katz & M. L. Inker (Eds.), *Fathers, husbands and lovers.* New York: American Bar Association. [Reproduced from original volumes of *Family Law Quarterly, 11,* 321-363 (1978).]

Gardner, R. A. (1970). *The boys and girls book about divorce.* New York: Bantam.

Gardner, R. A. (1977). *The parents book about divorce.* Garden City, NY: Doubleday.

Gasser, R. O., & Taylor, M. (1976). Role adjustment of single parent fathers with dependent children. *The Family Coordinator, 25,* 397-401.

Gatley, R. H., & Koulack, D. (1979). *Single father's handbook: A guide for separated and divorced fathers.* New York: Anchor Books.

Grollman, E. A. (1975). *Talking about divorce and separation.* Boston: Beacon.

Haynes, J. M. (1981). *Divorce mediation: A practical guide for therapists and counselors.* New York: Springer.

Krantzler, M. (1973). *Creative divorce.* New York: M. Evans.

Mendes, H. A. (1979). Single-parent families: A typology of life-styles. *Social Work, 24,* 193-200.

Olds, S. (1980, June). When parents divorce. *Woman's Day,* pp. 70, 108, 110.

Orthner, D. K., Brown, T., & Ferguson, D. (1976). Single-parent fatherhood: An emerging family life style. *The Family Coordinator, 25,* 429-437.

Roman, M., & Haddad, W. (1978). *The disposable parent.* New York: Holt, Rinehart & Winston.

Rosenthal, E. M., & Keshet, H. F. (1981). *Fathers without partners.* Totowa, NJ: Rowman & Littlefield.

Salk, L. (1977). On the custody rights of fathers in divorce. *Journal of Clinical Child Psychology, 6*(2), 49-50.

Soloman, P. F. (1977). The father's revolution in custody cases. *Trial, 13,* 33-37.

Tedder, S. L., Libbee, K. M., & Scherman, A. (1981). A community support group for single custodial fathers. *The Personnel and Guidance Journal, 60*(2), 115-119.

Tedder, S. L., Scherman, A., & Sheridan, K. M. (1984). Impact of group support on divorce adjustment of single custodial fathers. *American Mental Health Counselor Association Journal, 6*(4), 180-189.

U.S. Bureau of the Census. (1983a). *Child support and alimony: 1981* (Advanced report, CPT Series P-23, No. 124). Washington, DC: Government Printing Office.

U.S. Bureau of the Census. (1983b). *Lifetime earnings estimates for men and women in the U.S.: 1979* (CPR Series P-60, No. 139). Washington, DC: Government Printing Office.

Vail, L. O. (1979). *Divorce: The man's complete guide to winning.* New York: Sovereign Books.

Woody, R. H. (1978). *Getting custody.* New York: Macmillan.

19

Women and Men Together But Equal: Issues for Men in Dual-Career Marriages

Lucia Albino Gilbert

While the anger of women may be a necessary stimulus to any sex-role change in our society, our work with the male side of the universe will be more successful if it proceeds out of understanding of the issues, and if it includes a measure of compassion. (Napier, 1986, p. 1)

Men's and women's lives are inextricably linked. As the introductory quote from Napier indicates, recent changes in women's roles and self-perceptions have had and continue to have enormous impact on men. Nonetheless, aspects of both the male and female experience may make the dual-career family pattern difficult even for the well-meaning man and woman. Despite the large percentage of married couples in which both spouses are employed, the dual-career family pattern, as defined here, is far from normative (see Gilbert & Rachlin, in press, for a discussion of how the dual-career family differs from the broader category of dual-earner family, which is normative). A marital life in which a wife and husband are together in a personal, intimate, and economic sense *and* also equal in terms of aspirations, life choices, and personal worth is inconsistent with traditional concepts of marriage and often is difficult to accept cognitively and embrace emotionally. This chapter focuses on traditional and emergent views of masculinity and the male role that directly pertain to the dual-career family pattern. Key issues inherent in the psychosocial development of men are described first. Sources of stress in dual-career marriages and factors that promote effective coping and well-being are then addressed. Finally, recommendations are made for counseling and psychotherapeutic interventions.

The Male Partner in a Changing Society

Men are taught that they must achieve occupationally. In order to attain power, prestige, money, and other indices of achievement, many men readily sacrifice emotional expressiveness, intimacy, and interrelatedness. Because manliness, or one's sense of self as a man, is also tied to the "good provider role" (Bernard, 1981), men often become controlled by their occupational obligations and the economic structure. To be a real man, and a successful man, the male must be an effective breadwinner, whatever the physical and emotional costs involved. Finally, successful men are independent and do what is necessary to make their way in the world.

Such traditional socialization profoundly affects men's behaviors, attitudes, and emotional responses. In this section, the influence of male socialization in three areas—entitlement, dependency, and nurturance—is discussed.

ENTITLEMENT

I've heard complaints from many single women that they can't trust any man's willingness to promote their careers" (Mott, 1985, p. 58). Many men who advocate equality as an ideal in reality view a woman's career as secondary, and the emotional support they provide to their spouse and their level of involvement in family work reflect this view. Male prerogative demands that what men do or want to do should take precedence; and for many men, a successful husband should not have to do housework. Needless to say, being a supportive husband or involved father is difficult when so doing is experienced as infringing on a husband's needs to maintain his own dominance or as interfering with his own ambition. One man in a dual-career marriage described his struggle to live with his ambition and stay in his dual-career marriage as follows: "When I hold my daughter or brush out her hair or tell her stories, I am frightened by the side of me that wants to push ahead at her expense. At the same time, I feel that by taking on more of Roberta's [his wife] load I am losing ground in my career; it's like swimming with rocks in my pockets" (Wright, 1985, p. 166).

Feelings of entitlement may also engender feelings of competition between the spouses (Rice, 1979), which may have positive or negative effects for the marital relationship. On the other hand, an ambitious spouse can enhance a man's own ambition and encourage him to move into new and creative directions. He may be unable to get excited about his spouse's career success, however, when he views his advances and salary as lagging behind. Such a situation may cause embarrassment for the man and perhaps his spouse as well. Because men and women are socialized in the same social context, and therefore acquire many of the same views of gender-related status, both spouses may see husbands who are less successful than wives as unworthy (Blumstein & Schwartz, 1983).

Another important aspect of male entitlement—one that can cause particular stress for men in dual-career marriages—is described by Blumenthal (1985):

> As men, we have been like America itself—and still often are. Accustomed to immediate respect, attention, deference, flirtation when we walk into a room full of women (or by analogy, into a foreign country), it still comes, I think, as a shock to many of us that we are, in some measure, no big deal—in fact, are at times perceived as the enemy. (p. 74)

Women in dual-career marriages do not "need" men the way that men were traditionally brought up to believe they did. Women who can support themselves, and want to, can afford to have expectations for their marriage beyond financial security, and because they are more self-sufficient and have the social sanctions for being so, they can leave if these expectations are not met. And if, indeed, these women "need" men, it is as partners, not protectors; as someone to look across at, not up to.

DEPENDENCY

Gilbert (in press) argues that the struggle to achieve a healthy balance between passive dependent longings and active autonomous strivings is a lifelong developmental task for both genders but that traditional patriarchal views have hidden male dependency needs behind a cloak of power and dominance over women. Men's dependency on women is manifested as a need for power over women rather than a need for connectedness between equals.

The hidden nature of male dependency has been recognized by several other writers. Baumrind (1980), for example, believes that boys are bribed by promises of power and dominance to relinquish aspects of their dependency strivings prematurely and thus may depend more than they realize on unconditional acceptance and nurturance from a woman to sustain their pseudoindependent stance. Similarly, Pogrebin (1983) points out, "Contrary to the popular belief that women have the greater dependency needs, men's [noneconomic] dependency needs are far more insatiable. . . . Sex specialization in caring atrophies men's capacity to give comfort" (p. 197).

NURTURANCE

Men's difficulty in recognizing their dependency can cause immense problems in dual-career marriages because a sine qua non for the maintenance of such a marriage is spouse support (Rapoport & Rapoport, 1982). Spouse support not only involves valuing a spouse's abilities and ambitions, it also involves emotional support, empathic listening, and the ability to nurture. It requires putting aside one's own needs to be nurtured and emotionally sustained and doing so for another. It requires drawing out the emotions and feelings of the other person, something men have typically depended on women to do for them (Pleck, 1981).

Indeed, one of the most typical motivations of men who choose the dual-career lifestyle is the desire to nurture—particularly their children (Gilbert, 1985). Close emotional relationships have increasingly become a core part of these individuals' sense of self as a man. A value shift seems to be occurring in our culture toward greater involvement of men in parenting (although many men do not participate in housework to the degree that women do; Pleck, 1985). Gilbert (1985) reports that in her sample of men in dual-career families, 14% werre judged by raters to be more involved than the wife in parenting, 32% as involved, and 54% less involved.

In summary, when we look at "women and men together but equal" from the male perspective, we see that for men the attainment of more egalitarian roles by women generally involves more than sharing status and power with women. Because male power over women is central to extant views of masculinity and because wives traditionally sustained husbands' personal and work life, men in dual-career families also need to revise their sense of self. This is not a one-time task, and it is not easily accomplished. All the same, as we shall see later, some men are actively engaged in this process of change and they do find it personally rewarding.

Stress and Coping

It would be inaccurate to depict the dual-career family lifestyle as one replete with stress. Clearly, the choice to pursue a nontraditional lifestyle for which there are few societal supports and little precedence suggests that substantial benefits are possible for the individuals involved. The benefits for the female spouse are readily identified and include the opportunity to develop professionally and to establish a sense of self separate from a man and children, economic independence, greater intellectual companionship and contentment, and higher self-esteem (Blumstein & Schwartz, 1983; Gilbert, 1985; Rapoport & Rapoport, 1971, 1976).

The benefits of dual-career marriage for men, at this point, are less dramatic and perhaps less evident than those for women; men have experienced fewer constraints from their traditional roles and have not asked for change. As was mentioned earlier, men's involvement in careers was historically associated with what Bernard (1981) calls the "good provider role." The successful man provided well economically for his dependent wife and children but had little involvement in the home. Thus the foremost potential benefits of dual-career marriage for the male spouse are freedom from the mantle of total economic responsibility and family dependency and opportunities to involve himself in parenting and to express his inherent needs to nurture and bond. As was also noted earlier, men are raised to deny their normal dependency needs behind sex-typed needs for power and dominance; their dependency often gets projected onto women and children. A less direct benefit is learning to accept women as peers in work settings and recognizing women's abilities in the public sector.

Children in dual-career families benefit by having greater contact and involvement with both parents, being exposed to less sex-role stereotypic behavior in the home, and developing a greater sense of independence and competence by sharing responsibilities so that family life is successfully maintained (Russell, 1982; St. John-Parsons, 1978; Stephan & Corder, 1985). Adolescent and young adult children raised in dual-career families surveyed by Knaub (1986) viewed this lifestyle positively and rated their families high in family strength, especially in the areas of concern and support. The three most mentioned benefits of growing up in a dual-career family were having positive role models, financial security, and the opportunity to develop independence; time constraints was the most-mentioned problem. The comment of a 24-year-old male in the sample seems particularly apropos to this topic. He felt that the main advantage to him was "seeing my mother, and therefore, other women as my equal" (p. 435).

SOURCES OF STRESS

Whether, When, and How to Parent

Mary and Mike have been married for five years. Both are in their early thirties and have demanding jobs that require long hours. They are feeling pressure to come to a decision about having a child.

The traditional family structure is a reflection, or outgrowth, of an ideology that places the primary responsibility for direct care of children on women. Parenting is equated with mothering. Thus when dual-career couples consider whether to have children, they also face the additional question of who will care for them. The recent focus on men's capacity to nurture and care for young children (Lamb, 1982, 1986; Pleck, 1985) is a departure from the earlier focus on the potential negative effects of working mothers on children (Hoffman, 1979). Even with changing societal trends, however, this ideology dies hard. Traditional sex-role ideology places the responsibility for child care with the wife, and in practice this typically is still the case even among dual-career families. Moreover, given current employment benefits and policies, women are better able than men to ask for and receive the accommodations necessary for combining work and family (e.g., maternity leaves, flexible schedules). As Schroeder (1985) notes, "If the father would want to take off [to stay home with the newborn infant], if he even mentions it, it's like he has lace on his jockey shorts. You don't do that in America" (p. 16).

Perhaps most crucial to stress in this area is the importance of a child, and a close emotional relationship with a child, to each spouse's self-concept and life goals. For example, should this importance differ markedly between the spouses the stress associated with a decision to remain childless, or to have a first or second child, could be considerable, depending on which spouse wanted a child more and the type of role accommodations characteristic of the marital relationship. Still, today it is easier for the male spouse to admit a low desire to be involved in child rearing and then actually to remain relatively uninvolved than it is for the female spouse. Thus the decision to have a child would be made all the more stressful when one spouse feels she (or he) will have to do all the accommodating. For men, the psychological cost involved in deciding to have a child may be reduced by limiting the number of children to one or two (contrary to popular beliefs, only children fare well in life emotionally and intellectually; Falbo, 1984), by a strong commitment on his part to be involved in parenting, and by redefining traditional ideas of how a child should be reared.

Finally, for many parents, identifying quality day care is a particularly stressful task; although some corporations and communities provide some assistance in this area, the identification of suitable day care is by and large left to the individual family. In the vast majority of dual-career families some outside help is necessary to supplement the parents' care of children. The type of child care generally used depends on the age of the child. Most parents prefer group care for children older than three years, but they show no clear preference for individual or small-group care for children under three years of age (Kamerman, 1980).

Combining Occupational
and Family Roles

John is willing to help out when he can with his son and the housework, but his career is not nine to five. He feels that he is the one with the more demanding and financially rewarding career and that the effort he puts into his career entitles him to be freed from some household and family responsibilities.

How to combine occupational and family roles is a source of stress for both women and men in dual-career families. Neither gender has role models for doing so, and neither gets much encouragement or assistance from their professional world to do so. Typically, the family is expected to accommodate to the demands of one's profession. As Pleck (1983) notes, some conflicts between work and family are intrinsic and present choices that individuals and society must face.

In principle, couples representative of the egalitarian model have dual-career marriages in which both spouses have major commitments to a full-time professional career. Numerous studies (for example, Rapoport & Rapoport, 1976), however, indicate that many dual-career marriages are far from egalitarian. In an in-depth study of men in dual-career families, Gilbert (1985) found three marital types, which she labeled *traditional, participant,* and *role-sharing.* In a traditional dual-career family, the responsibility for family work is retained by the woman, who adds the career role to her traditionally held family role. In the participant type, the parenting is shared by the spouses, but the woman retains responsibility for household duties. In this situation, male dominance is muted and gender-based role specialization is less extensive. In role-sharing dual-career families, both spouses are actively involved in both household duties and parenting. This type of marriage, which is best understood as an ideal that some dual-career couples are striving for, rather than as a common pattern, is most successful in eliminating gender-based role specialization and power associated with male dominance, as evidenced by such indicators as spouses' salaries, sources of spouse support, and involvement in family work.

Factors influencing the type of marital role pattern adopted in dual-career families can be divided into three major categories—personal factors, relational factors, and environmental factors. Personal factors include personality characteristics, attitudes, values, interests, and abilities. Examples of relational factors are sources of power in the relationship (e.g., expert or coercive power) and tasks that need to be done to maintain the family system. Finally, environmental factors refer to the structure of occupations, societal norms and attitudes, and social networks and support systems. Satisfaction with the particular pattern adopted depends on these same factors, as well as on the degree of congruence and mutuality between spouses. Particular attention is given to these factors in the section on coping that follows.

Occupational Mobility and
Job Placement

Lisa returned to school to increase her career opportunities and Larry, her spouse, very much supported this decision. Lisa has now completed her degree and recently received an attractive job offer in a desirable area. The employment opportunities for Larry, however, are relatively unknown and would need to be worked out after relocation.

Job placement and occupational mobility may very well be the most difficult issue for members of dual-career families and one for which there is no ready or easy solution. Finding two equally attractive job offers within reasonable geographic proximity in a desired locale is no small feat and indeed may prove to be impossible. Although couples may wish to give equal weight to the interests of both partners in reaching decisions about new jobs or relocations, various factors often make a strictly egalitarian decision impossible (Wallston, Foster, & Berger, 1978). Husband-oriented career choices are still predominant, however (Bird & Bird, 1985; Gilbert, 1985).

Men's own sense of entitlement may come to the fore when decisions about relocation must be made. As one man remarked in a recent article, "Then it struck me where my fears came from. The man in the family— me—was putting his career at the mercy of his wife's. In the starkest psychological terms, I was following her and abdicating my traditional male role" (Mott, 1985, p. 58).

COPING

A satisfying, fulfilling dual-career marriage depends on the spouses' willingness to struggle with the difficulties of integrating work and family roles and of developing a sense of self, despite societal pressure to conform to gender-typed roles and behaviors. What are the resources needed to effectively weather difficulties, dilemmas, and stresses intrinsic to the dual-career lifestyle? Three conceptual categories particularly useful for understanding stress and coping in dual-career families are personal resources, family resources, and societal resources (Gilbert, 1985).

Personal Resources

Most salient among the personal resources for dealing with stressors are material or financial assets, education, physical health, and sociopsychological characteristics. Among dual-career families, however, the latter resource is most likely to influence coping. Sociopsychological resources include one's personality attributes, characteristic ways of coping, and personal beliefs and attitudes.

Men in dual-career families typcially report relatively high self-esteem, personal styles that reflect expressive (e.g., warmth) and instrumental (e.g., achievement-oriented) traits, and relatively liberal or profeminist views (i.e., belief in the social, political, and economic equality of women and men). Generally speaking, they are supportive of the women's career efforts and have the capacity to value strengths in their wives.

Family Resources

Two characteristics are central to the successful maintenance of a dual-career family lifestyle: (1) mutual spouse support and shared values and (2) coping strategies that reflect redefinition, compromise, and commitment. Because the dual-career family challenges traditional assumptions about family roles and functioning, spouse support is crucial to effective coping—particularly support by the male spouse. (Women are socialized to support men's occupational roles, whereas the reverse is not the case.) Numerous studies report that having a supportive husband is a key factor in successful dual-career marriages (e.g., Rapoport & Rapoport, 1982). Ideally, such support includes positive attitudes toward the woman's career as well as a willingness by the man to involve himself in household and parenting responsibilities.

Spouses in a dual-career marriage typically must struggle with their own sex-role socialization. For example, men committed to role sharing may find it embarrassing to "be caught" vacuuming or doing the laundry or to admit that their wives earn more of the family income than they do; their spouses, in contrast, may well feel reluctant to put their career needs ahead of the husband's or to waken husbands for 2 a.m. feedings. Functioning as a dual-career couple may at times also require behaving in ways that counter societal expectations and risk peer disapproval. A man who "follows his wife," for example, is likely to find that professional colleagues and friends cannot understand why he doesn't divorce her or put his foot down and say, "Stop this career nonsense, woman, and get into the kitchen!"

Finally, the sense of fairness or equity about the balance of family and professional roles achieved by the spouses is crucial. Equality of power is not the issue but rather the perceptions of equity or proportional returns in the exchange of personal and economic resources. That is, does each partner feel that the other is doing his or her fair share when all aspects of the relationship are considered? Successful dual-career marriages are characterized by communication and commitment; compromise, realistic expectations, and flexibility; and an apportionment of household and parental responsibilities that is viewed as equitable by both partners. As one man married to a businesswoman said in a recent study, "Both of us are accommodating people. If an expectation is not met, that is not cause for walking out" (Gilbert, 1985, p. 72).

Societal Resources

The norms and rules of a society provide individuals with a set of ready responses to problems. Unfortunately, for women and men in dual-career families the extant norms and rules often are incompatible or inapplicable to their situation and can themselves be the cause of the stresses and conflicts experienced. Clearly, this is the category of resource that is consistently deficient or unavailable for dual-career couples and the one over which they have the least direct control. Men in dual-career families need to recognize these limited societal supports and existing equities and do all that they can in their organizations to improve things. Also crucial is their ability to recognize those conflicts that are unique to themselves and those conflicts that stem from insufficient societal supports.

At the present time, dual-career couples must cope with the stressors in their lifestyle largely as individuals, negotiating stress-reducing changes and strategies on their own and in a "create as one goes" context. As has been repeatedly noted here, however, the long-term acceptance and maintenance of the dual-career family as a feasible option will require support from society as a whole. Changes in the structure of work, provision for adequate child care, rethinking of transfer and relocation policies, and increased career opportunities for women are all social policy innovations that would make it significantly easier for dual-career families to thrive. (For a detailed discussion of these issues, see Walker, Rozee-Koker, and Wallston, in press.)

In summary, stress in the various areas described is generally minimized by mutuality in spouse support, willingness by the man to be actively involved in parenting, and relatively comparable career opportunities in their present locale. Typically, the husband is more involved in family work when the wife contributes more financially and when greater meaning and importance are attributed to her work. Thus the smaller the difference between the husband's and the wife's income, the more involved the husband is in household and parenting responsibilities (Gilbert, 1985).

Recommendations for the Practitioner

Areas of conflict for men in dual-career families center on the issues discussed in this chapter under the theme "men and women together but equal." Both psychological and societal factors, it has been argued, can hamper and impede attempts to embrace this ideal in real life. How can those in the mental health field assist individuals with this at times thorny process? This final section first addresses what therapists must bring to treatment and then considers various approaches to treatment.

THERAPISTS' ATTITUDES, VALUES, AND KNOWLEDGE

Crucial to working effectively with men in dual-career families is the knowledge and attitudes therapists bring to the therapeutic situation and the conceptual models they use in working with clients. Providing effective therapeutic assistance to individuals in dual-career families may be impossible if the therapist has inadequate knowledge and/or holds negative attitudes about this lifestyle. Moreover, because therapists, not unlike the clients who seek their guidance and help, are products of a relatively traditional socialization process, they need to constantly question their attitudes and beliefs about what it means to be male (or female) in our society. Therapists who are opposed to or ambivalent about women pursuing careers, men being involved in family work, or changes in the traditional sex-role division of labor are not very likely to be able to understand and effectively work with individuals in a dual-career family relationship. Research indicates that men are generally more negative toward nontraditional careers than women; both men and women are more negative toward males pursuing nontraditional roles than females (e.g., Haring, Beyard-Tyler, & Grey, 1983).

In addition, the failure of therapists to recognize the salient internal (psychological) and external (structural) barriers to an egalitarian marriage can be counterproductive and work against understanding the limits and obstacles men in dual-career marriages may face. What is needed is a sensitivity to the real difficulties, both psychological and pragmatic, of developing new concepts of self and of coordinating career and family roles and a respect for the values implicit in the choice of a dual-career family lifestyle. Particularly crucial to effective therapeutic work is the recognition that the experiences of men in the dual-career situations are not the same as those of women. Because the gender-role socialization of women and men differs so dramatically, the areas they experience as problematic and the factors contributing to problem areas often differ markedly. Combining a career and family is a different process, involving different choices and changes for men and women.

For men, the traditional structure of professional careers and the assumptions associated with male entitlement and independence have presented obstacles to fuller involvement in family life. For women, the traditional division of labor and assumptions about female dependency and nurturance have presented obstacles to fuller involvement in professional careers. These differences show up in the day-to-day conflicts of men and women in dual-career families and the issues they bring to therapy.

Husbands typically struggle with esteem issues stemming from a perceived loss of power and prestige or decreased freedom in their occupational pursuits, competition with spouses, or involvement in "women's work" within the family. Some men discover a fundamental discrepancy within the marriage; it may be easier to be a supporter or advocate if one's own immediate life is not affected. Wives, in contrast, often struggle with esteem issues regarding conflicts between parenting responsibilities and career interests, legitimate expectations for a man's involvement in family work, and redefinitions of their roles of wife and mother.

EXAMPLES OF THERAPEUTIC INTERVENTIONS

There are many possible approaches to assisting men in dual-career families—at both the proactive and reactive levels of intervention. Most of us work at the reactive or treatment level. We see individuals or couples when they are having difficulties. In this section, issues that often emerge at the treatment level are addressed first. Programs possible at the preventive level are then considered briefly.

Therapists who work at the *treatment level* typically help their clients become aware of underlying feelings and attitudes related to problem areas. Particularly pertinent to this process are the various factors outlined in the earlier sections of this chapter. For example, understanding and acknowledging spouses' values about the prerogatives associated with being male is a sensitive and potentially explosive process, but one that is often essential to conflicts many clients experience. In the process of therapy some men may find that they are willing to make the changes needed and come to see them as benefiting themselves and their relationship. Others, however, may discover that to alter traditional sex-role behaviors and beliefs appreciably would be too great a cost given their career goals and life plans. Still others are cognizant of discrepancies between their attitudes and behavior and will continue to live this "double standard" until circumstances or their spouse push for change. As one client said, "I think it is entirely unfair that my wife does everything."

The handling of household responsibilities and parenting is another area frequently associated with relationship difficulties. Oftentimes men wish that they felt differently than they do or deny deeply ingrained beliefs and values. Helping clients to realize and acknowledge their inner emotional reality, regardless of how inconsistent it seems with cognitively held views, can free them of entrenched positions and allow them to consider alternate views and ways of being. Examining the implicit and explicit expectations of the marital contract and its relationship to traditional views of marriage is often an essential part of this process. Open, honest discussions of what is preferred, what is needed, and what is workable are then possible.

A case in point is a couple in which the male felt unappreciated by his spouse. He was preparing dinner three nights a week and doing what he considered to be his fair share of the family work. What emerged during the therapy was how his sense of male entitlements was getting in his way. He felt that he should be thanked for doing his share—after all, men typically have not done what he was doing. This attitude made his wife furious. Was she to be thanked for being a successful businesswoman because women typically have not done so? Even more upsetting to her was his then implicit assumption that she did not need to be thanked for preparing dinner the other four nights, because that is women's work. Important aspects of the therapeutic process for him were becoming aware of his unconscious attitudes about male and female rights and responsibilities in the marriage and assisting him in understanding how he and his spouse could feel the way they did. Crucial to this process was developing the self-knowledge and conviction that expanding his own perspective to include his wife's viewpoint did not mean abandoning his own position or life experiences. (For more details on this process, see Gilbert, 1984).

The proactive, or preventive, model—in contrast to the reactive model—educates individuals about the potential problems and challenges that men in a dual-career relationship may face. (The assessment schema developed by O'Neil, Fishman, and Kinsella-Shaw, in press, and the value analysis described by Walker et al., in press, provide material especially pertinent to proactive approaches.) The purpose of this type of intervention is both consciousness-raising and skills-building. Participants are given the opportunity to learn about the day-to-day realities of the dual-career family lifestyle, to examine their personal attitudes, values, and life goals vis-à-vis the egalitarian ideals of such a lifestyle, and, finally, to assess the likelihood of their being able to make the personal and attitudinal changes necessary to accommodate to a dual-career family situation as well as to develop strategies for problem solving and decision making. Daniluck and Herman (1984), for example, report that a workshop format was useful in facilitating parenthood decision-making—but of career women, not men. To date, few programs of this sort have been developed specifically for men. Moorman (1986), however, describes an organization called Father Focus, which provides fathers with an opportunity to talk about their lives and the choices they must make in integrating work and family demands.

Preventive programs can also take the form of marital enrichment and stress management programs. Marital enrichment is based on the premise that couples can provide support for each other and learn from each other if they have the opportunity to interact together as couples. As Mace (1982) points out, interacting as a couple in a couples' group is very different from interacting as an individual in a group. One of the key differences is that couples in a group interaction share their marriages by having a dialogue in front of other couples. This provides an experiential basis for sharing their marital experience. Also crucial is the cross-couple identification, modeling, and support underlying this model of intervention. Many men in dual-career families feel alone in their struggle with an emerging lifestyle, and hearing how other families deal with various conflicts and difficulties can be very helpful.

Like marital enrichment, stress management is particularly relevant to individuals attempting a nontraditional marital relationship. These individuals are coming to grips with new concepts of self and are pioneering a lifestyle with few societal supports. A key aspect of stress management for men in dual-career families is learning how to define and recognize stress and its physical and emotional effects and how to minimize or prevent its chronic development. Often individuals are unaware of how stressed they are because they are used to it or they assume it comes with the turf. Looking at some of the internal and external factors identified in this chapter, which mediate or cause the stress, can help in determining what behavioral or attitudinal changes could best alleviate or minimize the stress and promote more efective coping. Moreover, good nutrition, regular physical exercise, practice in self-assertion or time management, and an understanding of typical stressors for dual-career families can be effective preventive measures.

Summary

Some men are basing their self-evaluations less on work-related issues and more on family-related issues and are attempting to integrate work and family into their concept of career. This is especially true of men who live in a dual-career family situation. Although there is much evidence that these changes benefit and enrich men's lives, they also encounter resistance—both from within men themselves and from the society at large. Astrachan (1986), in his book *How men feel: Their response to women's demands for equality and power* concluded that although nearly all men approve of working wives, only 5% to 10% support women's demands for independence and equality. Although his findings may not accurately describe men in dual-career families, they do reflect the larger reality in which these men live. Mental health professionals need to be cognizant of these complex issues and how they affect men's lives. And, as was mentioned at the outset of this chapter, their therapeutic work with men in dual-career families needs to "proceed out of an understanding of the issues . . . and a measure of compassion" (Napier, 1986, p. 1).

References

Astrachan, A. (1986). *How men feel: Their response to women's demands for equality and power.* Garden City, NY: Anchor Press/Doubleday.

Baumrind, D. (1980). New directions in socialization research. *American Psychologist, 35,* 639-652.

Bernard, J. (1981). The good provider role: Its rise and fall. *American Psychologist, 36,* 1-12.

Bird, G. A., & Bird, G. W. (1985). Determinants of mobility in two-earner families: Does the wife's income count? *Journal of Marriage and the Family, 47,* 753-758.

Blumenthal, M. (1985, November 10). No big deal. *The New York Times Magazine,* p. 74.

Blumstein, P., & Schwartz, P. (1983). *American couples: Money, work, sex.* New York: William Morrow.

Daniluck, J. D., & Herman, A. (1984). Parenthood decision-making. *Family Relations, 33,* 607-612.

Falbo, T. (Ed.). (1984). *The single-child family.* New York: Guilford.

Gilbert, L. A. (1984). Understanding dual-career families. In *Perspectives on career development and behavior and the family: Family therapy collections.* Rockville, MD: Aspen Systems Corp.

Gilbert, L. A. (1985). *Men in dual-career families: Current realities and future prospects.* Hillsdale, NJ: Lawrence Erlbaum.

Gilbert, L. A. (in press). Gender issues in psychotherapy. In J. R. McNamara & M. A. Appel (Eds.), *Critical issues, developments, and trends in professional psychology* (Vol. 3). New York: Praeger.

Gilbert, L. A., & Rachin, V. (in press). Mental health and psychological functioning of dual-career families. *The Counseling Psychologist.*

Haring, M., Beyard-Tyler, K., & Gray, J. (1983). Sex-biased attitudes of counselors: The special case of nontraditional careers. *Counseling and Values, 27,* 242-247.

Hoffman, L. W. (1979). Maternal employment: 1979. *American Psychologist, 34,* 859-865.

Kamerman, S. B. (1980). *Parenting in an unresponsive society: Managing work and family.* New York: Free Press.

Knaub, P. K. (1986). Growing up in a dual-career family. *Family Relations: Journal of Applied Family & Child Studies, 35,* 431-437.

Lamb, M. E. (1982). *The role of the father in child development.* Somerset, NJ: John Wiley.

Lamb, M. E. (1986). *The father's role: Applied perspectives.* Somerset, NJ: John Wiley.

Mace, D. R. (1982). *Close companions: The marriage enrichment handbook.* New York: Continuum.

Moorman, F. B. (1986, May 18). Putting kids first. *The New York Times Magazine,* p. 114.

Mott, G. (1985, April 14). Following a wife's move. *The New York Times Magazine,* p. 58.

Napier, A. (1986). *Family politics theme for speakers.* National Council on Family Relations Report, Vol. 31, No. 3.

O'Neil, J. M., Fishman, D. M., & Kinsella-Shaw, M. (in press). Dual-career couples' career transitions and normative dilemmas: A preliminary assessment model. *The Counseling Psychologist.*

Pleck, J. H. (1981). Men's power with women, other men, and society: A men's movement analysis. In R. A. Lewis (Ed.), *Men in difficult times: Masculinity today and tomorrow* (pp. 234-244). Englewood Cliffs, NJ: Prentice-Hall.

Pleck, J. H. (1983). Husbands' paid work and family roles: Current resarch issues. In H. Lopata & J. H. Pleck (Eds.), *Research in the interweave of social roles: Jobs and families* (pp. 251-333). Greenwich, CT: JAI Press.

Pleck, J. H. (1985). *Working wives/working husbands.* Newbury Park, CA: Sage.

Pogrebin, L. C. (1983). *Family politics: Love and power on an intimate frontier.* New York: McGraw Hill.

Rapoport, R., & Rapoport, R. N. (1971). *Dual-career families.* Middlesex, England: Penguin.

Rapoport, R., & Rapoport, R. N. (1976). Dual-career families re-examined. London: Martin Robertson.

Rapoport, R., & Rapoport, R. N. (1982). The next generation in dual-earner family research.

In J. Aldous (Ed.), *Two paychecks: Life in dual-earner families* (pp. 229-244). Newbury Park, CA: Sage.

Rice, D. G. (1979). *Dual-career marriage: Conflict and treatment.* New York: Free Press.

Russell, G. (1982). Highly participant Australian fathers. *Merrill-Palmer Quarterly, 28,* 137-156.

Schroeder, P. (1985, December 29). Should leaves for new parents be mandatory? *The New York Times,* p. 16E.

St. John-Parsons, D. (1978). Continuous dual-career families: A case study. *Psychology of Women Quarterly, 3,* 30-42.

Stephan, C. W., & Corder, J. (1985). The effects of dual-career families on adolescents' sex-role attitudes, work and family plans, and choices of important others. *Journal of Marriage and the Family, 47,* 921-930.

Walker, L. S., Rozee-Koker, P., & Wallston, B. S. (in press). Social policy and the dual-career family: Bringing the social context into counseling. *Counseling Psychologist.*

Wallston, B. S., Foster, M. A., & Berger, M. (1978). I will follow him: Myth, reality, or forced choice—job-seeking experiences of dual-career couples. *Psychology of Women Quarterly, 3,* 9-21.

Wright, L. (1985, December). I want to be alone. *Texas Monthly,* pp. 164, 166, 168.

20

Men in Marital Therapy

Barry Graff

The greatest ordeal in life is marriage—it is the central focus for enlightenment and the natural therapeutic process in the culture.

—Carl Whitaker

Men are often more deeply involved in their marriages and families than is apparent. If masculine inexpressiveness and feminine symptom expression blind therapists to a couple's commitment, therapy will be greatly hindered. It is the marriage that is potentially the most therapeutic relationship; any intervention should recognize and facilitate this rather than ignore or try to replace it. When therapists recognize this, they are prepared to see caring, commitment, and hope where there appears to be only pain, conflict, and alienation.

Psychotherapy is a verbal, dependent, nurturing, and expensive experience. Therefore, women are traditionally allowed to want psychotherapy and men are not. If a man seeks help, especially from another man, he experiences himself as weak. Men, and their wives, are frightened by men not being strong and silent, so they silently conspire to protect the man from these feelings. Men do this by labeling wives (or children) as the problem, by providing them with symptoms, and by sending them for help. They do not mind if wives spend all that money; women are expected to spend money, men to conserve it. Women also spend words and feelings, and men conserve them. How nicely role expectations create conflict.

Assumptions

First, all symptomatology is part of a relationship complementarity. If one partner shows a symptom, this serves a relationship function, and the spouse will help keep the symptom in place. This helps to avoid labeling either partner as "patient" (usually the wife) or "villain" (usually the husband). It also makes it imperative that couples be seen together in therapy. Seeing one spouse alone, usually the wife, leads to maintenance of the role set-up or to divorce.

Second, couples come for help most often when trying to accomplish a transition in the natural development of their family. The "problem" may have existed for some time, but professional help is sought when it is serving to delay a stage of growth. These stages, according to Milton Erickson, are courtship, marriage, childbirth and dealing with the young, middle marriage, weaning parents from children, and retirement and old age (Haley, 1973). The case studies presented will relate to two of these stages.

A word of caution: This chapter is written from the point of view of a male therapist seeing heterosexual married couples. The basic principles will apply in other situations. These basic theoretical principles follow and will be illustrated through case studies. The two theorists who have had the most impact on my work are Virginia Satir and Carl Whitaker.

Theoretical Principles

VIRGINIA SATIR

In her classic work, *Conjoint Family Therapy*, Virginia Satir delineates a number of basic concepts that apply to work with couples. These concepts are family pain, the identified patient (IP), homeostasis, family triangles, and metacommunication. In addition, her thoughts concerning the appearance of symptoms and the inclusion of the absent parent will be useful to cite here.

Amending her definition of identified patient to focus on one of the marital partners, we have "a *spouse* who is most obviously affected by the painful marital relationship and most subjected to *family* dysfunction." This symptom carrier is "sending an SOS about the marital pain and resulting family imbalance; her/his symptoms are a message that s/he is distorting her/his own growth as a result of trying to alleviate and absorb the *marital* pain" (Satir, 1983, p. 2).

As stated, the IP in a marriage is usually the wife, fulfilling her societal role of keeper of the feelings. When the husband is the symptom carrier, it most often takes the form of alcoholism or physical illness, thus providing only an indirect entrance into therapy.

Satir further hypothesized that "when one person in a family has pain . . . all family members are feeling this pain in some way" (Satir, 1983, p. 1). This is not limited to the symptom of pain. Again, when the children are not used as IPs, the most likely carrier of family pain is the wife. Even when the symptom is male alcoholism, this seems to dull his pain and increase hers.

Family (marital) *homeostasis* is defined by Satir as "a process by which the family balances forces within itself to achieve unity and working order" (Satir, 1983, p. 1). Thus the IP's symptoms and behavior not only serve an individual function, they serve to maintain a balance in the marriage. The fears seem to be of extreme marital disharmony, abandonment, or a severe breakdown in the non-IP spouse. The particular sense of the symptoms or behaviors can only be understood in terms of the relationship. The case study of Mr. L. and his wife will later provide an illustration of this.

The *family triangle* is a construct by which Satir describes how the spouses and one child (the IP) form a three-cornered structure to alleviate, minimize, or divert attention from the marital conflicts. Again, this serves the purpose of preventing fantasized or real catastrophe resulting from intimate spousal interaction. The therapist (especially the male therapist) who innocently (naively?) accepts the IP wife into individual therapy is forming a "therapy triangle." Intimacy and energy are diverted into the client-therapist relationship, and "successful" therapy often leads to divorce. It is important to remember here that divorce is often a way of maintaining certain structural aspects of the marriage. Thus the therapist can serve the marital homeostasis by keeping the wife in long-term, anxiety reducing therapy that promotes no individual change, or by forming an intense, "productive" therapeutic alliance that helps avoid catastrophe through distance or divorce.

The great power of these maneuvers can be understood only if *metacommunication* is understood. The denotative level of communication is the literal content. The metacommunicative level is a comment on the content *and* the nature of the relationship between the communicators. Therefore, when words say, "I will be glad to help you with your anxiety and feelings of low self-esteem, Mrs. Smith," the metacommunication often is, "We will continue to see you and your symptoms as the problem, and protect your husband from breaking down and abandoning you. In return, I would appreciate it if you would adore me as if I had great potency and wisdom."

Because these latter messages are nonverbal and partially, or wholly, out of awareness, they are very difficult to respond to or change. When therapy is defined as couples therapy, a statement is being made on the meta-level of the importance of both spouses' participation.

CARL WHITAKER

Whitaker has four assumptions about marriage that underlie work with couples. They express his reverence for an optimism about marriage. They also convey his belief in the power of the marital system over the dynamics of the individual.

First, the choice of a spouse is "done with purpose and wisdom"(Neill & Kniskern, 1982, p. 164). This is accomplished on the unconscious level, and the reasons are therefore never totally understandable. This assumption should lead the therapist to appreciate the "rightness" of the marriage, and to understand the "joint responsibility couples have for all aspects of the marital relationship" (Neill & Kniskern, 1982, p. 164).

Second, marriage is "an attempt by the individual to complete himself or herself" (Neill & Kniskern, 1982, p. 164). There is deep yearning for intimacy and closeness, and marriage is the best chance to achieve this. Therefore, the "healthiness" or "viability" of a marriage is judged by its potential for intimacy. One can more easily accept many serious difficulties if this potential is seen.

Third, marriage functions at a primitive (unconscious) level most of the time, and does not need to be hampered by trying to make it orderly or consistent. For example, Whitaker would not see the need to teach communication skills to couples. While I do not take a stance quite as extreme as his, I strongly emphasize facilitating the natural structure and communications pattern of the marriage, rather than trying to impose a "right way" to relate.

Fourth, the pathology of the individual is not the focus. More specifically, he believes that "one partner carries the symptoms and the other partner carries the repression and stability" (Neill & Kniskern, 1982, p. 184) in the relationship. Therefore, no matter how extreme or obnoxious the behavior of one partner, the therapist should search until the system function of the symptoms and the stability are found. The case studies will serve to illustrate this.

Male Issues

Three recurring issues that confront male therapists and male clients in couples therapy are competition, sexuality, and adequacy. These themes will be indirectly addressed in the following case studies.

Competition has too often been seen in terms of victor and vanquished. Competition may be seen as two peers, most often friends, struggling together head to head. They experience their strength, and feel closer when the competition is over. Because verbal skills are in short supply, the competition provides a framework for learning to love each other. A usually unspoken rule is that the competition does not have a girl or woman as the prize.

This model has seemed to translate directly to work with couples. Male therapists often arm wrestle, figuratively, with the husband. This is an exhilarating, revealing experience that temporarily excludes the wife. It helps the therapist to bond, and to lay the foundation for resolving later differences. The case of Mr. and Mrs. P. provides a good illustration of this phenomenon.

This competitive bonding also seems to balance the sexuality that exists between male therapist and female client. Because the wife has been excluded from the male-male bonding, the husband feels less threatened when he is excluded from the male-female bonding. In addition, since the sexuality is experienced in the husband's presence, his fantasies do not tend to enhance it unnecessarily. Most often, the sexuality is acknowledged in some humorous way. One woman related a "Dear Abby" column about a therapist who asked his female client to take off her clothes in the eighth session. When I asked, "What number session is this?" we all laughed and never needed to address the issue any further. The primary function of addressing the sexuality between male therapist and female client is confirmation of its existence for the client, and usually requires only brief attention.

Male adequacy is often tied to competition and sexuality, but is best understood in therapy in terms of mutuality. Client and therapist can only be adequate together; if one feels inadequate, both do. The model for this is parental, rather than peer—parental, as in delight and approval given in response to a son's accomplishments, especially when they surpass one's own. When male clients assert a direction for their marriage contrary to one that the therapist has been fostering, one ought to feel like a proud parent witnessing a son's move toward independence.

The issue of adequacy seems also to be addressed effectively when feelings of inadequacy are shared openly. Husbands are often surprised by how bewildered and overwhelmed the therapist may feel in the sessions, but relieved as well to find that another man does not have all the answers for him and his marriage.

In my experience with couples, an issue that has not been a central one is commitment. Only when two people have not yet "coupled," or are about to "uncouple," does it get much attention. Men are consistently as committed to the relationship as their wives. If evidence of the commitment is sparse, the couple is helped to rediscover it. I have rarely been called upon to help a couple create it.

CASE 1: MR. AND MRS. P.

Bad fathers make it easier for the kids to leave home and family.

—Carl Whitaker

Mr. and Mrs. P. suffered for 25 of their 30 years of marriage before they sought help with a stage of development. Mrs. P. had been in individual therapy for two years with another therapist. She was involved in severe marital and family problems, but her husband had refused to come into therapy. The individual therapist had referred them to me, and they finally came for an initial consultation. Mrs. P. was friendly, gracious, and obsequious, while Mr. P. presented an extremely belligerent and hostile stance. His nonverbal message was, "I'd rather be anywhere than here; if you're not careful I will walk out; this certainly is our first and last meeting."

My own internal response was complex: I first thought, "I'd love to tell this mean S.O.B. to leave." That felt good; it helped me feel strong enough to tussle with him. My second thought was, "How can I connect with this man?"; and I began searching for parts of me that might empathize with him. As we began talking, I decided that letting them tell their story and show their relationship by talking to each other would be futile because of the alienation between them. I decided instead to alternate as an individual, person-centered therapist for each of them. It seemed that hope would come from a sense of empathic response and connection with me, rather than from their own relationship. I wanted both of them—but especially Mr. P.—to feel that I understood them because we were similar inside. As a pretermination discussion later indicated, this proved to be a fortuitous choice.

Mrs. P. began by telling of their long-term squabbles, most involving conflicts over the children. She presented herself as a soft, sympathetic mother. Mr. P. responded by confirming her implied picture of him as an unreasonable, raging bully. He cursed his children, became red-faced and rigid, and seemed to be frightening his wife. I wondered, "When have I felt or acted like this man? What has pulled the monster out in me?" Memories came immediately flooding in, of times when I was trying to discipline my children and be a "good father." When my wife saw me being too harsh, she became extra soft and permissive; an immediate coalition of mother and children versus father resulted. At these times I felt chastised, guilty, and, most important, on the outside. With this image, it was relatively easy to ally with Mr. P. When experiencing his guilt, hurt, and helplessness at being put on the outside, partly in response to his own excesses, I could easily understand his rage and manner.

As I reflected his feelings, I also used my tone of voice and choice of words to show him glimpses of the harsh, rageful husband/father in me. This was very risky for me; I don't usually show the negative sides of myself that quickly. However, it proved worthwhile. I began to feel a bond forming between us. By the end of the session he had relaxed, and the couple decided to continue therapy.

Mr. and Mrs. P. stayed in therapy for just over a year, attending weekly. They worked on resolving their great divergence over their children, and moving through the "weaning parents from children" stage of family development. We focused on helping Mrs. P. become angrier and setting more limits with the "children," some of whom were still dependent on the P's even though they were in their twenties. A major transition came when the parents decided to move out of state, leaving their six oldest children, aged 19 and up, to fend for themselves.

In a session a few weeks before termination, Mr. and Mrs. P. discussed their marriage, Mrs. P.'s individual therapy, and our therapy relationship. They presented a poignant picture of the breakdown of their marriage relationship. After two of their children had been born, the closeness that they had initially experienced began to disappear. The economic, physical, and emotional stresses of raising a family led to conflict and alienation. Mrs. P. found herself going to the children for comfort, and Mr. P. found himself alone, on the outside, usually seen by the rest of the family as the "bad guy." He related this in a soft, vulnerable, almost pleading tone. He was both mourning what he had lost, and relieved and glad that he and his wife had regained some of this closeness.

She related how individual therapy had helped her, but had also brought her to the brink of divorce. She had reached a point where she would have left if he had not come to therapy and changed. She then asked why he had been so resistant to therapy. He related that he had again felt on the outside, labeled as the bad guy. This had been exacerbated when the individual therapist told her not to talk with her husband about therapy. Her therapy had begun to feel like an affair to him, with the therapist preferred over him. Amazingly, she responded by saying that although she wasn't having an affair, she would have chosen therapy over her marriage. As deprived as he was on the outside, she was just as deprived on the inside. Therefore, with her children almost grown, she needed them to be close again, or she would have had to leave for her own survival.

I then asked him about our therapy. He remembered his resistant feelings entering therapy, and reminisced about our first session. He stated that he had trusted me from the beginning, that he didn't feel that I was on his wife's side. I replied that I had sensed his trust, and his pleasure at seeing my "son-of-a-bitch" side. He laughed, and confirmed my perceptions, saying that he had come in prepared not to return. He had changed his mind when he felt that I understood him and that we were alike.

MR. AND MRS. L.

Mr. L.'s first question when he came into my office was, "Am I in a midlife crisis?" He was depressed, most notably over his inability to motivate himself in his work. He was also disturbed by the fact that his wife was confused and upset by his depression and lack of motivation. He presented a tentative, insecure manner, and was clearly afraid to present himself in a definitive way. He was 41 years old, had been married for 9 years, and had a 4-year old daughter. He was in the process of leaving a successful job, and starting his own business.

Although the term "midlife crisis" accurately described the inner experience of the person involved, "mid-life transition" more effectively portrayed the developmental stage being traversed. "Crisis" focuses on the feeling of "ending," while "transition" also captures the sense of "beginning" of a new experience. Two interpersonal aspects of midlife transition for married men are a newly highlighted need for acceptance from their wives, and a need for a feeling of commonality with other men. Because of the role expectations men carry, many recognize this latter need much less readily. With this in mind, I decided to talk about my own midlife experience with Mr. L. in our first session.

I revealed that the most significant part of my experience of turning 40 was that I no longer had a sense of an older generation supporting me. My parents are alive and healthy, and I had not depended on them in any significant way for many years. However, suddenly I was more aware that there was no one to take over for me. This awareness was both frightening and exhilarating; it made me feel very alone, but also served to push me to seek more closeness and comfort from family and friends. I also told him that I had begun thinking about my conception of maleness, and my demands on myself. I related that this process helped me to feel stronger, more capable of taking the responsibility for myself, and sharing the responsibility of my family.

As usually happens, my openness stimulated similar self-disclosure in my client. Mr. L. revealed that his parents had both died within the past three years, his mother less than a year ago. He stated that though he had not been aware of it, he had been feeling isolated and without support. His mother had lived with his family during the last year of her life, and her struggle with illness had become very much a part of his family life. As he talked, he realized that he had not given himself a chance to mourn her properly. This awareness allowed him to continue and complete his mourning, both in our sessions and at home.

One ironically troublesome aspect of his mourning involved his inheritance. He had inherited a few hundred thousand dollars. At about the same time he had decided to go into business for himself. He had been slow to work at the business, and was concerned by his lack of motivation.

Specifically, he worried that he was too dependent on his inheritance, and would use it instead of his own energy and initiative.

He continued to talk about previously unexplored feelings when he returned for the second session. Before the birth of their first child, Mrs. L. worked in a professional capacity in the same company as Mr. L. She left her work to raise their child, and they were now planning to have a second. This set of circumstances left Mr. L. feeling all the more alone, burdened with being the sole "breadwinner." Because his wife had been successful herself, it was especially painful and confusing when she doubted his capacity to succeed.

He also talked about his father and father-in-law. He portrayed his father as a somewhat frightened man, definitely not a risk taker. When a challenge had come along, economic or otherwise, he had seen his father as very frightened, almost overwhelmed. His father-in-law may have felt as his father had, but he dealt with his fears differently. He provided a very secure, although somewhat narrow and rigid economic and psychological environment for his children. He did this by staying in the same government position for 40 years.

Mr. L. reported that these two role models compounded his feelings of inadequacy. He feared becoming frozen like his father-in-law, and failing as his father had. He also felt that his wife was getting very anxious because he wasn't providing the same worry-free environment that her father had provided.

Mr. L. was seeing himself as unmotivated, inadequate, and depressed, and he feared that his wife had also begun to doubt him. He had attempted to reframe this experience, calling it a "midlife crisis." At this point in the therapy, I decided to expand on his reframing to help ease his burden. I stated that he and his family were really attempting to accomplish three developmental tasks at the same time. The three were the stage of childbirth and dealing with the young, mid-life transitions, and the grieving process. I emphasized that three were more than anyone could accomplish easily. He responded with recognition and relief, and went on to discuss past transitions in his life.

When Mr. L. graduated from high school, he wanted a year off before starting college. Family pressure and fear of risk taking forced him to abandon his plans and enter a local college. He performed poorly, and temporarily saw himself as a failure. His advisor at the college reinforced this perception, telling him that he probably was not qualified for college at all.

He was initially very discouraged, and eventually left school and went to work. He then returned to school at a university away from home, did very well, and proceeded to get a graduate degree. He further reminisced about returning to his original college to see the advisor who had discouraged him. He intended to show him how mistaken he had been. Even though the advisor had left the school, Mr. L. was still able to experience his "moment of triumph."

After this recollection, we explored the relationship between the young man that he had been, and the person that he had become. He quickly portrayed himself then as independent, willing to follow his own ideas about himself, and as productively free-spirited. He was able to see his initial "failure" as an assertion of self, as a way to have the year off that he needed.

We then drew a parallel to his present situation. His lack of activity was redefined as taking another year off. He needed this time to grieve and to rediscover the parts of himself that he now needed. His depression occurred because he had turned the task of rekindling his self-esteem over to his wife. This redefinition excited Mr. L., and gave him a sense of relief, but was not sufficient to complete his therapy. Focusing on the last stage of therapy will demonstrate why this is a case study in couples therapy.

Systems theory would predict that unless the changes in effect and perception begun by Mr. L. were accompanied by contextual changes, the power of the marital homeostasis would negate the individual changes. The marital pain must be relieved so that the symptoms no longer have a function. Therefore, Mr. L. had to bring his wife into therapy to help her to reinforce his growth rather than his symptoms.

Mr. L. shared some of the content of the sessions with his wife at home, but saved the more anxiety producing issues for the safety of therapy. When he told her the meaning of his inactivity, lack of motivation, and depression, she responded with interest but with some doubt. She talked of her own fears, and her need to have him talk about what he had been experiencing. As his story continued to unfold, she shared more about her own experience. She focused on the contrast between her ultra-secure childhood, and the changes Mr. L. kept making in his work. Although she clearly saw their past as successful, his recent inactivity seemed different to her. She mentioned that the death of his mother, with whom she had become very close, left her feeling alone and grieving.

As their interaction continued, she relaxed more and more. Finally, she told him that she could be patient with his process if he would share it with her. She didn't need him to lessen her anxiety by being an efficient "breadwinner" like her father; in fact, she had chosen him for his willingness to be creative and adventuresome. However, when he did this silently, she felt alone and vulnerable. He was ready to hear this, and used it to solidify his regained sense of self. Responsibility for his self-concept was his again, with the support of his marriage.

Techniques

Avoidance of the "therapy triangle" identification with male issues, and attention to family developmental issues were crucial in helping Mr. and Mrs. P. In addition, two other techniques were used. First, the insertion of oneself into the relationship as a true intermediary, that is, to reflect one spouse's feeling to the partner, then helping the partner understand the underlying vulnerable feelings that are masked by confusing or hostile words. For example, when Mr. P. would say in a rageful voice, "You always take the kids' side!" the therapist might say to Mrs. P., "I feel so angry and hurt when I become the 'bad guy' over and over." Always ask the spouse spoken for to correct any misrepresentation; then check the partner's understanding, and relay the response back the other way. This is done instead of teaching communication skills, because the couple has lost contact with each other, not because they lack sophistication as communicators.

Mr. and Mrs. P. talked about the early part of their relationship just before termination. Usually this is asked of couples in the first session, which helps to assess the strength and feeling in their initial bonding. This is the major criterion for the later success of marital therapy. The second advantage of this reexploration is that the couple tends to reexperience both the positive aspects of their relationship, and the high intensity of feeling of that time of their lives. This often helps a wife become reacquainted with the feeling man underlying the cold, unavailable one that she has felt stuck with in recent years.

References

Haley, J. (1973). *Uncommon therapy: The psychiatric techniques of Milton H. Erickson, M.D.* New York: Ballantine.

Neill, J. R., & Kniskern, D.P.O. (Eds.). (1982). *From Psyche to system: The evolving therapy of Carl Whitaker.* New York: Guilford.

Satir, V. (1983). *Conjoint family therapy.* Palo Alto, CA: Science and Behavior Books.

21

Working with Men Who Batter

Don Long

National estimates suggest that half of American men become physically violent with a woman at least once. About 20% of men are violent regularly, perhaps once a month or more. Three out of four men use verbal abuse (psychological violence) as a mechanism of control in their homes (Gelles, 1974). Awareness of these statistics makes it extremely difficult to claim that men who use violence against women are deviant. They are neither unusual nor aberrant. This behavior is in fact part of the "normal" behavior of the American male. There is a great danger in any therapeutic approach that singles out men who batter as examples of psychological problems independent from the social origins of and support for male violence. This individuation of a social problem that is manifested by some, but not all, men is in essence a denial of responsibility by the professional who has not recognized in this violence a masculine behavior from which all men benefit through the perpetuation of power over women. Treatment of men who batter that remains focused on the culpability of the individual fails to deal with some very basic and essential elements in the search for men's health. This by no means is intended to deny that individual psychological problems are sometimes involved in men who batter. However, the social context of male power and control issues in an era of declining social and political power for many individual men often provides the more effective treatment modality.

What, then, are some of the social conditions that provide a context for battery? The simplest way to identify the core of the problem is to examine masculinity itself. What must men understand about the nature of their gender role to be able to begin changing it?

Robert Brannon's (David & Brannon, 1976) four factors that define contemporary masculinity ("no sissy stuff"; "the big wheel"; "the sturdy oak"; and "give 'em hell") inform us quite inadvertently about men who batter; in fact, they provide us a clear portrait. Fear of femininity is at the center of this man. All actions and views are taken in light of the need to demonstrate himself "not female" as completely as possible. No "real man" acts, thinks, feels like a woman. Interwoven with this is a behavioral pattern of egotism and self-centeredness, expectations of control and success, alienation from personal weakness, and the need to maintain separateness (independence) as more powerful than the desire to sustain unity (dependence) (see Rubin, 1983). Masculinity also permits the use of violence in a context of proving manhood through daring, courage, and aggressiveness. The individual batterer uses violence at the level he deems necessary to make up for his sense of inadequacy, his perceived sense of loss of power or control, or as an outlet for his sense of rage at an unfair world in which he can never live up to the expectations of being masculine. In line with his fear of, sometimes hatred for, and envy of the feminine, he carries out his violence against the woman in his life, fulfilling social prescriptions found in institutional sexism.

The need to educate in the realm of gender roles is clear, confronting traditional perspectives and providing alternatives to them. It is essential to counteract the myth of male superiority. Recent studies have demonstrated that the more a person adheres to traditional sex-role expectations, the more likely he or she is to approve of the use of violence against the female in personal relationships (Malamuth & Donnerstein, 1984). Challenging these traditional assumptions can be very fruitful in producing change. An atmosphere is necessary in which *appropriate* uses of power are modeled, confronting the inappropriate power-over mode of human relationships. *How* therapists interact with the clients is often more important than *what* is actually said. Control and competition are exceedingly important to address in this context, as is the "win/lose" syndrome, which applies modes appropriate to sports to our personal relationships. In fact, a constant reference to the social pressures for "John Wayne-Rambo" forms of masculinity is essential in leading men to a new model for being male.

Treatment

There are four perspectives that must be considered prior to the development of any treatment program for men who batter. Ignoring any of these issues can leave major gaps in the therapist's conceptual approach.

CHEMICAL DEPENDENCY

This issue *must* be confronted prior to any effective treatment for the issue of violence. As long as the chemical abuse continues, there is a "devil-made-me-do-it" denial that is available to the abuser. It is possible to attend an alcohol and drug treatment program concurrently with counseling to end violence.

DEPENDENCY ON THE WOMAN

There is more than one form that addictive behavior can take. Unhealthy dependency is often mutual; she on him for financial reasons, he on her for reasons of emotional expressiveness. As Pleck (1979) noted, many men perceive women's emotion-expressing ability as a power that women have over them. Men remain dependent on women to know and identify their feelings. There is also the dependency men have on the woman for her caretaking, nurturant role. He often arrives for treatment feeling lost and out of touch with his basic needs and feelings. This is a clear reflection of the emotional dependency men have upon women. It must be a focus of treatment to recognize that the socially and physically powerful male is emotionally dependent—in a sense, weak—and that this dependence can be a part of his control issues. Understanding this issue can also prepare us for the constant victim-blaming rationalizations used by men who batter.

CONTROL AND ITS CYCLES

The control issue is one of the most salient issues in this work. It stands far and above all else as a critical manifestation of male power confronting female power. Most men identify a major request in the entry interview. That request is to learn to "control" themselves. The best response is a paradox, "No, I will not teach you to control yourself. You already control far too much in your life. You control your feelings, you want to control your partner, your children. I want, instead, for you to learn to let go, even to surrender to what cannot be controlled. To let go of the need for control is essential in your search for health." Many claim they cannot control themselves in the moments leading up to the violent incident. It is essential to confront that claim, noting that the behavior is a control mechanism that is intended to bring the control back into the hands of the perpetrator of violence. (See Figure 21.1.)

Each man, in his search for some semblance of psychic health, denies the extent of his violence by noting that those who do worse things are the "real" wife beaters. "I never hit her with an open hand or nothin'. I just slapped her around a little." "I've never, like, put her in the hospital, you

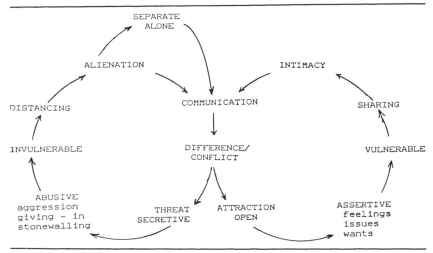

Figure 21.1   The Cycle of Intimacy

know. I only grab her, and push her and stuff." The denial is common; that other batterers, who go beyond *my* personal limits, are worse. Asking a man who claims to lose control, but who denies doing real damage, how he stopped himself from hurting her more seriously is quite instructive in identifying his behavioral limits. The sad part, of course, is that the longer the battery continues, the more a man feels compelled to do to gain the modicum of control his violent behavior gains him (Ptacek, 1985). Women consistently report the steady worsening of the levels of violence used against them.

A variety of programs that do this work focus on "anger control" or teach a man who batters to have better "impulse control." It is singularly inappropriate to teach control to men who use violence as a form of control over those who the sociosexual system claims to be less powerful than men. Anger expressed against injustice is a valid, liberating, and wholesome emotion. Anger alone does not need to be oppressive. Violence and abuse are oppressive inherently. And blaming poor "impulse control" denies the entire relationship of control, power, and sexism. Battery has utility. It accomplishes something, whether it gets exactly what the batterer wanted or not is hardly the point. Violence shows those upon whom it is perpetrated that it can happen again, that the perpetrator is more physically powerful when "necessary," and that rebelling can lead to such violence at any time. Using violence to control a woman is not a question of "impulse." The act is consciously derived, it is purposeful, and it is—even if only temporarily—useful (Gondolf & Russell, 1986).

FEELINGS AND
THE "MALE EMOTIONAL
FUNNEL SYSTEM"

Men are, quite simply, taught to be emotionally inexpressive, except for the emotions connected with anger. Awareness of one's other feelings as a male is a major step toward health, and toward the consciousness necessary to choose alternative behaviors. Traditionally, men are "testy" while women are "hysterical." Both emotional forms are rooted in our sex glands. Etymologically, testes are the source of such anger; wombs (hyster) are the roots of overwhelming negative emotions other than anger. With this sort of training, men tend to transform all negative or painful emotions into anger again and again (see Figure 21.2).

Men turn internal confusion and stress outward on the world, on their loved ones. Women tend to reverse the process, transforming angers into depression, turning worldly stress internally upon themselves. And men continue to label difficult feelings other than anger as female, girlish—as nonmale. In the attempt to ignore or deny such feelings, men keep themselves in a constant state of rage. Emotional literacy, then, is a major prerequisite to the environmental and physical awareness necessary to unlearn violent behavior. And emotional literacy requires an understanding of the gender system that limits our development as full human beings.

Points of Theory

Various theoretical points concerning the way one works with men who batter are important to consider. The first is use of a group format, as opposed to individual therapy (Adams & McCormick, 1982). In a group, men are able at least to begin to deal with one of the most common issues men face—isolation. For men are severely emotionally isolated in this society, unable to turn to another man for support, largely due to the interconnection of homophobia and sexism. Fear of being gay, or of being thought to be, is a major block to male sharing. This joins with the emotional dependence on women as cultivators and expressors of men's feelings to nearly forbid any emotional interaction among men, unless it is greased by the universal social lubricant—alcohol. Therefore simply being in a (sober) group helps teach a new form of communication in a highly emotional situation. It also enables men to comprehend the social source of this behavior in masculine prescriptive behavior. As a man looks around a room with men of all types of backgrounds, educational levels, races, occupations, he begins to under-

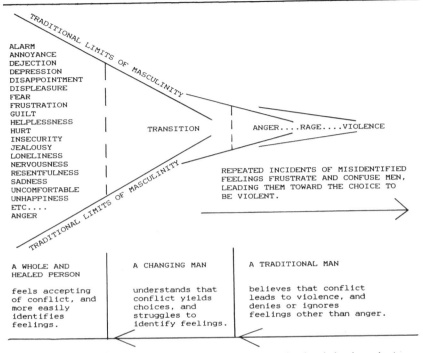

The task for men who wish to change old violent or abusive behaviors is to
move from the traditional model on the right where anger is the primary
negative or painful feeling identified, toward the left where anger is but
one of many clearly identified negative/difficult feelings. As men, we must
reclaim our right to the natural human emotiveness that is denied us by the
limits of traditional masculinity.

Figure 21.2   The Male Emotional Funnel System

stand the universality of the behavior and can reject the typical individualizing of battery that takes the broader society off the hook. Individual
work with man simply cannot do this.

The sex of the therapists is a second point of theory. Many believe that
men working with men is the preferred mode because of our experience
with modeling new behaviors, and the easy gender association of men with
men. Some programs utilize male/female teams in group leadership,
stating the goal of modeling male/female interactions to the group
participants. Others do not trust that male therapists alone can truly
communicate antisexism to an all-male audience. Yet there is reason for
concern that a solitary woman in a group of men is made too responsible
for the effective expression of male feelings, and is made the watchdog for
sexism in the group. Arguments run both ways. There are reasons for
trying each, since it is clear at this point that no one has all the answers.

An important consideration of men working with men is to provide a means by which men who are not batterers can communicate the concept that all men are responsible for some men's physical violence against women. Each man benefits from the existence of such violence whether or not that individual ever raises his fist in anger. It can prove very useful to redefine abuse, violence, and physical violence. As defined by Rape and Violence End Now (RAVEN, a St. Louis organization) *abuse* is any behavior that controls or dominates another person, or that prevents another from making an autonomous choice. "Peer" pressure, manipulation, name-calling or other verbal harassment, ignoring, lying, cursing, or mild threats all come under this heading. *Violence* is any behavior that *causes fear* in another person. These redefinitions are based on the *victim's* experience of the action, not on the *intent* of the perpetrator. Yelling, sudden movements, physical posturing, shaking of fists, threats of further violence, or breaking things are examples of violence—all clear violations of another person's psychic peace. But it is important to recognize that a look in one's eyes, or a tone in one's voice can instill fear with equal effectiveness, and should therefore be considered violent acts. Finally, *physical violence* is any of the above behaviors done with physical contact, and includes pushing and grabbing as well as hitting or using weapons.

At RAVEN, talking about abuse and violence in this manner permits us to move beyond the simplistic perception that physical violence is the only behavior we wish to change, and to move toward an understanding of power and control, which permits us to perceive the eternal dance of male and female conflict as a power struggle based in gender privilege and oppression. As women in the battered women's movement have pointed out, we will not have gotten very far if we only teach men not to use physical violence, permitting them to maintain their position of power over women by other means. Control by methods other than battery does not smell much sweeter, and decidedly does not contribute much to the emancipation of women from male power. Nor, for that matter, does the mere cessation of physical violence contribute to the removal from men of the felt need to exercise control over women and children. It is these perceptions that lead us to the awareness that all men benefit from the existence of physical battery, which enables some to maintain their positions of gender superiority without having to resort to the brutal forms of control; for some, it is quite sufficient, and equally effective, to maintain economic control. It is important that any therapist understand this concept, which forbids the scapegoating of the men who actually do commit battery as the only men who abuse women. It is this awareness that helps overcome the tendency to "individuate" the crime, which permits the male therapist to deny his own issues in the universal condition of gender inequality.

It is for related reasons that couple counseling is not advocated until a man has been through an extensive program, has given up his prerogatives to violence, and understands something of the nature of the gender power struggle. It is equally important that a woman has had time to reestablish trust in the man's ability to choose not to be violent. For, as Kathleen Carlin, an advocate for battered women, once said to therapists, "It takes a certain amount of trust to say, 'I don't trust you.' " As long as violence, whether physical or emotional, is a possibility when the couple leaves the relatively safe confines of the therapist's office, how can any of us expect that a woman can be honest about her fears, or about the man's actual behaviors? (Bograd, 1986).

Careful thought must be given to the difference between teaching self-awareness and self-control. Men are already too much in control of society, their bodies, their feelings, and strive for that same level of control over women, children, or other men. Similar issues arise when we examine race and class. The man who comes for help seeking to learn to control his anger needs to be challenged immediately with the paradox of choice in his violent behavior. He needs to be told that he will not be taught to control anything more than he already does; the thesis here is that he needs to learn to let go, to give up the need to control that has gotten him in trouble in the first place. More than likely, he will not immediately understand this; some men never quite grasp the concept. If he claims to be out of control when he does the violence, ask why he did not do worse things, why he has the sense that he *only* did this, but never that. EMERGE (a Boston group) learned to ask a simple question to shock the realization of choice: "Why didn't you pick up a knife if you were so out of control?" The man's reaction, often one of horror, can be simply, "I didn't want to hurt her; after all, she's my wife." The point of this is that every man does exactly what he thinks he needs to do to regain control of the situation over which he perceives he is losing control (see Figure 21.1). Once he understands that control is at the center of the problems he is having, it is easier to communicate the need to release it to attain health for himself and a better understanding with his current or future partner. Awareness, not control, is the essence of transformation of male violent behavior—awareness of gender issues, of one's own body sensations and feelings, of stress levels, of "hot topics," of alternative forms of conflict resolution. Education and consciousness, which yields more choice—not limitation or constriction of choice—is the path to help men who batter become men who no longer batter.

A Model of Structure and Practice

As a model for a program for men who batter, a man will be followed through the steps of the RAVEN program. His first contact is by telephone, through a 24-hour access emergency system, utilizing a professional answering service that will page a counselor on call for emergencies at any hour. The phone is answered in the office in normal business hours. It is useful to note that, contrary to initial expectations, a man normally calls for help the first time during the business day. It seems that men do not generally call during the crisis itself, but more usually after the woman has taken some step for her own protection, for example, after she has gone to a shelter, obtained divorce papers, or an order of protection. A woman calls the shelter during or very soon after the crisis, but the man has taken time to think, and has come to some realization that he'd better get help. Normally in this first contact, it must be explained to him that the counselor will not contact a missing woman who has allegedly gone to a shelter, will not inform her of the man's attempt to seek help, or intervene with her in any way. The helper is there to help him change the behaviors that led her to leave him, and that is all.

If the man is receptive to the services that we offer, he is invited to begin attending open group sessions immediately. RAVEN holds four of these open sessions each week, three on weekday evenings, one on a weekend morning. It is important that each man have an intake interview in the first week or so of his attendance. From long experience RAVEN decided that it is not necessary to have the intake prior to attendance in group. Some men prefer to have the individual meeting first; we are quite open to his own choice here. But it is very useful in prolonging attendance and in keeping men involved to permit them to begin instantly without any complications in scheduling. Previously, insisting that a man have the intake prior to attending group led to a dropout rate prior to intake that was much higher. It seems that responding to the crisis promptly has a beneficial effect on the man's attendance.

The Initial Interview

The intake session is primarily structured to explicate the program requirements, to set fees (which are based on income), to answer questions, to provide immediate "homework" and new ways of seeing the circumstance, to assess for substance abuse, to clarify group rules, to sign appropriate release forms, and to fill out demographic forms. It is important to give new information about the violence and his choices since about 20% of men who attend intakes never actually enter the group program. Realizing that this may be one's only contact with this new man necessitates that he be provided with the seed of a new idea to take with him. It is also of extreme importance to assess lethality—that is, to make your best judgment as to the partner's safety, especially in the situations in which the man and woman continue to live together.

The Safety Planning Course

The RAVEN program has created a series of four classes in which a new man is instructed in some of the basic concepts he will need to operate effectively within our system. The classes are titled "Responsibility I and II," "Safety Planning," and "Self-Care." This class system was created to separate out the beginning participants from the intermediate, which enables us repeatedly to offer the basics without boring those men who have already learned this preliminary level of our instruction. It permits us to teach new men the basic concepts, after which they join with intermediate men in a group format where the basic concepts are being utilized effectively by those who have been around longer. RAVEN has produced a Safety Planning Guidebook to lead men through this course. The guide is provided to each new man in the intake session.

The first of the two classes on responsibility presents the redefinitions of abuse and violence as noted above. Responsibility itself is redefined as "the ability to respond" to situations, rather than to rely on traditional concepts of duty, burden or accountability (see Schaef, 1981). Responsibility is a choice in the present, not guilt about the past. This helps to clarify the reality that change is made up of consciousness plus action. Awareness of choice is empowering; guilt is disempowering. The continuum of abuse and violence is then presented to exemplify the range of behaviors to be changed. The first class concludes with the introduction of the concept of anger logs in which each man is asked to chronicle his occurrences of anger, examining each incident for common behaviors or issues and overlooked feelings.

Responsibility II reviews the first class, in particular the redefinitions. Then the cycle of violence, as created by Lenore Walker, and the cycle of intimacy (see Figure 21.3) are presented. The cycle of intimacy, developed by Mark Robinson of RAVEN, is quite useful in showing past patterns and future possibilities in developing intimacy in close relationships. Men seem to find this particularly helpful in showing responsibility as ability to respond to the stresses of conflict in our lives. Then the group discusses ways we deny responsibility for our behaviors. Such denials include blaming the victim, blaming an outside force, minimizing the extent of violence, forgetting, or outright lying. The session ends by presenting the concept of self-disclosure as a path to health for men, emphasizing the necessity of disclosure in group if a man is going to make the group experience work for him.

The third session of class is the core of the RAVEN experience. "Safety Planning" is the creation of a concrete plan for avoiding the use of violence in the future through the examination of past incidents of violence to

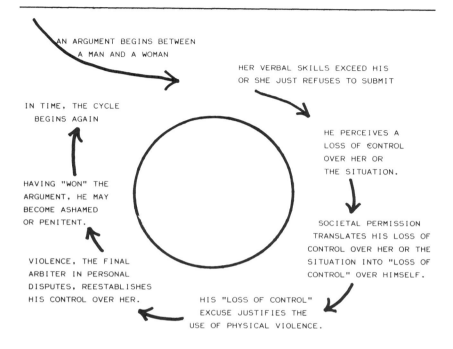

Loss of control over a man's partner or over the situation is translated by our social experience into a _felt_ loss of control over our selves. This subjective experience is a denial of the reality of men's use of force to maintain our control over another person through dominance.

Figure 21.3   The Cycle of Control

establish our own patterns in conflict, then to create a step-by-step path through stressful situations that illuminate as many alternative behaviors as possible at each stage of the way. RAVEN teaches the three-step mnemonic device called the ACE plan: _Anticipate_ the conflict, _Create_ alternatives for your behavior, and _Evaluate_ your success. Anticipation means to know when you become abusive or violent; what are the issues, what are the physical signs, how does it feel—and, of course, to know it beforehand. Creation of alternatives begins with the simple Time-Out Plan, in which either partner has the right to call for a break from the developing argument to reestablish clarity of thinking or to seek safety. The time-out must be agreed upon _in advance_ by the partners; it helps to agree upon time limits, the "safe room" that will be used, and the sign either partner can use that will indicate that a time-out is needed. Alternatives other than this one are individually developed according to circumstance. Evaluation is necessary in that it implies that some mistakes will be made.

Safety plans must be regularly updated. Quite probably, a safety plan that works in one situation will not work as effectively in another. As a man works to create a series of plans, he begins to come to the awareness that safety planning is really the development of a lifetime awareness of alternative choices to traditional behaviors that have been proven ineffective and hurtful. Awareness of the "right to choose" our conflict patterns is the key.

The fourth session of class is the self-care presentation. The session opens with a relaxation exercise that can be used anytime to defuse tension. As a means to increase physical awareness, ways are shown that men can better care for themselves (nutrition, aerobic exercise, sleep and rest, asking for help) as well as ways we usually don't take personal care of ourselves (drug abuse, workaholism, the fast-food habit, ignoring medical problems, etc.). Group members brainstorm ways they can add some caring activities to their lives, subdivided into four categories: physical, emotional, social, and spiritual. Some focus is given merely to asking for help from other men in the group. Exchange of telephone numbers by members in the group is encouraged. It is not done much initially; however, the longer men stay with your program, the more likely it is that they will make some personal contact with other members outside of group itself. This session concludes with another example of a relaxation exercise, and the use of such "vacations" is encouraged anytime a man feels stress in his day-to-day life.

The Group Session

Each RAVEN group session is approximately two hours in length. The session begins with the check-in. Each participant, including the counselors, are asked to state a few details of their past week. Including the counselors in the check-in provides both a model of a nonviolent lifestyle and the recognition that no one's life is completely free of abusive incidents and behaviors. RAVEN helps men realize that no one is ever "cured" of the influence of traditional male behaviors, but that men can make many changes in their lives that lead to a reduction in confrontive challenges that become or threaten to become abusive or violent.

By the time the round of check-ins is over, a few men have identified issues they need to discuss. Newer men need to tell their stories often to present the reasons they are attending RAVEN. This is a search for validation and often is a misguided attempt to shift blame for their violent behavior onto their partner by showing just how awfully she has treated him. It is important here to clarify the meaning of responsibility immediately, to give a stroke for actually asking for help, and at the same time to challenge the notion that anyone else can be responsible for his own chosen behaviors. More seasoned members who have learned the ways of using the group and the framework for presenting their problems will usually have more specific incidents to discuss. Part of the facilitator's job is to maintain the focus on naming and clarifying the problem instead of giving advice. It is better to help men "better feel" as opposed to "feel better." Do not paper over the realities of power struggles and traditional gender differences in a desire to help an individual leave for home smiling instead of frowning. Toward this end, RAVEN has developed a "discipline for reflection" on a problem. After a group member has described a difficult incident, the group responds by first asking questions of clarification, to obtain a more complete understanding of the situation. Then the group reflects on ways that incidents or patterns in our own lives mirror what the man has described, after which the problem is named. The problem that has been named in this manner becomes the center of the subsequent discussion. This method helps prevent the endless bog of advice-mongering that could, if permitted to happen, prevent any clarity from emerging out of the discussion. Giving advice is an excellent defense mechanism that permits the avoidance of recognizing the ways my problem is similar to your problem. Very simply, advice avoids self-disclosure.

Much of the group work is based upon the common needs expressed by the men in check-in. Group exercises can be easily developed out of commonly stated issues. Since group education is such a central aspect of our work, even work with an individual man can easily be used to educate the entire group by asking for group reflection and participation in the topic at hand. Many of the exercises led by the facilitator have to do with the immediate objective—modeling communication patterns and conflict resolution skills that can replace the old violent behavior. However, there are more diverse needs to be met. Men ought to leave having a better understanding of the gender system that places limits on the ability to choose behaviors not in keeping with prescribed rules of masculinity. A few exercises that facilitate that end follow.

MASCULINE-FEMININE BRAINSTORMING

"What makes a man?" is a good brainstorming session. Men are asked to describe the characteristics socially accepted as masculine. After a list is created, we review the list, noting characteristics that support violent behavior. We do the same for women, reviewing the list for characteristics that support victim behaviors or powerlessness. Then we create a list of characteristics that describe what we would like to become as men. This list usually includes positive characteristics from both of the earlier lists. After we discuss what our choices really can be, the men are asked to create a list of characteristics describing what we would like our partners to be. Very quickly, group members realize that we can use the same list that we created for ourselves. It is useful here to point out that the objective of such changes is not to make men and women the same, but to stop trying to make us so different. We are more alike than we are opposite; we are not opposite sexes, we are different sexes.

SUCCESS STORIES AND
THE NEXT STEP

Men are asked to note the types of things they have successfully learned since coming to RAVEN, and to give examples of their successful application. A column of these concepts is kept on one side of the board. After the realization that we can all share in the successes of our fellow group members, we then make a new list of the current struggles in which we are involved. As that list is made, again the realization is reached that we are more similar than uniquely separate in our attempts to change old behaviors. This exercise is a cohesive one for group development.

HOW DID WE LEARN
VIOLENCE?

Men are asked to talk about the ways they individually learned that violence was an appropriate male behavior, or what they think were the sources of their own violent behavior. Fathers, childhood abuse, street fighting, peer or family mistreatment of girls and women, the military, and media violence are commonly brought out. While this exercise is important to lay the foundation for understanding social supports for male violence, it is essential to make the point at the end of the exercise that many other men experience all these things and more, yet still choose not to be violent themselves. Not everyone who has all the traditional training actually decides to use violence against a loved one. This is yet another situation in which the awareness of choice can be brought to focal attention. The exercise ends with writing on the board, "We *choose* to be violent . . . or nonviolent." We assign 100% of the responsibility for men's behaviors to the men themselves, staying aware that none of us is entirely responsible for *beliefs* that allow us to choose to be violent. Confronting our attitudes—what we believe about the world— is a powerful catalyst for change. This awareness plus action will yield change. We can change our attitudes, and we can change our behaviors.

Summary

The counselor working with men who batter strives most obviously to become teacher for and brother to the men who come for help, and occasionally slips into the role of cop, parent, and therapist. Therapist is listed last here, which may seem an unusually low priority to admit. But it is placed last for a reason. It is not known what works best in facilitating nonviolence in men, but traditional therapeutic approaches are not the solution. In fact, some of the problems of psychology and social work—elitism, the hierarchy of knowledge and of health, individualizing of a social experience, inappropriate use of power—make that tradition as much a part of the real problem as any number of secondary factors. Therapy must change to help people—men—in the best way possible. The reality that all men have been involved in the subjugation of women in some form must be faced before they can truly begin to help themselves or the men who come to them for help. All the answers are not known. However, listening to the leaders of the battered women's movement can teach more than any school, any workshop, any conference. Extensive contact with battered women's shelters in our communities must be developed, as safety for women and children must be the first priority. The love for men that motivates this work with men who batter must never be used as permission to conceive of this work as antagonistic to safety for women. Yes, men hurt. But men's emotional pain must always be placed in the context of the life-threatening violence done by men to women as a result of not knowing how to express or alleviate that pain. It is after men who batter have given up the privilege of utilizing violence to obtain control that a host of other issues inherent in contemporary masculinity become appropriate to face.

References

Adams, D. (1986). *Counseling men who batter: A profeminist analysis of clinical models.* Paper presented to Annual Meeting of the American Psychiatric Association.

Adams, D., & McCormack, A. (1982). Men unlearning violence: A group approach based on the collective model. In M. Roy (Ed.), *The abusive partner: An analysis of domestic battering.* New York: Van Nostrand Reinhold.

Bograd, M. (1984). Family systems approaches to wife battering: A feminist critique. *Journal of American Orthopsychiatry, 54,* 558-568.

Bograd, M. (1986). Holding the line: Confronting the abusive partner. *Family Therapy Networker, 10,* 44-47.

Cook, D., & Frantz-Cook, A. (1984). A systematic treatment approach to wife battering. *Journal of Marriage and Family Therapy, 10,* 83-93.

David, D., & Brannon, R. (Eds.). (1976). *The forty-nine percent majority: The male sex role.* Reading, MA: Addison-Wesley.

Ganley, A. (1981). *Court mandated counseling for men who batter.* Washington, DC: Center for Women Policy Studies.

Gelles, R. (1974). *The violent home.* Newbury Park, CA: Sage.

Gondolf, E. (1984). *Anger and oppression in men who batter: Empiricist and feminist perspectives and their implications for research.* Unpublished paper presented to Third International Institute on Victimology, Lisbon, Portugal.

Gondolf, E. (1985). *Men who batter: An integrated approach for stopping wife abuse.* Holmes Beach, FL: Learning Publications.

Gondolf, E., & Russell, D. (1986). *The case against anger control for batterers.* Unpublished manuscript.

Hart, B. (in press). *Safety for women: Monitoring batterers programs.* Harrisburg, PA: Pennsylvania Coalition Against Domestic Violence.

Malamuth, N. M., & Donnerstein, E. (Eds.). (1984). *Pornography and sexual aggression.* Orlando, FL: Academic Press.

Pleck, J. (1979). Men's power with women, other men and society: A men's movement analysis. In E. Shapiro & B. M. Shapiro (Eds.), *The women say, the men say: Women's liberation and men's consciousness.* New York: Delta.

Pleck, J. (1981). *The myth of masculinity.* Cambridge, MA: MIT Press.

Ptacek, J. (1985). *Wifebeaters' accounts of their violence: Loss of control as excuse and as subjective experience.* Master's thesis, University of New Hampshire, Durham.

Roy, M. (Ed.). (1982). *The abusive partner: An analysis of domestic battering.* New York: Van Nostrand Reinhold.

Rubin, L. B. (1983). *Intimate strangers: Men and women together.* New York: Harper.

Saunders, D. (1984). Helping husbands who batter. *Social Casework, 65,* 347-353.

Schaef, A. W. (1981). *Women's reality: An emerging female system in a white male society.* New York: Harper.

Schechter, S. (1982). *Women and male violence: The visions and struggles of the battered women's movement.* Boston: South End Press.

Walker, L. (1979). *The battered woman.* New York: Harper & Row.

22

Counseling Men
in Prison

Jeffrey W. Aston

It is the purpose of this chapter to provide a therapeutic perspective for working with men in prison. Such work will occur in a most difficult environment with an often recalcitrant clientele. Even therapists skilled in intervention with other populations will discover prison work to pose problems and challenges that can fairly be termed unique. The criminal's skill at externalized blame and self-justification can make him seem at times impervious to change—it is others who are at fault, not he. It is the therapist who should be educated about the world's grim realities, not the inmate.

Counselors and therapists often become confused as to what sort of battle is being fought with their prison clients. Hoping to be of help, they are surprised to encounter ploys, deceptions, and manipulation that seem to serve no purpose. Some kind of struggle is clearly at hand, but its character and meaning remain hidden.

Men in prison are in conflict with themselves and others in part out of mistaken allegiance to an exaggerated and corrupt philosophy of masculine identity. There is a sense in which prisoners "should" act as they do in order to fulfill a peculiar notion of manhood. Since therapeutic change is impossible unless the client perceives growth to be significant in his own terms, that ideal of manhood must be understood by the therapist.

The terms *criminal* and *inmate* will be used in this chapter to refer to incarcerated men who evidence to significant degrees the cognitive-behavioral patterns described in Yochelson and Samenow's (1976) *The Criminal Personality*. While one encounters other men in prison who are not antisocial personalities, that smaller subset does not tend to present peculiar or unique problems for the therapist. The reader unfamiliar with *The Criminal Personality* (Vols. I and II) is advised to review that work in preparation for entering the correctional setting. The books convey in ordinary language a useful image of the sociopathic mentality. One gleans a portrait of individuals distinguished by the extremity of their concrete, short-range, selfish, exploitive, irresponsible thinking patterns. Without attempting a summarization of that lengthy material, I would note here that Yochelson and Samenow view criminality, as defined by cognitive errors and irresponsible behavior, as measurable in a single direction along a continuum. A particular individual will demonstrate some degree of these characteristics, ranging from the responsible person (who neither contemplates nor acts upon criminal ideas) to the severe sociopath (whose mind "races" with criminal thinking and who commits violations whenever possible). Criminals are thereby differentiated from each other, and from responsible citizenry, by the extent to which they manifest such exploitive thinking and behavior. This cognitive-behavioral definition of criminality leads naturally to the authors' prescribing a form of cognitive therapy as an intervention. The therapist is to aid the criminal in uncovering these cognitive distortions, in preparation for the subsequent task of correcting them.

While a knowledge of criminal thinking is important in working with inmates, a direct attempt to change criminal thinking errors one by one can be an arduous project. Equally important, the goal of simply reforming the self into a model of responsible citizenry will likely appeal to few prisoners. The challenge of a wider definition of manhood can however, become quite intriguing to them. To facilitate this process of redefinition, it is useful to understand more than one viewpoint from which criminals might experience the difficulties of masculine identity.

In contrast to viewing criminality as a phenomenon that varies in degree along a single continuum, I will describe the criminal's preoccupation with his masculinity as assuming two possible, and somewhat opposed, forms: He can believe himself to fall short of an imagined masculine ideal, and thereby engage in constant attempts to prove how tough he is, or he can image himself as actually embodying an extreme masculinity that excuses his callous treatment of others in a dog-eat-dog world. While both types evidence a common preoccupation with notions of "manhood," the former feels chronically anxious about his supposed hypomasculinity, while the latter lives in shallow comfort within a hypermasculine role whose limitations are not spontaneously recognized.

Each of the foregoing types will cherish an inward justification for his life of repetitive arrests and imprisonment. The hypermasculine criminal violates the law out of an indifference to social mores that are "soft" and beneath him, while the hypomasculine criminal strikes out against a world peopled by superior men and women who are "hard" and threatening. Each has his own dread of intimate relationships, which includes the therapeutic encounter. The hypomasculine inmate, while initially far more inclined to seek help and succor from a therapist, quickly sabotages the situation as his underlying fear of being revealed as unmanly emerges. The hypermasculine inmate is likely to come to therapy only through external coercion or a brief desire for respite from the boredom of typical prison games. The therapy game itself will be tolerated so long as it represents an amusing forum for manipulation and self-enhancement. The therapist who is penetrating and persistent enough to avoid distractions will lose his hypermasculine client as soon as the dialogue becomes intimate enough to threaten invasion of the tough-guy role.

It may seem at this point that the foregoing serves only to highlight the impossibility of doing any serious therapy with men in prison. I would instead suggest that while work with criminals who represent *extremes* of either type may be unproductive, the majority of inmates will exhibit more moderate tendencies.

It is similarly wise to be wary of those who are on the extreme end of the Yochelson-Samenow continuum of criminal thinking. For the purposes of this discussion, we can view that continuum as bearing an orthogonal relationship to the hypomasculine-hypermasculine construct. That is, one can be high or low in degree of criminal thinking while viewing the self in either hypo- or hypermasculine terms; the conceptual dimensions are independent.

It is important to emphasize that the distinction between hypomasculinity and hypermasculinity is phenomenological in character. The terms refer to an inner experience of one's manhood, which can seldom be directly inferred from the inmate's overt behavior. Hypomasculine types are no more or less socially competent, intelligent, strong, or attractive than their hypermasculine counterparts. Since everyone in prison "acts tough" while concealing inward reactions, behavioral discrimination becomes even more difficult for the casual observer. One will tend to see on the surface only a uniform code of hypermasculine role behavior among prisoners. The point for the therapist is to realize that *some* of those men have inner feelings that may be diametrically opposed to their efforts at maintaining the tough facade they believe they "should" embody. For others, that facade is experienced without dissonance, as entirely genuine.

A problem with much of the literature on criminality, from *The Mask of Sanity* (Cleckley, 1964) to *The Criminal Personality* (Yochelson & Samenow, 1976), is that it highlights the distinctive features of sociopaths at the expense of making them appear quite foreign to the reader. It is sometimes difficult to emerge from these volumes with any intuition as to how one might bond with such persons in therapy, assuming that the reader retains any interest in doing so. An advantage to viewing work with criminals as continuous with a general concern for men's issues, is that such a bond is implied.

For the male therapist in particular, one is joined with the inmate in a common quest for liberation from an imprisoning gender role. One's wisdom as a therapist consists precisely in having examined the issue of masculinity at a level of philosophy superior to the crude images that inform the inmate culture. Rather than playing the superior role of doctor to patient or good guy to bad guy, the therapist can relinquish such superficiality in favor of genuine collaboration. The nature of this collaborative concern with masculinity may be made quite explicit, or remain unspoken as one deals on the surface with other presenting issues. The therapist often exerts a more powerful influence by virtue of the model of masculinity he embodies, rather than through the clever interventions he dispenses.

The idea that a therapist's human qualities represent a critical variable productive of client change has certainly been well examined in the more general context of research on psychotherapeutic efficacy. In the prison setting, however, one discovers this variable to be peculiarly highlighted. Prisons are tight, hierarchical structures deliberately removed from fluid interaction with a larger society protective of its comparative gentility. The men who come to prison bring with them some form of exaggerated preoccupation with power, control, dominance, and other attributes of masculinity. Unsurprisingly, women who enter this environment feel themselves to be objectified, on stage. It is equally true, however, that male staff will describe the sensation of being watched, judged, and evaluated. One might term this an accurate paranoia (and inmates voice the reciprocal experience of being constantly observed by staff).

Other chapters of this volume have alluded to that competition aspect of male identity which places men at odds and creates in them an underlying sense of being constantly at war with one another. Beyond the war experience itself, this combative intuition is nowhere realized more clearly than in prisons. Power struggles between and within staff and inmate groups may be contained, in more advanced and human institutions, to the level of surly memoranda and frequent litigation. Still, conflict in some form is never long absent. More important to this narrative is the sense one will feel while working in prison of being constantly tested as "a man." Since the inmates (and many staff) experience each other in terms colored by a fascination with manhood, the therapist is similarly experienced. The therapist's ability to formulate a creative response to this awareness, can provide him enormous leverage. The following are some pertinent themes which inform the inmate's understanding of masculinity.

Strength

Whether the inmate complains about his subordinate role with staff, bemoans his unjust lot in life, recounts his successes (or frustrations) with women, or describes in rapturous terms his latest conversion to yet another religion, it is not difficult to detect in his monologues an underlying intrigue with visions of power. The very instability of the criminal's flirtation with so many jobs, schemes, women, roles, and ideas suggests a restless quest for some strong position in life that will guarantee him risk-free access to whatever promises fulfillment. That none of his enterprises prove truly fulfilling is an important insight, but for now the idea of "strength" as a vehicle for supposed success and survival is worthy of examination.

The hypomasculine criminal will engage in various maneuvers, or relate certain "facts" of his history, that are meant to convey an appearance of strength which exceeds his private estimation of himself. The therapist can often test for the presence of this discrepancy through straightforward inquiry. After listening to an inmate brag about himself, I have asked "How long have you felt so insecure about your image?" This tactic can refocus the dialogue toward exploring whatever subjective fears of being "weak" underlie the surface presentations. Once the subject is broached, the hypomasculine client often evidences relief at being able to talk about his anxious concern that he is a weak man born into a strong world. He will begin to speak of his crimes as efforts to prove that he couldn't be "pushed around by society." He may or may not describe an abusive upbringing, but there is usually the sense of his having felt inadequate as a man since childhood or adolescence.

How the therapist responds to these disclosures will depend upon the particular context, but it is important to shift at some point to a more flexible, humane, and evolved definition of what being a man is all about. The hypomasculine inmate will remain self-rejecting so long as he is tantalized by an image of masculine "strength" that seems unattainable. It is critical to demonstrate that this image is actually *undesirable*, and that a basic reformulation of the weak-strong polarity is necessary. Since the client will leave the office to ponder these matters in a prison cell, it is important to be aware of how the prison culture around him defines strength.

The best way to derive an understanding of prison culture is to deliberately recruit a few hypermasculine clients. Therapists invested in validating their own manhood might try placing a number of these men in group therapy all at once; it will prove an experience worthy of reflection. In any event, it is not difficult to elicit stories about the "tough joints," where inmates may literally measure strength in terms of one's ability to murder another human while remaining unmoved. Some hypermasculine types who have been transferred to a more moderate prison (perhaps nearing the end of their sentences) will voice a kind of nostalgia for the brutal clarity of such settings, where men "don't play games." The sincerity of that nostalgia is one index of an extreme type for whom therapy is likely ineffective. I am reminded of those Vietnam veterans who explain their power maladjustment by confessing that nothing can recapture the adrenaline rush of a good firefight.

One can sometimes confront the hypermasculine client's distaste for "games" (i.e., civilized discourse), by pointing out that a dominance hierarchy of ruffians actually constitutes the shallowest of games imaginable. The so-called strength that is tested by such hierarchies can be recast as a kind of fragility. The more sensitive and defensive one is about one's manhood, allowing violence to ensue from the most trivial of insults, the more insecure and "weak" one actually is. This theme, while providing reassurance to the hypomasculine type, should be used to challenge the hypermasculine inmate to develop that deeper experience of strength that abides in tolerance, forbearance, and eventual freedom from the need to prove oneself to others.

The therapist who is working with his client to reframe the construct of "strength" should be aware that both types will at times object that it is impractical to experiment with more liberated roles of manhood while in prison. Fail to be tough, and the others will get you. An appropriate reply is to differentiate between behavioral *tactics* and self-definition. While it may indeed be necessary at times to *act* tough in prison, one need not perpetuate the hypermasculine error of an inner identification with that superficiality. It is helpful to suggest that one of the hallmarks of a more evolved masculine identity is precisely such tactical, or situational, role flexibility. It is, however, critical to distinguish an evolved masculine flexibility from the mercurial inauthenticity of criminal role-playing, which is described in the next section.

The Objectified Self

Criminals lie and they do so for a number of reasons. Rather than viewing their deceptions either as purely pragmatic (to fool authorities) or pathologic and involuntary (pseudologica fantastica), we will focus here upon the life of the lie as it relates to gender role. The criminal's obsession with a simplistic image of masculinity actually requires that he use lies in order to maintain that distance from himself and others which is demanded by the role. To understand this, one must note that male identity in general has a certain contrived and artificial character to it. Externally, men seek to grasp the world at a distance, and to control that contact through the power of their images, concepts, and biceps. Their genius at this sort of manipulation seems coupled with a concomitant inability to create and share meaning with others at the closer quarters of interpersonal intimacy. This may be due in part to the male's internal tendency to try and grasp the self in terms of the same surface images that inform his view of the world. Prisoners in sex therapy will, for example, report being most aroused by the woman whom they objectify in fantasy as somewhat distant and challenging. Bring her too close, and a certain type of arousal dissipates at the same moment that anxiety increases.

The criminal's problem with women will be examined in the next section. It is worth emphasizing that criminal lying serves in part to sustain a contrived, objectified self that represents an exaggeration of the male image. Men have a chronic discomfort with intimacy, which is epistemological in character, and which can be seen highlighted in inmates. Psychologists sometimes are surprised by the interest shown by many criminals in psychological theory. They will read texts, attend lectures, and one is tempted at first to find this encouraging. It is not difficult, however, to discern in this interest merely one more effort to acquire a tool that will enable the criminal to understand and control the world, relationships, and himself at a safely analyzed distance. It is like learning to love by reading *Hustler* (which he will also do).

Criminal lying and role-playing appears pathological because of its pervasiveness, yet the inmate will tell you in candid moments that he is merely making a more conscientious effort than most to perfect the art of impression management that everyone practices. Inmates are notoriously adept at proving this by setting traps that will prompt the therapist to engage in some sort of defensive dissembling. This is sometimes achieved by asking unexpected personal questions, watching the therapist squirm or fib, and then concluding that indeed "no one is honest." This shallow maneuver is interesting because a significant issue is being tested.

All humans are ambivalent about the possibility of being truly known by another. The advent of telepathy would, for example, arouse enormous anxiety and force a virtual restructuring of everyone's identity. Assuming further that there is a particular masculine phobia about the prospect of honest self-disclosure, one would predict men to engage in approach-avoidance behaviors in connection with intimacy. While the initial approach is motivated by a desire to bond, avoidance comes into play at the point when the male epistemology, or objectified way of knowing, is threatened. The therapist will encounter this ambivalence in his criminal clients.

The inmate will approach out of a genuine hope of allowing the self to be known, yet as intimacy develops he encounters a curious blankness in that self if he makes a sincere effort at exploration. Beneath the lies and deceptions there seems no core from which to respond. It is at this critical point that the therapist may need to sustain the relationship by leading the dialogue. It is helpful to speak from personal experience about the curse of self-monitoring and self-control that binds the male's tight identity. Inmates will readily identify with this, as they have practiced it in spades, and one can then begin to explore with them the diminished experience attendant to living this objectified role.

I have taken the somewhat personal risk of speaking quite directly about common masculine role limitations to large groups of inmates in prerelease programs who are preparing for societal reentry. These talks are at times greeted with spontaneous applause, rare for such audiences. Mentioning to them the analogy of Vietnam veterans who, returning home, often felt such alienation that they found themselves alternately withdrawing or fabricating stories to placate their audience is helpful. Recommending strongly to these inmate groups that they not make too strenuous an effort to quickly connect with other people, men or women, in relationships is also useful. Having lived the life of the lie, and having suffered the added isolation of prison, it is far too tempting to submerge one's anxieties by "faking it" again with others. Emphasizing that there is no simple answer to the general male ambivalence about intimacy, is important, as is suggesting that those with the courage to risk themselves in defiance of authority might contemplate the still greater risk of relinquishing their shallow self-control in favor of real exploration with people.

The outcome of even a successful dialogue about these matters is scarcely the inmate's discovery of his real self. Such expectations should be discouraged, as any "self" that the criminal could quickly discover would merely be another fabrication. Unpracticed and fearful of spontaneity, he must learn instead to begin a *process* of defining himself through simple, straight talk. What he will discover is not an object, but freedom.

Women

This chapter has thus far explicitly alluded to the therapist as male. The themes of hypomasculine/hypermasculine preoccupation with strength, power, the objectified self and so forth, are intended to suggest areas in which the male therapist can establish a common explorative bond with the extreme men in prison. I frankly believe that female therapists, particularly attractive women, have a comparative hurdle to overcome in their efforts to penetrate the criminal facade. While male therapists may suffer the inmate's efforts to win a manly social-dominance game in counseling, women will encounter quite other complications. Before elaborating upon this, a general comment about the feminine role as "model" for criminals in therapy. Obviously a woman would not directly embody the model of evolved, flexible masculinity that was suggested for the male therapist. She can, however, seek to elicit such an evolution in the inmate by virtue of her own refusal to play the stereotypical female. Her disavowal of that role can force a complementary redefinition upon the criminal as he learns to interact with her. This relearning may then be generalized.

It is important to listen to the criminal's description of his women. One actual therapeutic advantage to the prison is its tendency to foster in the inmate a kind of monastic reflection upon his past, present, and future relationships on the outside. The fact of his incarceration usually creates serious problems in his relationships, and these are sometimes the most genuine of presenting issues brought to therapy.

Some incarcerated criminals have the good fortune to be involved with a woman who has become assertive in her overt intolerance for the criminal's lifestyle. This assertiveness may well be of recent advent, as she has been forced to learn a more independent role when relieved of his dominating presence in the home. He then recognizes that he must change or risk losing her while in prison. This dilemma provides a ready focus for proving his views of the man-woman relationship. One usually discovers that he has kept the woman protected from knowledge of his criminal enterprises. While he will present this as a noble and necessary tactic of secrecy, one must press for an examination of the deeper psychological function. His criminal thinking and behavior is usually the large portion of his character. To conceal this from the woman has been to deny her any awareness of who he really is.

On the surface, the supposed need for criminal secrecy excuses his pursuit of an underground (and underworld) life separated from the pseudoresponsible role he plays at home. This underground life handily allows him access to the excitement of drugs, deals, and other women. He may later offer the bizarre argument that all of this has been in the service of responsibly providing an income to keep the home intact. One must counter by defining real responsibility in terms of frank and open negotiations between man and woman. Even if he had been reliably paying the rent, to end by surprising her with his arrest and imprisonment is scarcely responsible or remotely fair. Other humans have the right to know what they are bargaining for when we draw them into relationships.

At a deeper level the criminal secrecy protects him from even addressing with the woman his phobia of self-disclosure. It will not suffice for him to shift to a legitimate occupation upon his release to the community. He must hear in his woman's distress a desire for the real intimacy he has denied her, or neither home nor the new job will endure, and he will become again a social predator.

Perhaps more common than the foregoing is the criminal whose woman does not directly challenge him to change, because of her unfortunate complementarity to his image. Listen for a description of his woman that suggests a magazine centerfold, and you are likely hearing of such a creature. If you are dealing with a hypermasculine client who uses this type of woman, the hope for change is remote. He has truly found his mate, and needs no therapeutic advice on how to continue to dominate and subordinate that willing stereotype.

More interesting is the hypomasculine type who is only fabricating a dominant, controlled role in order to contrive a supposed attractiveness. His success in such maneuvers is directly proportionate to the ambivalence he will feel about the fact of his pretense. He lives in continual fear that he will lose his woman to a superior competitor. The therapist can help him discover in this fear a sense that his "real" self would, if known, repulse his partner. I provoke hypomasculine clients by agreeing that there always *are* competitors with more money, bigger biceps, and flashier suits. If that kind of surface is what his woman really admires, he is destined to lose. Because he does not truly feel himself equal to that surface, he might consider the possibility that the woman who loves him has intuited this, and values what lies beneath more than he does.

The hypomasculine criminal who is willing to test this hypothesis with his woman almost invariably finds it confirmed. The woman has long awaited the opportunity to connect to him through his underlying sensitivity; it is the aspect she has been prepared to love. The fact that she did bond to a social rebel with buried sensitivity may suggest, however, her own conflicted attraction to the tough surface. In such cases there is much further mutual exploration and redefinition to be accomplished. One cannot, of course, conduct couples' therapy with one partner absent. One can advise the inmate as he communicates through letters, phone calls, and occasional visits, but much of the work consists in preparing him to engage with the woman in postrelease counseling. He can, at least, begin to formulate with the therapist a pertinent agenda of issues to be addressed in that forum.

Conclusion

It would be presumptuous to suggest that the viewpoint outlined in this chapter can be used by the therapist to render his work with men in prison unproblematic or easy. Still, experience of nearly a decade in the prison setting has led to a sense of considerable promise in the project of focusing with these men upon their concern with masculine identity. An unusual liveliness seems awakened in both group and individual counseling sessions when the topic is broached in a serious and sensitive manner.

Much of how this will go depends upon the therapist's ability to draw rather subtle distinctions for his inmate clientele. A problem with criminals is the fact that they are acutely sensitive to much of the game-playing that debases social interaction among men and women in the outside community. They move from this insight to a conviction that they possess a paradoxical kind of honesty in their forthrightly predatory behavior. The intellectual inmate will read Zen and conclude that he embodies *satori* in his detachment from the common man's investment in a workaday ego. Both hypermasculine and hypomasculine criminals will resist role redefinition because so many women still *do* respond to the romance of the rebel image. So why consider change?

The answer to these and a myriad other objections will depend, for better or worse, upon the therapist's own experience of evolving a new masculine identity. Yes, it is worthy to practice that detachment which protects the inner self from overidentification with social roles, but one must first *develop* a nonobjectified inner self, or there is no authority to protect. Yes, many women have yet to integrate their needs for a man who is both powerful and tender, but a narrow appeal to them in terms of power will only preclude true communion and rebound upon the self.

As difficult as these issues are, one has the saving grace of admitting that no one yet possesses the answer of defining where male liberation ought to lead. It is important at this stage to learn honesty as one searches to define one's problems. That it is possible to evoke such honesty among the company of men in prison seems hopeful indeed.

References

Cleckley, H. (1964). *The mask of sanity.* St. Louis: Mosby.

Hare, R. D. (1970). *Psychopathy: Theory and research.* New York: John Wiley.

Jacks, I., & Cox, S. G. (Eds.). (1984). *Psychological approaches to crime and its correction: Theory, research, practice.* Chicago: Nelson-Hall.

McCord, W., & McCord, J. (1964). *The psychopath: An essay on the criminal mind.* New York: Van Nostrand Rinehold.

Yochelson, S., & Samenow, S. E., (Eds.). (1976). *The criminal personality,* (Vols. I & II). New York: Jason Aronson.

23

Counseling Male Substance Abusers

Jed Diamond

"Give me librium or give me meth," John boomed in his best early American accent as he walked down the halls of the state mental hospital. John Thompson was young, articulate, and intelligent. He was also a drug addict.

"My whole identity is wrapped up with drugs. If I didn't take drugs I don't know who I'd be," John confided during a therapy session. In 1965 there were few resources available in hospitals for people like John and shortly after he left the hospital he was arrested for selling drugs and was sent to prison.

Gary never used drugs, though he drank a bit. He was the youngest chairman of the county board of supervisors and was looking forward to becoming the youngest senator in the country. Gary's rise in politics was slowed by the loss of a close election. He was killed in an automobile crash shortly before his thirty-fifth birthday. The newspapers said it was an accident. Only a few friends knew how despondent Gary was after losing the election, that the few drinks had grown to many, and how much of his manhood was tied up in his shattered dream of political power.

It is my belief that those who work in the field of substance abuse treatment came to the work because of some personal experience. Some grew up in families where one or both parents were alcoholic. Some are recovering alcoholics or addicts themselves and have a strong desire to help themselves by helping those in need. Others had close friends whose lives were ruined or lost as a result of drugs. John and Gary were the catalysts that drew me into the field.

In order to be most effective in counseling male substance abusers, expertise must be developed in six areas. First, we must become effective counselors. Second, we must develop expertise in the special issues that face men. Third, we must know about the various substances that men abuse. Fourth, we need to become expert in understanding and treating abuse or addictive relationships to these substances. Fifth, we must understand what does not work as well as what does. Finally, we must experience the fact that all healing is mutual.

Becoming an Effective Counselor

Until the advent of Alcoholics Anonymous (A.A.) there was little effective treatment for alcoholism and drug abuse. The 12 Step program of A.A. has been the most effective in helping substance abusers. According to William Mayer, M.D., of the American Medical Association, "A.A. by and large works better than anything we have been able to devise with all our science and all our money and all our efforts" (Brown, 1985, p. 25).

In 1975 a small handbook, *Becoming Naturally Therapeutic* by Jacquelyn Small (1981), began circulating within the alcoholism treatment community and has become a classic in stating clearly what is needed to be an effective counselor. Small lists the following 10 characteristics as being essential for those working in the field: empathy, genuineness, respect, self-disclosure, warmth, immediacy, concreteness, confrontation, potency, and self-actualization.

The primary difference between more traditional counseling approaches and this one seems to be the increased willingness of counselors to reveal aspects of themselves.

Brown (1985), while suggesting that all approaches have something important to offer, has developed a new theory of recovery that allows an integration of the various treatment practices. This is valuable for the therapist dealing with substance abuse.

Special Issues for Men

Although addiction does not discriminate against women, it does seem to be a disease that is closely associated with men. According to Richard O. Heilman, M.D., whereas 1 in 50 females become alcoholic, 1 in 10 males do (Heilman, 1973). A national study on mental health concluded that "throughout their life-time 19.2 percent of Americans will suffer from alcohol or drug abuse." The study went on to note that "men are four to eight times more likely to abuse alcohol than [are] women" (Time Magazine, 1984).

Men's special susceptibility to addiction was borne out by other studies that have shown that at least 25% of male relatives of alcoholics, but only 5% to 10% of female relatives, become alcoholic (Men's Health, 1986). As other drugs are used and abused by men we can expect similar patterns to those found with alcohol. Research on high school students has shown that males use and abuse all drugs more frequently than do females (Johnston & O'Malley, 1986). Although heredity undoubtedly plays an important part in the prevalence of male addictive behavior, the masculine role is very important.

We might think of male conditioning as a set of spoken and unspoken rules that dictate what a man must be and what he cannot be. Neitlich (1985) says that men are conditioned to be economically powerful, always sure, physically strong, courageous, controlled, cool and stoic, silent, protective, aggressive, and tough. She goes on to say that men are taught not to be loving, nurturing, tender, feeling, soft, passive, sweet, spontaneous, quiet, and giving. If addiction is a constant search for something one feels is necessary in order to be whole, a better understanding of why men get hooked on various substances emerges. If men think they have to be strong all the time, for instance, they will seek substances to give them the strength that they do not always feel. If men cannot be feeling, they will seek a drug that allows them to express emotions (Peele & Brodsky, 1975).

Cocaine, for example, is a perfect drug for men who cannot express feelings and think they need to be "supermen." It gives them a feeling of power. On cocaine men feel like superlovers, superachievers, superproviders, superathletes (O'Connell, 1985). The drug gives men the illusion of being all the things they "must" be, and at the same time offers them a chance to express the things they are taught they "cannot" be.

Substances Men Can Abuse

When Alcoholics Anonymous was started in 1935, the primary substance of concern in this country was alcohol. Shortly thereafter two federal hospitals—one in Lexington, Kentucky, and the other in Forth Worth, Texas—were started to deal with heroin addiction. Most theories of treatment and programs for help are still focused on these two drugs. Yet the "drug scene" has changed dramatically, particularly in the last 25 years.

In 1960, valium didn't exist. In 1980, 5 billion valium tablets were taken. The number of people who have tried marijuana has gone from a few hundred thousand to over 50 million. We are also in the midst of a cocaine epidemic unprecedented in the nation's history. Every day 5000 people try cocaine for the first time. "Crack," a very concentrated smokable form of cocaine, is a source of even greater concern (Mecca, 1984).

These drugs aren't just damaging kids on the streets but are threatening the stability of those who are supposed to be able to help. "Physicians have a rate of addiction that's four to six times higher than the general population's," says Dr. David Smith, founder director of the Haight-Ashbury Free Medical Clinic, and an authority on drug abuse treatment (Gallagher, 1986).

The advent of "designer drugs" will force us to change our entire way of thinking about drug abuse. Gary Henderson (cited in Gallagher, 1986), pharmacologist at the University of California at Davis, who coined the term *designer drugs* says, "There's just one bright aspect to the development of these drugs. They make it absolutely clear that the drug supply is now infinite, and that the measures we've used to deal with drug abuse have been to no avail."

Understanding and Treating Substance Abuse Problems

For those offering treatment it is important to understand the difference between "abuse" and "use." At present our national policy is virtually to ignore alcohol, nicotine, caffeine, and tranquilizer abuse as problems. We lump the use of all illegal substances together, regardless of the degree of impairment, and assume that any use constitutes abuse.

After 20 years of research into all aspects of substance use and abuse, Dr. Norman E. Zinberg, director of psychiatric training at the Cambridge Hospital and professor of psychiatry at the Harvard Medical School, had this to say:

> The leading recommendation to come from my years of research on controlled drug use is that every possible effort should be made—legally, medically, and socially—to distinguish between the two basic types of psychoactive drug consumption: that which is experimental, recreational, and circumstantial, and therefore has minimal social costs; and that which is dysfunctional, intensified, and compulsive, and therefore has high social costs. The first type I have labeled "use" and the second type "misuse" or "abuse." (Zinberg, 1984)

Although treating various substance abuse problems can be confusing, it is helpful to remember that if one becomes effective in treating one type of problem, such as alcoholism, then about 80% of what is needed to treat any abuse problem is known. What follows is an outline of the 12 steps I use in working with those with abuse problems.

WORKING WITH DENIAL

All those who have a problem with drugs at first insist that they do not, despite evidence to the contrary. Men who abuse alcohol usually insist that they can handle their booze, that they do not drink all that much, that they only drink because of a demanding wife. As the problem gets worse the denial increases. The first step in engaging people in treatment is helping them see that their use may be getting out of control. The therapist must be careful because pushing too hard may increase resistance and denial, while not pushing hard enough may allow continuation of an unhealthy pattern.

EXPLORING THE CONCEPT OF ABUSE OR ADDICTION

For most men the idea that there is something in their lives that they cannot control is very frightening. To admit that they have lost control brings up fear that they may be addicted. Everyone has a frightening image of addiction. For one it is the "man with the golden arm," a hopeless junkie. For another it's a skid-row bum slumped on the sidewalk, with a cheap bottle of wine stuck in his ragged coat.

Demystifying the notion of addiction is valuable; perhaps by telling clients that people can become addicted to anything (Wilson-Schaef, 1987). The addictive process stems from our desire to become a whole person. The desire is healthy and positive. The problem is that wholeness can only come from within. Whether it is alcohol, drugs, gambling, eating, sex, or love upon which one is dependent, that addiction occurs when people believe that happiness can be found or pain avoided through outside means. As the notion of addiction becomes less frightening, the therapist can help the person see what substances or processes are depended upon.

ASSESSING RISK

Having overcome the denial and fear, clients are now ready to assess the risk factors in determining how dependent they have become. Exploring how deeply they have become enmeshed in three related aspects (the 3 C's) of their relationship to their addictive substance is next. The first C is compulsion. The degree to which the person feels he needs the substance is assessed. How preoccupied is he? Does he think about getting high or having a drink when he is doing other things? To what degree does he begin to reorient his life around the substance of choice? Does he go to certain parties or begin to spend more time with certain friends because he knows his substance of choice will be available?

The second C is loss of control. In the late stages of chemical addiction, the loss of control is complete. One drink leads to a week of oblivion. One line of cocaine leads to the next, until all the coke is gone and all the money has been spent. In the early stages the loss of control is more subtle. A man may decide to have two drinks on a Tuesday night because he has to get up early the next day and he ends up having four and wakes up late with a hangover.

The third C is continued use despite adverse consequences. For most of us, if we have a bad experience with a substance, we stop using it in a negative way or stop using it altogether. Someone who has become dependent on the substance finds that he continues to use it even though it is causing problems.

The alcohol abuser continues to drink and drive even though he may have been arrested more than once, spent time in jail, paid a good deal of money for lawyers' fees, and so on. Despite his best intentions—and his intentions are usually genuine—he goes back to his destructive use.

This is one of the most difficult ideas for nonaddicts to understand. "Why doesn't he just stop drinking like that if it's causing so many problems?" they wonder. What they do not realize is that the characteristic of addiction is the inability to change use pattern despite the problems experienced.

GETTING READY
TO DO SOMETHING
ABOUT THE PROBLEM

Often a man realizes that he, in fact, is addicted to a substance. He recognizes the 3 Cs—compulsion, loss of control, and continued use despite adverse consequences—but continues to resist getting help. This can be a confusing time in the treatment process. It can be very frustrating for a counselor who has helped the man to admit he is having a problem, but not be able to help him to take the actions that would solve the problem. It seems odd that someone would continue to remain in a situation that is causing him so much pain.

The explanation may be found by exploring unconscious motivations. There are often hidden benefits derived from drinking, along with hidden fears of stopping. Once the therapist is able to bring to the surface these unconscious reasons for continued involvement with a problem causing substance, the client can intelligently weigh the positives and the negatives of continued use and have a clearer picture of the situation.

Trying to force the client to change before the whole picture is made clear often leads to a surface acceptance of the help offered with an underlying resistance. Dealing directly with the benefits and the drawbacks of change enables these issues to be dealt with early on in the treatment process with a much better prognosis for successful outcome.

FINDING A GUIDE

No one stops a longstanding pattern of relationship such as substance abuse without outside guidance, although frequently people at first try to do it on their own. The people who are successful have guidance. The guide may be a spouse who has gotten guidance, a counselor, a member of A.A. or some other self-help group, an employer, or a friend.

DECIDING WHERE ONE IS
IN THE ADDICTIVE PROCESS

There are nine possible positions that a person might occupy in beginning the treatment process:

(1) low risk/no problems
(2) high risk/ no problems
(3) minor problems
(4) serious problems, not ready for help
(5) serious problems, ready for help
(6) those in early recovery
(7) those in middle recovery
(8) those in late recovery
(9) those in continuing recovery

Traditionally, treatment began when people with serious problems, who were ready for treatment, voluntarily came for help. A period of intense medical intervention followed that focused on getting the person abstinent and involved with A.A. or other 12-step programs. Now counselors need to see the addictive process as beginning earlier and lasting longer if treatment is to be most effective.

DECIDING ON A
TREATMENT PROGRAM

I have found that there is a need for as many different treatment programs as there are people who need help. Most programs try to fit each person into an already existing program. However, no program has all the answers for everyone and a specific, custom-designed program for each person is generally best.

DOING THE PROGRAM
WITH GUIDANCE

Once an individual program has been decided upon, the guide helps engage the person in the program. Since a complete program may take as long as seven years, the guide needs to have a long-term commitment to this work to be most effective. A case example will illustrate the treatment process.

THE CASE OF BARRY S.

Barry S. was referred by the courts after being arrested for the second time on a drunk driving charge. Barry was 27 years old, married for five years, and had one small child. He had been drinking since he was 14, heavily in the last five years, and acknowledged that his father also drank heavily. Although he said he felt he was an alcoholic, he wasn't sure he wanted to stop drinking and hated the thought of going to A.A. "Those people are a bunch of losers. I don't want to associate with people like that."

Barry was seen once a week individually and every other week in a group therapy session with seven other men who were at various stages in their recovery. His wife, Nancy, was contacted and encouraged to get involved with Alanon (a support group for spouses of alcoholics). Barry was encouraged to keep an open mind about A.A. and to go to six or seven meetings before deciding whether it was useful. Over a period of six months, Barry began to talk about his fears of stopping drinking and the primary position alcohol had in his life. "Sometimes I think it's my only real friend." Gradually the times between drinks increased and one day he announced in group that he had attended an A.A. meeting and was planning to stay sober "one day at a time." "A.A. isn't what I expected," he said. "Those people really are just like me."

Group sessions ended after a year. Individual therapy continued for two years and Barry got quite involved with A.A., attending meetings three to five times a week. He said he felt it provided the social support to stay sober, while the therapy sessions helped him look at his life and deal with his feelings of anger, resentment, fear, and guilt. Gradually individual sessions were used for a once-a-month "check-in" and A.A. became the primary support.

Although A.A. encourages people to abstain from all mind-altering drugs, Barry continued to smoke marijuana occasionally during the first five years. He also drank a good deal of coffee laced with sugar, which was a staple at most A.A. meetings.

Barry returned again for weekly individual sessions to talk about his marijuana smoking and the effect it was having on his work. He had been a house painter since his early twenties, always made enough to get by, but now felt he wanted to become more successful and felt smoking marijuana was getting in the way. Over a period of six months he was able to stop smoking and also to stop drinking coffee, which kept him awake at night, and his work began to improve. Once again therapy sessions were spread out and Barry was seen every six months for a review session.

Six years after Barry started therapy, he returned for weekly individual sessions to focus on his sexuality. Although the marriage had improved greatly since he stopped drinking, he was unhappy that their sex life was so limited. He said Nancy didn't seem interested in sex and they made love once every three or four months. He found himself fantasizing about other women and said he was spending more and more time away from work following pretty women in his car. This brought up memories of early experiences with his mother and father. He remembered times his father had beaten him and his mother took him into bed with her after his father went to work. He said he always had a mixture of sexual desire and repulsion to women he became intimate with. Gradually he began to see how he contributed to the lack of sexual involvement between him and Nancy. As the issues became clear, they were worked with as a couple and their sex life began to improve.

The last time Barry was seen he invited the therapist to a special A.A. meeting where he was acknowledged by the group for being seven years sober. He seems to have worked out many of the issues that were causing problems. He no longer drinks or uses drugs. His work and family life have improved greatly. His feelings of self-esteem are at an all-time high. "Life," he said, "seems sweeter than ever before."

What Does Not Work in Counseling Male Substance Abusers

We can often learn a great deal about success by focusing on failure. Some of the most important lessons about being an effective substance abuse counselor with men have come from making mistakes. What follows is a summary of the most glaring mistakes I have made over the past 22 years:

(1) *Failure to address "drug use" as the primary issue in treatment.* Trained in "psychodynamic" psychotherapy I would focus on "underlying issues," believing that if I got at the root of the problem the person would stop using drugs. Meanwhile, the drug use continued and therapy was ineffective.

(2) *Failure to relate diagnosis and treatment.* In the early days working in a clinic, getting the proper diagnosis was important. I would spend hours reading manuals trying to decide if I should classify the person as having

"Alcohol Idiosyncratic Intoxication" or "Organic Brain Syndrome," for instance. There never seemed to be a relationship between how we labeled a person and what treatment we provided.

(3) *Failure to develop treatment that fits the unique needs of the client.* Positive I understood what treatment was most effective, I assumed that those who didn't fit in were "unmotivated" or unready for help. I came to believe that "substance abuse" was a unitary disease entity and my program was the right one for every one with that problem.

(4) *Failure to understand mutual support groups such as Alcoholics Anonymous.* At first I found it difficult to believe that no-cost "self-help" programs could be effective. When more clients reported success with these programs, I grudgingly sent a few people who could not afford to pay for treatment. I went to one or two meetings myself, but never tried to understand how these programs worked.

(5) *Failure to understand the different needs of women and men.* If a person has a broken leg, the pain is the same whether it's a man or a woman, and likewise, the treatment doesn't vary. I first assumed that alcoholism and drug addiction were problems that were experienced the same by both sexes. Later, as the women's movement spread, I could see that women had special needs, but was unable to see that men had unique issues as well.

(6) *Failure to discuss my own life experiences.* I was taught in school that a good therapist must keep a professional distance from the client. I never talked about my own life. I thought the experiences I had had with drugs and alcohol were private and of no value in helping the client. I worked in an office that revealed little about my own life and I saw my client's problems as different from my own.

Acceptance of Mutual Healing

The most effective counselors understand that all healing is mutual. Contrary to what many believe, the therapeutic process works both ways. Therapists' own lives are enhanced as they help those who seek their counsel. One of the primary reasons Alcoholics Anonymous is so effective in treating addictions is that members know that in helping each other they are helping themselves.

Sheldon Kopp (1971) reminds us that therapist and client can see each other as equals.

My pain hurts as yours does. Each of us has the same amount to lose—all we have. My tears are as bitter, my scars as permanent. My loneliness is an aching in my chest, much like yours.... You say you've had a bad time of it, an unhappy childhood? Me too. You say that you didn't get all you needed and wanted, weren't always understood or cared for? Welcome to the club!

References

Brown, S. (1985). *Treating the alcoholic: A developmental model of recovery.* New York: John Wiley.

Gallagher, W. (1986, August). The looming menace of designer drugs. *Discover Magazine,* pp. 24-35.

Heilman, R. (1973). *Early recognition of alcoholism and other drug dependence.* Center City, MN: Hazelden.

Johnston, L., & O'Malley, P. (1986). Why do the nation's students use drugs and alcohol? *Journal of Drug Issues, 16,* 29-66.

Kopp, S. (1971). *Guru.* Palo Alto, CA: Science and Behavior Books.

Kurtz, E. (1979). *Not God—A history of Alcoholics Anonymous.* Center City, MN: Hazelden.

Mecca, A. (1984). *Comprehensive alcohol & drug abuse prevention strategies.* San Rafael, CA: California Health Research Foundation.

Men's Health. (1986). *Alcohol: Men's special curse.* Emmaus, PA: Rodale Press.

Neitlich, A. (1985). *Building bridges: Women's & men's liberation.* Cambridge, MA: Building Bridges.

O'Connell, J. (1985). *End of the line: Quitting cocaine.* Philadelphia: Westminster Press.

Peele, S., & Brodsky, A. (1975). *Love & addiction.* New York: New American Library.

Small, J. (1981). *Becoming naturally therapeutic.* Austin, TX: Eupsychian Press.

Time (1984, October 15). *Report on national study,* p. 80.

Wilson-Schaef, A. (1987). *When society becomes an addict.* New York: Harper & Row.

Zinberg, N. (1984). *Drug, set, and setting: The basis of controlled intoxicant use.* New Haven, CT: Yale University Press.

24

Counseling with Veterans

Terry A. Carlson

"Is this client a veteran and, if so, are there special issues that may interact with the presenting problem, counseling techniques, and therapeutic goals?" That question is probably infrequently considered by counselors working with male clients unless one is a counselor in a Veterans Administration (VA) facility or a Veterans Outreach Center. Often men who are veterans are referred to VA sources since that is what the VA is "supposed to do." Unfortunately for many clients, a VA facility is not convenient and/or the veteran is not eligible for services. Thus the man seeking counseling may be a veteran with certain special issues originating from his service experiences that he may or may not present. Likewise, he may be a veteran whose concerns are addressed in other chapters in this book and are not specifically veteran related. This chapter is designed to (a) help the counselor understand the service and veteran experiences, (b) look at specific concerns of veterans, and (c) offer some suggestions about counseling with veterans.

So who are veterans? In the vast majority of cases they are males who have been drafted or who enlisted for a period of active duty in one of the military armed services (Army, Navy, Air Force, Marine Corps, or Coast Guard). Some may have served with national guard or reserve forces but also served for a period on active duty in order to be considered a veteran. According to data provided by the VA (1984), it is estimated there were 28,202,000 veterans alive in 1983. There have been four major conflicts/wars (Korea and Vietnam were never officially declared wars by the U.S. Congress) since the turn of the century. From World War I there are about 297,000 veterans still alive whose average age in 1986 is thought to be between 85 to 90 years old. For World War II there are about 10,978,000 veterans whose average age is 66 years old. From the Korean conflict the estimate is 5,294,000 with average age at 55 years old. Finally, from the Vietnam conflict there are 8,238,000 veterans with an average age of 39 years old. There are smaller groups from the peacetime periods, and some veterans also served in more than one war. What all these numbers may really mean is that 1 in every 6 male clients between the ages of 17 and 100+ is probably a veteran, and 1 in 3 over the age of 55 is probably a veteran. Most veterans served during one of the periods in which America was at war. It may therefore be important to understand the military experience.

The Military Experience

Every male who has served on active military duty has had a unique experience. Veterans during different wars had different experiences. It is probably unfair to generalize or describe a typical experience, but it becomes necessary to make the attempt for brevity's sake. The typical military experience begins in the late teens or early twenties. Erik Erikson (1950, 1968) in his eight-stage model of psychsocial human development, posed two important tasks for this life period. Erikson's stages that correspond to the time of entry into the military service are establishing one's own individual identity versus being involved in role confusion (14-20 years) and establishing intimate relationships versus being socially isolated (20-40 years). Most veterans had lived within a family context with a set of instilled values, mores, and beliefs until they made a break and were sworn into the armed forces. Culture shock began immediately.

Upon entry onto active duty, the young person goes through a period of basic training: generally an eight-week period of intense physical and mental indoctrination and training that is designed to turn a young civilian lad into a competent American fighting man whose job is to fight in wars. For most recruits (the name given to a new soldier in training) basic training is bewildering, scary, and physically demanding. There is much to learn, with immediate negative reinforcement for the slightest mistake delivered by a fierce-looking drill sergeant whose demeanor commands fear and respect. The young recruit is being trained for combat and his mission will be to kill the "enemy." This becomes the first major value conflict that a young man must resolve. For 18 years he lived in a society in which killing was wrong, and yet now killing is what he is supposed to do (cognitive dissonance to the nth degree; Festinger, 1957). The military helps to resolve this conflict by first depersonalizing the "enemy." The enemy is never referred to as a person or anything that gives humanlike qualities to the object of our violence. Nicknames are given to the enemy to dehumanize them. Second, the military (and ultimately the whole country) instills a cognitive set of "we are right, we are the good guys, we do no wrong, and our cause is just." An additional mindset is that "soldiers obey orders." Recruits are trained to respond instantaneously to an order from a superior without thinking about the order. Failure to obey can lead to judicial punishment. Besides no place for thinking, there is no place for emotions. Learning to shut emotions off becomes a required task to master. Finally, the group in which he now exists establishes a norm that killing the enemy is the right behavior for this group. If a young man resists this norm, he quickly becomes a group deviant, becomes singled out for "extra instruction" by his drill sergeant, or is discharged from military service because of failure to adjust.

Although a counselor may become angry, upset, or empathize with how awful that situation must be for the young male, one needs to remember that there are reasons for all of those resolving mechanisms. Primarily the training helps with the physical survival of the recruit and his fellow recruits when they enter a combat situation. A moment's hesitation as one stops to "think about" a situation may lead to a horrible wound or death. In the survivalistic environment of war, reactions are often more important to the individual soldier than are his cognitive abilities. The military trains reactions that save friendly lives while destroying the enemy. Most people want to live and so adopt the reactions. Almost of equal importance as the physical survival is the psychological survival that the training provides. If the military says to the recruit, "Your country wants you to go and kill 18-year-old boys, who just graduated from high school, who have a mother, father and two sisters, and who pray to the same God as you do," the value conflict would be so intense that the recruit would not function effectively in combat. A massive guilt complex would likely develop. Psychological survival would be in grave jeopardy. Instead, the coping mechanisms the military provides usually help young men to do what their country wants them to do: to fight a war, to kill the enemy.

Besides killing, there are other value conflicts that arise for young men. Many men had never lived outside their own community before entering the military. Suddenly, they are thrown into a new community with other young men from different communities and backgrounds. Values, beliefs, and mores different from one's own may become the new norm. One's individual identity, different from one's identity within the family, may create the role confusion Erikson (1950, 1968) proposed. To use alcohol, marijuana, or other street drugs may now become the "manly" thing to do. To engage in sexual activity with prostitutes may be the accepted group norm. To get into fights at local hangouts may be the merit badge required to show manhood. Many of these same dilemmas are faced by young men not in the military as well, but the group pressure of military "esprit de corps" and morale make it sometimes more difficult to resist. Finally, travel to foreign countries exposes young soldiers to new cultures with different customs, values, and mores that may also present value conflicts.

The most significant part of the military experience is being involved in combat. Combat strips away almost all vestiges of humanity. It is the ultimate "game of survival." Life and death occur randomly with little rhyme or reason. There may or may not be a geographical objective/purpose on the large scale; for the individual soldier the objective becomes kill or be killed. Most of the time nothing else matters. Men in combat are regressed to more primitive levels of thinking and behavior. The environment is no longer safe. Naturalistic dangers are often as deadly as man-made dangers. The most basic need on Maslow's hierarchy (1943) becomes threatened. Behavior becomes motivated to satisfy the physical needs for survival. Horrors, pain, and suffering beyond human comprehension occur routinely. After leading his famous Civil War "March to the Sea," General William Tecumseh Sherman is supposed to have stated, "War is hell." The destruction and devastation he witnessed in the aftermath of his army's movement became overwhelming for him to contemplate. For most people who believe in hell, combat surpasses their concept of what hell is. Combat is hell on earth but far worse. Nothing man does compares to it as a human activity. Think of the worst situation one can. Combat is worse!

One could write an entire chapter—an entire book—on describing what combat is like. That would only tell what combat, at that time, in that place, in that war, was like. The next war would be the same, yet different. Suffice it to say that war is, on the one hand, exhilarating for some men, giving them a God-like feeling of the power of life and death over another; and on the other hand, a feeling of the devastation and helplessness as the power of life and death is in the hands of the enemy. The adrenaline rush caused by the anxiety of combat can also become debilitating, making it difficult to cope with the stresses of everyday life. More will be stated about combat in the next section.

After a war, veterans either return to civilian life or continue with a career in the military. Reintegration into civilian life often leads to feelings of alienation and differentness. Friends and relatives who did not go to war have continued their lives without interruption. Their existence may not have been affected unless a son or brother or husband was wounded, taken prisoner, or killed in the war. The returnee wants to get on with his life, putting the war behind him. Unfortunately that may be easier said than done. The family may not want to talk about what happened in the war because they may have seen some of the horrors of war on the nightly news and do not want to explore the possibility that their veteran had been involved in such events. The veteran may quickly pick up on the unspoken message that talking about the war is taboo. Feelings of not being accepted or that by serving their country they had done something wrong may develop and lead to further isolation. The mundane activities of a noncombat world may be boring and unchallenging to the veteran. The tremendous responsibilities he had in the military may not transfer to equal responsibilities in civilian life. Finally, in terms of social interactions, the veteran may either want to "sow his wild oats" as he did in the military or feel that it is time to settle down and get married. Yet the lack of common experience may interfere with developing profound relationships. Also, the behaviors learned in a military environment, which were adaptive in that environment, may not transfer well into the civilian world. Thus the veteran may feel as if he does not fit in at home, on the job, on campus, or in relationships. He may not completely understand why he feels different; he just does, and it causes difficulties for him. Seeking counseling may not be on his list of possibilities of things he can do to change. As for many clients, counseling may be cognitively equated with being "crazy" to the veteran, and he does not want to be labeled "crazy" so does not seek counseling. He may eventually adjust or may turn to other ineffective coping mechanisms, such as alcohol or drugs, which may then lead to other problems.

Those veterans who remain in the military may experience many of the same problems as veterans who get out. Military life away from combat may be seen as "Mickey Mouse," which translated from military slang means "unimportant, comical, and inane." Spit and polish, strict discipline, and "fill the time" activities of a peacetime military do not compare with the excitement and meaningful activity of combat. Again, discipline problems may develop to include alcohol and/or drug abuse. The serviceman may be referred to counseling, may make an adequate adjustment, or be discharged from the service. If he stays in the service until he retires, he may then face adjustment problems in his move into the civilian world. The closed society of the military has provided a safe comfortable environment in which he has lived for at least 20 years. The customs and traditions within the military community may be different from those in the civilian world. The lack of common experiences, the military behavioral repertoire, and the different view of the world may also lead to adjustment difficulties. Retirement issues may also be encountered by veterans, as well as the difficulties of starting a second career in the middle years or older age level. A similar view of "counseling is for crazies" often prevents a retired veteran from seeking the counseling that could help him become as successful in civilian life as he had been in the military. The military experience generally ends for most males back in the civilian world from which they entered the military. That does not necessarily mean the same hometown in which they were raised, but the civilian world. They are now veterans and may appear as a client with any of the presenting unique problems because of their experiences as veterans. The next two sections present information on those unique problems.

Post Traumatic
Stress Disorder

The most common presenting problem of male veterans seeking counseling and psychotherapy may not be easily identified by the veteran or the counselor. A variety of symptoms or behavioral patterns may be presented that may lead to different conceptualizations or diagnoses. The veteran may be reluctant to tell every detail to the counselor unless asked and asked in the right way. Without the right questions, the core problem will not be identified and thus not addressed in counseling or therapy sessions. The right questions focus on military experiences, especially about combat or hazardous duty in which the veteran may have participated or had been in a support role in which he dealt with the carnage of war. Because of the reluctance to talk about the war, it may require an extended evaluation session or several sessions before the veteran (client) begins to develop the therapeutic trust in the counselor. Many veterans are not only afraid that they will be considered "crazy," they also fear that what they tell will either cause a feeling of disbelief in the counselor or the counselor will think they are terrible people for having done what they did in combat. Sarah Haley (1978) and Arthur Egendorf (1978) present excellent chapters on the therapist-veteran interaction during treatment sessions, especially when the horrors and atrocities are revealed. Carl Rogers's (1951) concept of "positive regard" may never be more greatly tested than when listening to a veteran talk about killing eagerly, as if he had enjoyed it, or with total lack of feelings. It is best if the counselor keeps in mind just how horrible the experience of combat is. In combat man often regresses to a more primitive man whose main concern is the survival of his physical and psychological self. The biggest legacy of combat is the experience of trauma. Trauma to the physical self and trauma to the psychological self. Combat trauma is often painful to even think about, let alone talk about with a stranger. The counselor needs to be aware of the veteran's issues about war as well as their own issues about war.

For many veterans the experience of combat trauma overwhelms them and results in a variety of symptoms. At various times throughout military medical history the cluster of symptoms has been called by different names such as "shell shocked," "combat fatigue," "combat exhaustion," "traumatic neurosis," "operational fatigue," and others. In 1980, a new disorder called "Post Traumatic Stress Disorder" (PTSD) was added to the DSM-III. The counselor is referred to DSM-III for a detailed description of the symptoms of PTSD (American Psychiatric Association, 1980).

Besides the symptoms of DSM-III, others have suggested that additional symptoms need to be included. Silver and Iacono (1984) reported depression and anger as additional symptoms, especially in Vietnam veterans. Horowitz (1986) discussed rage reactions and extreme irritability. The Roche Report (1980) reported cynicism, alienation, and anomie as common problems for some veterans. Another PTSD-associated symptom given by Jellinek and Williams (1984) is substance abuse, including alcohol abuse. The debate about PTSD symptoms will likely be a long one.

In closing this section, three symptoms that are frequently seen in counseling are reviewed. The first is anomie, which can be described as a loss of interest, a loss of a sense of purpose, or a loss of direction. After the combat experience, nothing else compares to it. In the best and worst senses, combat is probably the highest level of feeling alive. The best sense is in terms of the development of the greatest love between human beings undergoing the worst human experience. Every sense is heightened to the highest degree, and the combatants become mutually dependent upon one another for survival. The bond goes beyond family and marital love. It is a love in which one will sacrifice one's own life without thinking in order to save another. On the other hand, combat allows one to see the worst side of humankind in terms of the killing and atrocities one human being does to another. After reaching the acme and the nadir of human experience, many veterans present themselves in a depressed state. They go through the motions of living, yet appear almost zombielike, as if nothing seems to matter to them. It is as if they are burned out on life. A similar response is the veteran who is overly concerned, overly identified with another person. Often it is with a child, and the veteran's life becomes enmeshed with the child's life. The sole sense of purpose becomes the protection of the child. The counselor's investigation may lead the counselor to events from the traumatic experiences involving children, which helps explain the veteran's behavior. Finally, another symptom is the veteran who is a bomb waiting to explode. Rage reactions, super irritability, and continual anger become the norm for some veterans' behaviors. It appears almost as if they are addicted to this energized state, and some do seek the "thrill of combat" by frequenting places in which fights are more likely to happen. Their negative feelings are often blamed on others; yet this may only be a way to protect the psychological self from self-condemnation for actions performed during traumatic events. Often, acting-out behaviors are symbolic reenactments of the traumatic events. As counselors, it is important to see beyond our own emotional reactions when a client becomes enraged, and to understand what has happened to trigger such behavior. It is not an easy task but a necessary one when a client is in that much pain.

Counseling with PTSD Veterans

There have been several excellent books and articles published on doing therapy with war veterans, especially

Vietnam veterans. John R. Smith (1985) described four major themes of PTSD treatment that arise in psychotherapy from a cognitive therapy perspective. In the same book (Sonnenberg, Blank, & Talbot, 1985), Smith also described rap groups and group therapy, which have often been the recommended treatment milieu for survivors of traumatic events. A third chapter in the book, written by Candis M. Williams and Tom Williams, focused on family therapy. Keane and Kaloupek (1982) discussed using a behavioral approach of flooding in treating survivors. Silver and Kelly (1985) presented their use of hypnotherapy with both World War II and Vietnam veterans suffering from PTSD. Schwartz (1984) edited an entire book to the psychoanalytic interpretation and treatment of PTSD in combat veterans. Arthur Egendorf (1985) also presented his views on how to heal the trauma of war for veterans. Horowitz (1973) presented a phase model of treatment for stress response syndromes that can also be applied to the counseling of veterans with leftover symptoms of their combat experiences.

The list of references could go on for pages. Counselors will, however, pick and choose what method will work for them and apply it, just as they do with any client. With the male veteran who has PTSD, certain issues may be more prominent and so I will devote some time to each.

THE "I WON'T TALK 'CAUSE YOU AREN'T A VETERAN" ISSUE

Many veterans offer stiff resistance to entering into a counseling relationship. It may be sex, age, or a nonveteran status of the counselor that seems to be the stumbling block. Some veterans honestly believe no one who has not been through combat could understand what they still struggle with daily. Others use this issue as a defense against being rejected or viewed as animals because of what they did in order to survive while in a combat situation. Yes, it is true that most people who have not been in combat cannot fully understand it, but no one—not even another veteran—can completely understand what another's time in the hell of combat was like. My most competent professional associate, however, is a young nurse with a master's in counseling. Sue successfully treats many combat veterans not because she understands everything about combat, but because she cares and transmits that message to the veteran. When confronted with this issue, she makes statements along the line of, "You are right, I was not in combat and do not understand everything about it. I am willing to listen and understand what it is like for people to be in pain. I want to try and help. We can go at your pace until you feel comfortable with me." Such statements usually will begin to engage the veteran in the counseling relationship.

THE "LET ME TELL YOU
THIS HORROR" ISSUE

Sometimes veterans will attempt very early in counseling to test the counselor. In a bizarre kind of way, the veteran almost sets himself up for rejection, which is just the opposite of what he really wants. Because he has such poor self-esteem and may have had many rejections by people in his life, it is almost a form of self-punishment to relate an involvement in an atrocity or vivid description of the carnage of combat, hoping the counselor will be horrified and hence either reject or feel the pain of the veteran. His self-evaluation will be confirmed, and he may then continue to behave in social and / or antisocial ways. If the veteran gives gory details with enthusiasm, then further evaluation of an antisocial personality disorder needs to be considered. Most veterans who have horror stories take several sessions before they feel comfortable enough to begin to talk about a traumatic event. Instead of enthusiastically giving details, the veteran will do it matter of factly, without emotion, or become very labile and angry while recalling the events. Usually the anger is verbal but needs to be monitored for escalation, in which case the counselor may need to apply gentle but firm limit setting. The counselor needs to keep in mind that all veterans have been trained in the use of weapons and violence. Those that have been through combat learned that returned violence was a way to cope with intense fear and anxiety. By listening with a therapeutic ear and paying attention to one's own system, the counselor can prevent a blow-up that neither the veteran nor the counselor would find helpful. If this issue arises or even before it does, a reading of Haley (1978) can provide guidance.

THE "WHY" ISSUE

Many veterans spend a great deal of time ruminating about situations looking for the answer to a "why" question (e.g., Why did Joe, who was married and had a kid, get killed and I didn't? Why did Tom take my place on point? I should have been hit by the sniper. Why did that little kid have a live grenade and try to kill my friends?). As in everyday life, there is often no answer to be found. Why a bullet missed by an inch and killed the one behind is almost a random event in combat. Some fatalists will attribute it to "fate." One can almost never ask the person on the other end of the gun why and receive a response. Often the "why" questions center on traumatic events with many "shoulds" and "should not haves." This post facto second guessing may be treated with the cognitive therapy of the "shoulds" and "should nots" (Ellis & Grieger, 1977). Veterans want to change the outcome of the traumatic event and reduce their survival guilt. More global "why" questions may have a more existential basis and the treatment of such is discussed by Yalom (1980). For most veterans, the therapist may tell them "why" is the wrong question because they will probably never find the answer and hence nothing will change. After discussing the event, possibly more than once, the therapist may encourage them to change the question. Something along the line of, "Now that that event happened, what am I going to do about it?" By reshifting the focus away from the quagmire of the past onto the present, an attempt is made to help the veteran move forward with his life and to break the hold the past has on him.

THE "I FEEL LIKE EXPLODING" ISSUE

A common problem for veterans is the buildup of tremendous tension and anxiety. Some veterans turn to alcohol or drugs as a way to "keep a lid on." Some go looking for trouble in order to release tension by fighting. Others try to hold it in and control it but become very irritable and then go into a rage reaction. During the rage, they may direct much of their energy to verbal harangues, destroying furniture or structures (more than one veteran has told me about punching his fist through a plaster wall or kicking down a door), and unfortunately some have physically abused a significant other. The veteran reports feeling out of control, and after it is over, feeling guilty and self-deprecating. Teaching relaxation is invaluable. Helping the person learn the cues to increased tension and teaching other types of control can often defuse the imminent explosion. The cues need careful investigation to determine the etiology, the behavioral learning history, and the reinforcement potential for the explosion. By the time most veterans come into counseling, they realize their previous coping attempts do not work and often increase the problems, and they are now willing to try to learn some other techniques.

THE "I AM A VICTIM" ISSUE

This particular issue can take two forms. In the first form, a veteran will truly believe he is a helpless victim of traumatic events. There is nothing he can do about it, and so attempts to deny self-responsibility for his actions and for his efforts to change. He may express confusion as to what happened and to how he became involved. In the second way, the victim responds with much anger and frustration, often directed at those who sent him, those whom he fought alongside with and/or against, his family, and in some cases the nation as a whole. When the "boat people" refugees were brought into this country from Southeast Asia, many Vietnam veterans viewed it as a personal insult, an affront to their service. Many negative stereotypes were formed by veterans about the refugees, based upon lack of information or on overgeneralizations. It became easier to blame the refugees than for the veteran to accept the self-responsibility for not having achieved his own expectations. In either way the term *victim* gives a sense of helplessness to a veteran and keeps him oriented toward the past traumatic events. If veterans are viewed as "survivors" of a "hell on earth," it imparts a sense of strength to them. It also allows for an attitude of "Okay, that is over; now let's get on with life." A victim is not attributed control over his life, whereas a survivor is attributed a willingness to overcome adversity and hence has some control. When working with any PTSD client, talking about the experience in terms of being a survivor is therapeutically more beneficial. The counselor can attribute strength to the client in that since the client survived the traumatic event, he can survive his current life situations. The instillation of hope is important for many clients, and for PTSD clients it renews their willingness to try and readjust.

THE "I CAN'T GET TOO CLOSE" ISSUE

This issue focuses on difficulties with relationships that many PTSD veterans have. Many veterans will talk about how close they had been to certain guys they served with in their combat units. The comaraderie developed was frequently very strong because they were sharing life-threatening experiences and depending upon each other. Fighting not only the enemy, but the threatening elements of the environment, veterans learned to share their last bit of food or water, to talk about their plans for the future, and to huddle together to ward off the elements. Many veterans report feeling closer to their comrades than to any other friend or even their own brothers. Then in the suddenness of combat, a friend is killed or horribly maimed. The veteran may experience intense emotional pain at the loss, but military training does not support showing those emotions. Later in another engagement, another comrade is lost, and then another. Each time there is unreleased intense emotional pain. For many veterans, the emotional pain becomes too much and psychic numbing or a shutting down of emotions occurs. They no longer allow themselves to become friends because they do not want to care so much about anyone again. They develop a belief that if they get close to someone, that person gets hurt, and the intrapsychic pain is unbearable. That learning unfortunately becomes transferred to all close relationships. Upon return from combat, many veterans get on with their lives by marrying or living with someone. Because they have not resolved their PTSD issue, they do not easily share positive emotions or profess their love for their partners. Often the only emotions are irritability, depression, fear, or rage. Such an emotional environment is generally not conducive to long-term close relationships. Divorce is a significant problem for many PTSD veterans.

For Vietnam combat veterans, negative experiences in which children, women, and elderly were used as weapons by the enemy often led to a deep-seated mistrust for all strangers. Involvement in atrocities also instilled dysfunctional behavior based on guilt. Finally, for many veterans disenchantment and feelings of being used by their government and country caused feelings of suspiciousness. Then upon return to an unfriendly, unsympathetic country, strong feelings of alienation developed, and veterans tended to isolate themselves. Often these veterans talk about their desire to live "off up in the hills" or "out in the country," away from everyone. Another common statement is, "I just don't fit in here." Such a cognitive-affective learning experience makes relationships difficult. In some ways, it is almost as though the combat veteran went from age 19 to age 40 without the learning of the intervening years. The veteran's perceptions of relationships and of how to act his role within a relationship is clouded by his combat experiences.

The counselor may become involved in a long-term relationship (with many ups and downs) with a combat veteran. The workings of this relationship can be generalized to a significant personal relationship of the veteran. Communication skills, assertiveness skills, affective awareness training, and anger control may all need to be covered. Cognitive restructuring work, as well as couples and/or family therapy, may be needed. The psychological defensive wall erected to keep out emotional pain needs to be carefully taken down one piece at a time. Beginning to be aware of emotions may be the first true step in healing and breaking the chains of the traumatic events from the past.

Other Problems with Veterans in Counseling

Besides PTSD, there are a few other problems that often occur in counseling with veterans. These problems are not related to traumatic events. Instead, they are based on living in a military society with its peculiar rules and behaviors that can become deeply ingrained. Arguments could be made about certain personality characteristics that might lead an individual into the military service. A high psychological need for order, love of excitement and adventure, a desire for a camaraderie, self-sacrifice, and patriotism may be just a few. On the one hand, the military does everything and provides everything. Just do as one is told to do—don't think; just follow orders. It is a great provider; the ultimate parental figure. As some old-timers would say, "If the service wanted you to have a wife, they would have issued you one." Such mentality or belief system can create certain problems in counseling with veterans, and several of these problems will be discussed.

The biggest problem is that veterans *may not be in contact with their feelings.* Much of counseling focuses on the affective level. But millions upon millions of veterans have been trained to block out and deny feelings. Thus a veteran may not be able to discuss how he "feels" about some issue. He will tell the counselor what he "thinks" about the situation but seems at a loss to respond about effect. As a counselor, one may need to teach or offer affective alternatives to sensitize a veteran at the affective level. A veteran may talk about being uncomfortable but may need careful intervention to clarify whether he feels depressed, sad, tense, uptight, angry, frightened, anxious, irritable, explosive, or another affect. By taking the time to clarify, the counselor helps to educate the veteran and helps him better understand what is going on inside. A great number of veterans do not realize how tense/anxious they are until they are taught some relaxation skills. The idea of stress management provides therapeutic insight and treatment. Additionally, becoming aware of their affective self is beneficial, but scary as well.

The *fear of becoming emotional* is the second problem area often encountered. The military has trained the veteran to be in command, to show no weakness, and to know what is right. A super-masculine image is the standard by which veterans are judged. There is a place for women, and women should stay in their place. That place is not in the military and certainly not in combat. The male supremacy is reinforced constantly throughout their military career, and suddenly in counseling the veteran "thinks" of himself as a failure. There have been many times veterans have said to me, "I felt like crying but could not do it." Whether from fear of losing control or of viewing himself as weak if he cried, the veteran may initially resist getting in contact with his emotions because he wants to retain his self-image as a man. Instead of feeling anger at such a chauvinistic view, the counselor is recommended to view it as a part of the veteran with which he has not been in touch for a long time. The affective side is as important for a veteran as it is for any client. Just realize it may take time to help a veteran find and become accustomed to that new part of himself.

A third problem is the *anomie* that many veterans have following combat or an exciting career in the military. Nothing seems as important, as challenging, or as exciting as it was during his service time. His level of responsibility may have gone from being totally responsible for $30 million worth of equipment and personnel to being the low man in an occupational setting in which he has no input to decision making. The veteran may also be having problems adjusting into a "civilian" world. His entire lifestyle has abruptly changed, yet he may have little insight into any cause-and-effect relationship between such a change and how he feels. Often a true adjustment disorder as described in DSM-III is easily diagnosed for retired or recently released servicemen. Counseling can prove very beneficial to alleviate adjustment problems. Glasser's Reality Therapy (1965) is often effective in helping servicemen look at their expectations of what civilian life would be like. There are usually unrealistic expectations that can be corrected by soft confrontations. Encouragement of involvement in activities and/or organizations can also be helpful. Many retired servicemen move near military bases or into retired military neighborhoods, which can help to ease the transition. The anomie may be initially difficult to overcome, but once the stationary inertia is set into motion the problem generally resolves itself.

The final problem centers on issues of *authority*. Because counseling is often a new experience for a veteran, he may view the counselor as an authority figure. As an authority figure, the veteran may want the counselor to tell him what to do, just as his commanders in the military did. On the other hand, the veteran may have a need to resist the counselor because he is tired of "taking orders." In either case, the counselor will benefit from explaining what counseling or psychotherapy is about and what each member's role is in the therapeutic relationship. For many veterans the idea of counseling is anathema because in the military, seeking counseling was thought to lead to loss of a security clearance and hence the end of a chance for promotion. Difficulty taking orders may develop in a new work situation because the veteran may view the boss as inept or not knowing that there is a better way to do things. (Better in terms of the way it was done in the military.) The old military formula of instilling discipline— "kick ass and take names"—does not transfer to the civilian world. No longer does military rank provide power to command with the military justice system to back up orders with punishments for those who failed to respond. Again, reality therapy can be useful. Playing on the veteran's pride can also be used by the counselor. By pointing out to a veteran that in his long, successful career, he made many moves and served under many commanders, the counselor can point out to the veteran how he learned to adapt in each new situation. After achieving agreement with that point, the counselor can discuss with the veteran what the new environment is like and what he needs to do to succeed. Usually such an approach removes the blinders (resistance) for the veteran, and he can begin working on his adjustment. Not everything is "black and white," as many veterans believe. There are grays, and there are different ways of dealing with authority.

A subissue under authority is a veteran who runs his family as he did his military unit. Spit and polish, Saturday morning inspection, stern discipline, a "yes, sir; no, sir; no excuse, sir" environment often leads to family problems and needs to be dealt with in family therapy. There needs to be work done on the ego differentiation between the service and the family when the veteran becomes too authoritarian. It may be difficult to move him from his rigidity, but he would probably not be in counseling unless he wanted to change.

Other Resources

When faced with a veteran client whose main concerns are veteran related, it may be helpful to refer the veteran to a Veterans Administration facility within reasonable distance or at least provide a phone number to the veteran for him to call and check on his eligibility for treatment. It may prove beneficial for the counselor to call and consult with a psychologist, social worker, psychiatric nurse clinical specialist, or a psychiatrist about a particular case. If one is located in or near a large metropolitan center, there is probably a VA facility there. If not, then one can call the following telephone number to obtain the phone number of the nearest facility: VA INFORMATION—(202) 233-4000.

Similarly, if working with a Vietnam veteran or any combat veteran, a consultation with or referral to a local Vet Center may be of benefit. A Vet Center is an outreach counseling center providing free counseling services to veterans who are still struggling with their combat experiences. PTSD is the largest category of presenting problems and the reason the Vet Centers were created. Call the same VA information number and ask to talk with someone familiar with Vet Centers.

If the counselor wants or needs to do a PTSD evaluation, there are several available. Figley's (1978) Appendix B has a suggested format focusing primarily on Vietnam but is easily adopted to other traumatic events with a few word changes. Another format is provided by Scurfield and Blank (1985) to obtain a good military history.

Conclusion

Veterans are people who have been through some special experiences that have affected their lives. Although many veterans are resistant to counseling/psychotherapy, they often become appreciative clients who respond well to counselors' efforts. Do not try to fool them or not be "up-front" with them. Their experiences, especially in combat, seem to allow them to know when someone is not being honest with them. They often present a very stern, gruff exterior and much pain can be seen in their eyes. Combat certainly ages them beyond their years. Some problems they present may seem intractable because of the many intervening years. An empathic counselor can often ease their burden, simply by caring and showing a willingness to listen. As Fielder (1950) indicated, it does not seem to matter which therapy or technique of counseling is utilized, the concern of one human being—the counselor—for another—the client—appears to be the most important therapeutic factor. As with most clients, if treated with dignity, they respond with dignity. Veterans have shouldered the nation's burdens and at times may need help to unload a burden that has become too heavy. As counselors and therapists, we can help lighten the burden and in so doing, say thank you for the sacrifice the veteran made. Sometimes that is all that is really needed.

References

American Psychiatric Association. (1980). *Diagnostic and statistical manual of mental disorders.* (3rd ed.). Washington, DC: Author.

Egendorf, A. (1978). Psychotherapy with Vietnam veterans: Observations and suggestions. In C. Figley (Ed.), *Stress disorders among Vietnam veterans* (pp. 231-253). New York: Brunner/Mazel.

Egendorf, A. (1985). *Healing from the war.* Boston: Houghton Mifflin.

Ellis, A., & Greiger, R. (Eds.). (1977). *RET: Handbook of rational emotive therapy.* New York: Springer.

Festinger, L. (1957). *A theory of cognitive dissonance.* Palo Alto, CA: Stanford University Press.

Fiedler, F. E. (1950). A comparison of therapeutic relationships in psychoanalytic, nondirective, and Adlerian therapy. *Journal of Consulting Psychology, 14*, 436-455.

Figley, C. (Ed.). (1978). *Stress disorders among Vietnam veterans.* New York: Brunner/Mazel.

Glasser, W. (1965). *Reality therapy: A new approach to psychiatry.* New York: Harper & Row.

Haley, S. A. (1974). When the patient reports atrocities. *Archives of General Psychiatry, 30*, 191-196.

Haley, S. A. (1978). Treatment implication of post-combat stress response syndromes for mental health professionals. In C. Figley (Ed.), *Stress disorders among Vietnam veterans* (pp. 254-267). New York: Brunner/Mazel.

Horowitz, M. J. (1986). Stress-response syndromes: A review of post traumatic and adjustment disorders. *Hospital and Community Psychiatry, 30*, 241-249.

Jellinek, J. M., & Williams, T. (1984). Post-traumatic stress disorder and substance abuse in Vietnam combat veterans: Treatment problems, strategies and recommendations. *Journal of Substance Abuse Treatment, 1*, 87-97.

Keane, T. M., & Kaloupek, D. G. (1982). Imaginal flooding in the treatment of a post traumatic stress disorder. *Journal of Consulting and Clinical Psychology, 50*, 138-140.

Maslow, A. H. (1943). *Motivation and personality.* New York: Harper.

Roche Report. (1980). Cynicism, alienation, anomie linger among Vietnam veterans. *Frontiers of Psychiatry.* Nutley, NJ: Hoffman-La Roche.

Rogers, C. R. (1951). *Client-centered therapy.* Boston: Houghton Mifflin.

Schwartz, H. J. (Ed.). (1984). *Psychotherapy of the combat veteran.* New York: Spectrum.

Scurfield, R. W., & Blank, A. S. (1985). A guide to obtaining a military history from Vietnam veterans. In S. Sonnenberg, A. Blank, & G. Talbot (Eds.), *The trauma of war* (pp. 263-291). Washington, DC: American Psychiatric Press.

Silver, S. M., & Iacono, C. U. (1984). Factor-analytic support for DSM-III's post-traumatic stress disorder for Vietnam veterans. *Journal of Clinical Psychology, 40*, 5-14.

Silver, S. M., & Kelly, W. E. (1985). Hypnotherapy of post-traumatic stress disorder in combat veterans from WW II and Vietnam. In W. E. Kelly (Ed.), *Post-traumatic stress disorder and the war veteran patient* (pp. 211-233). New York: Brunner/Mazel.

Smith, J. R. (1985). Individual psychotherapy with Viet Nam veterans. In S. Sonnenberg, A. Blank, & G. Talbot (Eds.), *The trauma of war* (pp. 125-163). Washington, DC: American Psychiatric Press.

Smith, J. R. (1985). Rap groups and group therapy for Viet Nam veterans. In S. Sonnenberg, A. Blank, & G. Talbot (Eds.), *The trauma of war* (pp. 165-191). Washington, DC: American Psychiatric Press.

Sonnenberg, S., Blank, A., & Talbot, G. (Eds.). (1985). *The trauma of war.* Washington, DC: American Psychiatric Press.

Veterans Administration. (1984, February). *Trend Data: 1959-1983.* Washington, DC: Office of Reports and Statistics, Author.

Williams, C. M., & Williams, T. (1985). Family therapy for Viet Nam veterans. In S. Sonnenberg, A. Blank, & G. Talbot (Eds.), *The trauma of war* (pp. 193-209). Washington, DC: American Psychiatric Press.

Yalom, I. (1980). *Existential psychotherapy.* New York: Basic Books.

25

Counseling Physically Challenged Men

Patricia M. Carlton
Richard N. Maxwell

In an era where society worships youth, athletic agility, and the trim, perfect body, the physically challenged male is at a disadvantage. The very traits that society values in individuals are usually traits inconsistent with being physically disabled. Even at an unconscious level, both disabled and nondisabled individuals operate under the presumption that handicapped persons are dependent and helpless (Lindemann, 1981, p. 1). For the male the inconsistency is even more pronounced, because dependence and helplessness are inconsistent with society's view of the ideal male.

It is our purpose in this chapter to increase the reader's knowledge about the special characteristics of the physically challenged male. Initially, we will define disability and present our philosophical approach to counseling. Issues particularly pertinent to either an acquired, congenital, or progressive disability will be discussed. Emphasis will then be placed upon how the male role in particular has an impact upon an individual with a physical disability and the disabled man's relationship with others. Finally, there will be a discussion of general counseling issues applicable to the physically challenged male and suggestions to improve counseling rapport, pitfalls to avoid, and counseling areas to pursue.

Definition

Many individuals are viewed by others as disabled but do not consider themselves disabled. Whether or not one considers himself or herself disabled depends a lot upon how one defines disability. Wright (1980, p. 9, 68), in his definition of disability and handicap, says:

> A disability is any physical, mental, or emotional condition that is chronic or long-lasting (not acute or temporary), which is severe enough to limit the individual's functioning, and which results in, or threatens to be, a handicap to productive activity. . . . A handicap is a disadvantage, interference, or barrier to performance, opportunity, or fulfillment in any desired role in life . . . imposed upon the individual by limitations in function or by other problems associated with disability and/or personal characteristics in the context of the individual's environment or role.

Thus a person with a disability may not be handicapped given certain roles or in certain environments, for key words in the definition of handicap are "limitations . . . in context of the individual's environment or role." For example, the famous violinist Itzhak Perlman, who is mobility impaired, is not handicapped in his role as a violinist, but he would be handicapped as a soccer player.

The words "physically challenged male" may include much of the male population if used in its broadest sense. To limit the topic, emphasis will be placed on men who are mobility impaired, particularly those men who use wheelchairs.

Theory

Disabled men have been thrust into their disabling condition in a fashion that is out of their control; however, disabled persons have the potential to choose their way of life and therefore to change, to function more effectively, and to improve their quality of life. Certainly one would not choose to be mobility impaired; however, there are choices to be made throughout life.

As counselors for those who are mobility impaired, it is our goal to help facilitate change by dealing with issues that can interfere with a positive self-image, by focusing on what an individual can do, and by expanding on the existing personality. Focus should not be placed on limbs that do not function well but rather on the man as a total system. At the same time, ignoring the impairment would also be inappropriate. Linkowski and Dunn (1974, p. 31) suggest that "perceptions of disability are a significant and central aspect of the self-concept, relating to both self-esteem and satisfaction with social relationships." They go on to suggest that a Gestalt rather than an analytic approach is more appropriate for the understanding of the relevance of a disability for those who are disabled.

Acquired Disability

The professional who counsels individuals with acquired disabilities must be aware of the inherent demands—both physical and emotional—the psychological stresses, and the limitations and frustrations imposed by this type of disability. Acquired disabilities can come in several forms, including spinal cord injury, stroke, polio, head injury, and loss of a limb. For purposes of this section we will use the example of spinal cord injuries to exhibit many of the problems encountered with other acquired disabilities.

Those who experience spinal cord injury have many short and long-term needs that are over and above their physical/medical concerns. The severity of injury is the best predictor, at present, of the number of difficulties the person will encounter. Dew, Lynch, Ernst, and Rosenthal (1983) report that, in general, the severity of impairment increases the higher the level of the lesion; however, depending upon the area and degree of damage of the spinal cord, loss of sensory and motor functions vary.

According to Bray (1978) spinal cord injured individuals go through a lengthy four-stage adaptation process that resembles the mourning process. The actual time involved depends on the flexibility and motivation of the individual and the support services available. Anxiety, the first stage, lasts about nine months. During this time the person requires reassurance of survival, help in focusing on the present, and encouragement to function within present ability level. The second stage, which lasts about 14 months, is that of accommodation. This is a time for reconciliation of differences and realizing of a changing lifestyle. Three years postinjury is usually when one enters the third stage, assimilation. By this time the person has regained all the sensation and motor control possible. This stage centers on growth, challenge, and change. Assimilation continues throughout life. The fourth stage is referred to as reflux. It can be experienced at any time in the process but is not necessarily experienced at all. Reflux is a regression to an earlier time due to a serious physical, emotional, or financial difficulty. Successful adaptation requires a reworking of all subsequent stages. An understanding of the stages of adaptation facilitates more effective counseling of the spinal cord injured.

Each traumatically injured individual does not necessarily go through the four-stage adaptation process in exactly the same fashion. Each has his or her own set of problems. An example is a young man named John whose adaptation process illustrates the four stages as well as illustrates his particular problems. John was involved in an automobile accident as a college freshman that resulted in quadriplegia. John's initial hospitalization did not go well. He had developed several decubitus ulcers (bedsores) that had prevented his active participation in the therapy program. Despite reassurance from the rehabilitation staff and family about his future, John vacillated between bouts of severe depression, angry outbursts, and unrealistic expectations about walking again. Finally, at the rehabilitation center, John's decubiti began to heal to the point where he could use his motorized wheelchair. He was confronted with individuals in various stages of rehabilitation, and ultimately he began to realize the inevitable change in his future lifestyle. With support from staff, family, and friends and a positive but realistic environment, John began to adjust to his new circumstances. About a year or more later when John came back to the rehabilitation center for a routine urological checkup, he shared his plans to change his college major from physical education to business. He later graduated and got a job working at a bank. Unfortunately, his enthusiasm and desire to succeed in his new job caused him to overlook aspects of his skin care, resulting in a reoccurrence of decubitus ulcers. He then required extensive hospitalization for plastic surgery to heal his skin. Again, John became depressed and anxious about his future. He relived some of the initial stages of adaptation, but ultimately he recovered. John is presently a successful banker who now realizes that he must continuously monitor his own health.

The criteria for success and adjustment for those who are spinal cord injured may not be the same as the criteria for the nondisabled. Roessler (1978) suggested that some of the necessary components to successful rehabilitation include a positive orientation toward life, goals that are realistic, and a sense that the goals can be accomplished. However, a realistic goal for spinal cord injured persons may not necessarily be a return to productivity as indicated by employment. Dew et al. (1983) suggested that other criteria such as self-care skills acquisition, volunteer work, and recent employment of other family members may be better indicators of success for spinal cord injured persons.

Individuals with spinal cord injuries are frequently characterized as impulsive, rebellious, nonconforming, and difficult rehabilitation clients (Athelstan & Crewe, 1979). Malec (1985) found that the traumatically injured are extroverted. Athelstan and Crewe (1979) suggest a relationship between these personality traits—that is, impulsivity, rebelliousness, nonconformity—and the occurrence of the spinal cord injury. At the same time they found that the personality characteristics related to injury acquisition were correlated with successful adjustment.

Counselors for spinal cord injured individuals may be involved with formerly physical, rebellious, streetwise males who may defy traditional middle-class values. An understanding of personality characteristics may facilitate better adjustment success. Malec (1985) suggested that due to the personality characteristics of spinal cord injured individuals it would be better to encourage active participation in the rehabilitation process on the part of the clients rather than introspective counseling and psychotherapeutic efforts.

Congenital Disability

Children with congenital disabilities grow up to be adults with congenital disabilities. Cerebral palsy and spina bifida (or myelomeningocele) are the two most frequent congenital disabilities causing mobility problems.

Many of those with a congenital disability face problems similar to those with an acquired disability; however, there are in addition a unique set of concerns. Lindemann and Boyd (1981, pp. 127, 252) described the presence of increased maladjustment including anxiety, withdrawal, poor self-esteem, and dependence for those with cerebral palsy and spina bifida. They go on to describe difficulty with mother-child bonding, which promotes fearfulness, passive timidity, and withdrawal in any child. Parental overprotection can also incapacitate the congenitally disabled adult. Tarnow (1984, p. 70) suggested that a sense of autonomous, competent self cannot be fully developed if overprotection occurs. This may result in individuals who are unable to take care of themselves or exhibit acting-out behavior.

Individuals with a congenital disability may not have some of the same experiences or opportunities as the nondisabled. In some ways they may be culturally deprived because of the lack of experience. A study conducted by Hayden, Davenport, and Campbell (1979) suggested that adolescents with myelomeningocele take little responsibility for chores they could physically perform at home. Their investigation showed that these adolescents often have prolonged hospitalization and are behind in school. As a result they tend to interact with younger individuals. They participate in fewer team sports, group, and extracurricular activities and have fewer close friends than the control group that was part of the study. This type of experiential deprivation is detrimental to independent living and psychosocial maturation.

The individual who has a congenital disability may experience social isolation and as a result develop inadequate social skills. In addition, the quality of social relationships may be limiting since interaction with disabled persons may consist of patterns of support, assistance, and reduced expectation. A disabled individual may develop the attitude that he or she is the center of the universe, and thus the natural give and take of a relationship is not developed. This individual may not assume personal responsibility for a relationship and then expect others to initiate and maintain the relationship (Easton & Halpern, 1981, p. 147). As a result others may be reluctant to interact meaningfully with an individual who lacks social skills, is egocentric, and who does little to enhance and maintain a relationship.

When counseling those with a congenital disability one should consider that the disability can cause intrinsic psychosocial disabilities. For example, cerebral palsy can cause difficulty with retention, acquisition, interpretation, and application of information. Verbal receptive, verbal expressive, visual perceptual, and visual motor impairments can be present (Easton & Halpern, 1981, p. 147).

Despite the unique set of problems, congenitally disabled individuals frequently do not have some of the adjustment problems of the traumatically or progressively disabled. For those who are congenitally disabled, there is not the longing for what used to be. The congenitally disabled person may envy those who are able-bodied; however, they have never lost any abilities, as someone who is traumatically disabled.

Many congenitally disabled individuals are functioning as productive and well-adjusted adults. For one particular individual with spina bifida there has always been the focus on abilities rather than disabilities. Jim is mainstreamed in the public schools. His academic abilities allowed him to compete with his classmates. While able-bodied friends are participating in athletic pursuits, so is Jim. He participates in competitive swimming for the disabled and has won numerous awards across the country. He has been encouraged to baby-sit for neighborhood children. In the summer he volunteers at a center for autistic children, and eventually Jim would like to go into special education.

Progressive Disabilities

There are numerous chronic and progressive diseases that cause mobility impairment. The diseases that are often associated with a progressive nature are multiple sclerosis and muscular dystrophy. Both of these diseases, as well as others, are characterized by decreasing physical abilities, changes in appearance, loss of key roles, the need for medical attention, and an uncertain future (Pavlov & Counte, 1982). For these individuals there are continuous and unrelenting changes and adjustment occurring throughout life.

Individuals with a progressive disability vary. Pavlou and Counte (1982, p. 141) said, "There is considerable variability in adaptive success at any particular level of disability." Those who are mildly disabled may have more adaptive distress than those who are severely disabled, for the mildly disabled may be more anxious about the future. Tarbell (1980) suggested variability when she described a wide range of symptoms and differences in residual functional capacities. The course of a progressive disease is also variable. Some individuals exhibit a steady worsening condition without remission, and some experience many years between exacerbation (Kraft, 1981, p. 112). A counselor should consider the relationship with a disabled client in the light of remission or exacerbation. The behavioral expectations of the client may be different during remission than during exacerbation.

During remission individuals may more easily deny the disability, whereas during exacerbation increased depression may occur. McIvor, Riklan, and Regnikoff (1984) suggested that individuals with multiple sclerosis who experience at least one remission were less depressed than those who never experience a remission.

Individuals with a progressive disability have often been characterized by increasing social inhibition, passiveness, and depression (Harper, 1983). Social isolation is frequently associated with a progressive disability. These characteristics appear to be related to the realities of decreased mobility and reduced social interaction (Harper, 1983). Facial muscles may be affected in some individuals with some types of muscular dystrophy, and an individual may not be able to smile or give appropriate facial response (Lindemann & Stanger, 1981, p. 285). Motor weakness may interfere with nonverbal communication. An individual with multiple sclerosis may experience mental changes, that is, euphoria, intellectual deterioration, and lability of mood (Kraft, 1981). As a result of all these physical characteristics and situational characteristics, the individual with a progressive disability is often isolated and may be socially inhibited.

Another period that Lindemann and Stanger (1981, p. 286) suggested as a period that is particularly difficult is when those with a progressive disability are required to use a wheelchair. Frequently, these individuals become quietly depressed at this time (Lindemann & Stanger, 1981). The progression of the disease cannot be denied, and the individual must face the reality of the disease.

Finally, it should be emphasized that individuals with acquired, congenital, or progressive disabilities can be well-balanced, happy, and productive individuals. Again, the variability of those with disabilities must be stressed.

General Issues Related to the Physically Challenged Male

THE MALE GENDER ROLE

The gender role appears to play a significant part in an individual's adjustment to a disability. Our society's expectations for men make it more difficult for them to be disabled (Skord & Schumacher, 1982). Therefore, due to societal expectations, disabled men frequently behave in ways that are often contradictory to effective rehabilitation.

Liss-Levinson (1982, p. 326) states that "the traditional male sex-role dictates that men are rational, independent, and capable of handling any and all crises." "Men are . . . expected to be healthy, vigorous, strong, and sexually rapacious. . . . Men are generally expected to be powerful and in control of themselves and of their situations at all times" (Scher, 1979, p. 252). Men are not socialized to ask for help or accept help, to be emotional and dependent.

When a man changes from able-bodied to disabled, many of the roles he is accustomed to playing become inconsistent with the disability. This change can cause the individual to feel that he has lost control of his life. This loss of control is made worse by the disabled man's perpetual dependency. Dependency is in contrast to a society's image of the self-sufficient male.

THE DISABLED MAN'S
RELATIONSHIP WITH OTHERS

There is a strong correlation between a supportive family and the successful rehabilitation of disabled individuals. McIvor et al. (1984) found in their study of depression in multiple sclerosis that severely depressed individuals perceived less family- and friend-based support than those with less depression. Reagles (1982, p. 27) suggested that "the family's willingness to mainstream or reestablish a disabled person's role is an important source of motivation for rehabilitation." Thus the nature of an individual's relationship to significant others may strongly influence an individual's adjustment and ongoing life as physically disabled.

If family members, including the disabled male, can be flexible and adjust to new norms, expectations, resources, and roles, they will be better able to remain intact as a family and at the same time the disabled male's chances for successful rehabilitation will be increased. According to Reagles (1982), if one member of the family is chronically ill or physically disabled, roles need to change in order to facilitate family adjustment. As a family works toward developing new roles and status, care must be taken that new roles are acceptable to all involved. At the same time, the male as well as other family members must take care that the newly developed roles are not roles that are destructive. The disabled male must not be treated differently from other family members. He must be allowed to maintain or reestablish a major family role where he is a contributor, not just a receiver.

On a daily basis, disabled men interact with people who are not significant others. These interactions may be brief passing encounters or daily encounters, such as with a van driver or attendant. Frequently the individuals encountered are sensitive and caring individuals. There are many, however, who are caring but not sensitive. For example, in a restaurant setting, the waitress may ask a nondisabled companion what the disabled individual would like to eat. The implication is clear that the disabled individual is not capable of ordering his or her own meal, and this is demeaning to the disabled individual.

Also of importance to the disabled male are sexual encounters. For most disabled men, the ability to relate to others sexually is important to their identity of being male. Much has been written concerning the sexual issues of mobility disabled men, particularly for those who are paraplegics and quadriplegics. Despite this wealth of literature, the disabled individual is often considered sexless; however, Halstead (1984, p. 235) stated that it is a myth "that disabled people are uninterested in sex, do not function normally anyway, and might hurt themselves if they tried."

Stewart (1981, p. 348) said that, "disruption and disfigurement associated with a disability need not destroy the heart of sexuality—the capacity to share pleasure and vulnerability with a loved one." For all people there are no correct ways to have sex. For men who have experienced a spinal cord injury, there is a need to explore the body's sexual response both with and without assistance (Robbins, 1985). New erogenous areas become apparent. For many there is more planning and some preparation before sexual encounters can take place.

Men who are spinal cord injured have reduced or no sensation below the level of injury. Those individuals with incomplete spinal cord lesion may have some sensation, however, those with a complete lesion or those with spina bifida will have no sensation below the lesion (Sandowski, 1976). Most male paraplegics or quadriplegics will be able to have an erection; however, reports vary. It should be emphasized that the inability to have an erection and ejaculate does not mean that the disabled man cannot experience some form of sexual gratification.

"Healthy sexuality . . . is a part of a healthy self-image" (Cole & Glass, 1977, p. 586). Healthy sexuality and a healthy self-image are both possible for the disabled man who has a good sexual knowledge base and who uses remaining functions whether cognitive or physical.

APPROACHES TO
COUNSELING DISABLED MEN

There are some practical approaches to counseling the physically disabled male. One must definitely take into consideration that counseling a male must be somewhat different from counseling a female. Ignoring this difference may jeopardize the counseling relationship. Weinberg (1979) suggested that the disabled and nondisabled are socialized into similar gender roles. She says that an individual's gender has more influence on an individual's self-perception than a disability. Thus it is in the best interest of the counselor and client and their relationship to consider the needs of a male and the implications of male role expectations when counseling the physically challenged male.

Wong, Davey, and Conroe (1976, p. 59) suggested that a positive approach to counseling men would be "to start with the idea of strengthening and expanding on the already masculine base." Liss-Levinson (1982, p. 328) also suggested that a counselor should "work within the context of the traditional sex-role." For example, men are socialized to be in control. Exploring acceptable ways for a disabled man to be in control, whether over personal care and/or environment, will allow him to exert his masculinity.

Somewhat related to the idea of a male role is eye contact. Males do not generally like to be dominated or placed in an inferior position. As a counselor it is wise to stay in a seated position when conversing with an individual in a wheelchair so that the person will not have to look up to maintain eye contact.

Another pitfall to avoid when counseling the mobility impaired male is the avoidance of the parental role. There is no need to be condescending, protective, controlling, or too helpful. The parental role is inappropriate for the nondisabled and disabled as well. "If someone always insists on taking a difficult but learnable task out of the disabled person's hands, the person may be deprived of the opportunity to learn how to function alone (Ker, 1984, p. 153). It may be helpful to work together to set realistic goals or to explore activities and behaviors that have not been tried before.

Many disabled individuals have developed successful techniques on how to manipulate others. Some use secondary gains or learned helplessness in their efforts to control others and as a way of getting out of tasks they can do themselves. Often they are not aware of their behavior. Wright (1980, p. 546) stated that "'secondary gains' refers to the external, additional gains derived from disability." Learned helplessness is when an individual who is disabled picks up cues from those around him or her as to what he or she is able or unable to accomplish.

A disabled man requires good communication skills. Most people are dependent on communication skills. However, they are even more important for the disabled individuals. Maxwell, one of the chapter authors, learned this just shortly after his injury. Friends and family were very supportive of him, and they visited him while he was strapped to a circular electric bed with tongs and traction attached to his shaven head. Prior to the visitation the visitors would be briefed by a nurse, but no matter how well the visitors were prepared, they were uncomfortable with the "new" Dick Maxwell. After a brief exchange of recent news, there was silence, uncertainty, and possibly fright. Finally, Maxwell had to "break the ice." He had to help them to feel more at ease, and this has become a constant in his life. He had to react to able-bodied persons to help them adjust to his disability. Later, he had to work to help others see the man beyond the hum and chrome of a motorized wheelchair. The necessity of good communication goes beyond the disabled man's desire to get his needs met; it is vital for the securing and maintaining of good interpersonal relationships.

Finally, the counselor needs to focus on the entire person, not just the disability. At the same time, the disabled client needs to shift his perception of self from the disability as the major focus of identity to the periphery so that the true personality will be the major focus. By this acceptance of the basic personality as self, the disabled person will be better able to help those around him shift from focus on the disability to focus on the more positive aspects of self, as suggested by Cogswell (1984). Ultimately, disabled men do not want to be treated like disabled men. They want to be treated as individuals.

References

Athelstan, G. T., & Crewe, N. M. (1979). Psychological adjustment to spinal cord injury as related to manner of onset of disability. *Rehabilitation Counseling Bulletin, 2*(4), 311-318.

Bray, G. P. (1978). Rehabilitation of spinal cord injury: A family approach. *Journal of Applied Rehabilitation Counseling, 9*(3), 70-78.

Cogswell, B. E. (1984). Socialization after disability: Reentry into the community. In D. W. Krueger & L. B. Collins (Eds.), *Rehabilitation Psychology* (pp. 111-118). Rockwell, MD: Aspen Systems Corp.

Cole, T. M., & Glass, D. D. (1977). Sexuality and physical disability. *Archives of Physical and Medical Rehabilitation, 58*, 585-586.

Dew, M. A., Lynch, K., Ernst, S., & Rosenthal, R. (1983). Reaction and adjustment to spinal cord injury: A descriptive study. *Journal of Applied Rehabilitation Counseling, 14*(1), 32-39.

Easton, J., & Halpern, D. (1981). Cerebral palsy. In W. C. Stoler & M. R. Clowers (Eds.), *Handbook of severe disability*, (pp. 137-154). Washington, DC: U.S. Department of Education, Rehabilitation Services Administration.

Halstead, L. S. (1984). Sexuality and disability. In D. W. Krueger (Ed.), *Emotional rehabilitation of physical trauma and disability* (pp. 253-266). New York: Spectrum.

Harper, D. C. (1983). Personality correlates and degree of impairment in male adolescents with progressive and nonprogressive physical disorders. *Journal of Clinical Psychology, 39*(6), 859-867.

Hayden, P. W., Davenport, S. L., & Campbell, M. M. (1979). Adolescents with myelodysplasia: Impact of physical disability on emotional maturation. *Pediatrics, 64*(1), 53-59.

Ker, N. (1984). Help that is helpful. In D. W. Krueger & L. B. Collins (Eds.), *Rehabilitation psychology* (pp. 151-160). Rockville, MD: Aspen Systems Corp.

Kraft, G. H. (1981). Multiple sclerosis. In W. C. Stoler & M. R. Clowers (Eds.), *Handbook of severe disability* (pp. 111-118). Washington, DC: U.S. Department of Education, Rehabilitation Services Administration.

Lindemann, J. E. (1981). *Psychological and behavioral aspects of physical disability.* New York: Plenum.

Lindemann, J. E., & Boyd, R. (1981). Myelomeningocele (Spina Bifida). In J. Lindemann, *Psychological and behavioral aspects of physical disability* (pp. 243-271). New York: Plenum Press.

Lindemann, J. E., & Stanger, M. E. (1981). Progressive muscle disorders. In J. Lindemann, *Psychological and behavioral aspects of physical disability* (pp. 273-300). New York: Plenum Press.

Linkowski, D. C., & Dunn, M. H. (1974). Self-concept and acceptance of disability. *Rehabilitation Counseling Bulletin, 18*(1), 28-32.

Liss-Levinson, W. S. (1982). Clinical observations on the emotional responses of males to cancer. *Psychotherapy: Theory, Research and Practice, 19*(3), 325-330.

Malec, J. (1985). Personality factors associated with severe traumatic disabilities. *Rehabilitation Psychology, 30*(3), 165-172.

McIvor, G. P., Riklon, M., & Regnikoff, M. (1984). Depression in multiple sclerosis as a function of length and severity of illness, age, remissions, and perceived social support. *Journal of Clinical Psychology, 40*(4), 1028-1032.

Pavlou, M., & Counte, M. (1982). Aspects of coping in multiple sclerosis. *Rehabilitation Counseling Bulletin, 25*(3), 138-145.

Reagles, S. (1982). The impact of disability: A family crisis. *Journal of Applied Rehabilitation Counseling, 13*(3), 25-29.

Robbins, K. H. (1985). Traumatic spinal cord injury and its impact upon sexuality. *Journal of Applied Rehabilitation Counseling, 16*, 24-27.

Roessler, R. T. (1978). Life outlook, hopes, and fears of persons with spinal cord injury. *Journal of Applied Rehabilitation Counseling, 9*(3), 103-107.

Sandowski, C. L. (1976). Sexuality and the paraplegic. *Rehabilitation Literature, 37*(11-12), 322-327.

Scher, M. (1979). On counseling men. *Personnel and Guidance Journal, 58*, 252-254.

Skord, K. G., & Schumacher, D. (1982). Masculinity as a handicapping condition. *Rehabilitation Literature, 43*(9-10), 284-289.

Stewart, T. D. (1981). Sex, spinal cord injury, and staff rapport. *Rehabilitation Literature, 42*(11-12), 347-350.

Tarbell, D. J. (1980). Coping with multiple sclerosis: Strange encounters of the demyelinating kind. *Journal of Applied Rehabilitation Counseling, 11*(4), 179-182.

Tarnow, J. (1984). Pediatric and adolescent patients in rehabilitation. In D. W. Krueger (Ed.), *Emotional rehabilitation of physical trauma and disability* (pp. 63-78). New York: Spectrum.

Weinberg, N. (1979). The effect of physical disability on self-perception. In B. Bolton & M. E. Jaques (Eds.), *The rehabilitation client* (pp. 98-103). Baltimore, MD: University Park Press.

Wong, M. R., Davey, J., & Conroe, R. M. (1976). Expanding masculinity: Counseling the male in transition. *Counseling Psychologist, 6*(3), 58-61.

Wright, G. N. (1980). *Total rehabilitation.* Boston: Little, Brown.

26

Therapy with Men in Health-Care Settings

LaFaye C. Sutkin
Glenn Good

The stereotype of the male in our society calls for acceptance of injury and illness with courage and stoicism. To the extent that male patients expect to preserve this image, the health-care setting imposes severe threat. Cries of pain, tears of frustration, and honest expressions of fear are frequently seen as unacceptable. Male patients may employ alternative behaviors to secure the attention and care that might have been elicited by more direct expressions of feelings. A prominent alternative to direct need and feeling expression is an exaggeration of physical symptoms and an escalation of medical complaints. The male patient often views the presentation of needs in terms of an "objective" external reality as more acceptable (Eisenberg, Falconer, & Sutkin, 1981).

In fact, the health-care setting poses many threats to the accustomed roles of men. In accepting admission to a hospital, patients may feel stripped of control, robbed of status, and forced into a dependent role. The illness that precipitated admission, along with culturally inculcated attitudes toward hospitalization, are apt to leave patients feeling fearful, anxious, and depressed. Male patients may employ a variety of coping strategies to deal with the abrupt emotional challenges and role changes of illness. Some of these strategies are adaptive and assist them in feeling more secure and more in charge of the situation, while other strategies exacerbate the situational stresses of male patienthood, and may threaten health or even life (Eisenberg et al., 1981).

The majority of patients eventually adjust to the demands of the health-care setting and accept their physical condition as they come to understand the situation. However, in those instances in which maladaptive coping strategies persist, threatening the recovery of the patient, referral to mental health services may be indicated. Many hospitals offer a specialized group of mental health professionals who are specifically trained to meet the particular needs of the hospital setting (Olbrisch & Sechrest, 1979). For example, health psychologists must develop a rudimentary understanding of medical conditions as well as the contextual demands of the health-care setting. These areas of expertise supplement traditional psychological training to facilitate more accurate assessments and more effective interventions with medical patients than would be possible when such relevant factors are not well understood.

It is essential that a male medical patient referred to a mental health professional be evaluated in the context of his physical condition as well as his environment, that is, the hospital. A full appreciation of the interactions of both of these factors promotes the development of most appropriate treatment plans. Although long-term psychotherapy may occasionally be indicated, most often the interventions required of health psychologists are brief, and at times may not even involve direct contact with the patient (Tefft & Simeonsson, 1979).

This chapter will describe health behaviors commonly encountered in male patients and the demands and pressures imposed on patients by the medical environment. Subsequently, methods male patients employ to cope with iatrogenic (caused by medical treatment) psychosocial maladies, the implications of mental health referral, and counseling/therapy approaches will be discussed. The chapter focuses on male medical patients who may come to the attention of mental health services due to their maladaptive coping strategies; little attention will be given to those patients who promptly and successfully cope with stress, illness, and hospitalization.

Health Behaviors of Men

A major facet of traditional male socialization is the avoidance of vulnerability, particularly emotional vulnerability. Thus the male patient who has been subjected to such socialization avoids asking that his emotional needs be met. Although unable to communicate his hurt, loneliness, fear, or desire to be held and nurtured, such a patient is no less likely to have such needs. Traditional men often feel more comfortable seeking medical attention than mental health services. Complaints of back pains, headaches, or chest pains may be viewed as legitimate avenues for obtaining attention. Moreover, for the man who strives to model John Wayne's endurance and responsibility, illness or injury may be the only "legitimate" escape from overwhelming burdens. At best, the use of medical complaints as indirect expressions of emotional needs is inefficient; at worst, subjective experiences of distress may be intensified by this approach. The lack of response by health-care professionals, who may come to label the individual as a hypochondriac or malingerer, or by family members, who may tire of caretaking roles as they come to suspect that complaints are exaggerated, may contribute to his fears of neglect or abandonment (Eisenberg et al., 1981).

Those traditional men, however, who continue to "tough it out," unable to communicate their needs or their emotional pain, may suffer long-term consequences of a more serious nature. Continuous arousal of the body's stress responses often leads to irreversible physical damage and to the development of chronic illnesses, such as coronary artery disease, ulcerative colitis, and perhaps reduced resistance to cancer. Potentially reversible physical manifestations of constricted emotions and stress may also occur, such as reduced resistance to infection resulting in chronic "colds" or flu, allergies, asthma, and migraine headaches (Stone, Cohen, & Adler, 1980). Other men attempt to cope with the stresses of life in a manner consistent with the "strong, silent" image, resorting to the socially sanctioned anesthetic, alcohol. Chronic use/abuse of alcohol to manage stress multiplies the psychosocial stressors and may itself result in multiple health problems, for example, hypertension, gastritis, cardiac myopathy, cirrhosis, and dementia.

Demands and Pressures Imposed on the Male Patient by the Medical Setting

Preceding descriptions of the traditional male in this chapter, as well as in other chapters, suggest the probability that medical illness and hospitalization will produce extensive ramifications. The very nature of hospitals almost instantly imposes a "patient" role on admitted individuals. The process of becoming a patient requires that the person "voluntarily" surrender rights normally taken for granted by adults and most children. Perhaps the most efficient method for conveying this experience is a representative account of a patient's experience upon hospitalization.

Typically, disorders that are sufficiently serious to result in hospitalization are also sufficiently serious to provide some level of anxiety and depression. Thus it is with some level of emotional stress that the patient who is able to communicate is subjected to admission process. Throughout the admission and subsequent hospital experience, it is likely that he will be addressed by his first name but expected to pay appropriate "respect" to hospital personnel as demonstrated by formal address. As the patient answers the first of many sets of intrusive and personal questions, he will realize that a record is being prepared of every aspect of his life. This chart includes the intimate details of his financial, sexual, and lifestyle status, and the contents of "his" chart appear to be available to everybody *except* him. He is then provided a wristband that usually displays his name, hospital number, date of birth, and the ward to which he is assigned.

Eventually, the patient will be transferred from the admitting section to the medical or surgical ward. The patient will be given a pair of pajamas (regardless of the time of day) into which he is expected to change. He will be given a room, usually with a roommate not of his choosing. He will be told when and what he may eat and drink. Depending on the patient's condition, he may be required to depend on nursing staff for attendance over bodily functions that he has controlled since he was toilet trained. In addition, he may be forced to permit a stranger to bathe him and change his clothes.

Typically, a patient is protected, during hospitalization, from the necessity of making a variety of "trivial" decisions, such as when to get up, when to go to bed, when to have visitors, and when to take food or medications. More significant decisions may be removed from patient control as well, since often the information needed to formulate decisions regarding his care is withheld. Although most of the hospital personnel appear to own the privilege of collecting information from the patient, the role of "patient" precludes inquiry of staff, even in issues concerning the status of the patient's health. Although many of the above procedures are necessary or expedient for hospital operation, they do tend to strip the patient of a sense of control, status, and independence.

Superimposed on the necessarily restrictive environment of most hospitals, certain kinds of interpersonal experiences between staff and patient have a potential for intensifying the patient's sense of lost power. Hospital staff consists of individuals each with a set of needs—personal and professional—that may come into conflict with those of patients. Common conflicts between staff and patients center on "compliance" or power issues. Occasionally, a staff member may feel that a patient is not sufficiently compliant and therefore is not under staff control. In some cases, this has occasioned a struggle literally "unto death." More vocal patients may also acquire the ominous label, "noncompliant," a label that may follow the patient long after the conflict has been resolved. Moreover, the conflict and the allegation of noncompliance often stem from unilateral decisions on the part of staff regarding their view of the patient's needs without benefit of the patient's input (Eisenberg et al., 1981).

A frequent source of staff/patient conflict arises when a staff member gives mixed or double messages. This may occur because the staff member is attempting to avoid some discomfort, but, regardless of the reasons, the patient is apt to feel powerless when the information he receives is found to be unreliable. Moreover, a patient may experience similar confusion and distrust when staff members disagree and provide the patient with discrepant information regarding his diagnosis and/or prognosis.

In fact, there are an endless number of personal and idiosyncratic issues over which conflicts may arise. Some staff feel that patients "should be grateful" for the care they are receiving. The expression of gratitude necessary to satisfy staff may very well leave the patient feeling even more dependent and out of control. Some staff may feel that a patient who is not depressed is denying, and may attempt to encourage the onset of depression; others may feel that a patient who directly expresses depressed feelings—particularly tearfully—is weak, dependent, and unmanly. In either case, the patient's right to his own feelings ends up being attacked.

A common and time-honored conflict between patients and their nurses is that of the lag time between patients' requests for PRN (as needed) medications and the fulfillment of those requests. Some patients request medications well in advance, partly to assure that their need will be met before it becomes too intense; others regard it as a matter of pride to display their stoicism and wait until the last possible moment to ask for assistance. In either case, those nurses who uniformly delay responding to patient requests amplify the frustration and powerlessness experienced by their patients.

This discussion of factors in the hospital environment that contribute to the subjective distress of patients is only cursory. The possibilities for experiences that leave a patient feeling helpless are infinite. For those male patients who characteristically respond to stressful and anxiety-provoking experiences with an intensified need to be in control, the hospital environment has the potential of creating iatrogenic psychosocial maladies.

Methods Male Patients Employ to Cope with Iatrogenic Psychosocial Maladies

Although a variety of psychosocial maladies are possible, anxiety is likely to underlie them all. For this reason, reducing anxiety and sense of threat is the major psychological task confronting all medical patients. Most people attempt to master anxiety in ambiguous situations through assertion of control over the environment. The instrumental male is particularly prone to try and "do something" in an effort to restore his internal sense of control over the external environment. To this end, it becomes extremely important that he feel his actions will produce a response and that a sense of predictability can be achieved. Certainly, the majority of patients derive sufficient sense of control through direct expression of their needs and possess the capacity to tolerate relatively high levels of stress and ambiguity. However, as the mental health provider, one shouldn't expect to be called in to congratulate folks who adequately cope (Eisenberg, Sutkin, & Jansen, 1984).

The male patients most often referred for psychological services in medical settings are apt to employ an array of less adaptive mechanisms in their efforts to regain control (Wright, 1980). Several distinct types of male patients may be identified by the clusters of maladaptive behaviors that they exhibit. The most prevalent clusters to be referred to mental health professionals are those considered by the staff to be the "nasty patient," the "V.I.P." patient, the "poor me" patient, and the "tough-guy" patient.

For the patient who is unable to express his fear and who may feel that he is going to be neglected and overlooked, intimidation may be viewed as the only path to security. Although irritability may be present as a function of illness and depression, the patient who wishes to establish some control may use his testiness to communicate to staff that he is aware of what is happening and will not "take it lying down." This fellow experiences the need to be vigilant, distrusting staff to respond adequately to his needs unless voiced frequently and loudly. All complaints tend to be tendered at the same volume and tone. Furthermore, his low expectations of caretaking lead him to make excessive demands on staff, in part to exert control and in part to conduct tests that staff would respond if they are *really* needed. In actuality, however, this tendency toward being demanding is likely to produce a response in staff quite opposite to that desired by the patient; staff become less responsive or even antagonistic. An unfortunate dynamic is likely to develop in which patient and staff behave as though they are antagonists rather than colleagues working toward the same goals. The patient becomes determined to secure attention through escalating the behaviors that have led him to this point, and staff become increasingly resistant and seek to "break him" of his bad habits, often resorting to passive-aggressive maneuvers. A full-scale power struggle may develop in which the patient becomes increasingly angry and aggressive.

The more dependent the angry patient actually is on staff, the more he may resort to demands in order to determine his power (Eisenberg et al., 1981). For example, a patient who was newly spinal cord injured felt completely helpless and made unreasonable demands of staff to learn what tasks others could be intimidated into performing for him. Spinal cord injured patients (or any of a number of types of patients who have sustained a massive disability) are faced with the task of constructing new identities in much the same way that adolescents must establish an identity. They rely heavily on the feedback of those with whom they interact to establish a new self-image. When such patients use anger and demandingness as their approaches to having their needs met, staff may understandably react unfavorably. The patient, however, may lack the insight to recognize that the staff is reacting to his inadequate social skills (a correctable problem), rather than to him as a disabled person.

The "V.I.P." patient also feels out of control in the hospital environment, but marshals a different set of behaviors to secure some sense of control. Instead of attempting to overpower staff with aggression, this individual tries to intimidate staff by conveying to them how important, that is, personally powerful, he is. Essentially, he is saying, "Don't you know who I am? Surely you don't plan to treat me like just another patient. I'm entitled to special attention and consideration!" Therefore, the V.I.P. patient employing this strategy for control may tell anyone who will listen who he is, and will also tend to increase the frequency of this behavior as he feels more frightened and out of control. In some cases—perhaps where the patient does not feel that he is sufficiently important—significant exaggerations and falsifications of credentials may occur. In these cases, staff may find themselves feeling annoyed at the patient, but may be unable to identify the source of their annoyance.

This patient may parade a variety of credentials. One face is that of the professional, successful businessman, or celebrity, but there are many other ways of "displaying credentials" as well. Sometimes boasting of special knowledge or of the patient's relationship to a health-care professional are offered as proof that "you can't fool me. I know more than the average patient."

Financial status, personal contacts, spheres of influence, and personal attractiveness may all be deployed to assert a patient's merit of special service and attention. In Veterans Administration Hospitals, some unique kinds of credentials may be tendered. The patient may boast of, or even exaggerate, his military experiences, his rank, or his service-related health problems. Frequently, the patient who engaged most glaringly in this activity is the patient who feels uncomfortable accepting what he may consider "charity" from medical staff.

Patient efforts to make staff aware of "V.I.P." status are not always so direct. The patient who interacts collegially with the health-care team by calling members by first names, the patient who takes charge of other patients, and the patient who is seductive in his interactions with staff may all be seeking to communicate that they are slightly more worthy and important than the other patients.

The "tough-guy" patient shares some characteristics with the "V.I.P."; in fact, some patients may show both faces in efforts to feel secure. The "tough-guy" need not resort to external cards of identity, however, to assert his "specialness." He displays such stoicism that he appears to require no help whatsoever. He is the joker of the unit and appears invulnerable to anxiety. This is the guy who waits six hours before requesting his four-hour-acting pain medication. The difference between this patient and the man who truly is in no distress is that this patient is denying his own needs in the interest of gaining recognition and consideration. He hopes to achieve the admiration and respect of staff for his stoicism and courage, hoping that staff will rush to his aid in the event of an emergency.

Acting quite different from the two characters just described, but with the same agenda of gaining control, is the "poor me" patient. This individual acts as though staff can't hear him if his complaints are accurate and realistic; therefore, he exaggerates his symptoms and intensifies his sick role in an effort to *convince* everyone in earshot of his need for attention and care. The "poor me" patient usually appears depressed, anxious, or both, and is often withdrawn. Pronounced grimaces are likely in response to inquiries about the patient's condition, and exaggerated difficulty in movement is likely to be displayed. Such patients may come to be regarded by staff as hypochondriacal; as a result, staff may attend to them less than other patients, causing the patient to escalate complaints and symptoms and setting off a vicious circle of dissatisfaction on both sides.

All patients may from time to time behave in one of the ways cited above as maladaptive. Ultimately, the difference between adaptive coping and maladaptive coping in hospitalized patients is, not unlike in other contexts, determined by whether or not the patient is getting his needs met in the most efficient way. Moreover, the patient who is coping adequately with the situation is likely to have an array of responses from which he can flexibly draw when he determines that an approach is not working.

The Male Role and Mental Health Referral in Medical Settings

No attempt will be made here to supply an exhaustive list of issues for which medical patients are referred to health psychologists. There are presently a number of excellent texts devoted to this task (Gatchel & Baum, 1983; Stone et al., 1980). Rather, the objective of this chapter is to discuss specifically male issues as they appear in the health-care setting.

Occasionally, male patients in medical treatment will request help for mental health problems, such as depression or anxiety, or they will request assistance in adjusting to illness or a terminal diagnosis. These patients are generally similar to nonmedical patients seeking mental health treatment in that they are aware of the kinds of services available and recognize their need for treatment. However, such patients are relatively rare. Most commonly, male patients in the hospital for physical problems are not aware of the possibility of psychological services, *nor* do they recognize the need for such assistance. They are referred, often without their knowledge, by their primary physician at the request of staff or family members. Referrals may stem from concern for the patient, but also from complaints about the patient (Degood, 1979).

Staff and family *concerns* about male patients are reflected in consultation requests that ask the mental health professional to assist the patient in adjusting to a disability; in dealing with denial, depression, or anxiety; in coping with chronic pain or stress; in dealing with substance abuse; or in addressing family problems.

Staff/family *complaints* result in referrals for evaluation for hypochondriasis, psychophysiologic disorder, or questionable functional overlay in patients' physical ailments. Other consults usually provoked by staff/family distress include noncompliance with medical regimen, anger or abusiveness, or substance abuse as referral problems.

Often the real issue impelling referral is the necessity for adjustment, that is, the necessity for the patient to undergo a shift in his role. As discussed earlier, the patient may be involved in role changes on several levels simultaneously. A description of the course of a dialysis patient may serve as an illustration of some of the changes imposed on patients and some of the referral questions that might be asked of the mental health professional.

The kidney patient who has come to the hospital for examination and diagnosis is subjected to all of the demands of the hospital system described earlier, and may employ his most familiar coping style to contend with the stresses. If anger and noncompliance were selected, a consult might be directed to a health psychologist requesting help in securing the cooperation of the patient. Although the referral issue for staff may have been noncompliance, there is a strong possibility that the issue with which the patient will be dealing is a sense of powerlessness and a need to restore his control (Eisenberg et al., 1984).

Simultaneously, the dialysis patient must deal with changes in his life and in his role that extend far beyond the hospital and the temporary role changes imposed by hospitalization. The patient who had been employed often must deal with immediate retirement and loss of the breadwinner role. As noted in other chapters, this change alone may demand massive modifications in role expectations. In addition, the dialysis patient very likely has reduced physical strength and stamina, and may be unable to perform the heavier chores previously assigned to him in the family. Further, cognitive changes may have resulted from the accumulation of toxins (uremia) prior to dialysis, which threaten his ability to control household finances and his sense of intellectual competence.

Under these circumstances, it is not surprising that many patients experience an identity crisis, and search—almost frantically—for means by which they may regain control and wield some power. Anger, hostility, and even physical abuse may be directed at family members or hospital staff to demonstrate that he is still a person to be reckoned with. Again, the consult received by mental health professionals may fail to reflect the patient's concerns. The patient may exhibit very little direct concern over his physical health, especially if great energy is perceived as required to secure control. An absence of apparent patient concern regarding dialysis might lead staff to conclude that he is denying his medical condition, and requests might be submitted for assistance in helping the patient through denial. On the other hand, when the patient has discovered that his efforts to recover control have been only partially successful, and when he begins to experience the impact of his disability on his life, evidence of depression may appear. Ironically, staff members who were only shortly before concerned with denial, may quickly route a consult to the psychology department for treatment of depression, especially if the male patient is expressing his distress with tears or other "nonmasculine" emotionality.

Hospital patients do not enter the medical environment as blank slates; rather, they are individuals with long-term patterns of adjustment that may be incompatible with the new demands imposed by disability. For example, prior to renal failure a kidney patient may have been able to tolerate poor marital adjustment largely by avoidance. That is, through work, child rearing, and outside recreation, the couple may have spent only limited time together, and may have avoided the necessity of resolving relationship problems. When such a patient is faced with the prospect of retirement, almost continual contact with his spouse, and significant dependency on her for assistance with a home dialysis program, the need for marital conflict to be dealt with through counseling may be literally a matter of life or death. Poor communication patterns, obstacles to dealing with a spouse or a health-care professional, may require alteration.

Obviously, most patients are able to accept the conditions of hospitalization and the necessary accommodations to physical disability or chronic illness through their own efforts and resources. The question, then, is when to refer medical patients to mental health professionals and when the patient should be given the opportunity to adapt independently. It is our bias that where the question exists, a referral for evaluation is in order; however, the realities of private sector health-care systems may make this recommendation impractical.

Probably the most important criterion for referring the medical patient for psychological intervention is the clear evidence that the patient's behavior or his emotional status is impeding his ability to benefit from treatment. Often the intensity of emotion expressed—whether anger, sadness, or anxiety—is considered the determinant of intervention need; however, the intensity of emotional expression may be much more a personal or cultural characteristic than a reflection of need. The effect on the patient's acceptance of appropriate medical treatment, his receptivity to learning more about his disorder, and his ability to make required lifestyle changes are examples of criteria for referral to health psychologists.

In some instances, the patient's psychological status may not only hamper treatment, it may also directly exacerbate the health-care problem. For example, excessive anxiety that is poorly managed in the hypertensive or cardiac patient may have lethal results. In patients whose respiration is severely compromised by chronic obstructive pulmonary disease (COPD) or asthma, anxiety further restricts the transfer of air into the lungs, thereby increasing anxiety. Moreover, depression reduces respiratory capacities in such patients. Depression may also reduce the pain threshold in injured patients. It may also happen that a patient is in no apparent psychological distress, but that staff find him difficult and find themselves avoiding him for some reason. This patient, too, may have to modify his behavior in order to receive maximum benefit from hospitalization (Coombs & Vincent, 1971; DiMatteo & Taranta, 1979).

Medical patients who are identified *by others* for psychological referral are frequently in sharp contrast to patients who self-initiate their mental health treatment. Often, the problems noted by staff that prompt referral are not viewed as psychological problems by the patient. Rather, the patient may view the problem as being a physical complaint, a psychological problem of staff, or as not a problem at all. Further, since referral issues are often linked to the crisis of the hospitalization, many medical patients have never given thought to mental health treatment, and may have few or negative expectations of psychological treatment. It is not unusual to hear a patient ask if his physician thinks he is "crazy" since the doctor sent a "shrink" to see him. To many male patients, the consultation of a psychologist is a clear statement that *someone* believes them to be mentally weak and unable to cope independently. The notion of seeking assistance for lifestyle changes or adjustment to disability rarely occurs to medical patients.

Patients who have heretofore maintained privacy with respect to their personal lives—especially their sexual activities—may understandably consider intrusive those questions that the voluntary mental health consumer has come to expect. Mental health professionals who are naive to these considerations may find themselves facing a very resistant patient or being quickly ordered out of the room. Interpretations of patient resistance in this setting must be made very cautiously.

The implications of referral for somatiform disorders warrant special note. It is an unusual patient with somatiform features who has not already inferred from a physician's comments that his complaints were viewed as hypochondriacal. The subtle distinctions between psychophysiological disorders, conversion reactions, and functional disorders are frequently unclear to health-care workers; therefore, it is not surprising that patients are confused as well. The patient who believes that a "shrink" has dropped in to see him because a staff person does not take his pain or symptoms seriously will require preliminary education (and a great deal of tact) prior to any reasonable evaluation or intervention (Degood, 1979).

A man who is confined to the hospital bed with an acute illness and accompanying anxiety may come to view the warm, empathic mental health professional who visits him daily as a close friend. Having no previous expectations of a psychotherapy experience, the patient cannot be expected to understand the limited nature of this professional relationship. If he describes the time a therapist spends with him as "rap sessions," he is not necessarily trying to devalue the therapeutic experience. Likewise, the psychologically unsophisticated patient may not make a distinction between the therapist and other hospital visitors and may ask personal questions or offer compliments to the therapist. Therapeutic interpretations that might have been suitable in an outpatient mental hospital setting such as transference, dependency, weak ego boundaries, and so on are not directly applicable to the medical setting.

APPROACHES TO COUNSELING/PSYCHOTHERAPY WITH MALE MEDICAL PATIENTS

In view of the nature of men's socialization and the nature of the hospital environment, counseling conducted with male patients referred by staff clearly must be adapted somewhat from traditional approaches in more conventional settings. The importance of flexibility on the therapist's part cannot be overemphasized.

From the beginning, the medical patient calls for nontraditional psychotherapeutic approaches. The therapist comes to the patient, he or she stands, looking down at the bedfast patient who is clothed in hospital pajamas, and must be prepared to discuss what is for the patient the most relevant concern, his physical illness. However, conditions that allow the patient to feel comfortable in this contact with the mental health professional are quite diverse and require as much creativity as the therapist can muster. For example, one patient may need reassurance that the therapist is "not the usual kind of shrink" as he is informed, accurately, just what sort of activities are typical for this professional. Another patient may need to spend time telling the therapist just exactly why he would never have anything to do with a psychologist before he may be ready to spend time talking about the referral problem. One articulate patient had to inform the therapist that he considered psychologists "barnacles on the ship of life" before he could begin to form a close and meaningful therapeutic relationship that continued for the remainder of his life. However, it should be noted that early contacts with this patient were conducted over card games. For another patient, the therapist's willingness to string the patient's guitar established the required rapport to begin psychological work. More typically, meetings over coffee in the dining room are used to replace traditional, but also more threatening, office visits.

These types of activities may be required in order to stay within the patient's "comfort range." Although what ensues in therapy is often quite typical and traditional, and despite significant psychotherapeutic gain, it remains important for the patient to be free to characterize the intervention in a manner that is comfortable for him. Therapists new to the hospital setting are sometimes offended when a series of intense therapy sessions are casually referred to by the patient as "our classes," but veteran health psychologists recognize that construing the activity in this way may be the critical factor enabling the patient to receive benefit.

Similar flexibility may be called for in selecting modalities of treatment for hospitalized males. In fact, health psychologists must be prepared to accept that some interventions are most appropriately directed at staff, either through direct consultation or through in-service training. In other cases, interventions may be achieved by educating and instructing staff in patient management techniques or behavioral programs so that *they* might intervene. Usually these approaches to treatment require assessment of the patient, but in some cases staff education may be conducted in team meetings without the specific evaluation of the patient (Gatchel & Baum, 1983).

Presumably, all major therapy orientations are represented by mental health personnel practicing in health-care settings, and it is likely that some patients benefit from each of these approaches. However, the nature of the referral often dictates, to some extent, the type of intervention. Because the availability of the patient may be time-limited, only short-term, crisis-oriented activities are possible. Since the patient may be seeing the therapist involuntarily and for purposes clearly not seen as self-actualizing, nondirective approaches may be futile. In other words, the patient and the referral problem may dictate the type of therapy employed. For example, the "Type A" patient, for whom a feeling of control is all important, may be particularly averse to so nebulous an activity as therapy, despite obvious need for precisely that activity. Although the need to manage stress more adaptively may be as vital to this patient as medication or surgery, his intolerance of the ambiguity of "talking therapy" may preclude most types of intervention. In fact, the anger induced in some Type A patients by attempts at psychological intervention may be countertherapeutic and even dangerous. However, the same patient who objects to "senseless talking" may be intrigued by the technical aspects of biofeedback. Moreover, the technology provides, for this patient, pragmatic (and credible) evidence of stress, and of his capacity to modulate his body's response to that stress. Learning what is so visibly and audibly effective sometimes provides the patient with insight into the relationship between physical and psychological factors and allows him to progress subsequently via other therapeutic modalities (Gatchel & Baum, 1983).

For example, in many situations an initial interview affords opportunity for the therapist to offer permission for a patient to feel frightened, depressed, and so on. The unfamiliar feelings and behaviors that he may have been experiencing—especially when they evoked surprised reactions in family and staff—may create additional distress for the patient who questions his "sanity" or "rights" to his feelings until he receives permission to accept them. Occasionally, once permission is received, the patient can easily deal with the situation on his own without further help, and may prefer to do so.

However, many patients, having been victim to the hospital system described above, are overwhelmed with anxiety and other unfamiliar feelings. They perceive themselves as being unheard. The opportunity to ventilate those feelings in the presence of an empathic and understanding listener may reduce their stress sufficiently to allow the patient to get on with his recovery (Eisenberg et al., 1981).

Education is the most effective intervention for the patient who either has not yet received sufficient information regarding his condition or has not been able to accept or understand clearly that information. Education is also an effective intervention for the patient who takes pride in his strength and capacity to "take care of everything" but who currently worries that he has lost that capacity, feeling powerless to cope with the situation he faces. An explanation of the psychological process occurring within him may relieve his fear of "losing his mind."

Failing to understand the role that they play in their illness, their slow rehabilitation, or in their negative interactions with others, some patients require confrontation that may be delivered most appropriately by a skilled therapist rather than by family members or medical staff. Such confrontations should be direct and also at a level that can be tolerated by the patient who is ill, angry, and threatened by "shrinks."

All of the previously cited strategies are effective therapeutic tools in any setting, but rarely do each of them have as much potential for creating real and durable change as they do in the crisis that is engendered by illness and hospitalization. However, all of these techniques may be insufficient for some patients. For example, the patient who has repeated episodes of Crohn's Disease (a severe and dangerous inflammation of the bowel) every time his in-laws come to visit will require repeated intervention of these and other behaviors in order to develop insight and the ability to modify his response. Further, there are some patients whose psychological issues are well entrenched and extremely destructive in the face of their current health status. While in some cases, less intrusive strategies may have provided such patients with superficial insight into their brain-body connection, more extensive therapy may be required for long-term change.

While a variety of intervention strategies is available to the mental health practitioner, another issue worthy of consideration is whether they are to be applied in the interest of the patient or in the interest of the agency. Agencies differ in the extent that mental health professionals are given autonomy to decide on treatment contracts with the patient. In many instances, the goals of the patient may be in direct conflict with the agency or the referring party. For example, patients who are seeking greater control over their restrictive and threatening environment may be referred by a staff member who sees them as aggressive and noncompliant. The chronic dialysis patient or terminal cancer patient who is opting to refuse treatment may be referred to the psychologist by staff who clearly desire to have the patient talked out of his wish. The patient who may be seeking compensation from the treating agency is in obvious conflict with agency financial needs. Also, the patient who feels (with some apparent justification) that he is not being treated compassionately by staff may create a conflict of interest for the therapist. It is important for mental health professionals to clarify for themselves and for patients the degree to which they are free to establish goals based solely on patient needs.

The health-care environment can be seen as having important interactions with the traditional coping styles of men. Further, the referral to mental health services may also impinge upon the attitudes of many male patients. Innovative strategies for psychological intervention may be required for this population. However, the effort is generally well rewarded in that individuals seen in this context frequently are motivated (once they are convinced of the efficacy of psychological intervention) to make rapid and highly significant changes. In addition, a population that ordinarily would never avail themselves of mental health services is afforded the opportunity to receive valuable assistance.

References

Coombs, R., & Vincent, C. (Eds.). (1971). *Psychosocial aspects of medical training.* Springfield, IL: Charles C Thomas.

Degood, D. (1979). A behavioral pain-management program: Expanding the psychologist's role in a medical setting. *Professional Psychology, 10*(4), 491-503.

DiMatteo, M. R., & Taranta, A. (1979). Non-verbal communication and physician-patient rapport: An empirical study. *Professional Psychology, 10*(4), 540-548.

Eisenberg, M., Falconer, I., & Sutkin, L. (Eds.). (1981). *Communication in a health care setting.* Springfield, IL: Charles C Thomas.

Eisenberg, M., Sutkin, L., & Jansen, M. (1984). *Chronic illness and disability through the lifespan: Effects on self and family.* New York: Springer.

Gatchel, R., & Baum, A. (1983). *An introduction to health psychology.* Reading, MA: Addison-Wesley.

Olbrisch, M., & Sechrest, L. (1979). Educating health professionals in traditional training programs. *Professional Psychology, 10*(4), 589-595.

Stone, G. C., Cohen, F., & Adler, N. (Eds.). (1980). *Health psychology.* San Francisco: Jossey-Bass.

Tefft, B., & Simeonsson, R. (1979). Psychology and the creation of health care settings. *Professional Psychology, 10*(4), 558-571.

Wright, G. (1980). *Total rehabilitation.* Boston: Little, Brown.

V

Implications and Future Directions

It is difficult, if not impossible, to pull together adequately a volume so crammed with information, techniques, philosophical musings, and hope as the present one. However, that is just what we will attempt in this chapter. What will be addressed is the future for counseling and psychotherapy with men. We will also make some general observations about psychotherapy with men from a historical perspective, from a dynamic/process perspective, from an examination of outcome of and obstacles to therapy, and finally from the emerging perspective of masculist therapy.

In regard to themes that emerged in the handbook, they can be broadly broken down into what therapists need to be, what they need to know, and what they need to do. What therapists need to be is what they have always needed to be: insightful, empathic, warm, honest, congruent, genuine, and knowledgeable. What therapists need to know is the broad range of techniques that the last hundred years of writing on psychotherapy and counseling has provided, the major importance and impact of the male gender role on men and on therapy, the basic information about what affects the lives of the broad range of men depicted in this book, and the basic elements of knowing themselves. What therapists need to do is listen carefully, judge minimally, advise and respond adequately, accept generously, and work swiftly.

It was initially hoped that the present volume would be as comprehensive as possible. However, as it is impossible to include everything, it is worthy to note that which has been neglected. Assessment of men for therapy has not been addressed extensively as it is beyond the scope of this work to explore the limitations, liabilities, methods, and potentials of traditional and more recent assessment and diagnostic procedures. However, it is worth cautioning that traditional assessment and diagnostic procedures tend to perpetuate control, power, and competition issues while minimizing interpersonal connection between client and therapist. Motivational levels of men who are candidates for therapy as well as men in therapy have also not been dealt with completely. Motivational levels for therapy are low amongst the general population of men because of male unwillingness to

388

seek aid and nurturance, as has been indicated in this book. The therapist who works with men must be aware of this low motivation for therapy and attempt to broadcast the availability and desirability of services for men. The therapist must also monitor the motivational level of male clients, working swiftly because men often want to terminate therapy as soon as they feel better, even if they have not accomplished any deep amelioration of their problems.

There is a myth that men do not do well in therapy. The truth is that men may not do well in traditional therapy. However, after becoming involved in the therapeutic process, men in general do benefit from therapy. Men do want to get better; they are goal oriented. Most men are initially resistant to getting help, as that runs counter to the traditional male role, but once making the decision to seek help, they do make good use of it.

Almost all men come into treatment with problems or issues related to a restricting definition of masculinity. In other words, the psychological problems of male clients are frequently related to their view of themselves as either inadequately measuring up to traditional male role expectations; or conversely, to excessive conformity to traditional male role requirements when it is not in their best interest to do so. However, it is difficult to bring this information into the counseling session as well as to correct the client's current difficulty using that information. A sense of masculinity is a core identity issue, not a superficial one, and therefore most male clients are resistant to changing their definition of masculinity. Therapy may then optimally be viewed as an option for men in which they may expand their personal definition of masculinity rather than overhauling it or abandoning it.

In order to accomplish the deepest change of a positive nature in men, therapists must pay close attention to their relationships with the male clients. Men are most poorly prepared in the nuances, intricacies, and effects of interpersonal relationships. The therapist can greatly enhance the therapeutic gain for male clients by observing and using the relationship that is created, even if the relationship is mainly characterized by reluctance, hostility, or resistance on the part of the client.

Usually men change through cognitive interventions. This produces symptom relief but also reinforces the trait of excessive cognitive detachment from self and others. Men are thereby traditionally encouraged to objectify their problems and their role in them, thus increasing their detachment from self. Because self-awareness and self-exploration are narrowly defined in the cognitive-behavioral perspective, difficulties with therapy ensue. There is collusion with the restricting traditional male gender role. That is, the relationship component in therapy is ignored, and men are prematurely hooked into therapy for less valid reasons, for example, cognitive control versus the development of relationship awareness.

Affective experiential therapy, although potentially threatening to men at first, is a most valuable modality. It can help to create fundamental changes in the client that will be of greater utility in future situations. The relationship component of therapy helps men to move toward more rewarding relationships and to reduce objectification of self and others. If relationship is the focus in psychotherapy, cognitive-behavioral approaches can be effective supplemental aspects of the treatment.

Historically, psychotherapy has been criticized as being based on men and misapplied to women since theories and models for it were generally developed by men. In actuality, these theories were indeed usually written by, but were based on treatment of female patients as women were more likely to be in treatment. Models of therapy for men were based on helping men "adjust" to "correct" their deviancy from the traditional male role. A new model of therapy with men is becoming of increasing importance as this book makes clear. We call such a model masculist therapy.

Masculist therapy is an approach to psychotherapy built upon the vast theoretical and research literature on psychotherapy, which also incorporates the literature and knowledge about male gender roles and what the intersection of those roles with therapy is. Masculist therapy attempts to create an atmosphere where men will change and grow in ways dramatically different from the narrowly proscribed and prescribed directions that traditional therapy has in general provided. The emphasis is on relationships in masculist therapy. This directly contradicts the traditional masculine manner of dealing with the world in an instrumental manner. Thus the relationship between therapist and client is cooperative rather than adversarial, thereby reducing resistance and providing an appropriate model for men in the world. Issues specifically related to male gender roles—emotional constriction, dominance, low self-disclosure, competition—are focused on in masculist therapy and the client is helped to work through and integrate these issues in a more humane way than is typical. Masculist therapy seeks to use "male" issues to help the therapeutic relationship by working with gender-role issues in a positive way.

In this book, we have endeavored to provide the impetus to move from a collection of individual, separate approaches in working with men toward a consolidated and integrated approach to such work. It is clear that the manner in which therapy with men is done becomes a major, if not the most salient, therapeutic consideration for those therapists working with men, because men for the most part ignore the process of how they live their lives. Our hope has been to explore further the process of men's lives and men's therapy and to provide the beginning of an integrated approach to psychotherapy with men.

About the Contributors

Jeffrey W. Aston is currently a Staff Psychologist with the Federal Correctional Medical Facility in Rochester, Minnesota. Over the past few years, he has begun to apply an interest in men's issues to working with men in prisons and other correctional institutions. He was formerly a staff psychologist at the Federal Correctional Institution in El Reno, Oklahoma.

Augustine Baròn, Jr., received his B.A. in psychology, magna cum laude, from Loyola University, New Orleans, and his M.A. and Psy.D. in clinical psychology from the University of Illinois at Urbana-Champaign, where he was a Ford Foundation Fellow. He completed a predoctoral internship in clinical psychology at the Fort Logan Mental Health Center, Denver, Colorado. Dr. Baròn is currently a Staff Psychologist and Senior Lecturer in Educational Psychology at the Counseling and Mental Health Center, University of Texas at Austin. He is the editor of *Explorations in Chicano Psychology* (Praeger, 1981) and serves on the editorial boards of the *Journal of Counseling and Development* and *The Counseling Psychologist*. His professional interests include cross-cultural psychology, psychotherapy supervision, and the administration of university campus mental health services.

Nancy L. Carlson received her training in counseling psychology at the University of Kansas and has been a Psychologist at several university counseling centers and departments of psychology. She was Director of Counseling at SUNY, New Paltz, and then Director of Counseling and Career Services at the University of Rhode Island until 1986, when she moved into private practice and consulting in Portland, Maine. She is also a psychologist at the University of Maine Counseling Center. She earned the Diplomate in Counseling Psychology in 1981 and has been active in teaching, consulting, supervising, and training and development programs and services involving men's issues and women's issues for many years.

Terry A. Carlson is the Chief, Psychology Service, at the Veterans Administration Outpatient Clinic in Columbus, Ohio. He graduated from West Point in 1965 and served 10 years as a professional army officer, including tours of duty in Vietnam and Korea. After leaving the service, he received his Ph.D. in counseling psychology from the University of Missouri-Columbia in 1978. He joined the VA Clinic in 1979 as Staff Psychologist and began working with veterans, especially those with PTSD. He also has an Adjunct Clinical Assistant Professorship appointment with the Psychology Department of the Ohio State University.

Patricia M. Carlton is a Counselor in the Office for Disability Services at the Ohio State University. In this role she provides adjustment, personal, and career-counseling for the disabled student population. She has made numerous presentations to university faculty and special educators in the public schools concerning issues related to disability awareness and the facilitation of more effective teaching and learning strategies. Her background in rehabilitation counseling has provided her with varied experiences that include working with individuals with learning, physical, and emotional impairments. Recently elected as the Secretary of the Ohio Valley Association on Handicapped Student Service Personnel in Post-Secondary Education, she will be working with professionals throughout the state of Ohio. At the national level she has given presentations on counseling students with disabilities and facilitating successful support groups.

Sam V. Cochran is currently Director of Clinical Services and Service Staff Psychologist at the University Counseling Service, University of Iowa, Iowa City, Iowa. He received his Ph.D. in counseling psychology from the University of Missouri-Columbia. In addition to leading men's groups and providing workshops on men's issues at the University of Iowa, he has professional interests in psychotherapy with men, gender-role development, and brief and short-term approaches to therapy.

Brooke B. Collison is an Associate Professor of Counseling and School Psychology at the Wichita State University in Wichita, Kansas. He was elected President of the American Association for Counseling and Development in 1986 to take office in July of 1987. Dr. Collison received a Ph.D. in counseling psychology from the University of Missouri-Columbia in 1969. He contributed to a special issue of the *Personnel and Guidance Journal* on counseling adult men and has conducted frequent workshop sessions on gender-role issues in counseling.

Jed Diamond, Addictionologist, is Director of the Center for Prospering Relationships, San Rafael, California. Diamond, a 1968 graduate of the University of California, Berkeley, is a Licensed Clinical Social Worker and Certified Alcohol and Drug Abuse Counselor. He is the author of numerous professional and popular articles on men's issues and addictions, including his book, *Inside*

Out: Becoming My Own Man. His forthcoming book, *12 Steps for Curing All Addictions,* will help people effectively treat problems as diverse as love addictions and alcoholism.

Thomas E. Dubois received his doctorate in clinical psychology at the State University of New York in Buffalo in 1967. In 1969, he was awarded a postdoctoral fellowship at the State University of New York at Stony Brook, where he studied behavior therapy and behavior modification. Since that time he has been at the University of New Hampshire Counseling and Testing Center, where he is a Past Director. He has also been involved in community mental health work. Working within a humanistic-behavioral framework, he has consulted widely with parents, teachers, and school administrators, in addition to maintaining a private practice in psychotherapy. He has also extensively used self-induced altered states in reducing tension and pain, and increasing self-awareness and control. For over a decade he has been concerned with men's and gender-role issues, leading discussions, writing, and offering programs on different aspects of these topics.

Gregg A. Eichenfield received his Ph.D. in counseling psychology from the University of Utah, and is associate professor and licensed psychologist, Department of Professional Psychology, University of St. Thomas in St. Paul, Minnesota. He also conducts a private practice in counseling and psychotherapy in St. Paul, Minnesota, and has consulted with school districts, the federal prison system, and other institutions of higher education. He is the past Chair, Standing Committee for Men, American College Personnel Association, and the Task Group on Men and Mental Health, National Organization for Men Against Sexism (NOMAS). In addition to men and therapy, he has interests in suicide, crisis intervention, consultation, and clinical supervision and training.

Jeffrey C. Fracher received his Ph.D. in clinical psychology from Virginia Commonwealth University in 1979. He is currently in full-time private practice of clinical psychology in Metuchen, New Jersey, where he specializes in the treatment of sexual disorders. He is an Adjunct Assistant Professor of Psychology at the Graduate School of Applied and Professional Psychology at Rutgers University and an Adjunct Assistant Professor of Psychiatry at the University of Medicine and Dentistry of New Jersey. He is married with one child and lives in Highland Park, New Jersey.

Howard R. Fradkin works as a Psychologist in private practice in Columbus, Ohio. He works primarily with gay men and lesbians in his practice. He has served for the past two and one-half years as the Chairperson of the Support Services Committee and serves on the Executive Committee of the Columbus AIDS Task Force. He also has been elected as the Chairperson of the Support Services Committee of the Ohio AIDS Coalition. He has worked with a number of men with AIDS, ARC, as well as the worried well. He has trained more than 150 volunteers to work with people with AIDS.

Lucia Albino Gilbert is Professor of Educational Psychology at The University of Texas at Austin and teaches in the department's doctoral program in counseling psychology. Two of her major research interests are dual-career families and sexuality and gender issues in psychotherapy. She recently completed a book titled *Men in Dual-Career Families: Current Realities and Future Prospects* and edited a special issue of *The Counseling Psychologist* on this topic. She also just completed an invited chapter on the topic of gender and mental health for an edited book, *Critical Issues, Developments, and Trends in Professional Psychology.* She serves on the editorial boards of *Psychology of Women Quarterly, Journal of Counseling Psychology,* and *Professional Psychology.*

Daniel S. Gonzales is a doctoral candidate in counseling psychology at the University of Missouri. He received his B.A. from DePauw University in psychology and his M.A. from the University of Missouri. In addition to men's issues, he is also interested in substance abuse treatment, cross-cultural counseling, and ethical issues in psychotherapy.

Glenn E. Good is an Assistant Professor in the Department of Psychology and a Psychologist at the Counseling Center of the University of Missouri-Columbia. He received his Ph.D. in counseling psychology from The Ohio State University. He coedited a special feature of the *Journal of Counseling and Development* on gender issues in counseling, and served on the national council of the National Organization for Men Against Sexism. He presently works with men's issues as a therapist, researcher, and educator.

Barry Graff is a Clinical Psychologist in private practice in San Diego, California, and Las Vegas, Nevada. He specializes in the treatment of married couples and families, and teaches and consults with professionals in these areas. He and his wife, Bonnie, have been married for 19 years. They have two daughters, Erin, 15, and Allison, 11.

James Harrison is a Clinical Psychologist and cofounder of Harrison, Kooden & Associates, a psychological service organization in New York City. Through Intelligence in Media he is also a producer of educational videos for mental health professional and human services personnel. He has an M.Div. degree in theology from Yale University and a Ph.D. in psychology from New York University. Combining these interests, the focus of his work is men's sex roles, gay issues, and the relationship between religion and mental health.

P. Paul Heppner is an Associate Professor in the Department of Psychology and a Senior Staff Counseling Psychologist at Counseling Services at the University of Missouri. He has been involved in men's issues since the early 1970s, and has participated in and led a broad range of men's groups.

Michael S. Kimmel teaches sociology at SUNY at Stony Brook. He is the editor of *Changing Men: New Directions in Research on Men and Masculinity* (Sage, 1987), and edited a special issue of *American Behavioral Scientist* on men's roles. His articles on masculinity and sexuality have appeared in several anthologies, scholarly journals, and popular magazines, and he is currently working on a documentary history of pro-feminist men in American history (with Tom Mosmiller) and a book titled *Gender and Desire* (with John Gagnon). He is a member of the National Council of the National Organization for Changing Men.

J. Eugene Knott, a Counseling Psychologist with a practice in behavioral medicine, is currently Acting Director of the Counseling Center at the University of Rhode Island. He has taught, written, researched, and been a therapist with issues of dying and bereavement with all age groups for over 20 years. He received his Ph.D. from the University of Maryland, and is married with one teenage daughter and a son who died of leukemia in 1984.

Richard F. Lazur works with adolescents in outpatient, hospital, residential, and university counseling centers in Massachusetts and Alaska. A graduate of the Massachusetts School of Professional Psychiatry, he is active in exploring men's issues in both his personal and professional activities and has lectured on same throughout the nation. He presently is in private practice.

Daniel Booduck Lee is Associate Professor of Social Work at the Ohio State University and Executive Director of Transcultural Family Institute in Columbus, Ohio. He is clinical member of the American Association of Marriage and Family Therapists. He has founded and chaired the National Conference on Transcultural Family since 1984. He consults on intercultural processes and Asian mental health matters to various organizations. He is listed in the *Who's Who in Human Services Professionals* (1986 edition of the National Reference Institute).

Don Long, a cofounder of RAVEN (Rape and Violence End Now), has been counseling men and providing education and training toward the goal of ending men's violence against women since 1978. He also teaches a men's studies course at Washington University in St. Louis, and has been an activist in the national movement for changing men. He was the organizing coordinator for the Tenth National Conference on Men and Masculinity in June 1985.

Thomas M. Marino is a therapist who maintains a full-time private practice in Portsmouth, New Hampshire. He has published articles concerning men's issues and written a monthly newspaper column titled "About Men" for a local newspaper. His current interest in men's topics focuses on father and son relationships. Besides his work with men in transition, his other areas of specialization include chronic pain and stress management with expertise related to life changes connected to chronic pain. He works with individuals, couples, and groups from an existential, gestalt-oriented approach.

David R. Matteson received his Ph.D. from Boston University in 1968. He has taught at Boston University, Marietta College, the Royal Danish School of Higher Education in Copenhagen, and presently at Governors State University, where he is a University Professor of Psychology and Counseling. His research areas include adolescent identity, family dynamics, sex roles, and alternative lifestyles. He is a founding member and on the Council of the National Organization for Changing Men.

Richard N. Maxwell is the Assistant Director of the Office for Disability Services at the Ohio State University. In addition, he is a Clinical Instructor in the Department of Physical Medicine. He sustained a spinal cord injury in 1963. Although he is in a wheelchair, he was able to complete his undergraduate work, and in 1969 received a Bachelor's degree in business administration. He is involved in a variety of campus and community awareness and sensitivity activities regarding the needs of disabled persons. He has served as a trustee for state and local organizations including Creative Living, a unique assisted living apartment complex for quadriplegics in Columbus, Ohio. In 1963 he served in the United States Marine Corps. He is married and has a 14-year old stepson.

Ronald May is Director of the Student Counseling Center of the University of Oregon. Previous to this he was the Director of the Counseling and Testing Center and a graduate faculty member in the College Student Personnel Program at the University of Wisconsin-LaCrosse. Since receiving his Ph.D. in counseling psychology from Michigan State University in 1980, he has worked with men's issues as a psychotherapist, group leader, educator, researcher, and author. He has been actively involved in the National Organization for Changing Men and the Standing Committee for Men in the American College Personnel Association.

Joseph H. Pleck is the Henry R. Luce Professor of Families, Change, and Society at Wheaton College (Massachusetts). He is the author of *Men and Masculinity* (1974), *The Myth of Masculinity* (1981), and *Working Wives, Working Husbands* (1985). He was previously Associate Director of the Wellesley College Center for Research on Women, and holds a Ph.D. in clinical psychology from Harvard University.

Francisco Q. Ponce is Coordinator of Group Services at the University of Utah's Counseling Center. He is coauthor (with D. Douglass) of "A decision-making process" in *Career planning for Chicano-Latino students*, and coauthor (with D. R. Atkinson and F. Martinez) of "Effects of ethnic, sex, and attitude similarity on counselor credibility and influence" in the *Journal of Counseling Psychology*. His dissertation, "Effects of different levels of acculturation, counselor ethnicity and counseling strategy on client's perceptions of counselor credibility and influence," is being revised for publication. He received his B.A. in psychology with honors from the University of California at Santa Cruz, completed his Master's degree coursework in cross-cultural counseling from San Jose State University, and received his Ph.D. in counseling psychology from the University of California at Santa Barbara. He completed a predoctoral internship in counseling psychology at the Counseling and Mental Health Center at the University of Texas at Austin.

Frederic E. Rabinowitz is currently an Assistant Professor of Psychology at the University of Redlands in Redlands, California. He received his Ph.D. in counseling psychology from the University of Missouri-Columbia and his M.A. in clinical psychology from Loyola College in Baltimore, Maryland. His research interests include individual and group counseling with men, the supervision of counselors, and nuclear age education. He maintains a private psychological practice in Redlands, California.

Tuck Takashi Saul is a licensed psychologist in private practice in Columbus, Ohio. His professional background includes five years as a Senior Staff Psychologist at the Counseling and Consultation Services, The Ohio State University; five years, including a one-year tour in Vietnam, as a Psychiatric Nurse with the military; and experience as a Clinical Social Worker in a child-family mental health center. He is a member of the American Psychological Association and the Asian-American Psychological Association.

Murray Scher received the Ph.D. in counseling psychology from The University of Texas at Austin in 1971. He was Professor of Psychology at Tusculum College for 11 years before entering the full-time independent practice of psychotherapy. He has written and presented extensively on psychotherapy, especially the effect of male gender roles, including editing the special issue of *The Personnel and Guidance Journal* on counseling males. He was Special Projects Editor of *VOICES, the Art and Science of Psychotherapy,* for three years. He has been married for 29 years and has a 22-year-old daughter.

Avraham Scherman received his Ph.D. from Michigan State University in 1972 and is Associate Professor in the Department of Educational Psychology at the University of Oklahoma and Licensed Professional Counselor in the State of Oklahoma. He has devoted the last 10 years to the study of children's, males', and females' adjustment to divorce. Results of these investigations were published in the mental health professional literature. In addition, he offered group experiences for children of divorce, single custodial fathers, and noncustodial parents.

Edward W.L. Smith is in full-time independent practice in Atlanta, Georgia, specializing in adult psychotherapy, psychotherapy training, and case consultation. He is an Adjunct Professor in Clinical Psychology at Georgia State University. He has published poetry, numerous professional articles, book chapters, edited *The Growing Edge of Gestalt Therapy* (1976), and written *The Body in Psychotherapy* (1985) and *Sexual Aliveness* (1987). He has served on the editorial boards of two psychotherapy journals. Since 1971 he has traveled widely, offering workshops throughout the United States as well as Canada, the Caribbean, England, and Mexico.

Mark Stevens received his Ph.D. from the California School of Professional Psychology-San Diego and is presently Assistant Director and Coordinator of Training at the University of Southern California's Student Counseling Center. His previous position was as a Senior Staff Psychologist at The Ohio State University's Counseling and Consultation Services. He was co-chair of the National Organization for Men Against Sexism and is currently a member of the leadership collective. He is also active in developing and facilitating programs for college men on antirape and gender-role strain issues.

LaFaye C. Sutkin is a Health Psychologist at the Jerry L. Pettis Memorial Veterans Hospital in Loma Linda, California. She earned her Ph.D. in clinical psychology at Case Western Reserve University.

Sandra Tedder received her Ph.D. from the University of Oklahoma in 1982 and is an Adjunct Assistant Professor in the Department of Educational Psychology at the University of Oklahoma, as well as a licensed psychologist in private practice in the greater Oklahoma City area. Her practice specializes in assessment, divorce adjustment, and relationship counseling with children, men, and women, as well as working with men and women in transition. She has done research and conducted groups with single custodial fathers and children of divorce.

Luis F. Valdés received his B.S. in psychology from The University of Texas at El Paso, and his Ph.D. in counseling psychology from Texas Tech University in Lubbock, Texas. He completed a predoctoral internship in counseling psychology at The University of Texas at Austin Counseling-Psychological Services Center. He was employed at the University of Notre Dame Counseling and Psychological Services Center and Department of Psychology as coordinator of outreach and consultation services. He is currently a licensed Staff Psychologist at The University of Texas at Austin Counseling and Mental Health Center and is coordinator of program development. In addition, he is currently the President of the Texas College Personnel Association.

Craig S. Washington holds the position of Professor and Chairman of the Automotive, Engineering, and Public Services Technologies Division at Northern Virginia Community College. He earned his Ed.D. in counseling psychology from the University of Massachusetts in Amherst, Massachusetts, and his postdoctoral training in organizational and community systems at Johns Hopkins University. He is currently pursuing postdoctoral training in substance abuse at Loyola College in Baltimore, Maryland. He is also a counselor educator in the School of Continuing Studies at Johns Hopkins University, specializing in the teaching of group counseling to graduate students. He is the author of several publications and has research interests in the areas of multicultural counseling and diversity, counseling men, group counseling, and black student achievement.